THE HEGEMONY OF POLITICAL CORRECTNESS

and the rise of the woke-Right

Michael William

PREFACE

This book is a sequel to *The Genesis of Political Correctness: The Basis of a False Morality*, which was written prior to the populist rebellions of 2016, with the Brexit vote in the UK and the election of President Trump in the USA. This sequel takes a post-populist perspective.

The purpose of this book is to explain the resilience of political correctness, and how its hegemony survived the populist rebellions undisturbed. While it is true populism was politically incorrect, it would be wrong to describe the acts of voter defiance as being reflected in a political drive to defeat the power and ideology of political correctness – far from it. There was no such drive and both the UK and the USA paid a price for that failure, as the establishment desperately tried to thwart the will of the people.

It would, however, be wrong to assign the negligence to even try to remove political correctness from society as being solely the reason for its hegemony. The creed has many strengths. It enjoys establishment support. Political correctness is a belief system and the establishment are true believers.

This book aims to identify the creed's strengths and explain how and the extent to which it prevailed.

Michael William
December 2021

Also by Micheal William

The Ponzi Class: Ponzi Economics, Globalization and Class Oppression in the 21st Century

The Genesis of Political Correctness: The Basis of a False Morality

Multiculturalist Ideology (Part One), Second Edition: Race War Politics and the Rise of the Anti-Whites

Brexit Means Brexit: How the British Ponzi Class Survived the EU Referendum

Multiculturalist Ideology (Part Two): The Rising Tide of Race War Politics

Turbo Brexit: And the Case Against Brino

The Mosques Are Our Barracks: Will Turkey Join the European Union?

https://michaelwilliampg.com

Table of Contents

INTRODUCTION

In 2016, the Brexit referendum result in the UK, and the triumph of Donald Trump in the US presidential election, marked a new era in Western politics. 'Populism' became the new word of abuse targeted at those politicians trying to reflect the opinions and interests of ordinary people. By comparison, the establishment view, the politically correct view, was portrayed as being the summit of wisdom and as morally superior. This contemptuous attitude towards those deemed populists spanned the ruling classes including, importantly, the mainstream media.

The reaction of the powers-that-be to the voter rebellion, was one of astonishment and outrage. The voters had supposedly been misled. The rebellion had been due to underlying causes that had been ignored. The actual vote was only a protest. The voters did not really mean it. They did not understand what they were voting for. The votes could be ignored, not least, in the UK, because it was impossible to uphold the democratic decision. Things were far too complicated.

By the summer of 2019, in the UK, Brexit had still not happened and the May Government was in turmoil as Theresa May, the then prime minister and Tory Party leader, had lost the confidence of her party. Britain had even agreed to stay in the European Union (EU) until the end of October 2019, with many Tories keen to extend it beyond that date as well. The EU was relaxed and in control, having dictated a proposed withdrawal treaty May was eager to impose on the UK. That withdrawal treaty would subject the UK to EU dictatorship during a so-called transition period, and continued EU rule over many issues even beyond the transition period.

Eventually, Boris Johnson replaced May as Tory leader and he tweaked her withdrawal treaty with the EU and pushed it through parliament. The UK agreed to obey EU rules during a transition period due to end on 31 December, 2020. As 2020 progressed, the negotiations for a trade agreement did not, with the EU demanding control over the UK's state aid policy and the UK's fishing grounds. However, on this occasion, the British government made it clear there was to be no postponement of the Brexit date. Meanwhile, the Covid-19 pandemic dominated the political agenda across the West.

In the USA, President Trump had made progress on the USA's trade deficit, and had shown a willingness to impose tariffs to protect US economic interests. However, despite a government shutdown, and numerous court applications, the Trump administration had not ended mass immigration and made no meaningful progress in building a wall along the USA's border with Mexico. Failing to build the wall was a major blow to President Trump's credibility and a fundamental threat to the continued existence of the USA as a member of the West. A Third World populated country becomes a part of the Third World.

Political correctness played a part in this failure to implement the democratic decisions, and the orthodoxy remained intact, if not completely undisturbed by the democratic rebellions of 2016. Of importance are the creed's institutional aspects, the economic aspects (how the political correctness is funded), and the moral arguments (its false morality).

In my book, *The Genesis of Political Correctness: The Basis of a False Morality*, I asked and then answered the question whether William Lind's essay and speech made some time ago, 'The Origins of Political Correctness', was true. His central allegation was that political correctness was cultural Marxism and the Frankfurt School had crafted and promoted it. In examining the origins and evolution of political correctness, I concluded William Lind was correct. Cultural Marxism was always a part of the communism package from its inception and is contained in *The Communist Manifesto* of 1848 and the accompanying *A Communist Confession of Faith*. When the communist revolutions did not take off as Marx predicted, and

8

there was obvious economic ruin of communist-ruled countries, then the Frankfurt School, in particular, refocused attention on cultural Marxism to undermine the West and capitalism. They redeveloped it and fused it with Freudian thinking. In my book, I defined political correctness as being 'the mechanism for the enforcement of neo-Marxist ideology'.

This book takes the next step. It examines not the origins of political correctness nor its evolution, but the reasons for its continued hegemony. That examination will involve the interaction between the various basic concepts of political correctness with one another, and with the different aspects mentioned above. Obviously, without understanding the reasons for the creed's hegemony, it is very difficult to defeat it and halt the harm it is doing.

This book will firstly summarise the underlying thought process of political correctness. This is primarily a recap on the influence of the Frankfurt School, and the ideology it advanced. *The Basis of a False Morality*, being the subtitle of *The Genesis of Political Correctness*, is important. Political correctness is a false morality and the fluffy, candyfloss language that accompanies the intolerance is phoney. The language is deliberately designed to hide the evil that political correctness truly is: communism.

Secondly, this book will explore some different basic concepts of political correctness. Some of these are new. The purpose is to identify and understand how political correctness is structured. This structure is not wooden as different concepts affect many issues.

Thirdly, in the chapter 'The Hegemony', I take an overview and examine the three different aspects that enable the creed to triumph and prevail. Once again, there is some overlap.

Finally, in the conclusion I draw together the different concepts and aspects, and examine how they interact. The aim is to expose how the creed's concepts and aspects shape and influence individual issues. By understanding this, the manner in which the hegemony can be defeated is revealed. We need to target the strengths it depends on.

THE UNDERLYING THOUGHT PROCESS

In *The Genesis of Political Correctness: The Basis of a False Morality*, I examined the importance of the Frankfurt School in the evolution of political correctness, and focused on three key items. First, *The Authoritarian Personality* (1950), a book of pretend research by Adorno and his colleagues which sought to integrate Freud into Marxism. That Adorno's report was seriously flawed did not undermine its influence. Willing Left recipients seized upon it and were instantly convinced of what they wanted to hear: that conservatism was bad, that there was a new pre-fascist, far-Right that needed to be purged from society, and widespread indoctrination and thought control was needed.

Second, Herbert Marcuse's (1898–1979) 'Repressive Tolerance' essay (1965) was examined. This essay was important, as it openly advocated the banning of free speech for right-wing and even mainstream conservative opinion. The rationale being that the false consciousness of those deemed to be oppressed could only be broken if they were prevented from hearing conservative thinking. This approach not only reinforced the determination to impose widespread indoctrination and thought control but also justified the accompanying persecution of those deemed heretics.

In his essay, Marcuse was open from the outset that he was calling for intolerance: 'the objective of tolerance would call for intolerance toward prevailing policies, attitudes, opinions, and the extension of tolerance to policies, attitudes, and opinions which are outlawed or suppressed'. Marcuse was contemptuous of the tolerance for the 'systematic moronization' of the public. For him, the tolerance of right-wing views led to a perpetuation of the existing society, which he condemned for its supposed oppression and lack of freedom. For him, tolerance allowed discrimination and inequality; overthrowing the prevailing cultural hegemony required intolerance of existing views and the promotion of the Left and the views of minorities. Majority public opinion was invalid as it was prejudiced, derived, and influenced by the dominant forces of society ('tyranny of public opinion and its makers') and the process of moronization, and the people were suffering from false consciousness. For Marcuse, 'Liberating tolerance, then, would mean intolerance against movements from the Right and toleration of movements from the Left.'[1] He said:

> 'The false consciousness has become the general consciousness – from the government down to its last objects. The small and powerless minorities which struggle against the false consciousness and its beneficiaries must be helped: their continued existence is more important than the preservation of abused rights and liberties which grant constitutional powers to those who oppress these minorities. It should be evident by now that the exercise of civil rights by those who don't have them presupposes the withdrawal of civil rights from those who prevent their exercise, and that liberation of the Damned of the Earth presupposes suppression not only of their old but also of their new masters.'[2]

A postscript, written three years later, was unyielding and more virulent. Marcuse accused the majority of being 'self-perpetuating while perpetuating the vested interests which made it a majority' and 'the ideology of democracy hides its lack of substance'. Instead, Marcuse advocated support for 'radical minorities' who are 'intolerant, militantly intolerant and disobedient to the rules of behaviour which tolerate destruction and suppression'.

Marcuse, like Gramsci (who was not a member of the Frankfurt School), supported the 'long march through the institutions' and the strategy of 'working against the established institutions while working in them'.[3] This strategy allowed the wealth of Western society to be used to fund those whose aim it was to destroy it.

By the 1970s, Marcuse no longer regarded the working class as being the same instrument for a revolution as Marx had envisioned, the alienated proletariat, but hoped that other alienated groups – students, intellectuals, the unemployed, and racial minorities – would now act as 'catalysts' for revolution.[4] Marcuse sought to supplement class war politics with race war politics and regarded the Black population as being the 'most natural' force of rebellion.[5] The New Left was to be the vanguard.

Third, in *The Genesis of Political Correctness*, I examined 'Citizenship and National Identity: Some Reflections on the Future of Europe' (1995), where Jurgen Habermas (born 1929) argued there were three matters impacting upon citizenship and national identity: the future of the nation state, the EU, and immigration.

'Citizenship and National Identity' was an attack on the traditional nation state and on the understanding of nationhood. Habermas tried to impose a new concept of nationality. He failed to convince. There are differences between citizenship and nationality. Citizenship, to put it simply, is the entitlement to passports. Nationality is the pre-political identity of the nation and is inherited. Although the usage of the term nationality has been hitherto loose due to the homogeneity of the various European nation states, and the small numbers of non-European immigrants until relatively recently, this does not alter the differences of which people are increasingly aware. Habermas's contrived choice of words does not change this. It takes more than fancy language to create nations, as the failure to create an Ottoman nation over five centuries demonstrated. The Ottoman Empire culminated in the Armenian genocide.

Citizenship can be created easily, simply by issuing passports. Yet citizenship, passport identity, does not hold together a nation. This insufficiency is a dispute between so-called ethnic nationalists and those advocating civic nationalism (aka constitutional patriotism) – although the either/or distinction is simplistic.

Of importance is the concept of the Staatsvolk (an academic term), who created the state, its institutions, and culture. Uri Ra'anan, an Austrian/American political scientist, defined the Staatsvolk as 'the ethnic group that created the state, is largely identified with it, constitutes the bulk of its elite, and is responsible for the predominant culture'. For example, the English are the Staatsvolk of England. The nation which comprises the Staatsvolk confers upon the state the culture of the nation, as is reflected by the religion, the holidays, and the history. In this way, the civic institutions of the state reflect the culture of the nation. For the civic nationalists and multiculturalists, this is a problem. The civic nationalists respond by trying to drive out the nation's culture and influence from the civic institutions, while the multiculturalists seek to multiculturalise those institutions with immigrant cultures.

There are three positions regarding the problem of national unity. First, the ethnic nationalists stress the weakness of civic nationalism/constitutional patriotism and its likely failure to hold the nation together. Second, there is the liberal wing of civic nationalism/constitutional patriotism, which disagrees and promotes the idea that citizens can be taught to give allegiance to the state, devoid of any national culture. Third, there is the communist wing of civic nationalism/constitutional patriotism, the Habermasian view, that the likely weakening of national loyalty is desirable, should be encouraged, and is a prerequisite for a communist revolution. The communists support civic nationalism/constitutional patriotism for the same reasons the ethnic nationalists oppose it. With the Habermasian view, civic nationalism/constitutional patriotism is a mechanism for promoting the opposite of patriotism – that is, promoting a hatred of the country's history and, hence, the Staatsvolk. With the Habermasian view, the state is owed allegiance by all citizens; immigrants and other disaffected groups are to be encouraged to challenge existing national culture and tradition. The state owes no loyalty to the nation. Multiculturalists likewise reject the concept of a national culture; Bhikhu Parekh

14

and his supporters even advocate a 'multicultural post-nation' (see below).

No explanation is given why the Staatsvolk would agree to this, nor why they should owe any allegiance to a set of abstract universalist theories instead of their own culture. Such a statist approach, where state interests are the focus rather than the interests of the people, is unlikely to command support from the people.

In this way, civic nationalism/constitutional patriotism is a means of destroying the nation state and replacing the national culture, the culture of the Staatsvolk, with universalist values – i.e. abstract theories such as international human rights laws, with the state defining and implementing these theories in preference to defending the national interest. International and superstatist organisations are to be promoted. This anti-nation-state stance is at odds with the quadrupling of the number of nation states in the 20th century. The nation state is not defunct. It is the embodiment of civilisation.

There should be no doubting the malevolence of what Habermas advocated. This is especially so regarding immigration and the EU. He openly stated that immigration will 'give rise to social tensions', which if 'processed productively ... will enhance political mobilization in general, and might particularly encourage the new, endogeneous type of new social movements' such as 'peace, ecological and women's movements', which would in turn create pressures that could be resolved 'only at a European level'. This, in turn, would create a European-level civil society that would diminish the sovereignty of national governments, and 'cultural elites and the mass media would have an important role to play' regarding this – a concept that might appeal to the more vain. In simple language, Habermas openly advocated that immigrants should be used to attack nationhood. This is race war politics. Despite the carefully crafted forms of words and flowery language, what is being advocated is the fomentation of anti-White racial hatred. Race war politics should be used to generate a revolution, the overthrow of Western society, the overthrow of capitalism and the destruction of the nation state.

Habermas condemned the 'chauvinism of prosperity', which is a term as manipulative as it is dishonest. If a nation seeks to better itself by developing a thriving manufacturing industry and creating a welfare state, it is nothing to be ashamed of, and the nation is perfectly entitled to protect that which has been created. It is the process of civilisation. The Staatsvolk is entitled to protect itself, including the right to protect its culture, traditions and living standards. The nation is entitled to its own homeland – its place of safety.

Passports and abstract theories about human rights will not create the necessary national unity for a peaceful coexistence that has taken European countries centuries to establish. What Habermas advocates is the opposite of patriotism and is intended to create division and conflict.

These three key items (*The Authoritarian Personality*, 'Repressive Tolerance', and 'Citizenship and National Identity') comprise an underlying core of the thought process of political correctness.

BASIC CONCEPTS

*T*he *Genesis of Political Correctness* traces the evolution of communism and highlights some key concepts. It would be useful to recap those concepts before delving into new ones (the new concepts are points 13 to 16):

1   The three features of political correctness
2   The two wings of political correctness and the opposing patriotic stance
3   The barbarist
4   The Inquisition
5   Race war politics
6   The power of culture
7   Assimilation vs. integration
8   The corruption of human rights
9   Producer capture
10   The capture of state sector organisations
11   The need for a solidarity tax
12   Political AIDs
13   Antisense
14   Intergenerational equality
15   The plunder of the welfare system
16   Non-crime

The Three Features of Political Correctness

*W*ayne Mapp was a member of parliament and New Zealand's 'Political Correctness Eradicator' for a time, tasked with stamping out political correctness from public institutions. He made a speech in 2005 in which he identified three features of the ideology. First, political correctness is 'a set of attitudes and beliefs that are divorced from mainstream values'. Second, 'the politically correct person has a prescriptive view on how people should think and what they are permitted to discuss'. And third, which he regarded as most important, political correctness is 'embedded in public institutions, which have a legislative base' and 'coercive powers', and 'it is this third aspect that gives political correctness its authority'. For Wayne Mapp, the capture of public institutions sets political correctness apart from other ideas and ideologies. Furthermore, the consequence of this capture is that public institutions cease to represent the interests of the majority and instead 'become focussed on the cares and concerns of minority sector groups'.

Wayne Mapp continued (italics my own emphasis):

'The minority, therefore, has come to dominate the majority, which is an inherent feature of political correctness. This is not done with the intention of protecting minority rights, which is a legitimate aspect of any democracy. Instead, *the intent is to ensure that minority world views take precedence over the reasonably held views of the majority.*

Political correctness is a real challenge for National and other moderate centre-right parties. There is a natural abhorrence of the agenda of the politically correct, it being so rooted in leftist liberalism. *Simply railing against political correctness will not do. There needs to be a clear political programme to reverse it; to remove the viewpoints and language of the politically correct from the institutions of government.* Unless there is such a programme, the public who are intensely irritated about political correctness, are unlikely to believe anything will materially change, other than the most obvious examples of government silliness. There needs to be a commonsense strategy that deals with the central issue; what to do about those state institutions that foster the ideas of political correctness.

Political correctness is grounded in the capture of state institutions, with official spokespeople, legislative powers and ultimately sanctions for breach. Without these features, the attitudes and beliefs of the politically correct would be just another viewpoint in society, able to be debated and discussed in the same manner as any other set of ideas. Political correctness requires capture of state institutions by a minority so that the public institutions that deal with discrimination have now been taken over by people who are outside mainstream values. *Removing the power of the politically correct means removing their institutional and legislative base.*'

As the *Genesis of Political Correctness* states, political correctness is a belief system that has become a false morality, that is enforced upon society. Importantly, the politically correct have further used the power gained by capturing the legislative base, and the monies thus hijacked, to impose their views on society, irrespective of what anyone else thinks and believes.

The Two Wings of Political Correctness and the Opposing Patriotic Stance

In the *Genesis of Political Correctness*, I examined constitutional patriotism (a patriotism based on support for the institutions and laws and not based on a shared culture, history and national identity – detailed below) and the difficulty of maintaining national unity in the absence of genuine patriotism. I pointed out that constitutional patriotism (aka civic nationalism) had two wings: a liberal wing, and a communist wing. Then there were those described as ethnic nationalists (in reality, there is only nationalism, although the term ethnic nationalist distinguishes itself from the term civic nationalist). This distinction between the two wings of constitutional patriotism is important as the arguments about national unity

19

and social cohesion apply differently to the two wings. There is a three-way argument.

As mentioned above, first, the ethnic nationalists do not believe that civic nationalism/constitutional patriotism is strong enough to hold the nation together. Second, the liberal wing of civic nationalism/constitutional patriotism disagree and promotes the idea that citizens can be taught to give allegiance to the state devoid of any national culture. Third, the communist wing of civic nationalism/constitutional patriotism who believe that the likely weakening of national loyalty is desirable, should be encouraged, and is a prerequisite for a communist revolution. With the communist view, civic nationalism/constitutional patriotism is a mechanism for promoting the opposite of patriotism – that is, promoting a hatred of the country's history and hence the core nation (or Staatsvolk, to use the academic term). With the communist view, the state is owed allegiance by all citizens; immigrants and other disaffected groups are to be spurred on to undermine and eventually overthrow existing national culture and tradition of the core nation. The state owes no loyalty to the nation (Staatsvolk). Multiculturalists likewise reject the concept of a national culture as being discriminatory and racist (if there is a national culture, then other cultures are not that national culture and so have been excluded) and some even advocate a 'multicultural post-nation' (see *The Parekh Report* below).

The two wings of constitutional patriotism, the liberals and the communists, applies also to multiculturalism and political correctness. Its importance is that the liberals take the candyfloss language of political correctness at face value. Arguments about the damage done by political correctness might apply to the naivete of the liberal wing but are void when addressed to the communist wing, as doing harm is the communist intention.

The Barbarist

This is important. English philosopher, R. G. Collingwood (1889–1943), developed the concept of the barbarist in his book *New Leviathan* (1942). In *The Genesis of Political Correctness*, I examined the development of civilisation and the comparison between civilised peoples and uncivilised peoples. Several philosophers have delved into this issue.

Collingwood examined the different meanings of civilisation, the variety of civilisations, and civilisation's relationship to more backward peoples. He identified those who reject and wish to destroy civilisation as barbarists who seek to barbarise society. Collingwood's view was that the barbarists cannot succeed as 'there is no such thing as civilisation' and that it therefore cannot be destroyed. Like J. S. Mill (1806–1873) and Jean-Jacques Rousseau (1712–1778), Collingwood was concerned with civilisation's potential demise. In the *New Leviathan*, Collingwood began his examination of civilisation by identifying the term as the act of civilising and progressing a society towards civilisation and away from barbarism. Collingwood asserted that there is no clear distinction between civilisation and barbarism. The term is relative and changes over time as all societies progress. He therefore regarded civilisation as 'a process which has no absolute beginning and no absolute end'.

Collingwood accepted that civilisation is also used to denote a particular entity of society, such as the Chinese civilisation, European civilisation, or Roman civilisation. Collingwood believed that this distinction between different entities of civilisation means that each tries to be civilised in different ways, so that a Chinaman will attempt to be civilised in a way that might be regarded as barbarous to a European and vice versa. To Collingwood, 'civilisation and advancement of civilisation are one and the same', and he identified three senses of civilising: economic, social, and legal. The economic definition of being civilised is the ability to generate wealth by more advanced means than pure effort alone. The social definition is the manner in which people treat one another with civility, not force, and 'proper and seemly' behaviour. The legal definition means a society governed by law, in particular civil law.

Like other philosophers, Collingwood differentiated between barbarism and savagery. Savagery is not being civilised, and there is no such thing as absolute savagery. A savage people have a limited sense of being civilised relative to more civilised peoples. Unlike other philosophers, Collingwood also focused on barbarism. Barbarism was defined as either conscious or unconscious hostility to civilisation. It is a force to become less civilised and to promote others also to do likewise. Collingwood described this process as one to barbarise civilisation. 'To barbarise' is the opposite of 'to civilise'. In a conflict between civilisation and barbarism, Collingwood believed only civilisation can be the product of unconscious action, unlike barbarism:

> 'Barbarism can never be in this sense unconscious. The barbarist, as I will call the man who imitates the conditions of an uncivilised world cannot afford to forget what it is that he is trying to bring about; he is trying to bring about, not anything positive, but something negative, the destruction of civilisation; and he must remember, if not what civilisation is, at least what the destruction of civilisation is.
>
> Concentrating his mind on this question as he must do, the barbarist feels himself to be in one sense at least the intellectual superior of his enemy, and prides himself upon it.'[6]

Collingwood's rationale is that the barbarist must lose because:

> 'There is no such thing as civilisation. If there were, it could be exterminated, and the barbarist would have won; but in fact there are only innumerable and variously distant approximations to it, a kaleidoscope of patterns all more or less akin to the ideal ... what ensures the

defeat of barbarism is not so much the enormous diversity of existing civilizations, too numerous for any conqueror to dream of overcoming; it is the literally infinite possibility of varying the nature of the thing called civilisation, leaving it recognizable in this diversity; a possibility which will be exploited as soon as success in a barbarian attack stimulates the inventive powers of civilisation to look for new channels of development.'[7]

This assertion makes two assumptions. First, that civilisation is not distinct, and it is a process that will triumph in the end. Second, that the barbarist seeks to destroy the process of civilisation and not a civilisation as an entity. The assertion further overlooks the civilised status of the barbarist, who will himself be civilised, according to Collingwood's own logic, to some extent. It does not follow that the barbarist seeks to destroy his own degree of civilisation, nor does it follow he will not seek to benefit from the increased power more advanced economic civilisation brings, nor seek to use the law to legitimise and fasten any gains won. For example, the various invading barbarians of the Western Roman Empire sought to hold and defend their territorial conquests once they had settled down, rather than live in a lawless wasteland under threat from imperial forces.[8] Collingwood's assertion that 'there is no such thing as civilisation', and it is the variety of civilisation which guarantees its ability to defeat the barbarist, assumes the barbarist is at war with civilisation as a whole and civilisation as a whole is opposed to the objectives of the barbarist. However, the barbarist may only be attacking one entity of civilisation, and other civilisations may choose not to get involved, or may seek to support the barbarist for their own reasons (the Eastern Roman Empire did not fully mobilise in support of the West,[9] and the barbarians played one half of the empire off against the other).[10]

Collingwood cited four historical examples of barbarism. The Saracens were the first, and he asserted they were disgusted with the wealth and peaceful state of civilisation and responsible

23

for the destruction of civilisation in North Africa.[11] It is important that Collingwood, as did Mill and Rousseau, recognised the role of the disunity within civilisation which assisted the Saracens in their conquests.[12]

Collingwood identified the 'Albigensian heresy' as being the second barbarism (Collingwood described this as an anti-Christian aberration practised by believers who lived like hermits). The third barbarism was the Turks. The Turks conquered Asia Minor, then much of the Balkans, including Constantinople, thus destroying the Byzantine Empire (as the surviving eastern half of the Roman Empire was known). Collingwood portrayed the Turks as cruel, untrustworthy,[13] and piratical.[14] He said their failure to conquer Europe was a failure of barbarism and the success of civilisation, although he overlooks the Turks' retention of their conquests.

Collingwood's fourth barbarism was the Germans (he wrote during WWII). He believed that the benefit of hindsight reveals the German attitude to England at the time of the Boer War was barbarist.[15] He said German barbarism relied upon using diplomacy to divide any opposition to it[16] and that barbarists have no allies or loyalty; it is 'all fight against all'.[17] Collingwood reiterated that the barbarists exploit the slowness of civilisation to recognise its threat.[18] He said Germans had a tendency to 'herd-worship' and regarded this as 'a defect in civilisation where more civilisation is needed'.[19] While Germany was an advanced European country, civilised in many respects, Collingwood condemned them for 'incivility'.[20] This lack of civility was a key missing factor.

Collingwood summed up his account of the four arch-barbarists by saying they were all defeated, or withered away, for a variety of reasons.[21] That Collingwood was writing during WWII is pertinent and explains the case he is making. Collingwood's optimistic conclusion that barbarists will always be defeated is understandable, especially as victory against Germany was not assured, and defeat would have resulted in a definite victory for barbarism, given Nazi ideology.

Of the four barbarisms Collingwood cited, two were relatively backward peoples living on the edges of civilisation, the Saracens and the Turks, while the Albigensian heresy was internal to civilisation itself, and the fourth, the Germans, was a civilisation technologically and economically advanced but lacking the necessary civility to act responsibly. Three of the examples waged aggressive wars against civilisation, and the fourth, the Albigenses, who were plundering in southern France and described by Pope Innocent III as being 'worse than the Saracens', were vanquished in a crusade when peaceful means failed.[22] *All four examples have in common a strident ideology.*

Collingwood was concerned about the potential decay of civilisation, like many other philosophers and other inter-war writers.[23] He did not regard the barbarians as being the chief cause of the collapse of the Roman Empire.[24] However, the Western Roman Empire fell 1,000 years before the Eastern Roman Empire did.[25] Whatever failings the empire had, it was only in the west where those failings proved fatal. The Western Empire had twice the length of frontier to defend against the barbarians, while the Eastern Empire was strategically stronger, which meant the barbarians headed west.[26] The late 19th and early 20th centuries witnessed a sense of alarm at Britain's decline,[27] and the lead up to WWII was dominated by the threat of the rise of Nazism, and these factors undoubtedly influenced the concerns of Collingwood and the other inter-war writers.

If civilisations can fall, then it does not follow that barbarism must be defeated. Barbarism may triumph over a declining civilisation, not only as a result of the aggressiveness and opportunism of the barbarism, but also because of the civilisation's weakness. Collingwood, however, was optimistic that civilisation will always triumph. This optimism depends on what meaning is conferred upon the term civilisation. Collingwood identified three categories of civilisation: as a process of civilising; as distinct from savagery or barbarism; and as an entity, such as the Roman civilisation.

The Roman civilisation no longer exists. Various barbarian tribes in the west overran it, and the surviving Byzantine Empire was eventually completely overrun, too. The Turks conquered Constantinople and destroyed the Byzantine Empire. That they subsequently failed to conquer the rest of Europe may be true, but that does not help the Byzantines. Civilisation, as distinct from savage or less civilised peoples, is a relative phenomenon which can change. China, as Mill highlighted,[28] was once more advanced than many other civilisations, but the European powers surpassed it as it slid into decline. In this sense, too, civilisation can cease.

Civilisation as a process may be more difficult to destroy. But the process stems from the civilisation as an entity and depends on it. If the entity is destroyed, then so is the process. The Eastern Roman Empire was wealthier than the Western,[29] yet the eastern Mediterranean countries are not so now. Furthermore, to cite the failure of the barbarists to destroy the process assumes that is their intention. In fact, they are certainly keen on the wealth created by the process, as the Saracens, Turks, and all the other barbarians who overran the Roman Empire were keen to plunder and take whatever booty they could find. The Huns, Vandals (from whom the term vandalism originates) and Visigoths were equally keen to plunder. However, what distinguished the Saracens and Turks is that they were Muslim, and their destruction of Byzantine civilisation was more complete. Constantinople was plundered, its inhabitants were taken for or sold into slavery,[30] and the city was renamed and remained an Ottoman city.

Barbarists do not necessarily set out to destroy the process of civilisation, although their actions may harm and set back the process. They are more interested in the destruction of civilisation as an entity, either for territorial conquest or booty. Barbarist ideology is important and, when combined with the desire to plunder, poses a major threat to civilisation. Collingwood developed the understanding of the relationship between civilisation and barbarism with his attention to the barbarist. His definition of civilisation and his appreciation of its many forms are complete, as is his analysis of barbarism and his concept of barbarisation, being the goal of the barbarist.

Ideology is important. However, Collingwood's writing was influenced by WWII, and his optimistic assertion that the barbarist will fail because there is no such thing as civilisation is incomplete. Civilisation as an entity can be destroyed. The barbarists can win.

There is a danger that a civilised people takes its wealth and advancement for granted and becomes too soft and effete to defend itself. Society can become fragmented with vested interests and civilisation can decay.

Political correctness is a barbarist ideology. It, too, seeks to barbarise civilisation. Demanding money (or reparations), the toppling and defacing of statues and monuments, the debunking of civilised values, and trashing of literature and art is what barbarists do. The West needs to recognise the creed of political correctness for what it is, and mobilise to destroy it. The alternative is the destruction of the West.

The Inquisition

In *The Genesis of Political Correctness*, I wrote: 'Opposition to both the repopulation policy and political correctness is crushed. Free speech is restricted in Britain – unlike in the USA, where it is vigorously defended. In Britain, what is the British Inquisition even targets children for signs of political incorrectness.' The populist rebellions of 2016 showed I had spoken too soon. Opposition to political correctness had not been crushed (the voters rebelled), and so the Inquisition became more venomous.

The Trump election victory followed the UK's Brexit vote. The response from the establishment in the USA was very similar to that of the UK. Disbelief, followed by anger and a contemptuous dismissal of the vote. The wrong side won. People had been deceived. They did not understand what they were voting for. They had been misled by a populism that had promised easy answers. The vote had been rigged and could not be relied upon.

In the USA, the alleged Russian interference in the campaign went so far as to the setting up of the Mueller enquiry to investigate President Trump. Even when no evidence of the alleged collusion was found, many Democrats continued to call for impeachment. In July 2019, after plaguing US politics for some time in pursuit of the unfounded allegations against President Trump, Mueller replied 'yes' in Congress when asked if President Trump could be charged with a crime after leaving office. Mueller believed President Trump could be charged with obstruction of justice and could serve a substantial jail term if convicted.

In the UK, the focus was on an alleged breach of people's privacy by Cambridge Analytica via Facebook, supposed spending irregularities, and a court application to have Boris Johnson, the leader of the Vote Leave campaign, prosecuted and imprisoned for an abuse of public office – an application the judge refused to strike out as being vexatious or patently wrong. The judiciary, again, acted as the high priests of political correctness.

Less elevated political activists were likewise targeted. One, who had called Soubry 'a Nazi', in front of police officers who saw nothing wrong, was subsequently arrested, prosecuted and harassed by the police. Members of the dissident Right were imprisoned. Other pro-Brexit and anti-Islam activists were also targeted.

Internationally, social media came under pressure to close the various pages of those accused of spreading hate. Even political parties were affected. In Canada, a candidate for mayor of Ontario, Faith Goldy, was affected. In Britain, in the EU elections of 2019, the leader of UKIP, Gerard Batten was not afforded a fair hearing and UKIP was presented as being far-Right. Batten has been a long-standing critic of Islam. Also, UKIP had brought some internet activists into the party, one of whom had made laddish comments about a Labour MP.

This increasing oppression not only crippled the campaign efforts of various organisations and individuals but also filtered out to the wider public. Once social media had acquired a penchant for censorship, the habit grew, as did the demand from the politically correct for yet more censorship. Even ordinary users found their Facebook pages blocked with increasing frequency and little explanation.

Thus, the ability of those on the Right to communicate with one another and to the wider public was undermined. Meanwhile, as per Marcuse's demand, the Left were free to say and do as they like. The Left's control of the mainstream media facilitated a steady output of little more than propaganda passed off as expert opinion and news reporting.

The Inquisition was not confined to political opponents. Children were targeted to see if they abided by politically correct dogma. For example, in 2008-09, there were allegedly 10,436 racist incidents in primary schools in England and Wales, another 19,223 in secondary schools, and 41 in nursery schools. Most incidents involved name-calling. In 51 cases, the police became involved. Under the Race Relations (Amendment) Act 2000, teachers were required to name the alleged perpetrator of such incidents, name the alleged victim, and set out the alleged incident and punishment in reports to the Local Education Authority. Heads who sent in 'nil' returns were condemned for 'under-reporting'. The persecution of schoolchildren continued under the Tory/Liberal Democrats coalition. Using terms such as 'Chinese boy', 'Somalian', 'gay' or even 'girl' can be sufficient for a child, even a nursery child, to be branded as racist, homophobic, and prejudiced. The Office for Standards in Education (Ofsted) became the government's engine for the persecution. Ofsted placed a village primary school in Cumbria, with only 13 pupils, into special measures for having too many incidents of racist and homophobic bullying, stemming from one incident of children using the term 'gay' in a politically incorrect way. In January 2015, two schools fell afoul of Ofsted. One was put into special measures because a 10-year-old did not give a politically correct answer to a question as

29

to what lesbians 'did'; the other school was told it would be closed because one child gave a politically incorrect answer to a question as to what a Muslim was. An 11-year-old girl was asked if she was a virgin.

Incredibly, even during the UK 2015 election campaign, one primary school, with children as young as three years old, required pupils to sign a contract that they must 'Be tolerant of others whatever their race, colour, gender, class, ability, physical challenge, faith, sexual orientation or lifestyle and refrain from using racist or homophobic or transphobic language in school.' In guidelines from the government in October 2015, children were encouraged to spy on and report fellow children for using supposedly racist or sexist language. For example, the use of the term 'man up' was deemed sexist.

The sexualisation of children was not confined to the UK. In November 2019, Elizabeth Johnston, aka Activist Mommy, a home-schooling mother of 10 and a Christian family blogger, highlighted a video in which two female teachers explained 'self-love' to children of around 8-13 years old. First, the teachers started with 'different types of love' and that 'people fall in love at all different kinds of ages'. The children were asked if they were in love, to which the children answered they were in love with pizza, sour candy, or a favourite teen TV star. The teachers pressed on, saying, 'There are all kinds of different relationships', and 'all kinds of ways to show love', before telling the children, 'When it comes down to it, love is just love.' Then, one teacher said, 'What about things that could happen if you masturbate, since some people consider masturbation a form of self-love?' After talking about the masturbating not necessarily leading to sex, one teacher concluded masturbation is 'really pleasant and lovely that you can do for yourself and, if it's something you enjoy, that's definitely a way of showing yourself love'.

The objection to the use of words continued. For example, in the UK, the phrase 'ladies and gentlemen' was banned from the theatre under new guidelines. Maureen Lipman, a Jewish Labour supporter, spoke out to assert that she considered herself to be an actress and not an actor, the preferred term of the politically correct. Lipman said, 'In my new, blue, sadly no-longer EU passport, my profession will be stated as ACTRESS. Because asleep or awoke, that's the role for me.'

In March 2018, the Judicial College (which trains judges) issued new guidance, setting out a new list of words and phrases deemed politically incorrect. Terms such as 'West Indian', 'Afro-Caribbean', 'lady', 'homosexual', 'transsexual', 'ethnic minority', 'immigrant', 'queer', 'postman', 'businessman', and 'mental illness' were among those banned.

Universities remained in the forefront of the control of language permissible. In September 2019, the Oxford University Press (OUP) revealed it was considering changing the contents of its dictionary after complaints about the use of sexist words. Maria Beatrice Giovanardi, who had launched a petition to get changes, said:

> 'Have you ever searched online for the definition of a woman? "Bitch, besom, piece, bit, mare, baggage, wench, petticoat, frail, bird, bint, biddy, filly"– these are the words which the Oxford English dictionary online tells us mean the same as "woman". This sexist dictionary must change ... Sexism, just like racism, and any oppressive ways of talking, should have no place in society, and, of course, texts like the dictionary.'

OUP said, 'We appreciate feedback on our lexical content but it's worth reiterating that our dictionaries reflect rather than dictate how language is used, which means that we include terms that are often considered pejorative or have negative historical associations.' OUP are of course correct in pointing out that a dictionary is supposed to explain what a word means – not what the politically correct want it to mean. A dictionary should be objective and not political.

In May 2019, the quango Institute for Apprenticeships and Technical Education claimed women were being deterred from apprenticeships due to the use of masculine language.

Consequently, some words were to be banned, such as 'ambition', 'active', 'adventurous', 'analytical', 'challenging', 'leader', 'decisive', 'objective', 'competitive', 'independent', 'opinion', 'confident', and 'intellect'. Gender neutral words were to be used, such as: 'understand', 'support', 'dependable', 'cooperative', 'connect', 'interdependent', 'considerate', 'responsive', 'pleasant', 'committed', and 'communal'. Anne Osborne from the institute said, 'Research has shown that the language used in job adverts can make the job more or less appealing to one gender and therefore discourage women from applying for certain jobs.'

In July 2019, in the USA, the City Council of Berkeley, California, banned its employees from using 'man' words in an attempt to be gender neutral. Words such as 'manhole', 'manmade', 'manpower', 'ombudsman', 'fraternity', 'fraternal', 'repairman', 'pregnant women', 'heirs', 'craftsmen', 'master', 'sportsman', 'male' and 'female' were replaced. Council documents stated, 'In recent years, broadening of societal awareness of transgender and gender nonconforming identities has brought to light the importance of non-binary gender inclusivity.'

In the UK, the army banned soldiers from referring to one another as 'lads'. 'Mankind' and 'sportsmanship' were also banned. The orders came from the Ministry of Defence's joint equality, diversity and inclusion unit, known as Jedi.

Not to be left out, the UN called for the terms 'husband' or 'wife' to be phased out in the name of equality (that the UN had money to encroach into national and people's private affairs in this way proved they had too much money – that needs to be remedied).

In October 2019, the lyrics of *Baby, It's Cold Outside* were changed in John Legend and Kelly Clarkson's new version, after some radio stations banned the original. For example, 'Say, what's in this drink? – no cabs to be had out there' was replaced with, 'If I have one more drink? – It's your body, and your choice'.

In September 2020, the BBC banned certain words and phrases supposedly linked to slavery, including 'cakewalk', 'nitty gritty', 'sold down the river' and 'uppity'. 'Cakewalk' allegedly 'originated as a dance performed by enslaved Black people on plantations before the American Civil War' who 'competed for a cake'. 'Nitty gritty' is allegedly reference to nits (parasites) and grits (a cheap foodstuff used to feed slaves). 'Sold down the river' was banned because 'in the 19th century, Black slaves were literally sold down the river to plantation owners further south where brutal conditions awaited'. 'Uppity' was 'a word used by White people during racial segregation in the USA to describe Black people they believed weren't showing them enough deference'.

However, polite language was not required for the Left. In the UK, David Lammy, a Labour MP, said, 'Brexiteers like Nazis? I would say that wasn't strong enough.' In March 2019, David Lammy wrote on Twitter, 'The world does not need any more white saviours. As I've said before, this just perpetuates tired and unhelpful stereotypes. Let's instead promote voices from across the continent of Africa and have serious debate.' Lammy tweeted in response to the presenter Stacey Dooley's Comic Relief trip to Africa when she was photographed holding a Black child. She was accused of 'poverty porn' and of having a 'white saviour complex'. Comic Relief had previously been criticised for 'white saviourism'. Lammy had not accepted offers to be involved with the programme himself.

Another aspect was the determination to present women as being oppressed. In July 2019, the Commons Women and Equalities Committee called on the Equalities and Human Rights Commission to be given more powers and fine firms which did not pay women the same as men. Maria Miller, a Tory and chairman of the committee, said, 'Creating a society where people are not treated differently because of the colour of their skin, sex, gender, sexuality or religion is central to British values.' In October 2019, an Office for National Statistics (ONS) report disclosed that earnings peaked for both men and women in full-time work between 40-49 years. Men earned 11.4 per cent more than women in this age group. Figures showed that a record 75 per cent of mothers went out to work (including part-time) and the pay gap between men and women under 40 had disappeared: 'The gender pay gap for full-time employees is close to zero for those aged between 18 and 39'. For full-time workers over 50, the pay gap was more than 15 per cent in favour of men, which is to be expected given women also become mothers and hence spend more time looking after their children. Women are not oppressed victims. Outside of a communist state, it is not the role of government to impose equal outcomes by penalising men for the extra paid work they do and the resulting career advancement.

In August 2019, adverts from Volkswagen and Philadelphia Cheese were banned to prevent 'harmful' gender stereotyping. The ban was the result of three complaints against the Volkswagen advert (the men were supposedly in adventurous activities whereas the women were in a 'care-giving' role), and one complaint against the humorous Philadelphia Cheese advert (the man was apparently portrayed as not being able to care for children). This is a prime example of political correctness. The ads were banned because they were deemed to be not politically correct.

In September 2020, the Law Commission proposed that misogyny should be made a hate crime, and those designated as victim groups should include the homeless, sex workers, and 'alternative subcultures' such as goths. Hate crimes were introduced in 1986 and carry a maximum seven-year jail sentence.

The Inquisition continued and escalated beyond the politically corrects' wildest dreams. The trans issue is a good example, as is the purge of conservative opinions on social media. People could be prosecuted, lose their jobs or be subject to other forms of persecution for straying from the cultural Marxist narrative.

Incredibly, in the USA, given the trauma she had been through, one of those who fell victim to the inquisition was Mary Ann Mendoza, an Angel Mom, whose son was killed by an illegal immigrant drunk driver in 2014 (Angel Moms are mothers who have had family members killed by illegal immigrants). Mendoza's Facebook and Twitter posts were both censored. Facebook alleged a couple of her posts had breached their 'community standards on hate speech'. Mendoza told Fox & Friends:

> 'It was kind of surprising to me. This just isn't right. I sent the information to Facebook. Of course, I never hear back ... But it's becoming more and more apparent that the magnitude of crimes that illegals are committing in our country, and the information that myself and other angel families and organizations are getting out there is not settling well with the liberal ideas and pro-illegal, pro-open borders people.'

Mendoza's Twitter posts were censored when she spoke out against illegal immigration. Mendoza said:

> 'It is kind of disheartening ... they never tell me which words because all of my tweets, with Twitter, all of my tweets were different. There were six of them that I had to remove. So they never let me know what verbiage is wrong for them. And they talk about immigration status. You can't bring that up.'

Mendoza and the other Angel Mom families she represents were supporters of President Trump and wanted a border wall. She had resolved to spread her message in person and to launch her own blog.

Elizabeth Johnston, aka Activist Mommy, also fell afoul of the Inquisition. Her Facebook page was routinely suspended. In August 2018, Johnston received a message from Facebook telling her she could not post or use Messenger for seven days: 'This is because 2 of your posts go against our Community Standards on hate speech, and because you previously posted something that didn't follow our standards.' Facebook's Community Standards on hate speech is a highly subjective concept and nothing more than an opinion. Johnston had shared a post about an Ohio judge who refused to approve name changes for gender-confused teenagers, and had written on the post: 'This is what bullying looks like in 2018! Normalize our mental illness or we will sue you! Small minds must use these tactics. Pathetic!' and included the hashtag #GenderInsanity. Johnston responded by posting, 'That's right folks. If you don't bow to the trans agenda, you'll be muzzled and lose your platform. Free speech is dead in America.'

Activist Mommy highlighted another example in a post, 'Iowa Man Sentenced to 16 Years In Prison For Burning Church's LGBT Pride Flag – Activist Mommy: We must abide by the laws of the nation in which God has placed us, but how long will we stand by while those laws become increasingly more draconian, ever harsher, punishing anyone who dares to question the LGBT status quo? 16 years? Would such a sentence have been given to someone burning the Stars and Stripes? Of course not.'

A major development in recent years has been the growth of the transgender campaigners. Of importance, it was the campaigners who designated trans people as an oppressed minority in need of political intervention and not the doctors who treated them. There was some unease that children were being pushed into agreeing to medical intervention unnecessarily.

In March 2019, in the UK, psychotherapist Marcus Evans resigned as governor of The Tavistock & Portman NHS Foundation Trust, as he felt patients were being rushed and not given enough time for assessment and treatment before drugs and ultimately surgery for gender reassignment. The Tavistock Centre is England's only youth gender clinic and had been condemned as 'not fit for purpose'. Dr David Bell's report complained that the centre had not considered other problems such as bereavement or autism spectrum disorder.

In 2018 2,500 children were referred to the Gender Identity Development Service. Ten were aged three and four, and dozens were of primary school age. Bernadette Wren, of the Tavistock and Portman NHS Foundation, cited an example of a five-year-old whose parents changed his name from Billie to Ellie as he 'was always at his happiest when he could wear a dress'. The parents ignored medical advice and sent him to school as Ellie. The clinic warned that parents were pushing children into changing gender.

In July 2019, The Royal College of Paediatrics and Child Health asked its ethics and law advisory committee to investigate the increasing use of hormone blockers. The drugs were often used to prevent puberty in children who were deemed trans, and 'allows young people and parents to take time to weigh up and think about their options'.

In December 2019, an investigation by Sky News found that many of those at the Gender Identity Development Service (GIDS) at the Tavistock Centre were concerned at the 'over-medicalisation' of children. In the past decade, the annual referrals to the clinic increased from 77 to 2,590.

In June 2020, BBC's Newsnight reported clinicians were concerned children were receiving treatment too hastily at the Tavistock Centre, but that concerns were 'shut down'. One former patient, Keira Bell, 23, launched a legal claim that children were being administered life-changing therapy too soon. The Trust said:

> 'GIDS supports a wide range of children and young people grappling with distress about their gender identity. The Trust stands by its 2019 review of the service. We ... strongly refute the allegations put to us by Newsnight. Safeguarding is of the utmost importance to the Trust. In August 2018 a safeguarding lead was created specifically for GIDS.'

In 2010, the majority of those wanting to have a sex change were male. By 2020, that had been reversed with a 4,400 per cent surge in girls being referred for transitioning treatment, many of whom were autistic. The USA experienced the same. Studies showed that between 60 per cent and 90 per cent of gender dysphoric teenagers recover as they grow up.

In the UK, it had become possible for a man to obtain a Gender Recognition Certificate, and become legally female, without either taking female hormones or having surgery. Children could be given hormone blockers from the age of 11 to prevent puberty. From the age of 16, children can be administered oestrogen or testosterone. Surgical procedures can proceed after the age of 18.

One former Tavistock psychologist stated, 'Our fears are that young people are being over-diagnosed and then over-medicated. We are extremely concerned about the consequences for young people ... for those of us who previously worked in the service, we fear that we have had front row seats to a medical scandal.'

Another psychologist said that there was a fear of being accused of being 'transphobic' and that presently the medical pathway was the only pathway. Some had pointed out that female youngsters identified as transgender in response to anti-homosexual abuse. In some cases, medical procedures did not help and some de-transitioned.

A girl who told teachers that her parents were opposed to her changing gender was taken into foster care. The head teacher told the parents: 'I know she's not a boy but she's self-identified so my hands are tied.'

The case was cited, amongst others, by Professor Michele Moore, who previously worked at the Patient Safety Academy at Oxford University. She warned that children were being taken into care against the wishes of their parents, and that there had been a 4,500 per cent increase in girls who claimed to be transgender in the past decade. She was concerned that there was no investigation into the reasons for this or its consequences due to pro-transgender activists.

A change in the NHS memorandum of understanding in 2018 meant that doctors, health workers and teachers could not examine underlying issues behind a child's desire to transgender. Instead, they were required to accept the child's decision.

In November 2018, at one unidentified school, 17 pupils were transitioning. Other pupils were believed to be taking drugs to suppress puberty. In August 2019, leaked guidance from the Equality and Human Rights Commission (EHRC) stated that single-sex schools which disallowed trans pupils would be guilty of discrimination. The guidance further urged schools to install gender-neutral toilets. The guidance said:

> 'A refusal to admit a trans pupil to a single-sex school which is the same as the trans pupil's sex recorded at birth would be direct sex discrimination. Admitting such a pupil will not affect the school's single-sex status. A pupil who has transitioned, or wants to, must be allowed to continue to attend the school to remove them would amount to direct gender reassignment discrimination.'

In September 2019, police were called when angry demonstrators protested outside Priory School in Lewes. The school had introduced new rules requiring both male and female pupils to wear grey trousers, thus banning schoolgirls from wearing skirts. The demonstrators had been locked out as they were opposed to the gender-neutral school uniform. When schoolgirls had turned up at the start of the new term wearing skirts, they had been not allowed to enter.

In April 2019, the Brighton and Hove city council gave trans pupils stickers to prevent misgendering. The stickers had slogans such as 'trans ally', 'my pronouns matter', 'respect my pronouns, respect me', and 'gender is a spectrum'. A spokesman for the council said, 'The badges and stickers help raise awareness that you can't assume someone's gender identity and the pronouns they use. We know from a range of evidence that gender is more complicated than is traditionally recognised. We all define our own gender and we should respect other people's identities and rights.' The council had previously issued a 'gender guidance tool kit' to schools, to which staff were expected to adhere.

In October 2019, Clarissa Farr, a former top headmistress at St Paul's Girls School, and educational consultant, claimed at the Henley Literary Festival:

> 'The important thing is to have open conversations – to show that you're going to deal with them with respect and to distinguish those concerns which have longevity and some endurance where this is a genuine issue. It's what we, I'm afraid, in the staff room at the end of a long day called the "transtrender problem" where you've got these individuals adhering to the issue because they'd adhere to anything that was a bit radical and might cause a little bit of a turbulence in the school.'

However, also in October 2019, the judge-led Sentencing Council (responsible for recommending punishment levels) released instructions so transgender offences received more severe sentences than domestic burglaries.

By April 2020, there were signs of change. In a step away from the current thinking, Liz Truss addressed the Women and Equalities Committee about transgender surgery. She said that under-18s would be protected from irreversible decisions. In 2018, Theresa May advocated she wanted a 'more streamlined and de-medicalised' procedure. In September 2020, Liz Truss announced that gender self-recognition was 'not the top priority' for transgender people, and defended the 2004 Gender Recognition Act as providing 'proper checks'. There would, therefore, be no change in the law.

The heavy hand of PC Plod was exposed in the case of Harry Miller, a businessman contacted by Humberside Police who said they wanted to 'check his thinking'. The officer who spoke to Miller on the telephone claimed to represent the LGBTQ community and that he was investigating Miller about some tweets made the previous year that were being treated as a hate incident. Miller had questioned whether a transgender person could ever be a biological woman. One of Miller's tweets had said, 'I was assigned mammal at birth, but my orientation is fish. Don't mis-species me.'

Miller, a former policeman, was so angry he launched a judicial review into the training at the College of Policing. Miller told the *Daily Mail*: 'If ordinary people like myself don't stand up against what I see as the overreaching authority by the police, who will? It is definitely not the job of the State to restrict what we can or cannot talk about, either in face-to-face conversation or online.'

The PC claimed he had received a complaint about the tweets from a 'victim', who had alerted Scotland Yard's hate crime unit, who in turn had contacted the Humberside Police. The PC told Miller that although he had not broken the law, he had, nevertheless, committed a 'non-crime' hate incident. The PC had claimed: 'Sometimes a woman's brain grows in a man's body in the womb and that is what transgender is.' (The mind boggles). When Miller queried how someone could be called a 'victim' when no crime had been committed, the PC replied, 'that's just how it works'.

Miller received a police record for committing a 'non-crime' transphobic hate offence. He challenged the Hate Crime Operational Guidance issued by the College of Policing in 2014 and written with the help of lobby groups, which said a complaint must be recorded 'irrespective of whether there is any evidence to identify the hate element'. The police were to pursue 'any non-crime incident which is perceived by the victim or any other person, to be motivated by hostility or prejudice against a person who is transgender or perceived to be transgender'. The same rule applied to issues of race, religion, disability, or sexual orientation. Since the introduction of the guidance, the police had recorded at least 87,000 non-crime hate incidents. Scotland Yard had 900 hate crime officers.

The judge, Mr Justice Julian Knowles, presiding over the judicial review commented, 'Freedom-of-expression laws are not there to protect statements such as "kittens are cute", but they are there to protect unpleasant things. Their utility lies in exposing people to things that they do not want to hear.'

41

The trans agenda netted a few who dared to object. Another was Doula Lynsey McCarthy-Calvert, a birthing coach, who was forced to stand down from a charity after saying only women had babies, and for describing a woman as an 'adult human female'. Trans activists claimed this was a 'wolf-whistle of transphobia'. The charity caved in.

In another case, Miranda Yardley, who identified as a transexual male, claimed to have been put through 'ten months of hell' after the police accused him of harassing a transgender activist on Twitter. The judge dismissed the case after one day, saying there 'is no case and never was a case'. Yardley complained the police were out to 'enforce a political ideology'.

Trans activists called for a boycott of Tunnock's teacakes, after the LGB Alliance thanked them for supplying teacakes. It was believed Tunnocks did not understand the difference between the LGB Alliance, who are critical of the trans agenda, and the LGBT+ group who are not.

In another case, 45-year-old tax expert Maya Forstater lost her job because she had tweeted: 'Men Cannot Change into Women'. She failed in a legal challenge on the grounds that the European Convention on Human Rights protected her free speech. The judge at an employment tribunal ruled that her 'absolutist view' was 'not worthy of respect in a democratic society' and was therefore not protected under the law. The judge said, 'She will not accept in any circumstances that a trans woman is in reality a woman or that a trans man is a man'. (This issue is also a good example of antisense – see below). This infuriated the writer J. K. Rowling who tweeted: 'Call yourself whatever you like. Sleep with any consenting adult who'll have you. Live your best life in peace and security. But force women out of their jobs for stating that sex is real? #IstandWithMaya #ThisIsNotADrill.'

J. K. Rowling received abuse, demonstrators outside her home, and even death threats because of her stand. For example, she was told, 'Shut the fuck up, TERF [trans exclusionary radical feminist].' Regarding Maya Forstater, a Stonewall (an LGBTQ+ campaign organisation) spokesman said,

'This case was about the importance of Dignity and respect in the workplace. Trans people are facing huge levels of abuse and discrimination with one in eight having been attacked while at work in the last year.'

A source from Hachette, the publishing house dealing with J. K. Rowling's latest book, said:

> 'Staff in the children's department at Hachette announced they were no longer prepared to work on the book. They said they were opposed to her comments and wanted to show support for the trans lobby. These staff are all very "woke", mainly in their twenties and early thirties, and apparently it is an issue they feel very strongly about.'

Another source said:

> 'It was a handful of staff, and they are entitled to their views. If they were being asked to edit a book on domestic abuse, and they were a survivor of domestic abuse, of course they would never be forced to work on it. But this is a children's fairy tale. It is not the end of the world. They will all be having chats with their managers.'

Hachette issued a statement:

> 'We are proud to publish JK Rowling's children's fairy tale *The Ickabog*. Freedom of speech is the cornerstone of publishing. We fundamentally believe that everyone has the right to express their own thoughts and beliefs. That's why we never comment on our authors' personal views and we respect our employees' right to hold a different view. We will never make our employees work on a book whose content they find upsetting for personal reasons, but we draw a distinction between that and refusing to work on a book because they disagree with an

author's views outside their writing, which runs contrary to our belief in free speech.'

Four writers at The Blair Partnership, the literary agency used by J. K. Rowling, quit in protest at Rowling's views. One author wished to remain anonymous, but gender activist, Ugla Stefania Kristjonudottir Jonsdottir (known as Owl) and partner Fox Fisher (a 'trans queer artist'), as well as novelist Drew Davies (a friend) issued a joint statement which said:

> 'This decision is not made lightly, and we are saddened and disappointed it has come to this. After J. K. Rowling's ... public comments on transgender issues, we reached out to the agency with an invitation to reaffirm their stance to transgender rights and equality. After our talks with them, we felt that they were unable to commit to any action that we thought was appropriate and meaningful.'

The Blair Partnership said they could not compromise on the right of authors to free speech − 'a fundamental freedom'. A spokesman said, 'We believe in freedom of speech for all; these clients have decided to leave because we did not meet their demands to be re-educated to their point of view. We respect their right to pursue what they feel is the correct course of action.'

Jonsdottir, who is Icelandic and trans, was named as one of the BBC's 100 Women for 2019. Both Jonsdottir and Fisher claimed to be non-binary trans and preferred to use the pronoun 'they' rather than 'he' or 'she'.

In the *Daily Mail*, Julie Bindel, who also criticised the trans activists, wrote:

> 'I faced horrendous abuse from trans activists. I had death and rape threats. I was harassed and hounded in public, labelled a Nazi, a bigot, and accused of causing the suicide of young transgender people. The "Trans Taliban",

as I came to call them, would try to get events shut down at which I had been invited to speak about topics such as rape, child abuse or trafficking of women. Angry crowds would turn up, waving their placards, demanding that I be thrown out because I, like Maya [Forstater], believe that being born male of female is what makes someone a man or a woman.'

Gillian Phillip, 56, one of a team who wrote stories for Erin Hunter books, posted #ISTANDWITHJKROWLING on her Twitter handle. The result was a series of death threats, abuse, and complaints to her employer Working Partners. HarperCollins, which published the Erin Hunter books, also received complaints. In response to the threats, Gillian Phillip tweeted, 'Bring it on, homophobes and lesbian haters.'

In July 2020, James Noble, of Working Partners, announced, 'The worlds created by Erin Hunter are meant to be inclusive for all readers and we want to let you know that Gillian Phillip will no longer be writing any Erin Hunter novels.' Gillian Phillip said:

> 'I am disappointed that the hard work and professional attitude I have brought to my work for HarperCollins and for Working Partners counted for nothing in the face of an abusive mob of anonymous Twitter trolls. It is concerning that my concerns about women's legal rights and spaces have been presented as "transphobia", and that this accusation has been allowed to stand by my former employers.'

In Edinburgh, an imprint of J. K. Rowling's hands was daubed in red paint and a transgender flag was placed nearby. In August, after an attack from Kerry Kennedy, J. K. Rowling, who had been given an award by the Robert F. Kennedy Human Rights (RFKHR) group, said she would be returning it. Kerry Kennedy, the president of RFKHR, accused J. K. Rowling of 'undermining the validity and integrity of the entire transgender community'.

Despite the attacks on her, J. K. Rowling's latest book (using the pseudonym Robert Galbraith), *Troubled Blood*, topped the book charts with 64,633 sales in five days of its publication. This is despite calls from trans activists for a boycott. The book involves a male killer who dresses in women's clothes.

Forstater subsequently won an appeal against the employment tribunal decision.

In August 2020, Greater Manchester Police Chief Constable Ian Hopkins said, 'At vetting, applicants and serving officers must show that their behaviour and views are in keeping with the values of the service and the code of ethics.' He also said the 2010 Equality Act bound the police and they would treat gender reassignment as a protected characteristic as per the act. Also, the Police Code of Ethics stated officers must 'consider the needs of the protected characteristic groupings'. Rob Jessel, of the Fair Cop group said, 'The police are putting thousands of women in fear that they will not now be dealt with fairly and lawfully by their own force, simply because they share the same belief in biology as most of the population.' Two police forces had recently refused an application from a woman who said that she opposed discrimination against trans people, but did 'not believe you can change your biological sex'.

A Populus poll for the LGB Alliance found that 69 per cent of parents supported J. K. Rowling's stance regarding 'transgender activism'. The poll also revealed that only a quarter of parents were aware of a new curriculum for primary schools that promoted transgender rights. The Government Equalities Office supported the Stonewall 'LGBT inclusive primary curriculum guide'. The curriculum told teachers:

> 'Remember to teach children that "they", "them", and "their" can be singular as well as plural. You could use it as an opportunity to learn that a lot of non-binary people prefer not to be referred to as he or she ... Everyone has a gender identity. This is the gender that someone feels they are. This might be the same as they were given as a baby, but it might not. They might feel like they are a

different gender, or they might not feel like they are a boy or a girl.'

Stonewall lost some senior figures who disagreed with its adoption of a militant trans agenda. Its last accounts revealed it received £610,000 of taxpayer's money, including £234,000 from the Department of Education. A spokesman for the LGB Alliance said, 'Any curriculum that tells primary school children from age five upwards that they "may be born in the wrong body" is a bad idea. Young children are easily influenced and confused.' Liz Truss, the Equalities Minister, said, 'This document was not approved by Government. The Government Equalities Office logo should not be on it and I have asked for it to be removed.'

In November 2019, Sean Morris, 22, a student who made a 'call to arms' video that advocated that Muslims should be 'wiped off the face of the earth', faced a prison term when the judge said, 'People who incite religious or racial hatred create terrible trouble for our society. It will be a custodial sentence.' He was jailed for 18 months.

In October 2019, the Avon and Somerset Police's hate crime unit (yes, there is such a thing) encouraged Muslim women to report hate crime. Superintendent Andy Bennett claimed that there was 'still a substantial gap between reported and unreported crime and in some crime categories it can be as much as 50 per cent'.

In February 2019, Italy's Matteo Salvini ran into trouble when the senate voted to allow prosecutors to put him on trial. Salvini was accused of illegally keeping 147 illegal immigrants on a boat off Sicily for almost a week in August 2019. The trial began on 15 September 2021 with a procedural hearing (and the matter is ongoing at the time of writing). Salvini faced up to 15 years in prison.

The InfoWars site was banned across social media, as were some of the site's associates. In February 2019, the YouTube America First campaigner, Nick Fuentes, was likewise banned. Another, Steven Franssen, was banned from Twitter after tweeting about a Muslim committing rape at his old school. Katie Hopkins had her Twitter account suspended.

In addition, there were the casual attacks on high-profile personalities, including those who had passed away. The Royal Mint blocked the idea of an Enid Blyton coin, branding her a racist. John Wayne was denounced by students for a 'legacy of endorsing white supremacy'. The cartoon film, *The Jungle Book*, was accused of being racist.

Often, pressure was enough to impose the politically correct view. In the USA, television host Mario Lopez said:

> 'If you're 3 years old and you're saying you're feeling a certain way or you think you're a boy or a girl, whatever the case may be, I just think it's dangerous as a parent to make that determination then: "OK, well, then you're going to be a boy or a girl," whatever the case may be ... I think parents need to allow their kids to be kids, but at the same time, you gotta be the adult in the situation.'

For daring to express this common-sense opinion, GLAAD and PFLAG, two LBBTQ organisations, led a torrent of condemnation against Lopez. Fearing for his job, Lopez recanted.

A report from the Office for Students found that 35 per cent of universities, including Oxford and Cambridge, were imposing severe restrictions on freedom of speech. It advocated legislation to correct the situation. The lead researcher, Jim McConalogue said:

> 'Our findings suggest that 86 per cent of universities faced either severe or moderate free speech restrictions which need to be addressed. The fundamental issue must be dealt with because students and academics find themselves in educational institutions in which they cannot speak freely of the leading subjects of their day including on race, gender the outcomes of elections, their

views on religion, or on discrimination itself for fear of judgements that lead to eventual penalty or censorship.'

This report demonstrates the power of the Inquisition.

In August 2020, the rock star Nick Cave wrote in a newsletter on his Red Hand Files website:

'Political correctness has grown to become the unhappiest religion in the world. Its once honourable attempt to reimagine our society in a more equitable way now embodies all the worst aspects that religion has to offer (and none of the beauty) – moral certainty and self-righteousness shorn even of the capacity for redemption. It has become, quite literally, bad religion run amuck. Cancel culture's refusal to engage with uncomfortable ideas has an asphyxiating effect on the creative soul of a society.'

Up to a point, this is a legitimate criticism of the liberal wing of political correctness, but the 'religion' was formulated by communists with the purpose of doing harm. There is nothing 'honourable' about it.

There was some opposition. In September 2020, in the UK, the Department for Education issued new training manuals for teachers that included a slide that stated:

'Reinforce that everyone needs to show the same respect to others regardless of how different they are to them. Explain the harm caused by "cancel culture" and the importance of freedom of speech and freedom of association to a tolerant and free society. Teach that censorship and "no platforming" are harmful and damaging. Explain that seeking to get people "cancelled" (e.g. having them removed from their position of authority or job) simply because you disagree with them is a form of bullying and is not acceptable.'

Race War Politics and The Anti-Whites

The Frankfurt School, as did others on the Left, recognised that the focus on class war politics would not bring about a communist revolution. They therefore focused on culture and other means of revolution.

As stated above, by the 1970s, the Frankfurt School's Herbert Marcuse no longer regarded the working class as the alienated proletariat as Marx had envisioned. Were a communist revolution to be achieved, then other groups deemed not to be fully integrated into society – students, intellectuals, the unemployed, racial minorities etc. – would now become the 'catalysts' for that revolution.[31] Marcuse sought to supplement class war politics with race war politics and regarded the Black population as being the 'most natural' force of rebellion,[32] with the New Left as the vanguard.

The Frankfurt School's Jurgen Habermas also advocated race war politics. His 1995 essay, 'Citizenship and National Identity: Some Reflections on the Future of Europe' (Citizenship and National Identity), was predicated on the assertion that current history was in a state of flux, and three issues were impacting upon citizenship and national identity: (1) the future of the nation state; (2) the EU; (3) immigration.[33] The aim being to use immigrants to undermine social cohesion and ultimately to help overthrow Western societies. The growth of the various Black Lives Matter movements (BLM) across the West demonstrates the success of the Frankfurt School's focus on race war politics.

As can be seen from an examination of the Frankfurt School, they are hardened communists. Their every word is tailored to foment anarchy, division, strife and ultimately revolution. The failure of the proletariat to do what Marx predicted led to a whole new set of those deemed oppressed groups. Class war politics has given way to race war politics. This is a telling point. Instead of conceding that capitalism had evolved in a way unforeseen by Marx, and welcoming the higher standards of living and better quality of life that the proletariat enjoy, the communists dismiss the views of ordinary people as being false consciousness and then try to find new excuses for revolution. If class war politics does not trigger that revolution, then race war politics, with all the danger and hatred involved, is to be promoted. For communists, their hatred of society is all-consuming. Their motive is hatred and nothing more. They wish to destroy, no matter how bloodily, Western civilisation. They are barbarists.

A casual look at what has happened across the West, in particular the Anglosphere, shows that the barbarists, be they the politically correct or their allies, have been in the ascendency. Race war politics has been a useful tool.

Ilhan Omar, (D-Minn.), and her family moved to the USA as refugees from Somalia. A member of the so-called Squad, she is openly hostile to the West and the USA. For example, in an interview with *Vogue Arabia*, she said:

> 'It's an everyday assault. Every day, a part of your identity is threatened, demonized, and vilified. Trump is tapping into an ugly part of our society and freeing its ugliness. It's been a challenge to try to figure out how to continue the inclusion; how to show up every day and make sure that people who identify with all the marginalized identities I carry, feel represented. It's transitioning from the idea of constantly resisting to insisting in upholding the values we share – that this is a society that was built on the idea that you could start anew. And what that celebrates is immigrant heritage.'

For example, Ilhan Omar tweeted, 'I am Hijabi, Muslim, Black, Foreign born, Refugee, Somali', and 'easily triggering conservatives, Right wing bloggers, anti-Muslim bigots, tinfoil conspiracy theorists, birthers …'

Her Republican opponent, Dalia al-Aqidi, responded, 'I am an American. That's why I'm running for Congress.' Referring to Omar, al-Aqidi told Fox News:

'She needs to be stopped ... As an American citizen, my duty is to defend my country, and my duty is to stand up to her hatred and racism that she's spreading within her community, within the country, and even worldwide. Ilhan Omar is harming every American with her hatred, her standing against what we believe in, [and] against our own Constitution ... I came to the U.S. more than 25 years ago. So, basically, I'm not a refugee anymore. I'm not an Iraqi anymore. I'm an American. Period.'

Dalia al-Aqidi speaks as someone who is keen to assimilate and to defend the interests and people of her adopted country.

Palestinian-American activist Linda Sarsour, another member of the Squad, co-founder of the advocacy group MPower Change and national co-leader of the Women's March, has been accused of flirting with anti-Semitism, in part through her association with Nation of Islam leader Louis Farrakhan, whose publicly stated views on Jews and Israel have drawn wide condemnation.

In April 2019, Sarsour urged Muslims protesting outside the White House:

'Sister Ilhan Omar is the best that our community has to offer: She's black, she's Somali, a former refugee. She's bold, she's unapologetic, she's anti-war and anti-imperialist. She's a supporter of the [anti-Israel] boycott, divestment, sanction movement. She stands with poor people. She stands with the most marginalized people in America. And she represents everything that is beautiful about Islam.'

Linda Sarsour equated the State of Israel to White supremacy, 'Ask them this: How can you be against White supremacy in the United States of America and the idea of living in a supremacist state based on race and class, but then you support a state like Israel that is built on supremacy, that is built on the idea that Jews are supreme to everybody else?'

In response to one protest, Rashida Tlaib, another member of the Squad, tweeted then quickly deleted (but not quickly enough), 'Americans have spent decades raping and pillaging my people. What goes around comes around.' Rashida Tlaib further compared USA's border with Mexico to the Gaza Strip, as she demanded that Congress censure President Trump. Tliab told an American Muslims for Palestine conference in Chicago, 'When you think about the border, you have to got to understand how interconnected the oppression in Palestine is with the oppression taking place at the border.'

The Squad, and those other Democrats like them, were elected. They received strong support from the Left of politics and from their own communities. They are not voices in the wilderness.

A hatred of the West and their resident country was not confined to the USA. In the UK, the Labour MP, Rupa Huq, described the Union Jack as 'xenophobic'. When Benjamin Zephaniah, a poet, refused an OBE in 2003, he said, 'I get angry when I hear that word empire; it reminds me of slavery, it reminds of thousands of years of brutality, it reminds me of how my foremothers were raped and my forefathers brutalised.'

Thousands of years? Someone should tell Zephaniah, very slowly, that the British Empire did not last thousands of years and African colonies were only a part of the British Empire for around 80 years.

The commentator and BBC favourite, Yasmin Alibhai-Brown, once said, 'I don't like White men. I want them to be a lost species in a hundred years.' In February 2019, Kehinde Andrews, a professor of Black Studies at Birmingham City University, told Piers Morgan and Susanna Reid on ITV's Good Morning Britain show, 'The British empire lasted far longer, did more damage and in many ways paved the way for the Nazis and their genocidal ideology.' The fact the British Empire no longer exists did not deter Kehinde Andrews from his attack upon the UK and its people.

In keeping with what Habermas and other Frankfurt School members taught about people being indoctrinated to hate their countries, in the UK, the British Empire was a prime target. For example, there is a teaching tutorial for secondary school teachers called 'Winston Churchill: Hero or War Criminal?' prepared by a global education company, Tes. Chris McGovern, of the Campaign for Real Education, said of it, 'They are brainwashing kids and trashing our past. It's pitiful that we have planned strategy to demonise Churchill. We all know he was not perfect, but his views reflected the age in which he lived.' This comment, though true, does not acknowledge that the politically correct have to target Churchill. He is a national hero and engenders patriotism. That cannot be tolerated, and so Churchill is a target. He is targeted not because of his flaws, but because of his achievements. Citing his alleged flaws is merely the way the politically correct try to debunk his reputation.

Another teaching aid described Churchill as 'a warmongering, blundering reactionary' and 'responsible for such things as the disaster at Gallipoli, the callous treatment of exploited workers in the General Strike and a failed attempt to spark off World War Three against Soviet Russia in his "Iron Curtain" speech.' Tes claimed teachers wrote the lesson plans and denied responsibility for their content.

In fact, Churchill did not attempt to 'spark off World War Three' with his Iron Curtain speech, and the allegation is a lie. Churchill warned that the Soviet Union would split the European continent into two and bring Eastern Europe under Soviet rule.

Hatred of the British Empire and consequently of the British nation, reached to the very top. For example, the new Labour MP, Bell Ribeiro-Addy, made her maiden speech on the theme, 'Let's address the historic injustices of the British Empire.' In that speech she said of other ethnic minority and far-Left colleagues:

'They stand for a principled, unfaltering stance on opposing war, cuts and racism over decades. They have consistently supported peace, Palestinian human rights and LGBT rights, and they have opposed austerity, racism and bigotry, regardless of whether that was popular at the time, and regardless of being hounded by the reactionary press, or whether something would win in parliament. To me, they are socialist heroes. They have always been where I aim to be: on the side of the oppressed, not the oppressor, and always on the right side of history.'

Ribeiro-Addy described herself as 'proud to be the daughter of Ghanian migrants'. She continued:

'I cite my heritage not just because it is important to me, but because it underpins my experience in this country, my country, and my fear as racism and other hate crimes are on the rise. Today, we are debating global Britain. There is the saying that "if you don't know where you've come from, you don't know where you're going". It strikes me that as a country we cannot begin to fulfil the idea of global Britain until we first address the historic injustices of the British empire, injustices including slavery and colonialism; first, because it is the right thing to do, but also because we may soon find ourselves out in the cold if we do not.

...While we spent years debating Brexit and, as my hon. friend the member for Putney said, engaging in monumental self-harm, India surpassed the UK to become the fifth-richest economy in the world. India, a former British colony, where this country presided over a bloody partition, the Amritsar massacre and the Bengal famine. Countries in Africa, such as Ghana, Kenya and Uganda, are among the fastest-growing economies in the world; countries that Britain deliberately underdeveloped, stole resources from and brutally enslaved their people. Madam Deputy Speaker, were you aware that in the mid to late 1700s, over 50 members of this House represented slave plantations? Members of parliament just like me enslaved people that looked just like me.

I am someone who believes firmly that the only way to tackle an issue is at its very root, and the racism that I and many other people in this country face on a daily basis has its root in those very injustices. Not only will this country, my country, not apologise — by apologise I mean properly apologise; not "expressing deep regret" — it has not once offered a form of reparations. People see reparations as handing over large sums of money, but why could we not start today with simple things like fairer trade, simple things like returning items that do not belong to us, and simple things like cancelling debts that we have paid over and over again?'

The allegation Churchill is responsible for the Bengal famine is a smear against him. Professor Tirthankar Roy of the LSE, and an author about modern India, said, 'Churchill was not a relevant factor behind the 1943 Bengal famine. The agency with the most responsibility for causing the famine and not doing enough was the government of Bengal.' Churchill wrote to Lord Wavell, the Viceroy of India, saying 'every effort must be made, even by the diversion of shipping urgently needed for war purposes, to deal with local shortages'. The Japanese invasion of Burma had pushed hundreds of thousands of refugees into India and Japanese ships had sunk an estimated 100,000 tons of Allied shipping in the Bay of Bengal. The fall of Burma further ended the flow of rice to India.

Ribeiro-Addy might use the term reparations, but this is simply a redistribution of wealth, i.e. communism. It is the politics of envy. She rambled on to complain about the 'Windrush scandal'; borrowing centuries ago to 'pay off slave owners', tax dodgers; Grenfell Tower with '72 people dead and many more traumatised by the loss of their loved ones and the loss of their homes, a community scarred for generations'; cladding; even knife crime about which 'we cannot arrest our way out of this situation,' so what was needed was 'real investment in preventive measures'; and that if 'you are a young Black man who is caught or arrested with drugs, it is a very different outcome for you'.

After a few swipes at fake news, President Trump, and a complaint that 'half of the wealth of the world is hoarded by the top 1 per cent', Ribeiro-Addy made clear she opposed 'fascism rising across Europe' and wanted more immigration, and was 'very proud to have been appointed shadow immigration minister'.

Another, Dawn Butler, the Labour MP for Brent Central, accused Boris Johnson of being a racist, and complained:

> 'Sadly, some people seem to find me calling out racism more offensive than the racism itself ... I have come to the conclusion that we must be living in an Alice in Wonderland world, where it's become worse to call out racism than it is to be racist. I was made to feel in the wrong for calling out racism and my own lived experiences were disregarded. The other thing that is so often used to discredit me when I call out racism is to switch focus to Labour and anti-Semitism. I have said repeatedly that Labour failed on this issue and it is right that we apologised. Sorry to break the news to you. Boris Johnson is racist.'

The attacks on President Trump were not confined to the USA. One attention-seeking critic is the mayor of London, Sidiq Khan, who was prone to write articles and give interviews to air his views. For example, Khan said Mr Trump's actions, 'on many, many occasions ... (Trump) gives us the impression that all he cares about is White America ... When you see ... the President of the USA calling people rapists because they happen to be Mexican, having a travel ban against people of my faith, that leads to huge concerns across the world.' In September 2019, Khan wrote:

'Vulnerable, often minority, communities are being demonised and scapegoated for all society's ills. And, in appalling new parallels with the horrors of the past, migrants, refugees, people of colour, LGBTQ+ and Jewish communities are bearing the brunt. This comes as a new wave of extremist far-right movements and political parties are winning power and influence at alarming speed – fuelled by Donald Trump, the global poster-boy for White nationalism. Politicians across Europe are following his example by seeking to exploit division to gain power – from Matteo Salvini in Italy to Marine Le Pen in France. Hungary's Viktor Orbán has systematically destroyed the independence of both the judiciary and the press, institutions that are also under daily verbal attack from Trump and other far-right leaders around the world. The impact can also be seen in the UK ... Just last week we saw the disdain Johnson has for parliament and our democracy.'

Khan continued:

'Those spreading fake news in order to divide us must be challenged. And underlying causes of public discontent need tackling – a task that requires renewed global coordination to meet the economic, social and environmental challenges that are creating a breeding ground for the far right. This means recognising that economic inequalities between countries – made ever worse by the growing environmental catastrophe facing our planet – have contributed to the global migration crisis and cannot be tackled by any one country in isolation. It means tackling the frustrations of the growing numbers within western countries who have been left behind by globalisation, fuelling resentment. And, crucially, it means fighting against those trying to rewrite the darkest period in human history for their own political purposes. All this will require the UK to work more closely with other countries, not less. Instead of pursuing Brexit and poisoning our relations with the rest of the continent, we should be exercising our soft power and showing leadership in the fight against the far right.'

What a lot of deceitful, babyish rubbish! Khan sought to stir up a coalition of supposedly oppressed minorities while demonising those who do not share his cultural Marxist agenda as being far-Right. It was Khan who sought to foment and 'exploit division to gain power'. Khan then promoted a globalist agenda to excuse illegal immigration and to subvert democracy (e.g. by rejecting Brexit, which people voted for). Once again, Khan showed himself as an anti-West demagogue. A report from Euro News stated that Khan backed a housing project in London that was for Muslims only. Nine mosques in London were given permission to broadcast the call to prayer publicly. This is open colonisation.

In June 2019, prior to a visit by President Trump to the UK, Sadiq Khan wrote in *The Observer*:

'President Donald Trump is just one of the most egregious examples of a growing global threat. The far-Right is on the rise around the world, threatening our hard-won rights and freedoms and the values that have defined our liberal, democratic societies for more than 70 years. Viktor Orban in Hungary, Matteo Salvini in Italy, Marine Le Pen in France and Nigel Farage are using the same divisive tropes of the fascists of the 20th century to garner support, but with new sinister methods to deliver their message.'

A spokesman for the mayor's office said: 'Sadiq is representing the progressive values of London and our country, warning that Donald Trump is the most egregious example of a growing far-Right threat around the globe, which is putting at risk the basic values that have defined our liberal democracies for more than 70 years.'

Trump tweeted:

'Sadiq Khan, who by all accounts has done a terrible job as Mayor of London, has been foolishly "nasty" to the visiting President of the United States, by far the most important ally of the United Kingdom. He is a stone cold loser who should focus on crime in London, not me. Khan reminds me very much of our very dumb and incompetent Mayor of NYC, de Blasio, who has also done a terrible job – only half his height. In any event, I look forward to being a great friend to the United Kingdom, and am looking forward very much to my visit. Landing now!'

Not to be outdone, the Tories also had oppressed Muslims complaining about President Trump. For example, following the publication of a poll by the Commission for Countering Extremism, Sajid Javid, then Home Secretary, made a speech in which he criticised President Trump for telling the Squad to consider going back to their countries of origin. Javid said, 'I know what it's like to be told to go back to where I came from, and I don't think they mean Rochdale.' He accused extremists for using immigration 'as a proxy for race' and said, 'Anyone can challenge the myths. So tell your friends, shout it loud and proud: people from minority backgrounds did not steal our jobs, they're not terrorists, that there is no global Zionist conspiracy. We must confront the myths about immigration that extremists use to drive divisions.' He demanded further integration within society, more help for people to learn English, greater support for communities and a celebration of national identity. 'Everyone has a part to play – broadcasters who must not give a platform to extremists; police who must swoop on the worst offenders; public figures who must moderate their language,' he said. Javid did not explain why he should be the judge of who is an extremist, or why those so designated should be persecuted. Javid's determination to shut down free speech was entirely consistent with Marcuse's 'Repressive Tolerance' essay (see above).

Within days of the EU referendum vote in 2016, in response to claims of an increase in hate incidents in the UK, then prime minister David Cameron told MPs, 'We have a fundamental responsibility to bring our country together ... we will not stand for hate crime or these kinds of attacks.' The National Police Chiefs Council claimed there had been 85 reported incidents to a website from Thursday to Sunday, which was a 57 per cent increase from the previous year. In August 2016, the UN Committee on the Elimination of Racial Discrimination accused Leave campaigners of 'creating prejudice' due to their 'divisive, anti-immigrant and xenophobic rhetoric' during the referendum and further blamed them for the reported increase in so-called 'hate crimes'.

The much-repeated claim of a supposed post-referendum 57 per cent increase in hate crimes (mentioned above) was based on a press release from the National Police Chiefs Council on June 27, 2016, four days after the referendum vote. Although the press release stated there had been 'no major spikes in tensions' since the vote, a footnote said a website called True Vision had had 85 people alleging hate incidents during the four days, which was an increase from 54 from the same four days the previous month. The press release advised: 'This should not be read as a national increase in hate crime of 57 per cent but an increase in reporting through one mechanism' over four days. This caveat was instantly and totally ignored.

In July 2016, the government's 'anti-hate crime action plan' required head teachers to log every alleged anti-Muslim, anti-Semitic, homophobic, racist incident. Amber Rudd, the new Home Secretary, said:

> 'Those who practise hatred send out a message that it's OK to abuse and attack others because of their nationality, ethnicity or religious background; that it's OK to disregard our shared values and promote the intolerance that causes enormous harm to communities

and individuals. Well, I have a very clear message for them: we will not stand for it. Hatred has no place whatsoever in a 21st-century Great Britain that works for everyone. We are Great Britain because we are united by values such as democracy, free speech, mutual respect and opportunity for all. We are the sum of all our parts – a proud, diverse society. Hatred does not get a seat at the table, and we will do everything we can to stamp it out.'

Rudd did not expect immigrants to accept the national culture and focused on abstract theories. She did not defend English or British culture.

In August 2016, the Equalities and Human Rights Commission chairman, David Isaac, said, '[some people] were able to legitimise their feelings about race following the referendum result' and, 'We must redouble our efforts to tackle race inequality urgently or risk the divisions in our society growing and racial tensions increasing. If you are Black or an ethnic minority in modern Britain, it can often still feel like you're living in a different world, never mind being part of a one nation society.'

In October, the government ran a Hate Crime Awareness Week costing £2.4 million. The Met set up a £1.7 million 'crime hub' to target internet 'trolls'. Some universities set up centres for 'hate crime studies', and charities were funded to 'combat' or 'monitor' hate crime. The Crown Prosecution Service appointed a 'hate crime coordinator' in every region in addition to 'area-based Equality, Diversity and Community Engagement Managers' who 'contribute to the delivery of the Hate Crime Assurance Scheme'. A victim's perception that an incident is a hate crime is sufficient to make it so; intent is irrelevant.

The Labour MP and Shadow Home Secretary, Dianne Abbott, told a fringe meeting at the Labour Party conference in September 2016:

'The Brexit vote, whatever you think of that vote, has added another turn of the screw to rising racism. The Brexit vote and the Leave people winning seems to have given far too many people permission to racially abuse and attack people all over the country. People, not just East Europeans, but people of all colours, are being attacked and assaulted by people who talk about Brexit ... There has been this upsurge after this Brexit vote in horrible, horrible attacks.'

She also said, 'The people who complain about freedom of movement will not be satisfied because what they want is to see less foreign-looking people on their street and that's not going to happen.'

This was not Abbott's first outburst of anti-British, anti-White bile. In 1984, she said Ireland 'is our struggle – every defeat of the British state is a victory for all of us' and 'Though I was born here in London, I couldn't identify as British' and described Northern Ireland as 'an enclave of white supremacist ideologies'. In 1988, she told a US audience that Britain had 'invented racism' and parliament was 'the heart of darkness, in the belly of the beast'. In 1989, she described the Home Office as 'a fundamentally racist organization'. Shortly before 9/11, she voted against the banning of some terrorist organisations, such as al-Qaeda, Egyptian Islamic Jihad, the Armed Islamic Group, Harakat-ul-Mujahideen, the Palestinian Islamic Jihad, and the Islamic Army of Aden. She claimed some groups were 'not terrorist organizations, but dissident organisations'. In 2012, she tweeted, 'White people love playing "divide and rule". We should not play their game.' In 2015, she said, 'On balance, Chairman Mao did more good than harm ... he led his country from feudalism.' Mao was responsible for the deaths of 45 million people.

In April 2017, an attack on an Iranian asylum seeker in Croydon, London, led to Dianne Abbott claiming:

'Sadly, this is not an isolated incident but part of a sustained increase in hate crimes that this Tory Government is yet to offer any effective response to. With right-wing politicians across the world scapegoating migrants, refugees and others for their economic problems, we are seeing a deeply worrying rise in the politics of hate. We must make clear that there is no place for anti-foreigner myths, racism and hate in our society.'

She told Sky News: 'I'm not surprised in the attack because we have seen a rise in hate crime and anti-migrant feeling, particularly since Brexit. Much of the Brexit campaign was around fear of migrants, this now is being reflected in the rise in hate crimes.' This is all lies and pure race war politics.

The tolerance towards Abbott might be contrasted with the extreme intolerance shown to Marie Morris, the Tory MP for Newton Abbot, who, in July 2017, was suspended from the Tory Party after she used the term 'nigger in the woodpile'. The suspension occurred within hours, and she was further threatened with disciplinary action. Then Tory prime minister Theresa May said, 'I was shocked to hear of those remarks, which are completely unacceptable. I immediately asked the Chief Whip to suspend the party whip. Language like this has absolutely no place in politics or in today's society.' A recording of what Marie Morris said was circulated to the *Huffington Post*.

Marie Morris immediately issued a statement saying the comment was 'entirely unintentional' and 'I apologise unreservedly.' Tim Farron of the Liberal Democrats said, 'I am utterly shocked that this person represents the good people of Newton Abbot. Even if she misspoke, this is the nastiest thing I've heard an MP utter since Lord Dixon-Smith uttered the same awful phrase a few years ago.' The Tory MP Heidi Allen said, 'I'm afraid an apology is not good enough – we must show zero tolerance for racism. MPs must lead by example.'

The term was once common and originated in America. It was once in mainstream use up to the end of the 20th century and even appeared in an Agatha Christie novel. In the 21st century, Black people themselves still use the word 'nigger' frequently in films and rap songs.

In January 2017, David Isaac, chairman of the EHRC, a former chief executive of Stonewall, alleged, 'One of the things that concerns us greatly is the position in relation to the spike in hate crimes since June 23.' (see above). He also said:

> 'We are hugely concerned about what might happen in relation to an increase in hate crimes when Article 50 is triggered ... We are meeting with groups, we are seeking to ensure that there is as much police protection and understanding in relation to hate crimes as possible ... Britain needs guidance in relation to huge anxiety that reside, not just in relation to non-UK citizens and our visitors, but actually many of our own citizens.'

Isaac received £500 per day at the EHRC for one or two days' work a week; he was also a partner in the Pinsent Masons law firm.

Amber Rudd, despite being Home Secretary, was, laughably, hoisted by her own petard. In January 2017, police recorded her speech at the Tory conference in October as a 'hate incident' after physicist Professor Silver made a complaint. In a television interview, Professor Silver, who admitted he had not heard the speech, said it had 'discriminated against foreigners' so he had complained to the West Midlands Police.

In contrast to the demonisation of the British or English (in particular), a very different approach was evident regarding jihadists. For example, Ronald Fiddler, a Guantanamo Bay detainee for two years who the British government awarded £1 million after he denied any terrorist involvement (with monies from newspapers in addition), used the name Abu Zakariya al-Britani and was killed in an Islamic State suicide mission in Iraq near Mosul. ISIS issued a statement praising their 'martyrdom-seeking brother' along with a grinning picture of him in his suicide truck, laden with explosives.

The British Government also paid around £20 million to 16 ex-detainees of Guantanamo Bay, with the details kept confidential. An estimated one-third of those released from Guantanamo Bay returned to jihadist activity according to the Office of the Director of National Intelligence in Washington.

In March 2017, after another terrorist attack by Khalid Masood, May told the House of Commons:

'We meet here, in the oldest of all Parliaments, because we know that democracy – and the values it entails – will always prevail. Those values – free speech, liberty, human rights and the rule of law – are embodied here in this place, but they are shared by free people around the world.'

May's bald assertion that democracy would 'always prevail' did not match the reality of growing division, that was increasingly resulting in bloodshed and violence. She did not explain why she thought democracy would survive Britain becoming a Muslim majority country, as, ultimately, the policy of mass immigration would entail.

Khalid Masood, born Adrian Elms, committed various crimes, including grievous bodily harm (GBH), and served two prison sentences. He was allegedly radicalised in prison, where he converted to Islam. He used several aliases.

May's supposedly determined stance did not match policy. In July 2017, the Home Office published only a summary of a report into the funding of Islamist extremism in Britain. The suppression of the full report was believed to be motivated by a desire to hide the involvement of Saudi Arabia. The Home Office investigation discovered that extreme Islamist groups were raising hundreds of thousands of pounds in donations by pretending to be charities. They were also believed to be obtaining further funds from charitable foundations. In addition, the report said that a 'small number' of extremist organisations were getting a 'significant source of income' from overseas.

The Henry Jackson Society revealed Saudi Arabian government-linked groups were funding hard-line mosques in Britain. The society's spokesman, Tom Wilson, said, 'There is a clear and growing link between foreign funding of Islamist extremism and violent terrorism in the UK and Europe. While entities across the Gulf have been guilty of advancing extremism, those in Saudi Arabia are undoubtedly at the top of the list.'

The Labour MP, Sarah Champion, received death threats following her condemnation of the Pakistani grooming gangs in her constituency of Rotherham. The police arranged extra security for her. The Joseph Rowntree funded group Just Yorkshire accused Sarah Champion of 'industrial-scale racism'. Leading members of Rotherham's Pakistani community wanted a Muslim to replace Sarah Champion should she stand down or was deselected.

In August 2018, Boris Johnson sparked a politically correct backlash, including demands he apologise from fellow Tories, including May, when he wrote in the *Daily Telegraph*, 'It is absolutely ridiculous that people should choose to go around looking like letter boxes ... If a constituent came to my MP's surgery with her face obscured, I should feel fully entitled to ask her to remove it. If a female student turned up at school or at a university lecture looking like a bank robber then ditto.' The thrust of the article was the burka should be allowed and Britain should not follow other European countries and ban it.

At a time when it was important to encourage national unity and self-confidence, the politically correct denigrated Britain's past. For example, in November 2017, students at Liverpool University launched an online petition to have former four-term prime minister William Gladstone's (1809-1898) name removed from the hall of residence because his father owned a sugar plantation in the Caribbean and he had not been in favour of abolishing slavery.

Even academic analysis and research was affected for academics whose opinions were politically incorrect. Professor Bigger of Christ Church, Oxford, was targeted for an article he wrote in *The Times* in which he dared to say the British must 'not feel guilty about our colonial history' and complained that 'apologising for empire is now compulsory'. He urged for a more 'balanced' view of the empire. In addition to the online abuse and name-calling Bigger was subjected to, 58 of his fellow Oxford academics signed an open letter stating a 'firm rejection' of his 'agenda', and pledged to boycott Bigger's next research project. The 58 were a mix of anti-Israel campaigners, anti-Brexit campaigners and an assortment of lefties.

Students at Cambridge University demanded there be more attention given to ethnic minorities in courses and submitted proposals to increase the number of non-White authors as literature professors were supposedly 'perpetuating institutional racism'. The students also targeted the history, philosophy, and history of art departments. A 'Decolonise Cambridge' Facebook page was set up. Other universities came under similar pressure.

Ilyas Nagdee, the National Union of Students (NUS) Black student's officer, said that with the statues of historical figures 'remnants of Britain's imperial past continue to be celebrated without any context or challenge from the institutions which are meant to be Britain's centres of critical thought'.

Lola Olufemi, the Student's Women's Officer at Cambridge University, said, 'There needs to be a complete shift in the way the department treats Western literature in comparison to that of the global south, and non-White authors must be centred in the same way Shakespeare, Eliot, Swift, and Pope are; their stories, thoughts and accounts should be given serious intellectual and moral weight.' Olufemi had previously stated she wanted the 'decolonisation of the curriculum' and that 'Our curricula are White and they shouldn't be. People of colour, women and trans people are quite literally being written out of history, our contributions ignored.' In fact, it is natural for the curriculum of a Western university to reflect Western culture. What Olufemi demanded was not the 'decolonisation of the curriculum' but the colonisation of it with anti-Western propaganda. In July 2021, in a survey by the Higher Education Policy Institute showed only 23 per cent of the public supported so-called decolonisation of university curriculums. The General Secretary of the University and College Union, Jo Grady, reacted by saying the public 'hostility' showed 'how far we have to go to tackle systemic racism'. This is a prime example of the rejection of majority views and the promotion of minority views as a feature of political correctness Wayne Mapp highlighted (see above).

It was revealed in March 2018 that workshops at UK universities were being held to ensure lecturers could better understand 'White privilege' and how 'Whiteness' made them racist. One flyer stated: 'We discuss why White people accrue advantages and benefits simply due to the colour of their skin and how Whiteness as a discriminatory force is as prevalent today as it was 400 years ago.'

A workshop at Bristol University, hosted by the Black, Asian and Minority Ethnic Staff Advisory Group, said lecturers needed to 'examine and acknowledge the destructive role of Whiteness'. At Anglia Ruskin University, people were urged to ask 'how we benefit from a racist system'.

Despite around 20 per cent of new students being ethnic minorities, Oxford University was accused of 'institutional bias'. David Lammy MP was particularly outraged that some colleges had admitted fewer Black students than the national average, despite the overall total being in line with the national average. He said, 'The progress is glacial. The truth is that Oxford is still a bastion of White, middle class, southern privilege. Thirty Black pupils applied for computing last year. Not one of them gets in. Are we really saying there isn't a Black student in Britain who can apply for computing who is worth a place at Oxford? Surely not.' Other Lefties and Luvvies joined in the condemnation. The broadcaster Robert Peston announced on Twitter that, 'This morning I feel embarrassed to have gone to Oxford.' To be blunt, what was being demanded was anti-English ethnic cleansing in England.

Following her win of a Great British Bake Off contest, Nakiya Hussain, who sports a headscarf, complained to have been thwarted by Englishmen and 'there's no space for a five-foot brown girl who wears a headscarf.' She has been on several TV programmes, including some of her own such as 'The Chronicles of Nadiya' and 'Nadiya's British Food Adventure' etc. Her comments said more about her than of those of whom she spoke.

In March 2018, David Olusoga, a Nigerian immigrant and darling of the BBC, told the Oxfordshire Literary Festival that although he was glad Churchill led Britain in WWII:

> '...that doesn't mean that he wasn't responsible, or largely responsible, for the Bengal famine. It doesn't mean that he wasn't someone who took part in things we would consider war crimes in Africa. It doesn't mean that his views, the things he espoused, were shocking to members of his Cabinet, never mind to people at the time. Both of those things are true. Both of those Churchills exist. We're going to have to accommodate the fact that these things are true, and there are two sides to these stories and we're not good at it ... We have this conflict. I think these are the history wars we are having.'

Of China and India, Olusoga said:

> 'They haven't forgotten. We don't get the right to choose which bits [of history] we remember. This idea that these histories are dormant is naive. The holding back of the tide of acknowledging and apologising is doomed to the weight of what's coming. There are statues all over this country of people that have a different reputation in countries that are critical to our future.'

By 'we', Olusoga meant 'you', and was speaking *at* the British people. Olusoga had made specific reference to the statue of Edward Colston in Bristol. At the Hay Festival in May

2018, Olusoga said of the relics British museums had from other countries:

> 'A friend of mine, a TV producer, once came up with a brilliant solution: he said we should have a special version of Supermarket Sweep where every country is given a huge shopping trolley and two minutes in the British Museum. Maybe he's right, maybe that's the way forward ... If our relationship with the Commonwealth after Brexit is going to be more important, remembering they remember what happened, and they remember the things that were taken – and there are real senses of loss in those countries – it's beneficial to us as a nation to listen to those appeals.'

In fact, as an independent, sovereign country, Britain would not be answerable to any other country and certainly not answerable to those to whom Britain has donated so much in foreign aid.

Of bronzes taken from a Nigerian palace, Olusoga said:

> 'I think it's a very clear case of appropriation and theft. The palace was destroyed, they were taken and then sold to pay for the cost of the military adventure. Everyone was open about this – steal this stuff, send it to pay for the cost of the bullets. It's just such a stark case of theft. The idea that your national treasure would be in the museum of another country is something that as British people we would find absolutely impossible to get our heads around, but that's what Nigerians have to think about.'

As a Nigerian, Olusoga would not be so distressed about such matters were he to return to Nigeria, and Britain would be spared his anti-British hatred.

In July 2018, the Labour-run Bristol City Council made a planning application for a plaque to be sited next to a city centre statue of Colston. The plaque would highlight Colston's role in slavery. A Tory councillor dismissed the stunt as 'historically illiterate'. In March 2019, the plaque was scrapped. It was criticised for being insufficiently critical of Colston's involvement in the slave trade. Marvin Rees, who claimed to be a 'descendant of enslaved Africans', complained he had not been consulted as to the proposed wording on the plaque and, as mayor of Bristol, vetoed it. His office commented: 'It makes no reference to the descendants of Africans enslaved by merchants like Colston. It's an oversight to not have had a conversation with Marvin Rees, Europe's first mayor of African heritage. He is the descendant of enslaved Africans.' In fact, the African chiefs enslaved and sold Africans to merchantmen, and also to Muslim traders in east Africa.

In April 2018, Historic England circulated a video on social media showing a ball smashing Nelson's Column in Trafalgar Square. The stated purpose was to provoke a 'debate' about 'controversial' statues. Subsequently, Historic England advertised 'heritage training placements' for undergraduates and recent graduates who 'identify as having Black, Asian or other Minority Ethnic Heritage or mixed heritage' (i.e. non-English), and recently had a project to celebrate 'Britain's LBGBTQ heritage'. The campaign came following calls from Ghanian journalist Afua Hirsch for statues of Britain's heroes to be demolished. Hirsch even wrote an article in *The Guardian* titled, 'Toppling Statues? Here's why Nelson's column should be next'. Hirsch accused Nelson of being a 'White supremacist' who 'vigorously defended' slavery. Hirsch had previously condemned the British for the 19th century wars against the Ashanti, claiming the imperialists had turned her mother's family into 'refugees'.

To put Hirsch's attempted victimhood and her demonisation of British colonialism into perspective, the Colonial Secretary, Joseph Chamberlain, wrote in October 1895:

'The attempt to excite English sympathy for the King of Ashanti is a fraud on the British public. He is a barbarous

72

chief, who has broken the Treaty, permitted human sacrifices, attacked friendly chiefs, obstructed trade, and failed to pay the fine inflicted on him after the war; and the only proof he has ever given of civilisation is to be found in the fact that he has engaged a London solicitor to advocate his interests.'

The Ashanti King Prempeh had also recommenced slave trading.

Also in April 2018, Oxford University spent £20,000 on a project to 'confront its colonial history'. A part of the scheme was to build a statue of Cecil Rhodes (1853-1902), a prominent British statesman in South Africa after whom Rhodesia was named, on which students would be encouraged to scrawl 'graffiti, including swear words'. One presumes this is the academic equivalent of writing dirty words on lavatory walls.

Rhodes became a particular target. A plaque dedicated to Rhodes, a dominant figure of the British Empire and South African statesman, at Oriel College in Oxford, was to be removed after some students branded it as racist. Those students also demanded a statute likewise be removed. A so-called Rhodes Must Fall campaigner, Annie Teriba, claimed, 'There's a violence to having to walk past the statue every day on the way to your lectures, there's a violence to having to sit with paintings of former slave holders whilst writing your exams.' Another organiser from that organisation, Ntokozo Qwabe, a Zulu from South Africa, alleged that European tourists wrote African history and the reading list for political sciences ignored African scholars: 'The list was dominated by White male Europeans and Americans.'

Leading human rights lawyer, Sir Geoffrey Bindman QC, supported the campaign, arguing that to remove the statue would be 'no more than a symbolic and cost-free mark of disapproval of a man who manifested his racism in the commercial exploitation of those whom he considered inferior. The huge sum he gave to the college was its product.' Cecil Rhodes was a firm believer in the value of education and created a scheme whereby students would be funded to attend Oxford (Rhodes Scholarships) – the scheme was and remains open to all, no matter their ethnicity. The afore-mentioned Ntokozo Qwabe was himself a Rhodes Scholar – a fact that attracted some comment, leading Qwabe to proclaim he was 'no beneficiary of Rhodes' but 'a beneficiary of the resources and labour of my people which Rhodes pillaged and slaved'. Bindman also referred to Rhodes' alleged 'commercial exploitation' – a term that any Leninist would happily use.

It is important to note though that Rhodesia, even under its former prime minister Ian Smith after declaring a Unilateral Declaration of Independence (UDI), was the breadbasket of southern Africa and that South Africa experienced significant immigration even under Apartheid, whereas Zimbabwe became a typical communist basket case under Robert Mugabe (whose power stemmed from rigged elections) with Britain continuing to receive asylum applications from Africans from Zimbabwe.

The attack on Rhodes was merely a sideshow of a larger campaign, run by the Oxford Campaign for Racial Awareness and Equality, the co-chair of which, Chi Chi Shi, announced:

> 'It is very important to see the statue as a symbol of Oxford's colonial past and history but also how that relates to the experience of BME [Black and minority ethnic] students, especially in terms of the whiteness of the curriculum and Eurocentricity ... Challenging the narrative that the West discovered science ... rather than seeing it as a collaborative process in which Islamic science is fundamental.'

The slave trade was a favourite issue for the politically correct. In May 2019, St Catharine's College at Cambridge University had 'shuttered off' a historic bell as there was a 'significant possibility' it had once been used at a slave plantation. A college spokesman said, 'As part of the ongoing reflection taking place about the links between universities and slavery, we are aware a bell currently located at the college most

74

likely came from a slave plantation. A more detailed investigation is underway.'

Also in May 2019, Cambridge's vice chancellor, Stephen Toope, a Canadian human rights expert, announced a 'two-year inquiry' to examine whether Cambridge benefited from the slave trade 'through financial and other bequests to departments, libraries and museums'. Two full-time researchers, supervised by an eight-strong supervisory board, conducted the inquiry. Furthermore, there was an investigation into the work of generations of dons to see if they 'might have reinforced and validated race-based thinking' in the 18th, 19th and early 20th centuries.

Toope said:

> 'There is growing public and academic interest in the links between the older British universities and the slave trade, and it is only right that Cambridge should look into its own exposure to the profits of coerced labour during the colonial period. We cannot change the past, but nor should we seek to hide from it. I hope this process will help the university understand and acknowledge its role during that dark phase of human history.'

In August 2019, Glasgow University agreed to pay £20 million in 'reparation justice' over its alleged links with the slave trade. The university claimed it had received monies from those who had had involvement in the slave trade. The university further intended to put up a plaque at its Gilmorehill base saying the building is on the site of a house once owned by a slave owner.

In November 2019, Jesus College, Cambridge, announced, 'Following recommendations from our legacy of slavery working party, Jesus College has decided that a Benin Bronze statue of a cockerel will be returned, and that we will acknowledge and contextualise Tobias Rustat's role in our history.' Rustat was one of the college's largest donors, and had invested in the Royal African Company which had had slave dealings. Rustat died in 1694.

In November 2019, not to miss getting in on the act, Labour pledged to hold a major inquiry into the 'legacies of British imperial rule'. Jeremy Corbyn (the then Labour leader) had already demanded children be taught about the 'grave injustices' of the Empire and Britain should pay reparations to former colonies.

The Church of England was also supportive of the demonisation of British history. The Archbishop of Canterbury, Justin Welby, in March 2019 asked:

> 'How are British Christians heard when we talk of the claims of Christ by diaspora communities who have experienced abuse and exploitation by an empire that has seemed to hold the Christian story at the heart of its project? The ideology underlying the British Empire was largely predicated on the superiority of the British. The Church often colluded with that, and it was a thoroughly un-Christian worldview.'

Referring to the massacre at Amritsar, India in April 1919, Welby said:

> 'The machine gun magazines emptied on innocent men, women and children have left indelible marks on the site of the massacre and on the consciousness of Indian Sikhs, Hindus, and Muslims. This atrocity and so many others, were perpetrated by Christians and done in the name of Christian society. It's not good news; it's not God; it's not Christ-like.'

Welby further said, 'We need to take seriously the abuses of our history and engage other faiths with humility and empathy. Our mandate to witness will otherwise be disowned by a younger generation much more attuned to necessary demands for respect and cultural diversity.'

Welby did not see fit to remember the Cawnpore massacre of those British people who, besieged and starving, had surrendered in return for safe passage, during the Indian Mutiny of 1857. The British who surrendered did not get safe passage and were attacked. The surviving men were immediately killed. The women and children were killed days later and their naked bodies flung down a well, even though some were still alive. This savagery left indelible marks on the consciousness of the Christian British.

All the allegations about the slave trade ignored the fact that during the Empire, British officials and officers worked to end female infanticide, genital mutilation, widows being put on the funeral pyre, cannibalism, head-hunting, witchcraft, human sacrifice, tribal warfare and *slave trading*.

Allegations of racism were not confined to historical events and were casually peddled. In May 2019, the Zambian Tendayi Achiume from the UN on a 12-day investigation of racism and intolerance in the UK, said she would investigate 'discrimination and exclusion that may have been exacerbated' by the Brexit vote and 'xenophobic discrimination and intolerance aimed at refugees, migrants and even British racial, religious and ethnic minorities will be an important focus'.

In October 2019, to support of plans to force companies to reveal salary differences between White and ethnic minority staff, Theresa May said, 'Too often ethnic minority employees feel they're hitting a brick wall when it comes to career progression. The measures we are taking will help employers identify the actions needed to create a fairer and more diverse workforce.'

In May 2019, Dr Keith Wolverson was subjected to an investigation by the General Medical Council (GMC) after he asked a Muslim patient to remove her veil. Although the woman did not complain, her husband did. Dr Wolverston said:

> 'Unfortunately, I'm not able to work at the moment as I'm a locum GP and no-one will employ you while you're under investigation by the GMC. I feel I've been left with no alternative but to look at doing something else. I've received a lot of messages of support since announcing

my decision, which is a comfort. People have been almost unequivocal in backing me.'

In June 2019, the annual conference of the British Medical Association (BMA) voted overwhelmingly to stop charging foreign patients for NHS treatment. It was alleged that charging was 'complicit in racism'. Health tourism is estimated to cost the UK up to £2 billion per annum. Dr Omar Risk said at the conference: 'We are doctors not border guards. Charging migrants for accessing NHS services is a fundamentally racist endeavour – we are complicit in the oppressive regime.'

In September 2019, Tell MAMA (Measuring Anti-Muslim Attacks) claimed there had been a 375 per cent increase in Islamophobic incidents the week after Boris Johnson's comments about the burka, in which he had referred to 'bank robbers' and 'letter boxes'. Tell MAMA claimed the number of incidents reported to itself and the police had increased from eight the previous week to 38. This pathetic figure was typical. In December 2019, a Freedom of Information request revealed Scotland Yard's 'online hate crime hub' had recorded 1,851 incidents since its creation in April 2017, and had charged only 17, resulting in seven prosecutions. The £1.7 million unit created by Mayor of London Sadiq Khan cost £363,000 in 2019/20.

In December 2019, Nicola Williams, the Armed Forces ombudsman, announced on the BBC, 'I think racism is prevalent in the Armed Forces. Whether or not it is described as institutionally racist or there are racist incidents which are occurring with increasing and depressing frequency, the issue needs to be tackled.' An MOD spokesman said, 'Racism has no place in the military and … we are committed to stamping it out.'

In November 2019, George Mpanga, 'George the Poet', who enjoys a high profile on the BBC, turned down an MBE due to 'the colonial trauma inflicted on the children of Africa'. He said on his BBC podcast, 'I took a minute and reflected … Your forefathers grabbed my motherland, pinned her down and took turns … what [the empire] did was pure evil.' Mpanga, who grew up in London and is of Ugandan descent, demanded that Britain addressed the 'disruption' caused by 'her colonial exploits'.

In January 2020, regarding Prince Harry's wife, Meghan, on BBC's 'Question Time', a university lecturer on the show, Rachel Boyle, said, 'It's racism, she's a Black woman and she has been torn to pieces.' When the actor Laurence Fox, who was on the panel, rejected the accusation, Boyle replied, 'Says a White privileged man.' Boyle responded again by saying, 'What worries me about your comment is you are a White privileged male who has no experience of this.'

Also in January 2020, the Labour leadership contender, Clive Lewis, blamed racism for his failure to persuade more MPs to back him. He claimed, 'Structural racism is a reality of our society. The Parliamentary Labour Party isn't immune from the same forces that affect everyone. Do I think that's the only reason that I'm on the nominations that I am? That might be a factor, but I wouldn't sit here and say it was the only one.'

In February 2020, the British TV presenter Naga Munchetty explained why she had made a controversial remark about President Trump, 'My parents have always been absolutely professional and caring as nurses. They came to a country that wasn't always welcoming to people of colour, to be the best they could be. And they were told to go home all the time.' She further said, 'I grew up in Camberwell, then Peckham, then Streatham. Went to school in Tooting. I lived in south London until eight years ago. And I have been told many times: "Why don't you just fuck off to where you came from?"'

Munchetty's mother was an Indian immigrant and her father was an immigrant from Mauritius. In May 2020, she claimed she had temporarily changed her name to Nadia because of racism.

In May 2020, former 'Blue Peter' presenter, Konnie Huq, whose parents were from Bangladesh, said, 'I still have now people in their 20s or 30s going "I never saw Asians in that role or even Black people". You end up going through a thing where people may get called "token" but you have to have people doing it first for it to become the norm.'

In July 2019, US President Trump was accused of racism after, regarding 'the Squad', tweeting: 'Why don't they go back and help fix the totally broken and crime infested places from which they came. Then come back and show us how it is done.' Three of the four members of the Squad (Democrat congresswomen Rashida Tlaib, Ilhan Omar, Alexandria Ocasio-Cortez and Ayanna Pressley) were born in the USA.

The Squad advocated the payment of reparations to the descendants of slaves and the abolition of Immigration and Customs Enforcement (ICE). Ocasio-Cortez described US border detention centres as 'concentration camps'. Omar attacked Israel and blamed the USA for the crisis in Venezuela. In 2012, Omar tweeted, 'Israel has hypnotised the world, may Allah awaken the people and help them see the evil doings of Israel.' In February 2019, she described Democrat support for Israel as being 'all about the Benjamin baby' (i.e. dollars). Both Pressley and Tlaib condemned the USA's Declaration of Independence as being 'sexist, racist and prejudiced'.

After a crowd at a Trump rally chanted 'send her back', Senator Chuck Schumer accused Trump of having 'whipped up a toxic brew of racism, xenophobia and nativism'. House Republican leader Kevin McCarthy said, '[the chants] have no place in our party and no place in this country'.

During the Tory leadership race, of President Trump's tweet regarding the Squad, Boris Johnson said, 'If you are the leader of a great multiracial, multicultural society you simply cannot use that kind of language about sending people back to where they came from. That went out decades and decades ago and thank heavens for that, so it's totally unacceptable and I agree with the prime minister [Theresa May].'

In both the USA and the UK, leadership figures of both supposedly Conservative parties were opposed to telling those from the immigrant communities hostile to the West that they might consider going back to their countries of origin.

In the UK, in April 2019, Zamzam Ibrahim, 23, was elected president of the National Union of Students. She is a Muslim of Somali descent, and made these comments online when she was

16: 'I'd oppress White people just to give them a taste of what they had put us through.' Also, she said she wanted people to read 'The Koran. We would have an Islamic takeover.' Ibrahim subsequently said the statement 'do(es) not reflect my views today'.

Ibrahim succeeded Shakira Martin, a self-confessed former drug dealer's moll, who had faced a multitude of demands for her to resign amidst allegations of bullying. She dismissed the allegations as 'racism and classism' and that she 'did not give two shits' about the demands that she resign. Martin's predecessor, Malia Bouattia, had described Birmingham University as a 'Zionist outpost'.

In February 2019, the UK Government threatened universities with fines and sanctions unless they gave Black students better results. This came following a Race Disparity Audit that claimed only 56 per cent of Black students got either a 2:1 or a first compared with 80 per cent of White students. Black students were also more likely to drop out of university. The Universities Minister, Chris Skidmore, said:

> 'Universities need to reflect modern Britain, and ensure that everyone who has the potential, no matter their background or where they are from, can thrive at university. It cannot be right that ethnic minority students are disproportionately dropping out of university and I want to do more to focus on student experience to help ethnic minority students succeed at university.'

Universities would be required to publish data on ethnicity and gender. Put simply, either the universities fixed it so that non-White students got better results, or else the Tories would punish them. The Inquisition would be ratcheted up.

Chris Millward of the Office for Students said, 'Where we see lower proportions of ethnic minority students continuing with their studies, achieving the best degree outcomes, or progressing into graduate jobs, we expect universities to have a measurable plan of action to address this.'

In May 2019, Universities UK, comprised of vice chancellors, demanded in a report that universities include more ethnic minority writers and thinkers and complained 'some curriculums do not reflect minority groups'.

In January 2020, the Higher Education Statistics Agency revealed that of the 540 top university managers in 2018/19, 475 were White, and the number who were Black had fallen. Chris Skidmore said, 'It is unacceptable that the number has fallen as this does not represent our British society. Universities need to make more progress.' Of the 11,860 total, 10,510 were White, 185 were Black, 410 were Asian, 165 were mixed race, and the remainder were either of another ethnicity or unknown.

The National Archives finally agreed to withdraw a display entitled 'Empire & Colonialism', which described the Empire as being 'profoundly oppressive'. The exhibit had been criticised as unbalanced, 'Empire bashing' and 'unremittingly anti-British'. The National Archives admitted the display had not shown 'due impartiality'. One picture of slaves crammed on a ship's deck that was supposed to show slave-dealing was, in fact, a British ship rescuing slaves during the Empire's attempts to stamp out slave dealing. The slaves had been rescued from an Arab dhow in 1868. William Wilberforce's campaign to abolish the slave trade had not even been mentioned in the display.

When a sign was put up at Dollis Hill station commemorating the battle of Rorke's Drift, portrayed in the film *Zulu* (which was sympathetic to the Zulus and did not, for example, show their mutilation of the wounded British dragged from the hospital, nor the wearing of the lower jaws of bearded dead soldiers killed at Isandlwana), a few politically correct complaints were sufficient for Transport for London to apologise and remove the sign. This is despite the act of heroism that occurred in the battle when just over 100 British troops fended off an attack by more than 4,000 Zulus (who were known to disembowel their enemies), following the massacre of the

British column at Isandlwana. The battle at Rorke's Drift led to 11 Victoria Crosses being awarded.

The singer Lily Allen typically entered the fray, commenting 'Too right' to a video of the notice being removed along with a woman complaining of the notice 'celebrating colonialism'. However, there is no reason why Britain should not celebrate its empire or the bravery of its soldiers.

Even Rudyard Kipling became a target of the politically correct. Students at the University of Manchester painted over a mural of one of Kipling's most famous poems 'If'. The students objected to Kipling's other works as being colonialist, and so objected to 'If' even though it was not so.

One should regard the university students' attacks on Britain with the contempt they deserve. These people are not morally superior. For example, in September 2018, the LGBT student union at Goldsmiths, University of London, described the Soviet gulags as 'compassionate' with 'regular classes, book clubs, newspaper editorial teams, sports, theatre and performance groups'. They rejected the historical evidence that the gulag system resulted in the deaths of prisoners as a 'myth'. These people are nothing more than communists, and hatred is their currency. The gulag system was murderous, genocidal and totally beyond the pale.

The BBC was forced to withdraw a film for GCSE pupils about immigration following complaints of bias. The film contained allegations that Britain was 'multicultural long before curry and carnival' and that debate about immigration had created a 'huge rise in people going towards the EDL [English Defence League] and Britain First and reinforcing those nationalistic values'. Lord Green from Migration Watch UK said, 'The overall impression of the [film] is that anyone who questions the current scale [of immigration] is unreasonable and prejudiced ... the [film] seems designed not to inform and stimulate discussion but to promote a particular opinion.' In fact, Britain First was deregistered as a political party before the imprisonment of its two leaders, and had only been a very small entity attracting minimal electoral support (it subsequently re-registered as a political party). The

EDL was formed in response to Muslim protesters yelling abuse and threats at British soldiers returning home; it never had a membership and had not experienced a 'huge rise' in supporters. The BBC was wrong to misrepresent multiculturalism as anything other than a political policy.

The weakening of state patriotism affected public opinion, and the majority recognised the consequences of what was happening to their countries. For example, in May 2018, a report from Demos showed that 55 per cent of people did not believe the government was doing enough to promote traditional British values; 63 per cent believed life was better in the past; 43 per cent believed immigration had been positive for Britain while 44 per cent did not; and 71 per cent believed that immigration had left communities where immigrants had settled more divided. In June 2018, a survey by the BBC found that only 45 per cent of 18-24-year-olds felt proud to be English. Just over half of those in their 20s, 30s and 40s were proud of their English identity.

The Inquisition was not confined to White people. Another victim, Yusuf Kaplan, a Muslim interfaith adviser at Westminster University who was involved in the Prevent scheme to counter terrorism, was branded a 'fake Muslim' and hounded by protesters in a campaign of intimidation. At one point, using a megaphone, protesters chanted, 'Say it loud, say it clear, Kaplan not welcome here.'. Two ISIS terrorists had attended Westminster University, including Jihadi John.

Despite playing the victims in the West, the immigrant communities, especially Muslims, were the aggressors. Sharifa Alkhateeb said Muslims should use schools to convert the USA to Islam, 'The final objective is to create our own Islamic systems ... In that long-range process of making America Muslim – all of America Muslim – then we have to have some actual short-range goals. We have to have some way of dealing with them ... and be very calculated about it, or else we will not accomplish our goals.'

In the USA, a government-funded Muslim group worked with officials in Michigan, Minnesota and states across the USA to end 'Christian privilege' in schools. Instead, they wanted the government to 'infuse the curriculum' with Islamic 'intellectual traditions'.

In New Hampshire in the USA, around 100 business leaders, government officials and non-profit organisations met to discuss ways in which New Hampshire could be diversified. The state was 94 per cent White. Will Arvelo hailed the meeting as the first effort in New England to diversify an entire state.

An article in the *American Thinker* in June 2019, explained the consequences of Bill Clinton's decision, supported by 'Lutheran Social Services, Catholic Charities and World Relief Minnesota', to plonk '30,000 Somalis down into the midst of the kind, virtue-signalling, eager-to-help Midwesterners of Minneapolis'. Due to a continuing flow of refugees and chain migration, that Somali population grew to around 80,000 – 'or more like 79,000 if you subtract those who've left the country to join terrorist organizations like ISIS'. The article gave some examples of the violence and culture clash that had been created for that week, before asking:

> 'Will this cause anything to change in Minnesota? Will the city's leaders stop wearing the hijab in solidarity with the worst of Islam, incredibly, after they attack us!? Will Minneapolitans elect secular, assimilated Somalis rather than proudly Sharia-supporting, anti-Semitic, enshrouded Somali Muslims like Ilhan Omar? (80 per cent of Democrats picked her in the primary.) I doubt it. They did all that after the following events:
>
> • In 2018 it was uncovered that Somalis had perpetrated a massive, community wide scam against the welfare state of Minnesota, stealing an incredible $100 million from a childcare handout program by fraud and shipping that money to Somalia to fund God knows what. (Incidentally, though finally proven in 2018, this was an open secret for years. I knew about this scam when I left the state in 2014.)

- Dozens of Somalis, men and women, over the years arrested or tracked as they attempted to join terrorists overseas including ISIS. The feds are concerned it is still a rich breeding ground for Islamic supremacy and terrorist organizations.
- In 2016 the first Somali police officer murdered a woman in her pyjamas who had called in a disturbance. I guess it's not safe to call the cops when you see something and say something. He has been found guilty of that murder.
- In 2018 a Somali student at St Catherine University attempted to burn down the school and "hurt people," saying, "You guys are lucky that I don't know how to build a bomb because I would have done that."
- In 2017 a Somali man stabbed a young woman 14 times for no apparent reason – he didn't go after her purse – while she was walking home from her job at an Apple Store. He's still at large. Curiously no composite sketch was ever released to the media.
- In 2016 during Ramadan a gang of religious robed Somali men terrorized the city's affluent Linden Hills community "for three straight days, threatening to rape a woman, beating one resident's dog, and shouting 'jihad!' as they drove vehicles over residents' lawns and pretended to shoot people through their duffel bags. No arrests were made." (Seriously, read this account. You will find it absolutely horrifying and it's shocking that no arrests were made with all these people trying to get license plate numbers, all the likely surveillance cameras, etc. It makes one wonder if the city is protecting Somalis from being held accountable to our laws.)

- In 2012 90 per cent of Somalis worldwide said they think they agree with Sharia Law and think it should be implemented.

But Ilhan Omar wears such pretty headscarves when she's raising money for the Muslim Brotherhood.

I'm not sure what it would take for Minneapolitans to wake up and stop being so suicidal with their multiculturalism. Terrorism, arson, violent crime, murder, corruption, fraud, female oppression is apparently not enough.'

Someone commented online to the article, 'What did you expect, free camel rides?'

A record of around 3,000 Christian sites (including churches, schools, cemeteries and monuments) were attacked in Europe in 2019. Ms Fantini said, 'European governments and politicians, with a few exceptions, seem reluctant to address this problem', and agreed with former UK Foreign Secretary Jeremy Hunt that 'the UK and other Western governments have not grappled with the issue perhaps because of misguided political correctness or an instinctive reluctance to talk about religion'.

The Australian Federation of Islamic Councils, playing the victim, warned of 'increased intolerance towards Muslims' and complained that a draft of a Religious Discrimination Bill did not go far enough to combat Islamophobia.

Professor Saleem Kidwai, Secretary General of the Muslim Council Wales demanded ISIS fighters be allowed to return to the UK: 'They are our responsibility and we must have dialogue for peace.' He further alleged that Islamophobia, rather than extremism, is the new problem, with anti-Muslim abuse being the 'norm'. He considered there were problems such as poverty and lack of aspiration that needed tackling, and that youth poverty and unemployment needed to be addressed as the true Muslim population in Wales was closer to 75,000 rather than the census figure of 48,000 and 54 per cent of that population were under 35.

A reporter visiting the Al Hol camp in Syria, where ISIS wives and children were detained, was told by one child that 'we will slaughter you'. The reporter spoke to some who defended the caliphate about burning people alive and beheading prisoners only to be told, 'It says it in the Koran'. Some jihadi brides said, 'My son will grow up to be a jihadist.'

In New York, an ISIS jihadist was sentenced to 22 years in prison for plotting to behead people with a chainsaw.

In the UK, the authorities continuously make excuses for extremism and criminality. A school in Manchester required children to write an essay from the perspective of a parent of a Manchester bomb victim. The topic was, 'All terrorists should be forgiven.' The essay was supposed to allow students to formulate their own views about whether hate or forgiveness is the best response to even such terrible crimes. A spokesman said: 'I do understand that some people may find it difficult to understand why a school would ask students such a challenging question. However, having reflected on the matter we would in hindsight have posed the homework question in a different way.'

Murad Qureshi, a friend of Jeremy Corbyn, promoted antisemitism, met with Hamas, even stood up for leading Nazi official and evil co-orchestrator of the holocaust Adolf Eichmann, and led a small group of far-Left activists to protest against Trump visiting the UK. A former member of the London Assembly for the Labour Party, he was reselected as an official Labour candidate for the 2020 election – despite the party being fully aware of his previous actions.

An American Jewish tourist on the westbound platform of the Piccadilly Line at Green Park Underground Station, London, was waiting for the train to Heathrow when a Black male with a black beard and wearing a dark cap and a dark green jacket suddenly berated him: 'I hate you Jews, you are all full of bullshit, you fuck up the country – the only reason I don't kill you is because I just got my British passport and I don't want to lose it.'

The newsreader Alastair Stewart was accused of racism by Martin Shapland, 34, whose Twitter feed was found to be full of anti-White bigotry. He compared White people to 'cheesecake' and made comments about supposed White privilege. Shapland said he had faced a lot of abuse since his complaint against Stewart, and had been called 'nigger', 'ape', 'fucking idiot', 'cunt', 'fucking ape' and 'thick as shit'. Shapland said that a 'private apology would have been more than sufficient' from Mr Stewart, adding it was 'regrettable' that the presenter quit.

In response to an attempt to deport 50 immigrant criminals to Jamaica, Labour MP David Lammy said, 'We are almost now two years on and people watching see the way this government holds in such disrespect the contribution of West Indian, Caribbean and Black people in this country. When will Black lives matter once again?' Apparently, these criminals were doing the British people a favour. Once again, Lammy showed whose side he was on. He was consumed by race war politics.

To give but one example of an attempt to prevent the deportation of criminals, in June 2020, a Nigerian immigrant in his early 30s, who had a 27-month jail term for supplying cannabis, won the right to stay in the UK after he claimed his stepdaughter was seeking gender reassignment. He claimed his stepdaughter had mental health issues and was especially close to him. The immigration tribunal ruled the man's 'continuing support' was necessary for his stepdaughter's 'emotional and psychological well-being'. The Home Office lawyers had pointed out that the stepdaughter had managed to cope while the man was in jail, but this did not convince the tribunal. Judge Bruce further ruled that the man's identity be kept secret.

The Home Office refused to release a review into grooming gangs, claiming it was 'not in the public interest'. Instead, the Home Office said it would soon publish a national strategy to set out a 'whole system response to all forms of child sexual abuse.' These are race attacks against English girls. The Home Office was trying to blur the issue. Eventually, a report, described as a paper, was released. It included a foreword from Priti Patel as Home Secretary, in which she wrote, 'it is difficult to draw conclusions about the ethnicity of offenders as existing research is limited and data collection is poor'. The body of the paper betrayed that there had been a split between the Home Office, which wrote the report, and an External Reference Group, and a split in the External Reference Group itself as to the existence of Muslim grooming gangs. The paper was a brazen whitewash. The body of the paper stated (italics my emphasis), 'Based on the existing evidence, and our understanding of the flaws in the existing data, it seems most likely that the ethnicity of group-based [child sexual exploitation] offenders is in line with [child sex abuse] more generally and with the general population, with *the majority of offenders being White*.' That is a barefaced lie (an analysis of the paper is in Appendix One).

Jihadwatch.org published an article that stated:

'The Home Office some time ago banned Martin Sellner, Brittany Pettibone, Lauren Southern and Lutz Bachmann from entering, all for the crime of opposing jihad terror and Sharia oppression, and thereby made it clear that it is more authoritarian and unwilling to uphold the freedom of speech than ever – at least when it comes to criticism of Islam, Muslim rape gangs, and mass Muslim migration.

The bannings of Sellner, Pettibone, Southern, and Bachmann were just part of a long pattern. Pamela Geller and I were banned in 2013, apparently for life, also for the crime of telling the truth about Islam and jihad. Just days after Geller and I were banned, the British government admitted Saudi Sheikh Mohammed al-Arefe. Al-Arefe has said: "Devotion to jihad for the sake of Allah, and the desire to shed blood, to smash skulls, and to sever limbs for the sake of Allah and in defense of His religion, is, undoubtedly, an honor for the believer. Allah said that if a man fights the infidels, the infidels will be unable to prepare to fight."

And Syed Muzaffar Shah Qadri's preaching of hatred and jihad violence was so hardline that he was banned from preaching in Pakistan, but the UK Home Office welcomed him into Britain.

The UK Home Office also admitted Shaykh Hamza Sodagar into the country, despite the fact that he has said: "If there's homosexual men, the punishment is one of five things. One – the easiest one maybe – chop their head off, that's the easiest. Second – burn them to death. Third – throw 'em off a cliff. Fourth – tear down a wall on them so they die under that. Fifth – a combination of the above."

Theresa May's relentlessly appeasement-minded government also admitted two jihad preachers who had praised the murderer of an opponent of Pakistan's blasphemy laws. One of them was welcomed by the Archbishop of Canterbury. Meanwhile, the UK banned three bishops from areas of Iraq and Syria where Christians are persecuted from entering the country. The asylum application of a Christian family facing a death fatwa in Pakistan was three times rejected. But an ISIS bride was let back in and given a taxpayer-funded house, despite the fact she has an ISIS flag on her Twitter account. No terror charges for her, of course.'

And:

'Hadi Hamid, 40, was jailed for four years after ploughing his blue Dodge Avenger into Luke Mason and Matthew Lockwood outside the Empire club in Middlesbrough. The pair, who were both 18 at the time, had been enjoying a nightout celebrating a birthday when banned driver Hamid crashed into them both, leaving Mr Mason in an induced coma with a broken spine and Mr Lockwood with severe facial injuries.

Hamid, from Kuwait, in the Middle East, was jailed for four years in February 2018 – but it is understood he was released last week, having served less than half his term. The decision has provoked fury from Mr Mason's mother

Wendy and prompted Tory MP Simon Clarke to write to the Government calling for Hamid's deportation.

On Facebook, Mrs Mason described Hamid as "dangerous". She said: "He will be allowed to come back to Middlesbrough and live among us. After running over my son and his friend he drove over the top of my son's body. How do you do that? He broke my son's back, ribs, arms, collar bone and pelvis. His elbow was dislocated and his back and head was left without any skin. His lung had collapsed and we were told he needed immediate surgery but to be prepared that his body was so weak there's a chance he wouldn't make it. But he did make it and five operations later he's still here and still recovering. Yet this man fled the scene and then lied for months about it, blaming someone else."'

The major issue confronting the Anglosphere in 2020 regarding race was the militancy of the Black Lives Matter (BLM) movement. The killing of George Floyd led to mass protests against the USA and White people generally. This led to a breakdown in law and order. At the end of May 2020, President Trump tweeted, 'These THUGS are dishonouring the memory of George Floyd, and I won't let that happen. Just spoke to Governor Tim Walz and told him that the Military is with him all the way. Any difficulty and we will assume control but, when the looting starts, the shooting starts. Thank you!' Needless to say, many tried to blame President Trump for what had happened and the ongoing protests and riots.

To put the killing into perspective, in contrast to George Floyd, Captain David Dorn, who was murdered by looting rioters, had no marches held to remember him. Most will not even have heard of him. In 2019, 38 police officers were shot dead in the USA, according to the National Law Enforcement Officers Memorial Fund. In 2018, the number was 47. Some officers were killed responding to robberies or domestic disturbances. Others were ambushed.

In the USA, there was some pushback. For example, the American Conservative commentator, Candace Owens, tweeted, 'I've had time to reflect on my video about #GeorgeFloyd and you guys were right – I was very wrong. He went to prison 9 times, not 7. I missed two earlier convictions for theft and drugs. But he started a new chapter with meth & fentanyl – so let's throw our hero 2 more funerals!' Floyd's crimes included drug dealing, criminal trespass, theft and he served five years for armed robbery with a deadly weapon.

Not surprisingly, despite the profound differences between the USA and the UK, in the UK there were many keen to get in on the act. The saga laid out in detail above proves that this observation is not hindsight. The BLM protests and George Floyd provided an opportunity to be seized upon. It is not the case that the attacks on Britain's history and heritage are a reaction to the USA's BLM movement and George Floyd. It is a historical fact that the attacks on Britain and the British, in particular the English, preceded George Floyd, and the UK's adoption of the George Floyd and BLM agenda was a *consequence* of the promotion of anti-British, anti-English, anti-White hatred in the UK.

In early June, in breach of the Covid-19 lockdown rules, a reported 15,000 gathered in Hyde Park to support BLM. Placards read 'Enough is Enough', 'Black Lives Matter', and 'I Can't Breathe'. After the march, violence broke out with statues and even the cenotaph being desecrated. Police officers were injured. At the time, in Downing Street, Boris Johnson said, 'My message to President Trump, to everybody in the United States, from the UK is that ... racism and racist violence has no place in our society.'

In Bristol, the police stood and watched while a baying mob of BLM protestors tore down and defaced a statue of the philanthropist Edward Colston, before dumping it into a river. A woman yelled through a megaphone: 'We need to start a revolution!' Superintendent Andy Bennett said the police had taken a 'neighbourhood policing approach' to avoid 'causing any tension', and said the statue had been an 'emotive issue' for years. One protester, John McAllister, 71, said, 'I guess I'm the guy who kicked it off. The police did nothing. I saw some of them there, but they didn't lift a finger. It was so dangerous. The first duty of the police is to protect the health and lives of the public, but they did nothing.'

More than 130 protesters were arrested following 200 BLM demonstrations across the UK attended by 135,000 supporters. Of George Floyd's death, Boris Johnson said:

> 'In this country and around the world his dying words – I can't breathe – have awakened an anger and a widespread and incontrovertible, undeniable feeling of injustice, a feeling that people from Black and minority ethnic groups do face discrimination: in education, in employment, in the application of the criminal law. We must also frankly acknowledge that there is so much more to do in eradicating prejudice and creating opportunity, and the Government I lead is committed to that effort.'

According to the charity Inquest, in the UK, 1,741 have died in police custody since 1990, of which 14 per cent were ethnic minority – roughly in proportion to the proportion of the population. In London, despite constituting 13 per cent of the population, 58 per cent of murder suspects were Black.

A couple of days after the Edward Colston episode, the statue of Robert Milligan was removed from the Museum of London Docklands. Milligan had had 500 slaves on his plantations in Jamaica. The Labour councillor, Ehtasham Haque, had launched a petition for the statue's removal, and had threatened to protest on a daily basis.

The removal came after No 10 issued a statement saying the police should make their own minds up whether they should intervene to stop protesters bringing down statues. The Church of England described the racism in the UK as 'horrifying'.

BLM and other activists drew up a list of 60 'racist statues' they accused of 'celebrating slavery'. Statues included Sir Thomas Picton (who was killed at the Battle of Waterloo), Sir

Thomas Guy, Sir Robert Peel (a prime minister and founder of the police), Sir Francis Drake (the Elizabethan naval hero), William Beckford, Henry Dundas (a home secretary), Robert Baden-Powell (founder of the scouts) and Clive of India.

A crowd gathered in Oxford to demand the removal of a statue of Cecil Rhodes. Ndjodi Ndeuyema, who organised the protest, a former Rhodes scholar, said, 'The statue remaining is an affront on the university's support for movements such as Black Lives Matter. Rhodes is not worth of veneration or glorification because of the racism and subjugation he represents.' Protestors chanted, 'De- De- De- Decolonise!'

In June 2020, the governing committee of Oriel College at Oxford University voted to remove the statue of Cecil Rhodes. A statement said the college had 'voted to launch an independent commission of inquiry into the key issues surrounding the Rhodes statue'. Furthermore, 'They also expressed their wish to remove the statue of Cecil Rhodes and the King Edward Street plaque. This is what they intend to convey to the commission of inquiry. Both of these decisions were reached after a thoughtful period of debate and reflection and with the full awareness of the impact these decisions are likely to have in Britain and around the world.'

There was speculation that Historic England might rescue the statue. The body had the power to refer the matter to the Secretary of State for Housing. The body's policy, hitherto, was that 'the best way to approach statues and sites which have become contested is not to remove them but to provide thoughtful, long-lasting and powerful reinterpretation ... [which preserve] the structure's physical context but can add new layers of meaning, allowing us all to develop a deeper understanding of our often difficult past'. In other words, they are politically correct up to the eyeballs.

As some Tory MPs objected, MP Sir Iain Duncan-Smith said:

'I feel like we are on the edge of 1984, where we are trying to expunge our history. Our history is who we are, our past is what we are. The money Rhodes made has funded students from the Third World to go to Oxford, and if they take the statue down because people today don't like imperialism, they should also reject the money. My question is: Will they do that?'

David Lammy said, 'Good decision. Stick it in a museum alongside information detailing the awful acts Cecil Rhodes committed. This is not erasing history. It's understanding it.' In fact, it is communism.

The Rhodes Must Fall group admitted they also aimed to remove a number of statues in Oxford, saying, 'This is a potential epoch-defining moment ... we can, potentially, offer a powerful example of the decolonial project in higher education – in the UK and beyond.'

Oriel College ignored a student poll on the issue of removing the Rhodes statue in 2016 that found a majority in every ethnic group wanted to keep the statue. By voting to remove it, the college pandered to a mob. In the event, citing cost reasons, the decision was made not to remove the statue. This triggered a protest by 150 academics who signed a petition that they would 'refuse requests from Oriel to give tutorials to Oriel undergraduates', to 'refuse to assist Oriel in its outreach and access work' and to 'refuse to attend or speak at talks, seminars, and conferences sponsored by Oriel' amidst other claims and threats. The academics claimed that the statue 'glorifies colonialism and the wealth it produced for the College'. This was a bit rich given that, as Lord Jones (a former trade minister tweeted), 'Memo to Kate Tunstal, interim provost of Worcester College Oxford, who is leading the boycott. Worcester took a huge donation from the Sultan of Perak in 2018. Homosexuality is illegal in Perak.'

Cecil Rhodes wrote, 'My motto is equal rights for every civilised man south of the Zambezi. What is a civilised man? A man, whether White or Black, who has sufficient education to write his name, has some property, or works.'

Elsewhere, a memorial to Winston Churchill was daubed with 'was a racist'. Part of the M6 motorway was closed because 100

BLM protestors blocked the carriageway. Several police officers were hurt, despite their softly softly approach.

Dianne Abbott tweeted, 'Solidarity with the people protesting outside Parliament today. The death of George Floyd in the United States was an atrocity. But the police brutality is real here in the UK.'

In reference to a policewoman who was knocked off her horse and seriously injured when she collided with a traffic light during protests, Hasan Patel, a schoolboy who won a £76,000 scholarship to Eton, tweeted, 'The traffic light is my new best friend.'

A letter in the *Daily Mail* from a woman who described herself as a 'Haitian–American immigrant' who had moved to the UK as an employee of an investment bank and was now a British citizen, complained that when she arrived in the UK 21 years ago, there were few 'professional, middle-class black British people'. She wrote: 'Yes, we must show solidarity with the peaceful demonstrators in the US, but we must also address the racism in Britain that is as ruthless and cold in slowly killing the aspirations of Afro-Caribbean British people and making them feel excluded from capitalist society.'

In a fortnight, 33,000 donated to a GoFundMe page for Black Lives Matter UK, to the tune of almost £1 million. The fundraising page stated that the BLMUK would be 'guided by a commitment to dismantle imperialism, capitalism, White supremacy, patriarchy, and the state structures that disproportionately harm black people in Britain and around the world'. BLMUK said they would spend the money raised on 'developing and delivering ... strategies for the abolition of the police'.

BLMUK was formed in July 2016 (well before the death of George Floyd). They demanded the closure of all prisons and detention centres. They supported veganism, pay strikes and peddled a swathe of allegations of racism. They were anti-Israeli and supported a boycott of Israel. Its Facebook page stated BLMUK was opposed to 'homophobia, lesbophobia, biphobia, queerphobia, transphobia, sexism, misogyny, misogynoir, enbyphobia, ableism, racism, anti–Blackness, Islamophobia, whorephobia, ageism, fatphobia, eugenics, discrimination, stereotypes, respectability politics, the stigmatisation of HIV and the stigmatisation of addiction'.

The leadership of BLMUK was not known. There was no physical address, no constitution, no chief executive or governing board and it was not a registered charity nor a non-profit organisation. It had never produced accounts.

Meanwhile, in the UK, English football recommenced with players wearing BLM on their tops and kneeling before the start of the match – in contrast to the FIFA objection to wearing of Remembrance Day Poppies. In English rugby, the anthem 'Swing Low, Sweet Chariot', often sung at matches, was under review by the Rugby Football Union on the grounds of cultural appropriation. In reference to 'Swing Low, Sweet Chariot', a spokesman for RFU said, 'The song has long been part of the culture of rugby and is sung by many who have no awareness of its origins and sensitivities. We are reviewing its historical context and our role in educating fans to make informed decisions.' The song was written in America in the mid–19th century by a slave, believed to be Wallace Willis and his wife Minerva, who worked on a Native American owned plantation in Oklahoma. The late Dr Horace Boyer, an expert on Black US spiritual and gospel music, believed that the song's message was, 'I would rather die than be here, Lord just come and take me right now.' It is believed that the English rugby fans' interpretation of the lyrics was more crude.

Top independent schools, including Winchester, Fettes, Ampleforth, and St Paul's Girls, were reported to be 'formulating new approaches' to teaching students about Britain's colonial past. Winchester College said, 'We have initiated a review into the school's culture and practices, and it is our intention that this review will conclude next term. A major focus will be our curriculum and our desire to teach beyond the traditional syllabus by applying a global perspective and a broader range of source material.' Fettes said that current events had produced 'a catalyst for real change, and we are working with staff to produce an action plan.'

Eton College's head, Simon Henderson, in response to a letter of complaint from 635 parents and present and former pupils, pledged to teach pupils to understand the 'historic roots' of inequality, and that the school was 'actively auditing' its curriculum so pupils 'learn about the history of racism, the legacy of colonialism and the civil rights movement'. The letter of complaint demanded that Eton's curriculum 'attempts to address and reveal systemic racism within society'.

In September 2021, the private Haberdashers' Aske's Boys' School and Haberdashers' Aske's School for Girls confirmed they would be renamed. The schools had been named after Robert Aske, who bequeathed £20,000 to found the schools in 1689. The schools objected to Robert Aske being a shareholder in a slave trading company.

The Bank of England also issued a statement saying, 'The 18th and 19th-century slave trade was an unacceptable part of English history. As an institution, the Bank of England was never itself directly involved in the slave trade, but is aware of some inexcusable connections involving former governors and directors and apologises for them.' Some of the bank's directors and governors had been involved in the slave trade. Sir Humphry Morice, governor between 1727 and 1729, had owned more slave vessels than anyone else in Britain.

Lloyds of London said they would give substantial financial support to ethnic minority charities. The British Museum removed a bust of its founder, Sir Hans Sloane, over alleged links to slavery. His family had a sugar plantation. The City of London Corporation launched a public consultation regarding the removal of statues of those with alleged links to the slave trade. A spokesman said, 'We want to understand how people feel about this aspect of our cultural history.'

In August 2020, Dr Joseph Hartland of the Bristol Medical School told the BBC, 'Historically, medical education was designed and written by White middle-class men, and so there is an inherent racism. We are teaching students how to recognise a life-or-death clinical sign largely in White people – and not acknowledging these differences may be dangerous.' The school was attempting to 'decolonise' its curriculum.

The 'cancel culture' caught up with one of its own when the liberal left-leaning newspaper, *The Guardian*, had the embarrassment of 12,000 people signing a petition to have it shut down due to historical links to slavery. During the American Civil War, the pro-Black Lives Matter newspaper reportedly sided with the Confederate states, opposed the abolition of slavery and called Abraham Lincoln 'abhorrent'. The paper was founded by a cotton merchant who had slaves.

Needless to say, Labour MPs, including Keir Starmer, posted photographs of themselves on their knees. Linda Meehan, the chairman of Watford Labour Party, tweeted, 'Fuck Churchill. He was a racist, narcissistic imperialist scumbag. I'd happily piss on his grave.'

Mayor of London Sadiq Khan announced the creation of a new commission 'for diversity in the public realm'. The role of this commission is to decide which statues should be removed and which streets should be renamed. In London, anti-English ethnic cleansing would be reinforced with cultural cleansing. Khan said, 'Our capital's diversity is our greatest strength, yet our statues, road names and public spaces reflect a bygone era.' In other words, London was too English.

Elsewhere, 130 Labour councils committed to review the 'appropriateness' of statues in their areas. Joe Anderson, Liverpool's mayor, immediately announced he wanted the renaming of all roads and buildings allegedly linked to the slave trace. Liverpool University announced it would rename a Gladstone Hall (dedicated to William Gladstone) on the grounds that Gladstone's father had once owned slaves.

The Bristol mayor, Marvin Rees, said the Colston statue would be placed in a museum alongside placards from the demonstration that tore it down. Meanwhile, Colston Hall in Bristol was renamed the Bristol Beacon in a £49 million refurbishment. The renaming was a response to the BLM movement and Colston's links with the slave trade.

It should not be forgotten that between 1808 and 1860, the Royal Navy set free an estimated 150,000 slaves who were being shipped across the Atlantic, and then there was the fight against the slave trade elsewhere in Africa and the Indian Ocean. Many Royal Navy sailors died in the struggle.

Madeline Odent, a curator of the Royston and District Museum in Hertfordshire, tweeted:

'From an art conservation perspective, it's honestly fine to throw paint on memorials of genocidal racists! Paint is pretty easy to clean off. What would be an absolute shame is if people threw certain household items that cause irreversible bronze disease. Of course then the artefact can't really be on display, which is a shame. Because, like, if somebody were to throw a tin of tomatoes at a bust of a genocidal racist, nobody would probably notice the chemical reaction until it was too late to save the artefact. And this isn't a "pretty" deterioration either. The metal starts flaking off in the gross white fungus type thing – you've seen coins dug up in a garden? Like that. Once the damage is done, it can be paused or stopped but can't be reversed. In 150 years, we haven't found a way to restore artefacts that this happens to.'

The tweet was accompanied by a photo of Winston Churchill's statue daubed with 'was a racist'. Her comments prompted some complaints and a police investigation. Royston Town Council said, 'We have been made aware of tweets on a private Twitter account and are currently investigating the issue. The town council does not endorse the comments or views.' However, Odent, in response to her critics, wrote further: 'a) my boss thinks I'm funny. b) she also supports BLM. And c) I'm the one reading [your messages of complaint]'. She further claimed her contract allowed her to 'decolonise and diversify' the museum, that her 'boss has my back', that she 'got given a safe platform' and urged others to join her to 'piss off some racists'. She subsequently left her employment.

The Tory MP, Nadhim Zahawi, said, 'My opinion is any slaver should not have a statue, but I wouldn't be breaking the law to take statues down.' The Labour MP Hilary Benn called for an end to the vandalism of statues following the desecration of a statue of Queen Victoria in Leeds. He said, 'I don't think we should be commemorating slave traders. But let's have that debate in a proper way, and not by acts of vandalism like this.' In Edinburgh, a statue of Sir Henry Dundas was vandalised.

On BBC's Radio 4, the Archbishop of Canterbury, Justin Welby, responded to a BLM activist saying traditional statues of Jesus were a form of White supremacy, and in reference to the 165 countries of the Anglican faith:

> 'When you go into churches you don't see a white Jesus, you see a black Jesus or a Chinese Jesus, or a Middle Eastern Jesus, which is of course the most accurate. You see a Fijian Jesus, you see a Jesus portrayed in as many ways as there are cultures, languages and understandings. I don't think throwing out everything we have got in the past here does it, but I do think saying that is not the Jesus who exists, that is not who we worship, it is a reminder of the universality of the God who became fully human.'

Archbishop Welby said he was in favour of removing statues and plaques of those guilty of wrongdoing. Regarding forgiveness, he said, 'We can only do that if we've got justice, which means the statue needs to be put in context. Some will have to come down. Some names will have to change. You just go around Canterbury Cathedral, there's monuments everywhere, or Westminster Abbey, and we're looking at all that, and some will have to come down.'

St Peter's Church, in Dorchester, Dorset, voted to remove a plaque that celebrated John Gordon, citing his 'bravery' and 'humanity' in suppressing an uprising in Jamaica. David Rhodes of the Stand Up to Racism Dorset, said, 'It is good that the church is taking steps to acknowledge our "shameful past". The plaque is a celebration of white supremacy and racism.'

More statues were defaced, including ones of Oliver Cromwell and Nancy Astor. The statue of Cromwell in Manchester was daubed with the words 'cockroach' and 'racist'. Protesters objected to Cromwell due to his actions in the Irish civil war. In Plymouth, where she had been an MP, Lady Astor's statue was daubed with the word 'Nazi' based on allegations she was anti-Semitic.

The BLM targeted a statue in York of the Roman emperor Constantine the Great. The statue outside York Minster, on the site of a former Roman army barracks, stems from when his troops declared Constantine emperor when he was stationed in York in 306AD. As emperor, he founded Constantinople (now Istanbul) and allowed the promotion of Christianity to which he converted on his deathbed. The statue was put up in 1998. The BLM wanted the statue taken down as the Romans kept slaves in the fourth century. Archbishop Welby compared the BLM with those who, in Moscow in 1991, pulled down a statue of Felix Dzerzhinsky – the man responsible for Lenin's red terror. Officials at York Minster were reportedly reviewing the matter.

In August 2020, Jae Ikhera, 19, a student who had sprayed the 'V for Vendetta' anarchist logo on a statue of Lord Nelson and blacked out the face with spray in Norwich, was given a 12-month conditional discharge by magistrates. She did not have to pay any compensation. She even returned to the statue to spray 'Down' on the plinth three nights later. A spokesman for Save Our Statues said, 'Thanks to our legal system for handing another victory to the mob.' Ikhera said, 'I wasn't really frightened all that much. I knew it was going to end one of two ways but to me that doesn't really matter. I'm not going to do anything illegal again but I'm not afraid to use my voice as I have one.'

The Topple The Racists campaign group described Nelson as a 'known White supremacist'. In October 2021, a village in Wales was added to a dossier of sites connected with slavery on the grounds it was named after The Lord Nelson Inn, so-called as the admiral had visited the area in 1803.

In the USA, when a BLM column of thousands of protestors marched past the home of Mark and Patricia McCloskey in St Louis, Missouri, some of the protestors encroached onto the McCloskey's property and made threats. The McCloskeys, personal injury lawyers, had lived in their home – a mansion they had been restoring over many years. As the protestors' drum beat and some shouted abusive comments, the McCloskeys stood their ground. Mark McCloskey was armed with an assault rifle, and Patricia McCloskey had a handgun. They told the protestors to move on. The confrontation was filmed, naturally, which led to a persecution of the McCloskeys, who were even accused of racism. They were charged with unlawful use of a weapon, a class E felony, which can carry a sentence of up to four years in prison and a fine of $10,000. This decision drew national attention and criticism from Republican politicians. The McCloskeys pleaded guilty to misdemeanour offences. On August 3, 2021, Missouri governor Mike Parson pardoned the McCloskeys.

In August, a Trump supporter was shot dead at a BLM protest in Portland, Oregon. In the USA, Ashleigh Shackelford, a lecturer and BLM activist, was pictured next to a white board with 'All White People Are Racist' on it. She said White people were not welcome at BLM rallies.

The riots in Minneapolis, spanning several nights, were so destructive the city mayor, Jacob Frey, wanted $55 million in state aid to rebuild hundreds of gutted buildings.

Even the Formula One racing driver, Lewis Hamilton, got in on the act, demanding that 'racist symbols' should be removed. War memorials were daubed with BLM graffiti, like the Highland Light Infantry, who served in both world wars.

In Australia, a Greens staffer and her friend defaced a statue of Captain Cook. Two women were found with a bag containing spray cans following the incident. In the UK, in Whitby, a statue of Captain Cook was also sprayed with graffiti. A group called Topple the Racists campaigned for three statues of Captain Cook to be removed. They claimed he was a racist murderer who 'invaded' Australia and New Zealand.

In Leeds, a statue of Queen Victoria was defaced, and the words 'racist' and 'slave owner' were sprayed on the memorial. In fact, Queen Victoria did not own slaves and was very liberal. The Brighton and Hove council announced there would be a review of all statues and street names in response to BLM. In Poole, the council removed a statue of Baden-Powell, who formed the scouts.

In the USA, a Pawtucket Public Schools teacher was put on leave after she was charged for vandalising a statue of Christopher Columbus. Even a memorial Tomb of the Unknown Soldier was defaced in Philadelphia's Washington Square. There was a comprehensive effort to remove all Confederate monuments across the USA, and the Confederate flag was deemed no longer acceptable. Even the memorial to the 54th Massachusetts Regiment was defaced with graffiti – even though they were a Black regiment. In Washington, DC, a multitude of memorials, including the Lincoln Memorial, were vandalised and defaced.

In the UK, a demonstration in London to protect statues was described by the *Daily Mail* thus: 'Police fear far-Right thugs could descend on London this weekend to take on anti-racism protesters, with football hooligans planning counter-protests to "defend" memorials and statues.'

In the UK, Jake Hepple, a Burnley supporter, was the man primarily responsible for an aircraft flying a banner stating 'White Lives Matter Burnley' at the start of a football match between Burnley and Manchester City. The stunt occurred moments after players from both teams were on their knees. Afterwards, Hepple posted on Facebook, 'I'd like to take this time to apologise ... to absolutely fucking nobody. It's now apparently racist to say White Lives Matter, the day after three White people got murdered in Reading, but all we've seen on the TV is Black Lives Matter after George Floyd got murdered. What a mad world we live in.'

The police, after initially threatening prosecution for a banner that 'caused offence', decided not to charge Hepple, as no crime had been committed. The Burnley football club said they would ban all those involved. Hepple was sacked by Paradigm Precision, an engineering company where he had worked.

When someone put up some stickers in Ipswich saying 'Reject White Guilt', the police condemned them as 'deplorable' and launched an investigation. In another case in Southport, stickers and graffiti were condemned as a 'racial hatred message'. The stickers and graffiti said: 'It's OK To Be White'. Allegedly shocked residents demanded that the council and the police sort out the matter.

Meanwhile, Dr Priyamvada Gopal, an academic at Cambridge University (a fellow of Churchill College), tweeted, 'I'll say it again. White Lives Don't Matter. As white lives.' Twitter deleted her post as being hate speech. However, she did not lose her job, and in fact was promoted to full professorship. This was despite her being totally unrepentant. She complained loudly about receiving offensive comments (as she should have expected) and said: 'I would also like to make clear I stand by my tweets, now deleted by Twitter, not me. They were very clearly speaking to a structure and ideology, not about people. My Tweet said whiteness is not special, not a criterion for making lives matter. I stand by that.'

Gopal further wrote: 'Now we have the opportunity to carry out a resolute offensive against the white, break their resistance, eliminate them as a class and replace their livelihoods with the livelihoods of people of colour and LGBTQ.'

A statement released by the university said, 'The University defends the right of its academics to express their own lawful opinions, which others might find controversial. [It] deplores in the strongest terms abuse and personal attacks. These attacks are totally unacceptable and must cease.'

The Cambridge branch of the University and College Union (UCU), also showed their solidarity with Dr Gopal, writing: 'Solidarity with Priyamvada Gopal – being targeted with vile sexist and racist abuse for speaking up against white supremacists. We are proud to be your colleagues both on the picket line and off it. BlackLivesMatterSolidarity.'

A week earlier, Gopal had tweeted, 'With deep regret but with 17 years of consideration behind it, I have finally decided on my behalf & of other people of colour @Cambridge_Uni to refuse to supervise any students at @Kings_College. ENOUGH IS ENOUGH of the consistently racist profiling & aggression by Porters.' King's College responded:

> 'We have investigated the incident and found no wrongdoing on the part of our staff. Every visitor was asked to show their card during the course of that day, as the College was closed to everyone except King's members. Non-members such as Dr Gopal were asked to take alternative routes, around the College. This was a matter of procedure, not discrimination ... We categorically deny that the incident referred to was in any way racist.'

In February 2021, Gopal turned on the Home Secretary when she tweeted, 'Priti Patel is also a reminder that many Asians in British Africa had ferociously anti-Black attitudes and were used by colonial administrations to keep Black populations in their place. An attitude she brings to government.' She subsequently tweeted: 'My criticisms of the hawkish present Home Secretary and her participation in anti-Blackness are also a matter of public record. I had been under the impression that criticism of politicians was allowed in a democracy.' Gopal proceeded to claim that her right to free speech had been infringed when an invitation to give a speech to Home Office officials was withdrawn. She was due to speak about how the department's policies were linked with colonial history. Why the Tory Government was organising a communist immigrant to instruct Home Office officials about her interpretation of colonial history was not explained. That they were doing so demonstrates that the Tories are woke-Right.

107

In April 2021, Gopal accused: 'The monarchy is deeply implicated in the project of empire, a lot of what it possesses came right out of the imperial project. This is not a monarchy that has ever talked about its ties to empire – or to slavery for that matter.' She had previously described the monarchy as 'an institution invested in Whiteness ... and where Whites dominate'.

Gopal was born in Delhi, India, in 1968. After completing her education at the University of Delhi and Jawaharlal Nehru University in 1991, she moved to the USA, where she taught and completed a PhD in colonial and postcolonial literature at Cornell University in 2000. She moved to the University of Cambridge in 2001. She is cited as being interested in a number of issues, including 'gender and feminism, Marxism and critical theory, and the politics and cultures of empire and globalisation' – i.e. she is a communist.

So, in the UK in the 21st century, under a Tory Government, saying 'White Lives Matter' is a sacking offence, whereas saying 'White Lives Don't Matter' is OK. Furthermore, an immigrant who is openly anti-White and stirring up trouble is lauded and promoted, rather than being sent back whence she came.

Although Ministers ordered that government departments cease 'unconscious bias' training after an official study found that it did not work, large parts of the government and charity sectors took no notice. The Inquisition continued throughout 2020 and into 2021. Following a report from the EHRC that alleged there was an 'alarmingly high rate' of racism in universities, and following the BLM protests, the organisation representing the university vice-chancellors published a series of recommendations. These included demands that universities admit they 'perpetuate institutional racism' and pledge to confront 'White privilege'.

The student's union at the De Montfort University demanded the university be renamed. They objected to Simon de Montfort, the 6th Earl of Leicester, after whom the university was named, as he was an alleged anti-Semite.

Leicester University introduced a new English course that would largely ignore traditional English works and authors, such as Chaucer. Instead, the course comprised 'a chronological literary history, a selection of modules on race, ethnicity, sexuality and diversity, a decolonised curriculum, and new employability modules.' In March 2020, the university re-branded International Women's Day as 'International Womxn's Day' with the aim of appealing to the transgender community. As the university charged off into its politically correct hole, student numbers fell continuously as did revenues. On top of which, the university declared a loss of £43.6 million after paying £46 million into its pension fund.

In July 2020, in the USA, a Black group calling itself the Not Fucking Around Coalition (NFAC), who were all armed, were kept separate by the police from those, also armed, who called themselves the Kentucky Three Percenters in Louisville. The Three Percenters were seriously outnumbered. Three people were injured as a result of gunfire.

In September, in Louisville, on the day of the Kentucky Derby (the USA's equivalent of Ascot races), two armed militias faced off. Protesting about the shooting of a Black woman (Breonna Taylor) some months previously, the NFAC chanted 'No Justice! No Derby!' and were met with a local pro-police, pro-Trump militia. The pro-Trump militia were led by Dylan Stevens, who calls himself 'Angry Viking', and describes himself as 'a staunch supporter of Trump, police, our troops, Second Amendment, America, and the flag'.

In August, in England, a Black militia, donning stab vests and a black uniform, calling itself the Forever Family Force (FF Force), marched through Brixton, London. The march marked 'Afrikan Emancipation Day' and the 186th anniversary of the Abolition of Slavery Act. The FF Force called for an All-Party Parliamentary Commission for Truth and Reparatory Justice.

One leader of FF Force was Khari McKenzie, who shared a variety of conspiracy theories on social media. He had further repeatedly appeared on the BBC's Victoria Derbyshire Show. In one Instagram post with images of the Israeli Defence Force, he wrote, 'Research who funded the trans-Atlantic slave trade biggest holocaust and crime against humanity, with no reparations. Look at who is behind training police in the USA and the UK to put there (sic) legs on our necks.' In an Instagram video, he declared:

> 'Every Zionist is an Islamophobe. It don't make me anti-Semitic if I don't agree with the oppression in Palestine. That's foolishness, year. So when we're talking about Zionists, and even talking about if I don't agree with the people that run the banks, yeah, and by them running the banks the rich get richer and the poor get poorer; if I don't agree with that, that don't make me anti-no one. I'm just anti-oppression.
>
> If I look in my history book and see there were people with Zionist blood that were heavily involved in the transatlantic slave trade, me pointing that out doesn't make me anti-Semitic.'

Children watching cartoon film favourites on the Disney+ streaming service were subject to a warning as to their alleged 'harmful' cultural stereotyping. The films included *Dumbo*, *Peter Pan*, the *Lady and the Tramp* and *Jungle Book*. The warning stated, 'This programme includes negative depictions and/or mistreatment of people or cultures. These stereotypes were wrong then and are wrong now. Rather than remove this content, we want to acknowledge its harmful impact, learn from it and spark conversation to create a more inclusive future together.'

Hilariously, the film *Gone With the Wind* became the number one bestseller after HBO announced it would be blacklisted. On Amazon, the film's DVDs and Blu-ray discs sold out. HBO described the film as 'a product of its time' and depicted 'ethnic and racial prejudices' that were 'wrong then and are wrong today'. There were plans to re-release the film with an opening commentary, putting forward a politically correct critique that viewers would have to sit through and this duly happened. HBO returned *Gone with the Wind* to its streaming service with a four-minute introduction, including a panel discussion, about the film. The introduction stated:

> 'The film's treatment of this world through a lens of nostalgia denies the horrors of slavery, as well as its legacies of racial inequality. Eighty years after its initial release, *Gone with the Wind* is a film of undeniable cultural significance. It is not only a major document of Hollywood's racist practices of the past but also an enduring work of popular culture.'

The film won eight Oscars, including best picture.

Yorkshire Tea caused a stir when they tweeted a message to someone deemed not to be politically correct or a supporter of BLM, who had expressed a preference for their product: 'Please don't buy our tea again. We're taking some time to educate ourselves and plan proper action before we post. We stand against racism.'

In November 2020, curators at the British Library alleged that Ted Hughes, the late Poet Laureate, had links to slavery. They alleged that the London Virginia Company, set up to establish colonies in North America and with slavery involvement, had connections to Ted Hughes's distant relative Nicholas Ferrer, who had been born in 1592. Even the Tory MP Richard Drax faced calls to pay reparations for his family's sugar plantations in Barbados and Jamaica between 1640 and 1836, which had around 30,000 slaves.

The Tory Party's response to the BLM onslaught was predictable, given the prevailing mood of certain members of the party. In April 2019, Baroness Warsi, a former Tory co-chair and Cabinet minister, yet again, claimed the Tory Party was guilty of 'institutional Islamophobia', and said, 'The party line is to deny [Islamophobia], ignore it and bury one's head in the sand.'

In June 2020, announcing the launch of another racial inequality commission, the Commission on Race and Ethnic

Disparities, Boris Johnson said, 'What I really want to do as Prime Minister is change the narrative so we stop the sense of victimisation and discrimination. We stamp out racism and we start to have a real sense of expectation of success. That's where I want to get to but it won't be easy.' Shadow justice secretary, David Lammy told the BBC, 'This was written on the back of a fag packet yesterday to assuage the Black Lives Matter protest. Frankly, when you watch a man die like we did in eight minutes and 46 seconds – I'd like to ask Boris Johnson why he thinks the way to commemorate his death is to announce yet another commission.'

Mohammed Amin, chairman of the Conservative Muslim Forum, said the Tory's support among Muslims increased to around 25 per cent under David Cameron, but had fallen to only 11 per cent under Theresa May. Amin said of Ilford North constituency, 'It was a rock-solid Tory seat for decades, but now has swung to Labour. One reason is that there are more Muslim voters there, who have moved out of the East End. We narrowly lost the seat in 2015, then in 2017 were beaten by far more. If we want to win back seats like this, the party has to do far more.'

Although the non-White minorities were portrayed as victims, in reality, Whites were. For example, in June 2019, Damian Hinds, the education secretary, warned that two-thirds of the most disadvantaged children were White British. He said:

> 'There is another group of children who we often mention, but sort of in passing, sometimes, which is white British children. Among the disadvantaged population, the lowest performing group is white British children. Just among those who are classed as disadvantaged, if you separate out the ethnicities, white British children are least likely to reach the expected level at reading and writing and mathematics and then make the lowest progress when it comes to secondary school ... Almost two thirds of the cohort of disadvantaged children are white British children.'

The Power of Culture

The Collins English Dictionary defines culture thus:

> 1. the total of the inherited ideas, beliefs, values, and knowledge, which constitute the shared bases of social action. 2. the total range of activities and ideas of a group of people with shared traditions, which are transmitted and reinforced by members of a group: the *Mayan* culture. 3. a particular civilisation at a particular time. 4. the artistic and social pursuits, expression, and tastes valued by a society or class, as in the arts, manners, dress, etc. 5. the enlightenment or refinement resulting from these pursuits.[34]

The first three definitions are the ones associated with culture's understood meaning in the debate about multiculturalism, although the fourth and fifth definitions are not totally irrelevant. The key aspects of culture are threefold: it is inherited; it consists of 'ideas of a group of people with shared traditions, which are transmitted and reinforced by members of a group' – it binds the group together, distinguishing the group; and it is self-perpetuating in that it is 'transmitted and reinforced' by members of a group. This is a big issue for the neo-Marxists and, as they see it, is the manner in which false consciousness is maintained. The attachment of a people to their culture is a major obstacle to the much hoped for communist revolution. Political correctness aims to break that attachment and, if possible, to destroy the concept of a national culture.

The power of culture should not be underestimated. For example, the importance of culture, or subculture, is demonstrated by the YouTube videos of various rival gangs revelling in their violence, drug culture and their rejection of civilised values. Comments such as 'This bitch needs to die legit' can be routine, as is the promotion of knife culture. A rap soundtrack can accompany a video of violence, sometimes committed by teenagers. In October 2021, a Policy Exchange report revealed that drill music was linked to around a quarter of London's gang murders in 2018. Drill rappers often taunt rival gangs in their music videos. Around 80 per cent of gang-related murders were committed by non-Whites.

Organisations have their own cultures, and this can be a reason for their failure. Different sectors have different cultures. A government organisation will have a different culture to a private sector one.

Culture cannot be changed like changing a pair of shoes. It is deeply ingrained, and changing culture is difficult, takes time and a great deal of effort, and may even be impossible. That is all the worse if the culture involved is a religion, as someone's belief in a particular god is an ingrained belief and not something subject to reason. Islam is by far the most difficult religion to deal with, as it is supremacist and Muslim immigration into the West has caused friction and violence.

The recognition of Islam's violence is long-standing. Max Weber (1864-1920), the German sociologist and philosopher, wrote 'Islam was never really a religion of salvation. Islam is a warrior religion.'[35] More recently, Ayaan Hirsi Ali, an ex-Muslim and now a critic of it, wrote 'Islam is not a religion of peace', and that its violence is 'driven by a political ideology ... embedded in Islam itself', including the Koran and the hadiths (supposed teaching set out by Muhammad).[36] It is 'theologically sanctioned violence'.

Islam is not determined solely by the Koran, but also by hadiths. Hadiths are a record of Muhammad's sayings, teachings and an account of his activities.[37] Hadiths, supposedly, can be sourced back to Muhammad himself (this 'chain of transmission' is known as an isnad). The writer Peter Townsend said, 'A typical isnad will read like this: "I heard from A, who heard from B, who heard from C, who heard from E, who heard from F that the prophet did such and such a thing".'[38] The problem is that there are 'literally hundreds of thousands of hadiths floating around'.[39] Muslim scholars have therefore had to identify more reliable hadiths from the more fanciful ones, with books of supposedly more reliable hadiths having been compiled – both for Sunni and Shia Muslims.[40]

Following Muhammad's death, those who wanted to justify something, or their own status, tended to do so by citing some hadith or other, or simply invented one. There were so many false hadiths – many were described at the time as lies told for gain or ideological reasons – that in the ninth and tenth centuries, efforts were made to extract those deemed more reliable.[41] For example, the stoning of women has no basis in the Koran, but has stemmed from a hadith Umar claimed, who justified his tribal views by citing Muhammad.[42] Thus, the Koran and the evolution of the Muslim faith were subject to the cultural attitudes of medieval Arabia. Hadiths were divided into sound and weak ones, although some of the later hadiths were more cleverly contrived and were not as sound as they were presented to be, with the Muslim expert, Joseph Schacht, remarking that 'the more perfect the isnad (chain of transmission), the later the tradition'.[43]

The problems with hadiths are worsened by Arabia's powerful clan system in which more powerful clans could emerge as a result of marriages and political alliances.[44] When people married in their mid-teens, then the generational gap was small and the number of descendants grew. The bloodline held together the tribe.

Muslims believe in the 'superhuman perfection' of Muhammad and the 'literal truth and sanctity' of the Koran as 'the direct revelation of God'.[45] Muhammad is the last prophet until Judgement Day and the end of time, and the Koran is the last word spoken by God.[46] Many Muslims still believe that the Koran must be read in the original Arabic in order to experience the proper spiritual word of God and a translation is not sufficient.[47]

The four main schools of Islamic jurisprudence agree the Koran advocates war until non-Muslims either convert to Islam, pay jizyah tax or are killed, and this is endorsed by the 25 leading approved Koranic interpretations.[48]

A key aspect of Islam is Sharia. Sharia reflects both the Koran and the hadiths (and their Arab tribal background) and clerics adjudicate and enforce Allah's will.[49] Ulema (Muslim scholars) developed Sharia as a basis of judgement. There are five categories of behaviour: obligatory actions, which are rewarded and for which punishment is meted for non-performance; meritorious actions that should be rewarded, but punishment is not required for non-performance; actions that require no response; actions that are undesirable, but not punishable; and actions that are forbidden and punishable. The purpose is to reward virtue and punish wrongdoing.[50] The ulema have a number of roles; they act as judges in Sharia courts, are administrators in mosques, they are preachers, act as lawyers and other roles.[51] In Islam, religion and politics are inseparable, and the ulema can come down hard on any view to the contrary.[52]

Among the crimes contrary to Sharia are apostasy (giving up Islam), blasphemy, adultery, homosexuality, the drinking of alcohol and gambling. These remain crimes in Muslim states and, apart from the last category, the death penalty is the common punishment.[53] Sharia punishments include amputation, stoning and crucifixion.[54] Apostasy includes a failure to continue believing in Allah, and conversion to other faiths.[55] Although earlier verses of the Koran condemned but did not criminalise gambling and drinking, later verses prohibited this, describing them as an 'act of Satan'.[56] Muslim scholars regard this as abrogation and the later verses override the earlier ones.

Sharia has spread across Islamic countries and in the West. In Brunei, for example, Sharia is being phased in with adultery being punishable by stoning, theft by amputation, and the death sentence for homosexuality.[57] A survey by Pew Research in 2013 revealed that 72 per cent of Indonesian Muslims, 84 per cent of Pakistani Muslims, 82 per cent of Bangladeshi Muslims, 74 per cent of Egyptian Muslims, 71 per cent of Nigerian Muslims, 91 per cent of Iraqi Muslims, and 99 per cent of Afghan Muslims wanted Sharia as state law.[58]

Sharia is incompatible with democracy and human rights. Egypt and Pakistan have tried to ignore it, although it is accepted as legitimate civil law. Saudi Arabia applies it.[59] In Saudi Arabia, churches and synagogues are outlawed and beheadings are a legal form of punishment (in August 2014, there was a beheading a day). Iran uses stoning for punishment and homosexuals are hanged. In Brunei, homosexuality also results in the death penalty.[60]

That Sharia is drawn from the Koran and the hadiths is a major problem. It is the code for the perfect Islamic life and its laws are not a matter for debate or revision. Islam claims to be the final religion.[61] As 'Islam' means 'submission',[62] Sharia is therefore not a legal system as such, but the implementation of Allah's will by the clerics. Those who disagree with any aspect of Sharia are defying the will of Allah.

This 'blind obedience to God' is not only a problem in itself, as it renders Islam difficult to reform, but also is compounded by the interpretation of the Koran and that the later, more violent verses, are superior due to abrogation. It also means Islam will not integrate into Western society. The Koran actually *instructs* Muslims not to integrate into non-Muslim society: 'Let not the believers take for friends or helpers unbelievers rather than believers.'[63]

Ayaan Hirsi Ali identifies those she describes as Medina Muslims as those who focus on Muhammad's activities when in Medina, 'call Jews and Christians "pigs and monkeys",' 'put women in burqas', and 'believe that the murder of an infidel is an imperative if he refuses to convert voluntarily to Islam.' She said, 'They preach jihad and glorify death through martyrdom. The men and women who join groups such as al-Qaeda, ISIS, Boko Haram, and Al-Shabaab in my native Somalia – to name just four of hundreds of jihadist organisations – are all Medina Muslims.'[64] She further believes that the number of Medina Muslims, although a small minority, is underestimated and growing rapidly. Ayaan Hirsi Ali wrote in *Heretic* (2015):

'Look at photographs of any of the Muslim cities of the world in the 1970s: Baghdad. Cairo. Damascus. Kabul. Mogadishu. Tehran. You will see that very few women in those days were covered. Instead on the streets, in office buildings, in markets, movie theatres, restaurants, and homes, most women dressed very much like their counterparts in Europe and America. They wore skirts above the knee. They wore Western fashion. Their hair was done up and visible.

Today, by contrast, a mere photo of a woman walking on the streets of Kabul with a knee-length skirt becomes a viral happening on the Internet, and sparks widespread condemnation as "shameful" and "half-naked", with the government criticised for "sleeping". When I was a girl in primary school in Nairobi, those who covered their heads were the exceptions – fewer than half of all girls. A few years ago, I googled my old primary school. In the photos posted, nearly every girl was covered.'

The Science Center Berlin conducted a report on the attitude of Muslims in 2008. The report's author, Ruud Koopmans, stated, 'Almost 60 per cent agree that Muslims should return to the roots of Islam, 75 per cent think there is only one interpretation of the Koran possible to which every Muslim should stick, and 65 per cent say that religious rules are more important to them than the laws of the country in which they live.' Fifty-four per cent believed the West intended to destroy Muslim culture.[65]

The difficulty for the West is the sect of Islam that is promoted. Saudi monies promote Wahhabiism and it is, arguably, the most extreme version, and arose out of a deal done between the Saudi royal family and the Wahhabiists. In forming their alliance, Ibn Saud agreed with Abd al-Wahhab that he would lead the Muslim community while al-Wahhab would be a leader in religious matters.[66] This agreement has continued.

The vast Saudi oil wealth has facilitated the funding of Wahhabi schools, mosques, Muslim charities, and literature. Most mosques in Britain and across the West are built with foreign money. Saudi Arabia has used its oil wealth in this and promotes the extreme Wahhabism sect of Islam. Iran, Turkey and Qatar also fund the building of mosques overseas.[67]

Another key aspect of Islam is jihad. Jihad literally means 'a struggle', 'a striving' or 'a great effort'. This can be an inner struggle to be a devout Muslim or an external struggle such as war.[68] Muslim apologists try to differentiate between 'greater' and 'lesser' jihad, where greater jihad refers to the struggle of oneself to lead a more holy life and lesser jihad; 'Jihad in the Way of Allah', is the waging of war.[69] Peter Townsend wrote:

> 'This idea is based upon a story mentioned in a 12th century book *The History of Baghdad*, by Yahya ibn al 'Ala', who said: "We were told by Layth, on the authority of 'Ata', on the authority of Abu Rabah, on the authority of Jabir, who said, 'The Prophet returned from one of his battles, and thereupon told us, "You have arrived with an excellent arrival, you have come from the Lesser Jihad to the Greater Jihad – the striving of a servant (of Allah) against his desires"'.".
>
> The first thing to note is that the first time this hadith appears is in the 12th century, a full five centuries after Muhammad died! It is totally absent from the major hadith collections ... The idea that "inner struggle" is the primary form of jihad also directly contradicts the (Koran).'[70]

Consequently, classic Islamic scholars regard this hadith as 'weak' or 'fabricated', particularly its chain of transmission. Someone simply invented it and it has been fixed upon to pass off jihad and Islam as peaceful. Even so, to the Muslim fundamentalist, jihad means war. The Koran itself is warlike in many parts. For example, the Koran states, 'Fight in the way of God those who fight you, but do not begin hostilities; God does not like the aggressor' (2:190). It further states, 'permission to fight is given only to those who have been oppressed ... who have been driven from their homes saying, "God is our Lord"' (22:39). Elsewhere, it says, 'Slay the polytheists wherever you confront them' (9:5); and 'fight those who do not believe in God and the Last Day' (9:29). This was intended to refer to war against the Quraysh.[71]

The Koran strongly advocates Jihad and war. It says, 'I will instil terror into the hearts of the Unbelievers: smite ye above their necks and smite all their finger-tips off them.'[72] Chapter 9 of the Koran is the most violent and is among the last to be revealed. It contains the following two examples, 'But when the forbidden months are past, then fight and slay the Pagans wherever ye find them, and seize them, beleaguer them, and lie in wait for them in every stratagem (of war)'; and 'Fight those who believe not in Allah nor the Last Day, nor hold that forbidden which hath been forbidden by Allah and his Messenger, nor acknowledge the religion of Truth, (even if they are) of the People of the Book, until they pay the Jizya with willing submission, and feel themselves subdued'.[73]

Ayaan Hirsi Ali wrote, 'Islam teaches that there is nothing so glorious as taking an infidel's life – and so much the better if the act of murder costs your own life.'[74] The focus for Muslims is on the hereafter rather than life itself; paradise is what matters. This is reflected in the term 'martyrdom' that Muslims use rather than 'suicide' to describe the bombings. Saudi Arabia and Qatar charities further encourage this violence by sending money to the families of Palestinian suicide bombers.[75]

The West prefers not to recognise Islam's violence or extremism. Critics of Islam are subject to name calling and the Inquisition. Muslims are quick to allege Islamophobia. Reports of supposed Islamophobia can be exaggerated if not falsified. For example, the British pressure group Tell MAMA had its government funding cut after a report on its website entitled 'wave of Islamophobic incidents' reporting an alleged 192 'Islamophobic incidents' was found to be false. Only eight per cent of the supposed 'incidents' involved an alleged physical event (none of which needed medical treatment), with the overwhelming majority of 'incidents' constituting chatter on Facebook and Twitter, including many from outside Britain.[76]

More dangerous, the denial of the true nature of Islam has been the opening response to actual terrorism or the threat of it. In response to the bombings in London in July 2005, Tony Blair said, 'In the end, it is by the power of argument, debate, true religious faith and true legitimate politics that we will defeat this threat. That means not just arguing against their terrorism, but their politics and their perversion of religious faith'.[77] The former US President Barack Obama said in Cairo in 2009, 'The enduring faith of over a billion people is so much bigger than the narrow hatred of a few. Islam is not part of the problem in combating violent extremism – it is an important part of promoting peace.'[78] David Cameron, the British prime minister, said in response to the murder of a British aid worker by ISIS, 'They boast of their brutality. They claim to do this in the name of Islam. That is nonsense. Islam is a religion of peace. They are not Muslims. They are monsters.'[79] François Hollande, the French president, after the Charlie Hebdo killings said, 'Not to be divided means we must not make any confusion concerning these terrorists and fanatics that have nothing to do with the Muslim religion.'[80] Former US President Barack Obama also said, 'We are not at war with Islam but with those who "perverted Islam".'

In reality, the threat was embedded in Islam and growing. After 9/11, worldwide, there was an average of five terrorist acts that resulted in deaths every day. This totalled 27,000 attacks in about 15 years. For the month of November 2014, the BBC and King's College London reported that there were 664 jihadist attacks across 14 countries, with 5,042 people killed.[81]

In 2012, the National Consortium for the Study of Terrorism and Responses to Terrorism at the University of Maryland found the six deadliest jihadist terror groups were the Taliban (2,500 killed); Boko Haram (over 1,200 killed); al-Qaeda in the Arabian Peninsula (over 960); Tehrik-e Taliban Pakistan (over 950); al-Qaeda in Iraq (over 930); and Al-Shabaab (over 700).[82]

In November 2014, the UN estimated around 15,000 foreign fighters (around 25 per cent from Western Europe) had joined the 'radical jihadists' in Syria.[83]

Groups such as Boko Haram, which has openly stated it intended to kill all Nigerian Christians (roughly half of Nigeria's population),[84] grow from within the existing Muslim community. They begin by preaching and establishing support from the community before turning to violence.[85] More examples from this can be found across the West where a mosque is found to be at the centre of the growth of extremism, and extremist preachers from the Middle East can be invited to speak in many Western mosques.

This terrorism has wide support among Muslims. An ICM poll in February 2006 found that 20 per cent of British Muslims had sympathy with the 'feelings and motives' of the 7/7 London underground bombers and 40 per cent wanted Sharia in Britain. In 2007, a poll for Pew Research found 26 per cent of US Muslims aged less than 30 supported suicide bombings. A Pew Global survey revealed that only 57 per cent of Muslims had an unfavourable view of al-Qaeda. In 2013, a Pew Research poll found that 76 per cent of South Asian Muslims and 56 per cent of Egyptian Muslims advocated the killing of apostates who had deserted Islam. A COMRES survey in 2015 revealed that 45 per cent of British Muslims considered clerics preaching anti-West violence represented 'mainstream Islam', and 27 per cent supported violence against cartoonists who drew pictures of Muhammad.

A US Center for Security Policy survey in 2015 revealed that 25 per cent of American Muslims believed that 'global jihad' justified violence against Americans in the USA.[86] A Pew survey in 2007 revealed that seven per cent of American Muslims aged between 18 and 29 had a favourable view of al-Qaeda. The survey found that young American Muslims were twice as likely to support suicide bombings as older American Muslims.[87]

The Pew Research Centre estimated that, due to immigration and higher birth rates, the USA's Muslim population would increase from around 2.6 million to 6.2 million by 2030, a figure higher than in any West European country except France. Approximately 40 per cent of these Muslim immigrants would be from Pakistan, Bangladesh and Iraq.[88] A 2013 Pew Research poll found that 75 per cent of Pakistanis, 43 per cent of Bangladeshis and 41 per cent of Iraqis supported the death penalty for apostates, and the respective figures are 81 per cent, 65 per cent and 69 per cent for those who hold that Sharia is the revealed word of Allah.[89] Other extremist views were likewise shared.

Turkey is a good example of the power of culture. Turkey was born out of the Ottoman empire. Five centuries of the Ottoman empire failed to produce an Ottoman nation. There was an Ottoman citizenship. Even so, that empire was repressive, experienced bloody wars sparked by rebellions and ultimately collapsed following WWI. It also played a leading role in the slave trade.

The Ottoman Empire had special slave markets called 'Esir' or 'Yesir' in most towns and cities. Slaves were paraded naked for the inspection of potential buyers. A Portuguese missionary, João dos Santos, reported that some Somali slave traders had a 'custom to sew up their females, especially their slaves being young to make them unable for conception, which makes these slaves sell dearer, both for their chastitie, and for better confidence which their masters put in them'. Although the Italian colonial administration abolished slavery in Somalia at the beginning of the 20th century, the practice continued into the 1930s. In neighbouring Ethiopia, eunuchs were traded. Eunuchs had a high price as they served in the harems.

The Arab slave trade pre-dated the trans-Atlantic slave trade by around 700 years. The Portuguese and Spanish traders copied the Muslim possession of slaves in Islamic southern Spain and Morocco as they explored West Africa. From the end of the 15th century until the mid-19th century, the trans-Atlantic slave trade is estimated to have transported around 10 million African slaves, with another two million believed to have died in the crossing. Unlike the Muslim slave-traders, the Europeans bought their slaves. The mainly male slaves were mostly put to work on plantations. The slaves were allowed to marry and their descendants make up a sizeable proportion of the present-day populations of the Americas, including the Caribbean.

By comparison, the majority of slaves taken by Muslims were females and young boys. The females were used as sex slaves or housemaids and were placed in harems either for sex or to act as attendants; the young boys were castrated, although some 60 per cent died in the act. Some male slaves were traded, mainly to be used as galley slaves, and some were used in the army. The caliphate in Baghdad in the 10th century reportedly had 7,000 Black eunuchs and 4,000 White eunuchs in his palace.

It is believed the Muslims traded up to 100 million African slaves (one estimate puts the figure at 180 million, although other estimates are lower), and the death rates during transportation were far higher. While the trans-Atlantic slave trade spanned three centuries, the Arab slave trade lasted fourteen centuries and continues to this day in some parts of the Muslim world (most obviously in ISIS-controlled territory, and there are also reports of the slave trade continuing in The Sudan). Of tragic importance is that despite the preponderance of female slaves trafficked, there is the absence of their descendants today. While the male slaves were castrated or put to work where they could not reproduce, many female slaves were used for sex at a time when there was not contraception so the only explanation for their lack of offspring is the practice of infanticide on a genocidal scale. An article in the *New York Daily Times*, dated 6 August 1856, entitled, 'Horrible Traffic in Circassian Women – Infanticide in Turkey', stated:

> 'In Constantinople it is evident that there is a very large number of negresses living and having habitual intercourse with their Turkish masters – yet it is a rare thing to see a mulatto (someone of mixed Negro-Caucasian race). What becomes of the progeny of such intercourse? I have no hesitation in saying that it is got rid of by infanticide and that there is hardly a family in

124

Stanboul where infanticide is not practised in such cases as a mere matter of course, and without the least remorse or dread.'

Furthermore, once the sex slaves reached a certain age, they faced the prospect of being disowned by their masters and left to fend for themselves or die; reports of desperate women begging on the streets of cities across the Muslim world was evidence of this cruelty.

Turkey was keen to develop its Western status following the end of the Ottoman Empire, adopting 'western culture, nationalism, secularism and republicanism'.[90] The founder and first president of the Republic of Turkey, Kemal Ataturk, introduced sweeping reforms including the abolishment of the Islamic caliphate, legal reforms, women's rights, the Latin alphabet, and new dress codes, and educational, political and economic reforms including a firm commitment to being a secular state despite an overwhelmingly Muslim population.[91] The view of the Turkish elite could be summarised as: 'civilisation is the European civilisation. There is no other one.'[92]

Despite this determined effort, Turkey's secular status was dependent upon the military either directly, or via a constitutional court, imposing that secularism on a Muslim country. Ordinary Turks held the military in respect and the military would quickly restore civilian rule whenever a coup had been deemed necessary. This continued for around a century, with Islamist politicians being blocked and banned when necessary, with the odd coup along the way. Current Turkish president Recep Tayyip Erdoğan was one politician who was blocked. However, Turkey's application to join the EU changed the balance of power, as the EU required that the military was subordinate to politicians and not vice versa. Once the military-backed constitutional court was reformed, in order to comply with EU rules, the Islamists quickly rose to power. A century of imposed secularism was insufficient to change the culture of Turkey.

Under the Erdogan's AKP, Turkey has experienced a policy of Islamisation and Jews and Christians have been threatened by extremists.[93] Assyrians are targeted despite there only being around 25,000 remaining in Turkey.[94]

Turkey also involved itself in the Syrian civil war, which was a very vicious affair. In March 2013, the extent of the barbarity the civil war had reached was demonstrated when the rebel commander Khaled al Hamad (aka Abu Sakkar) was recorded as eating the heart and liver of a dead Syrian soldier. Hamad said, 'I swear to God, you soldiers of Bashar, you dogs, we will eat from your hearts and livers! O heroes of Bab Amr, you slaughter the Alawites and take out their hearts to eat them!' The Free Syria Army (FSA) took no disciplinary action against Hamad. The FSA were regarded as the moderates.

By April 2015, the FSA had all but disappeared in northern Syria, with some fighters defecting to Islamist factions such as Ahrar ash-Sham, and some units destroyed by the al-Qaeda affiliated al-Nusra Front (both ISIS and al-Nusra began as being a part of al-Qaeda, and split in a power struggle between al-Nusra and the ISIS leadership who had set up al-Nusra[95]), which took control of significant amounts of Western-supplied weapons. The Islamist factions, including al-Nusra, Ahrar ash-Sham, and the Muslim Brotherhood, united in a loose coalition known as the Army of Conquest, which attracted the open support of both Saudi Arabia and Turkey. Recruits for al-Nusra would travel to southern Turkey before slipping across the border into Syria.[96] The Russian foreign minister, Sergey Lavrov, described the FSA as being 'an already phantom structure', and ISIS fighters described it as being their best source of weapons. In May 2015, video footage from the newspaper *Cumhuriyet* showed Turkish intelligence shipping arms to Syrian rebels.[97]

Both ISIS, the Kurds, and a variety of experts and journalists claimed Turkey had provided support to ISIS. The support, according to David Phillips of Columbia University's Institute for the Study of Human Rights, allegedly ranged 'from military cooperation and weapons transfers to logistical support, financial assistance, and the provision of medical services'. An

ISIS member claimed, 'ISIS commanders told us to fear nothing at all because there was full cooperation with the Turks'. Turkey allegedly regarded ISIS as an ally against the Kurds in Syria. Turkey was much criticised for allowing free passage for recruits to ISIS to cross its border with Syria, labelled the 'Gateway to Jihad'. The payment of a small bribe was sometimes made to border guards. An ISIS commander stated that 'most of the fighters who joined us in the beginning of the war came via Turkey, and so did our equipment and supplies'. ISIS fighters received treatment in Turkish hospitals. For example, in July 2015, it was reported that a former nurse had been working in a secret Turkish hospital to treat ISIS wounded. The hospital was near the Syrian border and was run by Sumeyye Erdogan, the daughter of the Turkish president, Recep Tayyip Erdogan. The nurse was a member of the Alawite faith. She said, 'I was given a generous salary of $7,500, but they were unaware of my religion. The fact is that I adhere to the Alawi faith, and since Erdoğan took the helm of the country the system shows utter contempt for the Alawi minority.' The nurse was forced out once the hospital officials discovered her faith. The nurse explained:

> 'No sooner did they become cognizant of my faith than the wave of intimidation began, for I knew many things as who was running the corps, I saw Sumeyye Erdoğan frequently at our headquarter in Sanliurfa ... I am indeed terrified, I rue the day I enrolled in that program. Almost every day several khaki Turkish military trucks were bringing scores of severely injured, shaggy [ISIS] rebels to our secret hospital, and we had to prepare the operating rooms and help doctors in the following procedures.'

It was only after terrorist attacks in Paris that the USA prevailed upon Turkey to close its border. A senior US official told the *Wall Street Journal,* 'The game has changed. Enough is enough. The border needs to be sealed', and 'This is an international threat, and it's coming out of Syria and it's coming through Turkish territory.'

By comparison, the US plan to train 15,000 fighters for the Free Syrian Army collapsed into a farce and only a handful of fighters were actually trained. It did not help the recruitment that the CIA only paid its fighters half what ISIS was, and had an extreme rationing of ammunition with one local commander complaining his fighters were restricted to an average of 16 bullets per month[98] when by comparison al-Nusra was well funded.[99] Turkey hindered the exercise by supplying information of a US-backed unit known as 'Division 30' to al-Nusra who attacked and kidnapped many from it as they entered Syria from Turkey. The Turkish motive was to destroy the US initiative and allow the jihadist factions to become the only opposition to Assad.[100] A desire not to upset relations with Turkey and other supposed friendly Sunni states such as Saudi Arabia, Pakistan and Gulf monarchies compromised the Western policy.

Turkey openly supported jihadist groups, including Ahrar ash-Sham (ideologically very similar to al-Qaeda) and al-Nusra (which is banned in the USA and most of Europe). Jihadists, including those belonging to al-Nusra and ISIS, were allowed to move freely between Turkey and Syria.[101] The Russian president, Vladimir Putin, said, 'ISIS has big money, hundreds of millions or even billions of dollars, from selling oil. In addition, they are protected by the military of an entire nation. One can understand why they are acting so boldly and blatantly. Why they kill people in such atrocious ways. Why they commit terrorist acts across the world, including in the heart of Europe.' Both Western and Russian intelligence sources claimed to have evidence of ISIS oil shipments into Turkey. In June 2014, Ali Edibogluan of the Turkish opposition in parliament claimed ISIS had smuggled oil worth $800 million into Turkey from both Syria and Iraq. According to Russian sources, ISIS used Turkey to traffic Afghan heroin into Europe and profited by around $1 billion.[102] ISIS had even traded human organs in Turkey. Wayne Madsen, a former intelligence analyst at the US National

Security Agency and an American investigative reporter, stated that ISIS had been, and was, involved in organ trading: 'The Uyghur battalions of ISIS are heavily engaged in this. They are also known to be involved in organ harvesting in China.' Reportedly, a kidney could be sold in Turkey for $4,000 and a heart for $6,000.[103]

Russian Prime Minister Dmitry Medvedev said, 'Turkey's actions are de facto protection of Islamic State', and 'This is no surprise, considering the information we have about the direct financial interest of some Turkish officials relating to the supply of oil products refined by plants controlled by ISIS.' Iraqi Prime Minister Haider al-Abadi said the bulk of the oil produced by ISIS was being smuggled into Turkey. Moshe Ya'alon, the Israeli defence minister, said Turkey bought oil from ISIS, funded them, and 'permitted jihadists to move from Europe to Syria and Iraq and back'. James Clapper, former US Director of National Intelligence, said, 'I think Turkey has other priorities and other interests' apart from defeating ISIS, and opinion polls in Turkey showed most Turks did not see ISIS as a major threat. An opinion poll in August 2014 revealed 11.3 per cent of Turks, or nine million people, did not regard ISIS as a terrorist organisation.[104]

A senior Jordanian official accused Turkey of training ISIS fighters. An Egyptian security official stated Turkey supplied satellite information to ISIS and 10,000 passports to ISIS supporters to facilitate their free movement. The Armenian Defence Minister, Seyran Ohanyan, also accused Turkey of supporting ISIS.

The Gatestone Institute, Norddeutsher Rundfunk and Sudwestrundfunk, alleged ISIS was even selling women in Turkey. The Consortium of Public Broadcasters in Germany produced a film showing the ISIS slave trade in Turkey.

The day after ISIS abducted more than 90 Assyrian Christians, Jacques Behnan Hindo, the Syrian Catholic Archbishop of Hasakey-Nesibi, said on Vatican radio, 'In the north, Turkey allows through lorries, (ISIS) fighters, oil stolen from Syria, wheat and cotton: all of these can cross the border but nobody (from the Christian community) can pass over.'

The trade in oil was of critical importance. The EU reports deftly ignored Turkey's role in ISIS sales of oil. Redur Xelil, a YPG (Syrian Kurds) spokesman, said, 'Turkey is helping ISIS and facilitating their moves in and out of Syria, as well as aiding them in logistics and other levels'. ISIS was estimated to earn around $500 million per year from oil. Turkey turned a blind eye to the oil dealing, failed to seal its border and profited from the trade.[105]

Iraqi intelligence officers said ISIS sold crude oil to smugglers who then sold it on to Turkish middlemen. ISIS was estimated to be extracting 30,000 barrels of oil per day in Syria and another 20,000 barrels from Iraq, mainly from oilfields outside Mosul. At the time, ISIS controlled 253 oil wells in Syria, of which 161 were operational.[106] The capture of Mosul in June 2014 was a breakthrough for ISIS. On paper, they faced an Iraqi army of 60,000. That substantial force, in reality, was only a third of its supposed strength with the officers pocketing the salaries of non-existent soldiers or half of the salaries of others, provided they did not have to show up or don a uniform. Mosul fell to ISIS, with the officers scarpering at the outbreak of fighting. The soldiers who were captured were immediately executed.[107] This corruption in the Iraqi army was not unique. According to an Iraqi politician, who subsequently inspected an Iraqi armoured division, there were only 68 tanks and 2,000 soldiers instead of the supposed 120 tanks and 10,000 troops.[108]

Satellite images on 18 October 2015 of Deir Ez-Zor showed hundreds of oil tankers carrying oil towards Qamishli. Satellite photographs on the 13 November 2015 showed convoys of tankers waiting at the Turkey/Syria border on the motorway at Azzaz. After entering Turkey, oil was sent to the 'Tupras' refinery in Batman. Another satellite photograph on 14 November 2015 showed 1,104 trucks at Cizre.[109]

Putin told journalists at a G20 meeting in Antalya, 'I've shown photos taken from space and from aircraft which clearly demonstrate the scale of the illegal trade in oil and petroleum products'. In the two weeks following Russia's disclosures, airstrikes destroyed 1,300 ISIS tankers and trucks.[110]

On 15 December 2014, Aykut Erdogdu, a CHP (the Kemalist Republican People's Party, founded by Ataturk) member of parliament, alleged that partner companies of Berat Abayrak (Erdogan's son-in-law) and Ziya Ilgen (Erdogan's brother-in-law) were involved in the ISIS oil trade. Aykut Erdogdu was charged with 'insulting the president'.[111] Ali Edisoglu, a Turkish opposition MP, said:

> '$800 million worth of oil that ISIS obtained from regions it occupied this year (the Rumeilan oil fields in northern Syria and most recently Mosul) is being sold in Turkey. They have laid pipes from villages near the Turkish border at Hatay. Similar pipes exist also at the Turkish border regions of Kilis, Urfa and Gaziantep. They transfer the oil to Turkey and sell it at a discount for cash. They refine the oil in areas close to the Turkish border and then sell it via Turkey. This is worth $800 million.'[112]

Russia's Deputy Defence Minister Anatoly Antonov said Turkey was the biggest buyer of 'stolen' oil from Syria and Iraq. Antonov produced satellite images showing oil tankers travelling from ISIS-held territory to three locations in Turkey, including refineries. Some oil was sent to a third country. Antonov said, 'According to available information, the highest level of the political leadership of the country, President Erdoğan and his family, are involved in this criminal business.'[113] In November 2015, Berat Albayrak, Erdogan's son-in-law, was appointed Minister of Energy and Natural Resources.

Gürsel Tekin, CHP vice-president, said:

> 'President Erdoğan claims that according to international transportation conventions there is no legal infraction concerning Bilal's illicit activities and his son is doing an ordinary business with the registered Japanese companies, but, in fact, Bilal Erdoğan is up to his neck in

complicity with terrorism. As long as his father holds office he will be immune from any judicial prosecution.'

Tekin said Bilal's maritime company trading oil for ISIS, BMZ Ltd, is 'a family business and president Erdogan's close relatives hold shares in BMZ and they misused public funds and took illicit loans from Turkish banks.'[114]

Syrian Information Minister Omran al-Zoubi said, 'All of the (ISIS) oil was delivered to a company that belongs to the son of Erdogan. This is why Turkey became anxious when Russia began delivering airstrikes against the ISIS infrastructure and destroyed more than 500 trucks with oil already. This really got on Erdoğan and his company's nerves. They're importing not only oil, but wheat and historic artefacts as well.'[115]

In October 2015, Bilal Erdoğan allegedly took $1 billion to Italy. Lawyer Massimiliano Annetta filed a petition with the Bologna prosecutor's office about alleged money laundering by Bilal Erdogan, and requested an investigation.[116]

A captured ISIS fighter, Mahmud Ghazi Tatar, said he crossed the border from Turkey into Syria to be trained along with other recruits. He said, 'At the training camp in May 2015, our commander told us that the group sells fuel to Turkey. That income covers Islamic State's costs. The oil trucks crossing into Turkey every day carry crude oil, as well as petrol', and that ISIS had 'enough oil to last them a long time'.

On 26 January 2016, Israeli politician Moshe Ya'alon told reporters, 'As you know, Islamic State enjoyed Turkish money for oil for a very, very long period of time.' US State Department spokesman Mark Toner said ISIS sold oil to intermediaries who, in turn, were involved in smuggling that oil to Turkey.'[117]

Turkey's state-funded Directorate for Religious Affairs (*Diyanet*) boasted that nearly 9,000 new mosques were built in Turkey between 2005 and 2015. The total number of mosques in Turkey was estimated at around 90,000, or one mosque per 866 people. Iran, with a similar population to Turkey, had 48,000 mosques, giving Turkey around twice as many mosques as Iran per capita. Egypt, with a larger population, had 67,000 mosques.[118] Turkey had also a policy of building mosques abroad, in countries across the EU and even in Russia, Cuba and the USA. Erdoğan attended the opening of a cultural centre and mosque in Maryland, USA, which was the only one in the United States to feature two minarets and was constructed in the style of 16th century Ottoman architecture, with a central dome, half domes and cupolas. At the ceremony, Erdoğan said, 'Unfortunately, we are going through a rough time all around the world. Intolerance towards Muslims is on the rise not only here in the United States but also around the globe.'[119] In Germany, with the mosques came 'spook-imams', Turkish police patrolled Turkish areas in Berlin (the German authorities claimed they could not stop them), and spy even on Kurds living in Germany.[120]

Of importance was the new constitution that the Erdoğan government pushed through in a referendum in 2017. This new constitution created a presidential republic in which the role of prime minister was abolished, there was a new post of vice president, the president became the head of the executive as well as being head of state and party political, and the president had the power to appoint ministers, senior judges, control the budget and enact certain laws by power of decree. In the new constitution, the president alone could declare a state of emergency and dismiss parliament. It also dictated that the presidential and parliamentary elections would take place on the same day every five years, increasing the number of MPs from 550 to 600, and removing parliament's ability to scrutinise ministers, although it was able to impeach the president if there was a two-thirds majority.

With a referendum turnout of 85 per cent, 51 per cent voted to accept the new changes. The three largest cities (Istanbul, Ankara and Izmir) rejected the changes, but Erdogan's rural heartlands in Anatolia voted in favour, as did the Turkish emigrants living in European countries. Sixty-three per cent of voters living in Germany, 71 per cent of those in the Netherlands and 65 per cent of those in France voted in favour. The number of Turks in Europe could be as high as five million.[121]

There were further reports that, following the coup, Turkey's spy network, MIT, monitored and pressured Germany's large Turkish population. Erich Schmidt-Eenboom (a German intelligence expert and writer) described MIT's activities as 'intelligence service repression'.

After the count started, the election authorities announced they would accept unstamped ballots. Previously, these unstamped ballots were rejected to avoid corrupt officials rigging the vote. Up to 2.5 million votes were believed to have been affected by this change. Erdoğan responded to complaints from foreign observers that they should 'know their place'.

The narrow victory was achieved after the Yes side manipulated the count with the unstamped ballots, and with a campaign supported by the power of the state. Some No campaigners, such as the pro-Kurdish Selahattin Demirtas, were imprisoned. A Kurdish song calling for a No vote was banned. Yes supporters enjoyed 90 per cent of the campaign coverage across 17 national stations, according to one study. The campaign came against the backdrop of the coup clampdown, in which anyone Erdoğan deemed an enemy was sacked from their jobs and/or arrested.

Culture cannot be changed as if changing a pair of shoes. The power of culture is extraordinary: not even after five centuries could the Ottoman empire forge an Ottoman nation out of the empire's various peoples and religions; over one century, Turkey's Kemalists could not embed a secular society that would survive the instinct to vote for Islamist politicians, such as Erdogan; despite living in European countries for many years, and decades, and being surrounded by Western culture, the Turks in those European countries supported and voted for the Islamist Erdogan; and despite one century of imposed secularism, Turkey involved itself in the Syrian civil war to support the bloodthirsty barbarists of ISIS.

The policy of multiculturalism is designed to prevent assimilation. The greater the incompatibility there is between

134

the host culture and the incoming immigrant ones (such as between a liberal Christian country and fundamentalist Muslims), then the greater the conflict between cultures and hence the greater the prospects of the immigrant communities overthrowing the status quo. This is, of course, what the politically correct want. Behind the candyfloss language of celebrating diversity and difference, there is a communist revolutionary agenda.

Assimilation vs. Integration

Although there is little difference between the meaning of assimilation and integration, with the terms being used interchangeably, for multiculturalists, there is a major difference. This difference lies at the core of multiculturalist ideology. The communist and liberal wings of multiculturalism are united on the issue.

In his essay 'Cultural Diversity and Liberal Democracy', Bhikhu Parekh (born in 1935 in Gujarat, and awarded a life peerage in 2000), a leading multiculturalist, asserted that most modern states are culturally diverse, and there was an issue about how to establish common citizenship in such states. Parekh believed different cultural peoples required different treatment. His essay concentrated on those he described as 'ethnic, cultural and religious minorities' within society.

Parekh asserted these groups wish to preserve their identity and then examined three possible alternatives about how this might be achieved: assimilationist liberalism, cultural laissez-faire, and cultural pluralism. Parekh favoured the latter.

Parekh's argument has four major flaws: he accused liberalism of separating government from society when, in fact, it was he; he favoured minorities but neglected the rights of majority nations (the politically correct and the multiculturalists are consistently unconcerned as to the rights and interests of the nation and the majority); he ignored that minority cultures exist worldwide, and so liberal society cannot destroy them; and his goal of a 'community of communities' and 'multicultural post-nation' (as set out in *The Parekh Report* – see below) is against the interests of the core nation, who formed the state. From a multiculturalist viewpoint, multiculturalism being a political process, Parekh advocated a coherent programme to achieve his goal. There is a large overlap in the multiculturalist ideology he set out with Habermas' constitutional patriotism. Parekh defined the purpose of his essay as to analyse the problems of territorially dispersed 'ethnic, cultural and religious minorities' seeking to preserve their distinct ways of life.[122] This included immigrants. Parekh stated:

> 'These groups wish to participate as equal citizens in the collective life of the community, but they also wish to preserve their way of life and demand recognition of their cultural identities. This raises the question as to how a liberal state should respond to their demands.'[123]

This description makes two assumptions: first, the minority groups wish to retain their distinctive ways of life, and second, that the onus is on liberal society to respond to minority demands. The first potential response which Parekh analysed was assimilationist liberalism. He said this model 'presupposes and is a custodian of a way of life centred on such values as personal autonomy, freedom of choice and independent thought'.[124] Parekh said, '[Minorities] threaten the integrity of the liberal way of life. Being self-contained communities they also prevent their members from fully integrating into the wider society. Furthermore, their demand for the recognition of their differences is incompatible with their demand for equality.'[125]

According to Parekh, an assimilationist is therefore in favour of a culture-blind or colour-blind equality and opposed to special treatment for minorities, and will refuse to recognise cultural diversity in favour of integration. However, Parekh rejected assimilation for four reasons. First, according to him, liberalism recognises individuals and not their culture, which is disrespectful due to the importance of culture.[126] Second, the assimilationist liberal equates equality with uniformity, which leads to inequality.[127] He cited the effect of a requirement to wear trousers at work on Muslim women, who are culturally forbidden to expose their bodies in public when society needs to be discriminating. Third, a diversity of cultures enriches society and assimilation is detrimental to that enrichment.[128] Fourth, if minorities are confronted with a process of assimilation they are likely to exploit whatever freedoms liberalism offers in order to preserve and promote their own cultures, leading to friction with wider society. Parekh highlighted religion in this context, 'It is not often appreciated that fundamentalism is often provoked by liberal intolerance, and that once it arises, liberalism feels mortally threatened and unwittingly takes over many of the characteristics of its enemy.'[129] This assertion blames the majority for the actions of the minority. Parekh dismissed the notion that immigrants, by entering another country, should be prepared to accept the national culture of that country, as such is tantamount to treating them as second-class citizens.[130]

Parekh's cultural laissez-faire model would divorce the state of culture and allow individuals to choose a culture. This would extend to the education system, too. While Parekh saw some merit in the proposed cultural neutrality of the state, he nevertheless rejected the laissez-faire approach for four reasons. First, culture is pervasive and intrinsic and cannot be chosen as one might choose clothes. Furthermore, Parekh asserted that some cultures cannot properly survive in an individualist culture.[131] Second, if the state is to maintain an individualist culture, then doing so would result in the state promoting that culture and it would be unable to maintain total neutrality.[132] Third, liberalism would have an advantage in the competition of cultures as it is the product of several centuries of history. It is embedded in society, and people are attached to it. By comparison, other cultures would be at a disadvantage not being a part of the development of society. Liberal culture would therefore remain dominant.[133] In other words, for example,

Britain would remain British, and England would remain English. Fourth, a state's authority and constitution must be founded on some moral basis. Parekh said, 'Whatever its structure, the state is inescapably grounded in and biased towards a specific way of life.'[134] Furthermore, the laws of the state must reflect cultural bias – be it the legalisation or not of slavery, capital punishment, abortion, polygamy, etc. Therefore, 'A morally neutral state, making no moral demands on its citizens and equally hospitable to all human choices, is logically impossible. And since every law and policy coerces those not sharing the underlying values, a morally non-coercive state is a fantasy ... no state can be wholly free of a moral bias and of the concomitant coercion.'[135] Parekh sees the concept of state morality as a problem. His view is an attack on the existence of the nation state, since he regards state morality as unavoidable and unacceptable.

Parekh then came to his preferred option, that of cultural pluralism. Parekh described people as 'cultural beings' who are 'culturally embedded'[136] and stated:

> 'Cultural diversity, then, is a collective good ... it cannot be safeguarded by a policy of cultural laissez-faire. Since it is a valuable public good and since it cannot be left to the vagaries of a distorted cultural market, the state needs to play an active part in promoting it ... Respecting and promoting cultural diversity requires action at several levels. It requires that cultural minorities should be protected against conscious or unconscious discrimination.'[137]

Parekh believed liberals are likely to assume only their interpretation of morality is correct.[138] He condemned this and the concept of a division between public and private culture as it weakens cultural diversity.[139] The result of a prevailing public culture, according to Parekh, is that minorities tend to be nervous about their culture and choose to conform to the host society, which is undesirable, as cultural diversity is a collective good. Therefore, the state should promote minority cultures, including minority schools.[140] Parekh even advocated minority self-governance, 'There is much to be said for the state encouraging self-governance among [minorities] and becoming a community of communities ... there is no obvious reason why [decentralization] should be based only on territorial and occupational and not on communal grounds as well.'[141]

Parekh cited the Jews as a precedent.[142] In examining the limits on cultural autonomy, he summed up the liberal position as consisting of three elements: the autonomy principle, which needs to be sustained and minority cultures that threaten it should be discouraged or banned – Parekh dismissed this as assimilationism; the no-harm principle, which Parekh saw problems with if it includes matters that conflict with minority cultures; and finally, the concept of fundamental or core values of society, which Parekh rejected, believing the concept should be redefined to 'operative public values'. This included 'respect for human dignity, equal respect for persons, secure spaces for self-determination, freedom of dissent and expression, and the pursuit of collective interest as the central *raison d'être* of political power',[143] and all should be obliged to conform. The definition of these values should be open to change, and Parekh said '[society] ought also to bear in mind that the values are a product, of historical consensus and need to win the allegiance of and be revised to meet the legitimate grievances of new groups'.[144] This is almost identical to Habermas's constitutional patriotism, albeit looking at matters from an immigrant point of view, and would give immigrants a veto on the values of society. Parekh proposed his operative public values displace the current national culture or fundamental values, and the product of history be replaced with theory.

In Part One of *Multiculturalist Ideology (Part One), Second Edition: Race War Politics and the Rise of the Anti-Whites*, I compared the communist wing of multiculturalism with the liberal wing. For the communist wing, I examined *The Parekh Report*, with its objective of a 'multicultural post-nation', and for the liberal wing I examined the 'thinking' of Will Kymlicka – a

Canadian academic who has written several books on multiculturalism and is considered an authority on the subject – as set out in his two books, *Multicultural Citizenship: A Liberal Theory of Minority Rights* (1995) and *Politics in the Vernacular: Nationalism, Multiculturalism and Citizenship* (2001), in which Kymlicka took a more stridently politically correct view.

In *The Parekh Report* (produced by the Commission on the Future of Multi-Ethnic Britain that had been set up by the Runnymede Trust in 1998), Parekh went further than in 'Cultural Diversity and Liberal Democracy' – especially regarding assimilation: (i) the report denied Britain is or has ever been a homogenous, unified whole, and so integration is impossible as there is no culture to integrate into; (ii) it dismissed assimilation as immoral as it suppresses difference and renders those who do not share majority norms to second-class citizenship; (iii) it stated that assimilation is impossible due to globalisation.[145] None of this addresses the interests of the host nation or takes into account the need to maintain national unity.

The Runnymede Trust boasted that the commission consisted of '23 distinguished individuals drawn from many community backgrounds ... with a long record of active academic and practical engagement with race-related issues in Britain and elsewhere.' The commission was very much the establishment and took two years deliberating its report. The Labour government not only acted on the report, but subsequently promoted several members of the commission. Both Parekh himself and Sir Herman Ouseley were awarded peerages. Trevor Phillips, described by *The Times* as the key man behind the setting up of the report, was promoted to chairmanship of the Commission for Racial Equality and then appointed as chairman for the replacement EHRC. In promoting the report, Parekh wrote in *The Independent*:

> 'National identity is not given once and for all and cannot be preserved as if it were an antique piece of furniture. The so-called white majority itself consists of groups of people divided along cultural, religious and other lines.

This is equally true of the minority. Since Britain does not consist of cohesive majorities and minorities, we should think of it as a looser federation of cultures held together by common bonds of interest and affection and a collective sense of belonging.'

One could easily have written something very similar in the name of constitutional patriotism rather than multiculturalism. In response to the howls of outrage that greeted the report's launch, Black communist Gary Younge of *The Guardian* wrote:

'*The Telegraph's* front page headline yesterday: "Straw wants to rewrite our history" begs two central questions. Who do they mean by "our" and precisely what version of history are they talking about ... The "our" *The Telegraph* refers to is essentially white, English and nationalistic. For huge numbers of Scots, Welsh and Irish, not to mention those of Caribbean, Asian, African and Chinese descent the idea that 'the description of British will never do on its own" is not news ...

Unlike the French tricolore or the American stars and stripes, we do not have a national emblem that stands for a set of notional egalitarian principles or a constitution that would give it meaning. The union flag is a conqueror's flag that owes its design to the subjugation of England's neighbours and its reputation to the predatory expeditions which saw Britain steal huge amounts of land, labour and natural resources ... So "Britishness" like the union flag is not neutral.'

The Parekh Report asserts there are different versions of racism: 'many varieties of racism and exclusion that disfigure modern Britain and that have been woven into the fabric of British history for many centuries'. It is unashamed in its condemnation of British society as racist:

'Britain continues to be disfigured by racism; by phobias about cultural difference; by sustained social, economic, educational and cultural disadvantage; by institutional discrimination; and by a systematic failure of social justice or real respect for difference. These have been fuelled by a fixed conception of national identity and culture. They are not likely to disappear without a sustained effort of political will. Is it possible to reimagine Britain as a nation – or post nation – in a multicultural way?'

It also condemns the whole of Europe, saying 'European societies, it is sometimes said, are multi-racist societies' and have 'race-based nationalism interacted with a race-based imperialism. In Britain, for example, the Empire was frequently celebrated as the achievement of "an imperial race". The revival of rabid antisemitism, leading to the pogroms against Jews in central and eastern Europe and Hitler's Final Solution, was the product of this pan-European trend'. In fact, Hitler's Final Solution was a product of Nazi ideology and not part of a 'pan-European trend'. Britain bankrupted itself fighting Nazi Germany, and many millions of people died in WWII fighting against Nazism. The allegation is as vile as it is untrue and can only help stir up anti-European hatred.

The Parekh Report is a long attack on Britain, with a multitude of allegations of racism. Three paragraphs (amongst others) which caused outrage state:

'3.28 Does Britishness as such have a future? Some believe that devolution and globalisation have undermined it irretrievably ... It is entirely plain, however, that the word "British" will never do on its own.

3.29 Where does this leave Asians, African-Caribbeans and Africans? For them Britishness is a reminder of colonisation and empire, and to that extent is not attractive. But the first migrants came with British passports, signifying membership of a single imperial system. For the British-born generations, seeking to assert their claim to belong, the concept of Englishness often seems inappropriate, since to be English, as the term is in practice used, is to be white. Britishness is not ideal, but at least it appears acceptable, particularly when suitably qualified – Black British, Indian British, British Muslim, and so on.

3.30 However, there is one major and so far insuperable barrier. Britishness, as much as Englishness, has systematic, largely unspoken, racial connotations. Whiteness nowhere features as an explicit condition of being British, but it is widely understood that Englishness, and therefore by extension Britishness, is racially coded. "There ain't no black in the Union Jack", it has been said. Race is deeply entwined in political culture and with the idea of nation, and underpinned by a distinctively British kind of reticence – to take race and racism seriously, or even to talk about them at all, is bad form, something not done in polite company. This disavowal, combined with "an iron-jawed disinclination to recognise equal human worth and dignity of people who are not white", has proved a lethal combination. Unless these deep-rooted antagonisms to racial and cultural difference can be defeated in practice, as well as symbolically written out of the national story, the idea of a multicultural post-nation remains an empty promise.'[146]

The term 'multicultural post-nation' is appropriate. A post-nation is the ultimate logic of multiculturalism, to which English or British nationhood is an obstacle. Taken to its conclusion, as Parekh advocated, multiculturalism will destroy the British nation state, regardless of how the English might react, being England's Staatsvolk, and despite overwhelming hostility to multiculturalism even in traditional immigrant countries.[147] What entity someone would be a citizen of if Parekh achieves his goal is unexplained – possibly the EU, or a global parliament, or a state bureaucracy completely detached from the nation. This

143

national destruction is entirely in keeping with the communist agenda set out in *The Communist Manifesto* of 1848 (written by Karl Marx and Friedrich Engels), and entirely in keeping with the neo-Marxism promoted by the Frankfurt School.

Kymlicka also condemned assimilation. Regarding immigrants, he contrasted the pre-1960s expectations with the present arrangements:

> 'Prior to the 1960s, immigrants to these countries were expected to shed their distinctive heritage and assimilate entirely to existing cultural norms. This is known as the "Anglo-conformity" model of immigration. Indeed, some groups were denied entry if they were seen as unassimilable (e.g. restrictions on Chinese immigration in Canada and the United States, the "white-only" immigration policy in Australia). Assimilation was seen as essential for political stability, and was further rationalized through ethnocentric denigration of other cultures.'

Kymlicka dismissed any notion immigrants would become national minorities and described such as colonialism, being 'the systematic re-creation of an entire society in a new land'.

In *Multicultural Citizenship: A Liberal Theory of Minority Rights*, Kymlicka revealed his underlying political correctness with the casual allegation that those who opposed multiculturalism were motivated by a 'racist or xenophobic fear' of immigrants. In *Politics in the Vernacular: Nationalism, Multiculturalism and Citizenship*, Kymlicka focused more upon immigration (as opposed to indigenous national minorities), and produced a list of points for integration that took no account of the views and interests of the majority host nation. The list treated immigrants as victims and, in response, offered special treatment, quotas, etc. He did not believe in democracy (or 'majoritarian decision-making') and openly wanted the creation of global bureaucracies to which democratically elected

144

governments would be subordinate. He promoted the idea of people being 'citizens of the world'.

Kymlicka insisted immigrants wanted to fit in, would not create their own separate communities, and would be peaceful. That was completely wrong. Kymlicka dismissed the policy of Anglo-conformity assimilation. The abandonment of that policy has had profound, adverse consequences for the security and even existence of the West. 'Descent-based approaches to national membership', which Kymlicka condemned as having 'racist overtones' and as being 'manifestly unjust', would not have led to the present ethnic conflict.

Kymlicka said, 'Enabling immigrants from poor countries to re-create their societal culture may be a way of compensating for our failure to provide them with a fair chance at a decent life in their own country.' The mind boggles. It is not the West's responsibility to provide independent Third World countries with 'a decent life'.

Kymlicka baldly asserted 'there is strikingly little evidence that immigrants pose any sort of threat to the unity or stability of a country', and 'It has become clear that the overwhelming majority of immigrants want to integrate, and have in fact integrated', and 'they want the mainstream institutions in their society to be reformed, so as to accommodate their cultural differences, and to recognize the value of their cultural heritage', but they still have 'a desire for inclusion which is consistent with participation in, and commitment to, the mainstream institutions that underlie social unity'. Behind this lies Kymlicka's innocent view of Islam and the millet system (which he described as 'generally humane' and 'tolerant' – the Ottoman millet system divided the population into autonomous religious groups, which were subordinate to Islam, with Muslims having preferential status and privileges), with his bald assertion the 'overwhelming majority' of the Muslim immigrant communities accept Western culture and the 'majority of their demands are simply requests that their religious beliefs be given the same kind of accommodation that liberal democracies have

145

historically given to Christian beliefs'. This is dangerously untrue.

The policy of multiculturalism certainly does not work for the peoples of the West. The Anglo-conformity model of immigration should be the only form of immigration for the Anglosphere, and that immigration should be strictly controlled. Mass immigration must end, as must the inflow of asylum seekers and the acceptance of those asylum applications, no matter how ridiculous they are. To reject the reasoning of Kymlicka is not a matter of opinion. One needs only to examine a handful of facts to compare reality with the various pronouncements Kymlicka made, besides the power of culture and the backdrop of the race war politics cannot be ignored. This is not a matter of abstract theories.

In Part Two of *Multiculturalist Ideology (Part One), Second Edition: Race War Politics and the Rise of the Anti-Whites*, I focused on what multiculturalism had become by 2021. I examined three race theorists: Shola Mos-Shogbamimu, Kehinde Andrews, and Afua Hirsch. It is striking that they broadly sung from the same hymn sheet. As Kymlicka ideologically moved into step with *The Parekh Report*, so the new theorists acted in unison. This gave them greater impact.

A casual glance at the output of such race theorists reveals Kymlicka's bland assurances that immigrants want to fit in and that 'there is strikingly little evidence that immigrants pose any sort of threat to the unity or stability of a country' is bunkum. They most definitely do mean harm to the West and its peoples, and that rabid hostility, at an ideological level, is not confined to fundamentalist Islam, but is also found in 'Black radicalism' and is advanced as anti-racism.

To help understand the current different terms of racism bandied about, the UK report from the Commission on Race and Ethnic Disparities sets out its understanding of the different aspects of racism:

1   Explained racial disparities: this term should be used when there are persistent ethnic differential outcomes

that can demonstrably be shown to be as a result of other factors such as geography, class or sex.

2 Unexplained racial disparities: persistent differential outcomes for ethnic groups with no conclusive evidence about the causes. This applies to situations where a disparate outcome is identified, but there is no evidence as to what is causing it.

3 Institutional racism: applicable to an institution that is racist or [has] discriminatory processes, policies, attitudes or behaviours in a single institution.

4 Systemic racism: this applies to interconnected organisations, or wider society, which exhibit racist or discriminatory processes, policies, attitudes or behaviours.

5 Structural racism: to describe a legacy of historic racist or discriminatory processes, policies, attitudes or behaviours that continue to shape organisations and societies today.

These five types of racism are not concerned with an expression of racial hatred, but are based on outcomes and/or a critique of organisations or society. Types three to five (institutional, systemic and structural racism) are collectively new, interlinked and theoretical; they are not a description of a factual event (such as an expression of hatred by someone). The 2021 race theorists go far further than either *The Parekh Report* or Kymlicka. They are anti-White.

Shola Mos-Shogbamimu set out her concept of racism in detail in her book, *This is Why I Resist: Don't Define My Black Identity*: 'To begin with, racism is only perpetuated by White people and cannot be pigeon-holed into a neat box. It is far more complex and nuanced than just hate against a person because of the colour of their skin.'[148] She described racism as 'a power construct created by White nations for the benefit of White people', and that: 'Racism is the belief that one's race is superior to another race and the imposition of that belief through an act, thought or words of racial prejudice, hate and discrimination.' This, she alleged, was 'the direct result of the transatlantic slave trade from the fifteenth century to the nineteenth century'. The focus on the slave trade is a common thread for the anti-Whites. In her book, *Brit(ish): On Race, Identity and Belonging*, Afua Hirsch made a great issue of Britain's involvement in the slave trade.

For Mos-Shogbamimu, 'White privilege is a by-product of racism – an advantage solely based on being White and not predicated on socio-economic status, class or heritage.' And, 'The abolishment of slavery wasn't the end, as it was replaced with the colonisation of African countries.' The anti-White case is that slavery caused racism, and that both created the systemic racism of the West. Meaning, non-Whites are the victims. She also said, 'It is White privilege when White people try to impose their definition of racism on Black people.'[149] The supposed White privilege clouding the perception of racism is a new version of the Marxist concept of false consciousness. As with false consciousness, since White privilege means that White people are prejudiced, then the views of all White people are invalid. For Mos-Shogbamimu, there are no exceptions and she described herself as being 'anti-racist and unapologetic in my condemnation of systemic structural inequalities and institutional racism ... To the whataboutism of "racism against White people", I can tell you categorically that it does NOT exist.'[150]

Mos-Shogbamimu alleged that as racism was 'powered by an unparalleled economic and political structure controlled by White people to dehumanise, marginalise, commoditise, misrepresent and criminalise the Black identity' then it was impossible for Black people to be racist towards White people as there was no evidence that Whites were similarly being persecuted: 'Black people cannot and do not utilise power to negatively impact the quality of life and choices of White people as an entire race.' According to Mos-Shogbamimu, White privilege benefits all White people:

'The question of racism is no longer about what racism is but about how it manifests itself in the understanding of White people. White privilege whitewashes racism and whitewashing is the act, intentionally or not, of covering up, glossing over and/or excusing racism. There are two fundamental truths about racism. First, it is not the job of Black people and Ethnic Minorities to educate White people on racism perpetuated by White people. White people must educate themselves on the racism they perpetuate. Secondly, not all White people are racists. Some are, but all White people have and enjoy White privilege. This White privilege is what enables and enforces White supremacy.'[151]

Kehinde Andrews, in his book *The New Age of Empire*, made a direct attack on the West: 'But nothing short of a revolution that overturns the very foundations of empire can ever undo the problem of racism' and 'Police brutality, health inequalities, thousands of children dying a day are all symptoms of the disease of racism caused by the machine of Western imperialism'. He also sought to debunk the idea the West was the most advanced civilisation: 'We urgently need to trace how genocide, slavery and colonialism are the key foundation stones upon which the West was built. The legacies of each of these remain present today, shaping both wealth and inequality in the hierarchy of White supremacy.'

Andrews laid great emphasis upon what he alleged to be genocide in the West, the USA and Britain in particular, committed against Third World natives. He was scathing towards the USA:

'European expansion into the Americas was vital to the development of the West. And yet explorers like Columbus did not "discover" a new and empty land to be exploited. When they arrived, they found millions of people living in complex societies who needed to be erased in order to create the clean slate necessary for

149

Western progress. The genocide in the Americas is without precedent, wiping up to 99 per cent of the natives off the face of the earth. The bodies of those slaughtered are the foundation of the current social order. Westward expansion was the key that unlocked the bounties of European domination. Slavery, colonialism, industry, science and so-called democracy are all indebted to the tens of millions sacrificed at the altar of "progress".'[152]

The West, as a whole, fared little better in Andrews' estimation:

'In truth, the West was birthed by genocide and relied on the slaughter of millions of Black and Brown bodies to develop and enrich itself. You cannot separate genocide and the West, which is by far the most brutal, violent and murderous system to ever grace the globe. Rather than come to terms with the centrality of genocide to the West it is understood as a process alien to the progressive society built on science. Understanding genocide through the lens of the evil perpetuated by Nazis, or backward savages in Rwanda, allows the West to maintain its moral superiority. In truth both examples were products of the West, born out of the logic of empire.'[153]

This line was also taken by the American race activist, Robin DiAngelo, who said, 'Our country was founded on the wealth produced from the enslavement of Africans and the genocide and land theft of Indigenous peoples.'[154] DiAngleo believed 'all colonial powers, such as those of Spain, Portugal, France, and England, need to come to terms with the legacy of slavery'.[155]

Since the role of slavery was alleged to have provided the wealth of the West, then the reparations deserved are deemed to be substantial:

'Various calculations have been done based on damages and loss of earnings to arrive at an estimate of just how much the West owes. For the Caribbean alone, one estimate back in 2005 was $7.5 trillion. In the United States the estimates range from $3 to $14 trillion. What is clear from these figures is that if we were able to calculate a figure owed it would be so large that it would be impossible for the West to pay.'[156]

Mos-Shogbamimu was unwilling to accept that the British Empire no longer exists: 'Britain today can't be divorced from its colonial past'. Far from being relieved that the African former colonies are now independent, she seeks to purge Western culture from the West itself:

'In Britain, decolonising the curriculum would address the structural legacy of colonialism, which in most parts excludes the whole picture of what it cost to build the British Empire on the backs of slaves and the exploitation of the British colonies, particularly African nations. In America, decolonising the curriculum means to centre the consequences of slavery and the contributions of African Americans in its historical narrative ... British and American children must be taught all of their history, without exclusion, especially the brutality, deaths, blood and sacrifices of slavery that were the human cost that built the foundations of the British Empire and America.'[157]

In short, Mos-Shogbamimu proposed that historical facts should be replaced with communist propaganda. The version of history she set out is rubbish. She defiantly seeks to teach White children to be ashamed of their countries, and teach non-White children that a hatred of White people is justified. There is no comparison between the UK and the USA. With the end of the British Empire, the colonies became self-governing, providing countries for their people. That does not apply to the

USA as it had no empire. What is proposed is that people from those independent countries should deny the British their own independence. So, Mos-Shogbamimu aims to colonise the school curriculum.

Andrews was clear that his ultimate intention was revolution and the destruction of the West: 'The West simply cannot end racism through reparations because racial hierarchy is the fuel that feeds the system.'[158] Andrews endorsed the inevitability of the ultimate revolution: 'But make no mistake, whether spurred by revolution or tipped into collapse under its own weight, the West will eventually fall. Malcolm [X] was right when he warned that it will be "the ballot or the bullet, liberty or death, freedom for everybody or freedom for nobody".'[159]

Andrews, Hirsch and Mos-Shogbamimu advance a pan-Black revolutionary attack upon the West and White people. Their stated objective is the destruction of the West, and they are not content to simply allow demographic changes to achieve this. They are communist revolutionaries.

Andrews believed that revolution 'is absolutely essential if we truly want freedom':

> 'Revolution is possible, but we have to accept that it will not come from those who benefit from Western imperialism. There are centuries-long traditions of radical politics emerging from the oppressed. The bulk of my work is about developing the politics of Black radicalism, which centres on uniting Africa and the African diaspora to create a true revolution, which remains the only solution to the problem of racism.'[160]

This is an unambiguous commitment to a Black nationalist, anti-White race war politics. For Andrews, even reparations are a means of destroying the West:

> 'The West remains built on these foundations and to transfer the wealth necessary to repair the damage would destroy the West, not only because of the money

involved, but also because if the Black world had freedom that would mean the end of the Western project. Reparations are due, and tearing down Western capitalism is an utter necessity if we are serious about ending racism. But to realize the revolutionary politics necessary for this transformation we first need to recognize that the West can never pay full reparations for slavery without destroying itself.'[161]

In *Multiculturalist Ideology (Part One), Second Edition: Race War Politics and the Rise of the Anti-Whites*, in the chapter 'In Defence of the West', I give a full response to the lurid allegations of the West's supposed historical misdeeds, especially regarding North America and the slave trade.

The hostility to assimilation is not confined to abstract debate. For example, Neil Basu, the Scotland Yard Assistant Commissioner, said, 'Assimilation implies that I have to hide myself in order to get on. We should not be a society that accepts that.' He further opined, 'Don't forget that 70 per cent-80 per cent of the people we arrest, disrupt or commit an attack here, are born and raised here. Born or at least raised here. That has got to tell us something about our society. I want good academics, good sociologists, good criminologists ... to be telling us exactly why that is.' The answer is because the immigrant communities are rejecting the norms of Western society, if not being positively hostile to Western society. That is, they have not assimilated.

It is Third World immigration into the West that is the primary problem, the scale of it, and Islam. An Egyptian woman, using the pen name Magda Borham, wrote an open letter (the original being in Arabic) to the West warning of the danger of Islamic immigration. Having lived in Egypt for over 30 years, she stated:

'Nobody else in the world knows Islam and the mentality of Muslims more than those who have suffered by having Islam as a part of their life.

153

If you listen to the cries of the Copts of Egypt, the Christians of Syria, Iraq, Sudan, Pakistan and all the other Muslim countries, you will hear the descriptions of the horrors of Islam.

See and feel the tears of the minorities in every Islamic society. These tears will tell you the true stories of Islam. Hear the blood of the ex-Muslims pounding. It's their blood that is shouting out every single second, asking the rest of the world to "Wake up"!

Like so many others, I have been burned by this transformation. This transformation has seen me witness and experience Islam turn my home country to ruins and its followers are now threatening to bring the same fate to your own country.

Islam is a supremacist, racist political and social ideology wrapped in a thin peel of religious rituals. It seeks domination and supremacy over all other systems and religions. Islam is worse than Nazism and fascism systems combined without any doubt.

Muslims use your own democratic laws and values against you, and they do it successfully while you keep sleeping as if as in a deep coma. This is why the leftists are the people who are worthy of the title "useful idiots". They are in a perpetual state of shame and self-loathing and will be the first victims of Islam once it takes over.

Muslims use them as a stick to beat you with, but even they will never ever be accepted as friends to the Muslims after, and they will definitely be their first victims. Leftists, liberals, progressives, Antifa, Code Pink and so on are all appeasers of Islam. Appeasing evil is cowardice. They are fooled people who feed crocodiles, hoping they will eat them last. They are the enemy within your countries.

Your country is like your house; you expect visitors who come to your house to respect you and respect your rules, not the opposite. Visitors must appreciate your kindness and your generosity for receiving them into your home and not imposing their own rules on you. This is your house, you own it, so you have the obligation to protect it and defend it.

If the visitor doesn't like your rules, all he has to do is to leave. Nobody obliged him to visit you, and nobody will prevent him from leaving. As he came to your house by his own choice, he can leave your house freely or by force, if required.

One final thing you must be aware of. Muslims are projectors of themselves. They accuse you of what they truly are. They accuse you of being racist, while they are themselves racist. Islam is all about racism. They accuse you to be a hater, while they themselves hate unconditionally. Islam is full of hatred, incitement and violence. They accuse you of being a bigot, while Muslims act supremacism and are bigotry themselves.

Remember, Muslims love and need to portray themselves *always* as "victims". This is their greatest weapon against you in the West. Victimhood enables them to act violently and give them the pretext to attack non-Muslims around the world. It fuels them more and more with hate.

This hate generates more violence. Additionally this victimhood allows them to silence you and stop you from resisting their agenda. This is why the easiest thing for them is to label those who criticize Islam or reveal its reality as "racist" an "Islamophobe" or "bigot".'

The supremacist nature of Islam has led to its aggressive promotion across Western countries. The Muslims are well organised and relentlessly present themselves as oppressed victims. The Council on American Islamic Relations (CAIR), which the United Arab Emirates has designated a terrorist organisation, held its 25th Annual Gala in Washington DC, during which the co-founder and executive director, Nihad Awad, declared: 'So I'm telling you tonight we are going to work in the

155

next years, Inshallah (God willing], to elect at least 30 Muslims in the Congress.'

CAIR's promotion of radical Islam was evidenced as far back as July 1998, when its co-founder Omar Ahmad told a Californian audience in July 1998: 'Islam isn't in America to be equal to any other faith, but to become dominant. The Koran ... should be the highest authority in America, and Islam the only accepted religion on Earth.'

CAIR is the foremost Islamic supremacist group of influence in the USA. In Canada, it is the NCCM, formerly named CAIR-CAN – an offshoot of CAIR. The NCCM's earlier press releases identified the group as 'Council on American Islamic Relations Canada.'

A good example of not only the failure to assimilate immigrants, but of their open hatred of the West and the danger posed was demonstrated by the death of Iran's Shaheed Haj Qasem Soleimani. Following the USA's strike against Shaheed Haj Qasem Soleimani, a brutal army leader behind many atrocities, the Islamic Centre of England posted:

> 'The Islamic Centre of England hereby offers its condolences to the Imam or our time (atf), to the Supreme Leader of the Islamic Revolution and the Ummah at large on the martyrdom of the great soldiers of Islam, Shaheed Haj Qasem Soleimani, Shaheed Haj Mahdi Al-Mohandes and the companions. We will be holding a Majlis on Saturday 4th January 2020 at 5:15 to 7:00 pm, immediately after Maghrib prayers. There will be some keynote speakers addressing the gathering. We request your kind attendance. Muslim Communities in Britain.'

At the meeting, an imam said:

> 'I would like to give you all my condolences but I would also like to congratulate you. We are lucky enough to live in a time where we can see, touch and feel a man like

156

Qassem Soleimani and we hope and we pray and we work hard to make sure that there will be many many more Qassem Soleimanis. We aspire to become like him, we are jealous and we want the same thing for ourselves and our loved ones.'

Soleimani's successor, Esmail Ghaani, warned, 'Be patient, and you will see the bodies of Americans all over the Middle East.' This was not untypical. For example, after yet another Muslim extremist terror attack, the following statement was issued:

'Statement of the Muslim Council of Britain, 03 February 2020. Harun Khan, Secretary General of the Muslim Council of Britain, comments on the terror attack in Streatham on Sunday 2nd February:
    "Our thoughts are with the victims of the incident in Streatham and our solidarity is with the people of that area. Streatham is a vibrant community where Muslims find common cause with fellow residents on a range of issues. Only recently, the people of Streatham came together to speak out against the vandalism against a local mosque.
    We must continue to celebrate this strong community spirit, whilst also remaining vigilant. We encourage everyone to report any hate crime and suspicious activity to the police to help keep our communities safe.
    Now, as we wait further details from the police about what appears to be a terror-related attack, we stand firm with the people of Streatham against division and hatred from all quarters."'

The Muslim Council of Britain (MCB) did not condemn the attack nor the attacker. They sought to blur the issue and hid behind generalities about hate.

The Tory Government did not concern itself with the thought processes that led the Islamic Centre of England to be

157

so sympathetic to an anti-Western, brutal killer such as Shaheed Haj Qasem Soleimani, or for them to be so sympathetic to Iran. Nor did the government investigate the wider Muslim communities in the UK about where their allegiances lay. Nor did they, or the security services, consider the risk of the potential consequences of this open hostility.

In the USA, the Associated Press reported that Jason Brown, leader of the AHK drug-dealing gang in Chicago, was recorded by the FBI admiring the ISIS beheadings and saying that if anyone insulted Muhammad, then 'his head gotta go'. According to prosecutors, AHK dealt drugs all over Chicago, and was 'comprised of former members of the Black P-Stone, Gangster Disciples and Four Corner Hustlers who converted to Islam, the court filings say. The gang requires all new members to convert'.

In response to a poll in 2016 for a report from British Muslims for Policy Exchange, the Labour MP Khalid Mahmood, co-author of the report, said it proved British Muslims were 'loyal and patriotic'. But he said it was clear there was still a sense of 'victimhood' that allowed conspiracy theories to flourish.

The poll revealed nearly half of British Muslims would not go to the police if someone they knew was involved with supporters of terrorism in Syria; only 26 per cent of British Muslims did not believe 'extremist views exist'; one in 25 British Muslims believed Osama Bin Laden and al-Qaeda were responsible for the 9/11 attacks; 31 per cent believed the US Government was behind the atrocity, while seven per cent said the attack was a plot by the Jewish community; 40 per cent wanted Sharia; and 40 per cent were in favour of gender-segregated classrooms, while a further 44 per cent thought schools should force girls to wear traditional Islamic dress.

In response to the Tory general election victory in 2019, one Muslim remarked: 'It would have been a huge benefit to all communities if Labour won, but particularly the Muslim community where in some traditional households only one person works. Also, culturally, when someone gets married to

158

someone who comes from back home, it can be difficult for them to get a job when they don't know the language.' Zainab Patel, a 20-year-old university student, told the *Huffington Post*, 'As a Muslim, it makes me feel we are not welcome in this country any more.'

On Friday after the election, Harun Khan, of the MCB, said:

'Mr Johnson commands a majority, but there is a palpable sense of fear amongst Muslim communities around the country. We entered the election campaign period with long standing concerns about bigotry in our politics and our governing party. Now we worry that Islamophobia is "oven-ready" for government. We understand that the prime minister insists that he is a one-nation Tory. We earnestly hope that is the case and urge him to lead from the centre and engage with all communities.'

The English are now a minority in London, particularly in inner-London. Despite the Tory election victory, the inner-outer London divide remained. The Tories held only three central seats, and most of its support was in the suburbs. Tory London Assembly member Tony Devenish admitted it had been a 'difficult night' in the capital.

The Independent reported MCB comments that British Muslims had held 'long-standing concerns about bigotry in our politics and our governing party'.

Baroness Warsi, a former Tory co-chair and Cabinet minister, said the party 'must start healing its relationship with British Muslims'. She tweeted, 'Endorsements from #TommyRobinson & #KatieHopkins & colleagues retweeting both is deeply disturbing. Independent Inquiry into #Islamphobia is a must first step. The battle to root out racism must now intensify.' The Tories subsequently appointed the Singh Investigation to examine the allegations the party was guilty of Islamophobia. Professor Swaran Singh was an immigrant who previously complained to have 'experienced first-hand the pernicious manifestations of racism within certain parts of

British society'. The investigation found that out of a claimed membership of 200,000, there were around 122 incidents per year – around 0.0006 per cent of the membership. The investigation concluded that although 'anti-Muslim sentiment' remained 'a problem within the party', there was 'no evidence' the party was institutionally racist. Warsi responded, 'I think we now need an independent Equality and Human Rights Commission investigation because there are flaws to this report.' (See Appendix Two).

Australia, like other Western countries, has had to contend with honour killings. One such example was Mohamed Naddaf, who had the affront to appeal his eight-year jail sentence for the manslaughter of 25-year-old Ashlee Brown. Medics discovered Naddaf trying to resuscitate Ashlee Brown, whose post-mortem revealed she had injuries to her head, torso, buttocks and limbs, with stab wounds to her thighs and bruising on her right side, including her breast. Naddaf claimed he did not think she would die and pleaded guilty to criminally negligent manslaughter.

Problems were not confined to the West. For example, the Sri Lankan President Maithripala Sirisena approved the ban on all burkas and face coverings after a recent bombing campaign. Denmark's decision to ban the burka provoked the usual outrage of Muslims.

In the UK, a Syrian immigrant, named only as Ghazia, claimed £320,000 in benefits annually for his four wives and 23 children. Fida Hussain, 49, from Small Heath, Birmingham, demanded compensation after biting into a pork sausage McMuffin.

Mohamed Omar, an illegal immigrant in Texas and a 'prominent Muslim religious leader' who 'frequented several mosques in Fort Bend County' and 'greater Houston', was arrested and charged with child sex crimes. He had entered the USA in 2013 from Somalia.

This was not an aberration, but a continuance of Islamic culture as practised in Islamic countries. For example, in Pakistan, a ruling of the Sindh High Court in Karachi declared men can marry girls, provided they have had their first period. The declaration was made during a hearing into the alleged abduction, forced conversion and marriage of Huma Younus to Abdul Jabbar. He took the Catholic teenager from her home on 10 October 2019. Her parents said she was born on 22 May 2015 and provided a baptismal certificate and school testimony as evidence she was only 14. In Pakistan, Sharia trumps the rule of law. For example, In October 2019, Shimaa Qasim, an Iraqi TV host and former Miss Iraq, was told 'you're next' after a spate of killings of glamorous Iraqi women. Tara Fares, 22, was shot dead while in her Porsche at traffic lights. Islamic extremists were outraged at the supposed lack of modesty.

The aggressive imposition of political correctness and multiculturalism reinforced these matters. For example, in the USA, a former marine and his wife commenced legal proceedings after they discovered that their daughter's high school required students to complete assignments that endorsed Islam and its lifestyle. For example, one assignment was about 'Shahada', which means, 'There is no god but Allah, and Muhammad is the messenger of Allah'.

The Australian TV presenter, Sonia Kruger, was condemned for voicing the opinion that Australia should not allow Muslims to enter the country. A tribunal had ruled that Kruger had not engaged in racial vilification because to have Muslim people living in Australia was not a matter of race. But the Australian National Imams Council spokesman Bilal Rauf was angry that the comment was not unlawful and advocated a change in the law. He said, 'In the same way that someone shouldn't be able to paint a swastika, Islamophobia should not be acceptable.'

Apparently, since 2016, Ontario, which has Canada's largest Muslim population, has had an 'Islamic History Month':

'Across Canada, October has been proclaimed Canadian Islamic History Month, a time to celebrate the valuable role Muslim Canadians play in this country. Recognising October as Islamic Heritage Month in Ontario reiterates Ontario's commitment to embracing diversity and allows

Ontarians an opportunity to celebrate and educate future generations about the important contributions Muslim Canadians have made in their communities across the province.'

Kentucky, of all places, was proud to hold its first-ever 'Muslim Day' on 22 January 2020 to celebrate the wonders of Islam.

The political correctness continued even under Scotland's proposed protection orders against the barbaric practice to 'safeguard women and children who might find themselves under pressure to undergo FGM [female genital mutilation]' was condemned as being 'racially motivated' (*The Times,* September 13, 2019):

> 'A law to tackle female genital mutilation is racially motivated because it excludes intimate piercings and cosmetic surgery, Black and Muslim campaigners have claimed. Proposals to seize passports and detain anyone suspected of the practice have angered Africans and Muslims in Scotland who fear that they are being racially profiled.
>
> Genital mutilation has been carried out for more than 5,000 years in different cultures and religions and still occurs in 30 countries, including Egypt, Ethiopia and Indonesia. It is usually conducted on young girls and ranges from removing all or part of the clitoris and labia, which are considered 'unclean' in some cultures, to sealing the vagina to maintain virginity or fidelity...'

A diversity council in Australia urged businesses to stop using the word 'Christmas', alleging it might offend non-Christians.

A Twitter user, Harvington TR, tweeted: 'Saying #MerryChristmas is worse than fornication, drinking alcohol and killing someone says #muslim cleric! #Islam.' Gerard Batten, the then UKIP leader in the UK, tweeted in response, 'Anyone who thinks like this should fuck off back to the 6th century shit hole they came from & stay there to fester in their own stupid backward ignorance.'

In the Netherlands, a Muslim councillor demanded a halal beach in The Hague, as 'Muslims feel uncomfortable with scantily clad, ugly people'. One Muslim preacher in the UK circulated a YouTube video in which he said he did not go out much because he saw 'sisters' who were dressed inappropriately.

The UK stands out in its tolerance of Muslim grooming gangs. In the UK, official figures revealed that 19,000 children had been sexually groomed in the past year. There are instances of gang rapists shouting 'Allahu Akbar' in court as they are jailed.

When prime minister Theresa May said the number of Black and Asian police officers in the UK was 'simply not good enough'. As a part of the drive to increase ethnic minority numbers, Amjad Ditta, aka Amjad Hussain, was appointed diversity officer in West Yorkshire in 2016 'to boost numbers of Black and Minority Ethnic (BME) people applying to join the force'. In 2019, Ditta 'was charged with sex offences against children aged between 13 and 16'.

The lecherous attitude of Muslims towards women, infidel women in particular, is entirely consistent with their behaviour in their own countries. For example, girls as young as nine have been sold for one-hour-long 'mutaa [pleasure] marriages' under Islamic law in Iraq. Clerics were pocketing money for selling children and girls for such marriages, and anal sex was allowed to preserve the girl's virginity.

A Saudi Arabian women's conference attracted attention when a picture of those attending showed not a single woman amongst them. In Iran, one female activist was jailed for 16 years for taking off her hijab.

CBN reported on the massacre of an entire bridal party in December 2019 by suspected Boko Haram insurgents in Gwoza, Nigeria. The victims were beheaded. There have also been several recent abductions in the Borneo state.

The Western populations do not support what is happening to their countries. For example, a poll revealed 61 per cent of French people believe 'Islam is incompatible with French values and society'. *The Telegraph* reported British people would ban the burka by a margin of two to one.

In the USA, CNN's Anderson Cooper said it was 'exciting' that whites would no longer represent the 'majority'. 'Exciting' for some, it might be. But if immigrant communities can expect to form a majority, there is no reason for them to either assimilate or integrate. They will simply retain their own culture and enforce it upon everyone else. A report in the *Washington Times* predicted that if current demographic trends continued, within 40 years, Muslims would be the majority in Europe. *The Sun* reported in March 2019:

> 'If current trends continue the areas could become majority Muslim within ten years. Official ONS figures for 2018/19 that were released in December show that there are 3,194,791 Muslims living in England, with over a third aged under 16.
>
> English Muslims make up the vast majority of the 3,363,210 currently living in England, Scotland and Wales. They make up 5.9 per cent of the 2018 English population (55.16 million) ... 2018 figures show that London was home to nearly 1.26 million Muslims, making up 14.2 per cent of the capital's population. 74 per cent of Londoners are listed as Christian or a-religious.
>
> Following the migrant crisis that started in 2015, there were reports that Islamic populations would triple by 2050 as refugees headed west.'

One consequence of this trend was the impact on schools. An inquiry disclosed that there were 1.1 million children who speak 311 dialects. In some schools, English speakers were the minority and in other schools, no pupil had English as a first language. Reports showed that the overall number of pupils in state-funded schools in England was projected to increase by 13 per cent to roughly 8.2 million as a result of a baby boom and immigration.

In one English school, 342 of the 360 pupils said Punjabi was their first language, while just six were recorded as speaking English. Official statistics revealed there are classrooms in the UK where Polish, Bengali, Somali, Guajarati, Arabic, Tamil and the Afghan language Pashto were spoken ahead of English. Schools where foreign languages had overtaken English were spread across England, including areas of London and major towns and cities such as Oldham, Rochdale, Birmingham, Slough, Sheffield, Bolton and Bradford.

Christopher McGovern, of the Campaign for Real Education, said, 'Schools spend a lot of time and attention looking after children who do not speak English as a first language. We must make sure that native speakers of English are not neglected.'

One commentator, Mark Steyn, warned the demographic changes in Europe would happen faster than many realised. He said Muslims were having 3.5 children on average per couple whereas Europeans only had 1.3 children per couple: 'People think this is a slow process ... It happens very fast. The catching up is well under way.' He pointed out: 'This is the biggest story of our time, and yet hardly anyone ever writes about it. This is the biggest demographic movement/transformation in history, and it's about to accelerate.' He warned it would take about two generations before the Muslim population would have as many grandchildren as the Europeans.

This is colonisation. There is no reason for the immigrants to assimilate as they expect to take over and become the majority. Their views and culture will prevail, whereas that of the West will perish – unless something is done.

This issue of the immigrant birth rate was raised in a Migration Watch UK study in 2005, which examined the effect of foreign-brides from the Indian subcontinent on ethnic minority areas in England. The number of spouses entering the UK from India, Bangladesh and Pakistan doubled between 1995 and 2001 and reached 22,000. The main cause of this were arranged marriages and the Labour government's loosening of immigration rules relating to such marriages.

The study revealed that an estimated 48 per cent of Pakistani, 60 per cent of Bangladeshi and 38 per cent of Indian males marrying in the UK were wedding a bride from the Indian subcontinent. In Bradford in 2001, 30 per cent of children were born to immigrant mothers and the figure in London's Tower Hamlets was 68 per cent. In Bradford in 2001, it was estimated that 60 per cent of Pakistani and Bangladeshi marriages were with a spouse from the country of origin. The study also quoted from an annex to a report by Lord Ousely, a former chairman of the Commission for Racial Equality called *Race Relations in Bradford'*, which stated:

'[The high rate of marriages to spouses from the Indian subcontinent – ISC] has a major impact on population growth. About 1,000 Bradfordian Muslims marry each year. If most of those marriages were internal to this country, it would lead to 500 new households which would be likely to average 4 children per household. (This is based on experience from other immigrant groups where family size usually halves that of the first generation by the second generation.) With 60 per cent of marriages involving a spouse from overseas, the number of households goes up to 800 and, with many of the spouses being first generation, family size is likely to be significantly larger. So whereas 500 internal marriages might be expected to produce 2,000 offspring, the 800 marriages are likely to produce 4,000 offspring. This leads to very rapid population growth. In the eighties the Council estimated that the Muslim population would reach 130,000 by 2030 and then level. Now the projection is for 130,000 by 2020 and rising. The number of separate households is predicted to rise from 16,000 now to 40,000 in 2020. This rate of growth concentrated in particular areas puts severe demands on the public services. It has other ramifications. Many of the children arrive at school with little or no English. Many of those who come from overseas have little education and do not possess skills which are transferable to a Western economy. The high family size means overcrowding will be a persistent problem.'

The Ousely annex was not published as it was deemed too 'sensitive'.

The 2005 Migration Watch UK study revealed that mothers from the Indian subcontinent (ISC) formed a high proportion of mothers in the ethnic minority communities (e.g. 40 per cent for Bangladeshis), and mothers from the ISC had a high total fertility rate (2.3 Indian, 4.7 Pakistani and 3.9 Bangladeshi in 2001). The study compared the numbers of children born to mothers from India, Pakistan and Bangladesh in the five years from 1996 to 2000 inclusive with the numbers of children aged zero to four described as being of ethnic Indian, Pakistani or Bangladeshi origins in the 2001 census. This showed that nearly half ethnic Indian children aged zero to four have an Indian born mother and over three-quarters of ethnic Pakistani and Bangladeshi children aged zero to four have a mother born in those countries.

The study found in Bradford, which had an ethnic minority population of 22 per cent (of whom two-thirds were of Pakistani descent), the percentage of children born to foreign-born mothers was 30 per cent. In Tower Hamlets, which had an ethnic minority population of 49 per cent (of whom just over two-thirds were of Bangladeshi origins), the percentage of children born to foreign born mothers was 68 per cent. (According to the 2011 census, only 47.2 per cent of the Muslim population is UK-born. Of the non-UK born Muslims, the majority are from Asia and Africa. The Muslim population is an immigrant community.)

Consequently, the high numbers of arranged marriages involving spouses from the ISC had 'a major impact on the ability of these communities, particularly the Bangladeshi and Pakistani communities, to integrate into British society', because:

167

'The communities are being constantly refreshed by new immigrants, many of whom do not speak English, who will have little contact with other ethnic groups and whose children may well arrive at school unable to speak English. The rapid growth in households puts pressure on the housing supply in "ghetto" areas. There is also, of course, a substantial effect on the ethnic population. Between 1991 and 2001 the Pakistani population of Manchester, Birmingham and Bradford increased by between 46 and 53 per cent.

Employment prospects for immigrants from Bangladesh and Pakistan are very poor. New immigrants from Bangladesh and Pakistan have employment rates of 42.8 per cent and 44 per cent respectively (compared with 73 per cent for the British born population). The percentage of new Bangladeshi and Pakistani immigrants earning less than 50 per cent of median earnings are at 63.3 per cent and 35.4 per cent respectively compared to 21 per cent for the British-born population.'

MigrationWatch UK therefore advocated stricter rules for arranged marriages, pointing out there was a sufficiently large number of Asians in the UK for there to be arranged marriages with other UK Asians. Nothing was done.

The malice of *The Parekh Report* and Kymlicka were superseded by an openly anti-West and anti-White stance. The previous definitions of racism have been added to with new and greedier ones. The previous determination to prevent assimilation has given way to the open demands for reparations and the destruction of the West. The scale and sources of the ongoing mass immigration render any attempt to maintain social cohesion futile. The continued refusal to put a stop to all this poses an existential threat to the West. What is needed is patriotism and an end to political correctness.

The Corruption of Human Rights

An insidious aspect of political correctness is the manner in which it is passed off as human rights, and the manner it has corrupted the understanding of human rights. Human rights have become the foremost of politically correct holy words, the definition of which is the preserve of the politically correct, and the judges act as the high priests. The consequence is that human rights have become perverse and even antisense.

For example, whereas in previous centuries Britain and the Royal Navy were directly engaged in asserting the rule of law, abolishing the slave trade, and combating piracy, now they are more 'concerned' for the human rights of pirates and illegal immigrants. In 2008, European navies trying to control piracy off the coast of Somalia would neither arrest nor hand over pirates to the Somali government. The navy commanders did not believe they could successfully prosecute the pirates if they brought them back to Europe, and there was a real prospect the pirates would then claim asylum. They would not give them to the Somali authorities because the pirates might be executed. Nor were they allowed to simply sink the pirates.

The Americans did arrest and transfer Somali pirates to the USA to stand trial. Those convicted received life sentences; those acquitted or convicted of less serious offences were granted asylum.[162]

People smugglers, including ISIS and al-Qaeda, earn considerable wealth from their criminal operations, no matter the number of deaths they cause. This wealth is gained because illegal immigrants and those calling themselves asylum seekers are prepared to pay to be smuggled into the EU and Britain, in particular, from where they are almost certain not to be deported no matter how spurious their claim for asylum or how heinous the crimes they commit are. The judiciary and a whole host of lawyers and human rights groups are on hand to ensure the flow of money to organised crime rackets and terrorists, which is what the people smugglers are, continues undisturbed. In 2015, the Royal Navy was even engaged in the Mediterranean, helping immigrants get safely to the EU. In recent years, UK border patrol vessels were doing the same for illegal immigrants crossing the English Channel. The days of Palmerston are long gone.

The activities of the judges and lawyers are anti-democratic, and they display a scant regard for the interests and views of ordinary people. This is openly stated and is a long-standing viewpoint, as the judge Lord Bingham showed when he described the Human Rights Convention as 'intrinsically counter-majoritarian' and that decisions to uphold the rights of minorities 'should provoke howls of criticism by politicians and the mass media. They generally reflect majority opinion.'[163] Britain has become a lawyers' dictatorship.

In a speech in Melbourne, Australia, Lord Neuberger, the President of the Supreme Court and Britain's most senior judge, said that the Human Rights Act allowed judges to:

> '...interpret statutes in a way which some may say amounts not so much to construction as to demolition and reconstruction. We can give provisions meanings which they could not possibly bear if the normal rules of statutory interpretation applied. Parliament has written us judges something of a blank cheque in this connection ... this new judicial power of quasi-interpretation can be said to involve a subtle but significant adjustment to the balance of power between the legislature and the judiciary ... The [British] approach can be seen as effectively conferring a law-making function on the judiciary.'

In June 2015, Neuberger said in a speech to commemorate the Magna Carta: 'The need to offer oneself for re-election sometimes makes it hard to make unpopular, but correct decisions. At times it can be an advantage to have an independent body of people who do not have to worry about

170

short term popularity.' In reference to 'judicial aggrandisement', Neuberger highlighted that the EU law and the Human Rights Act had given the judges a 'quasi-constitutional function'.

Britain's judges embraced their own interpretation of their new-fangled human rights role with eagerness. In reference to his decision to allow a Bangladeshi murderer to move to England, overturning a Home Office decision, Judge Peter King proclaimed, 'There seems to be an expectation that the public interest trumps everything else. It seems to me that is not necessarily the case.' The Bangladeshi was further granted anonymity to protect his identity and his criminal record.

Judicial largesse can be expensive. In November 2014, an illegal immigrant from Sri Lanka who had committed 35 criminal offences in Britain while fighting deportation was awarded £600 compensation after being supposedly unlawfully detained for eight weeks in 2008. His legal costs from a 22-year fight to remain in Britain were £1 million.

In 2015, the High Court judge Justice Nicol, ruled as unlawful the government's fast track system to decide those asylum claims deemed to be totally without merit. The Labour government introduced the Detained Fast Track process in 2003. The judge objected to 'serious procedural disadvantage' to the asylum seekers and their lawyers who had limited time to prepare their cases.

In July 2014, High Court Judges ruled that to limit entitlement to legal aid to those living in Britain was 'unlawful and discriminatory' and the justification for such was 'little more than reliance on public prejudice'. The ruling rendered proposed government reforms to the legal aid system illegal, such as restricting legal aid to those who had lived in Britain for at least one year. Lord Justice Moses dismissed the reforms as a 'joke'.

The treatment of British servicemen is another example. In October 2015, it was announced the police would investigate claims of over 100 Afghans, including Taliban, that British troops had mistreated them. The investigation, Operation Northmoor, involved the Royal Military Police, Greater Manchester Police, and the National Crime Agency. The investigation was launched after allegations were presented to the police by the Public Interest Lawyers firm, who were believed to have had Pashtun-speaking workers approaching local Afghans, asking them if they considered themselves to have been mistreated and inviting locals to report allegations of mistreatment to them. This was similar to the experience in Iraq, where a 145 strong team from the Iraq Historical Allegations Team toured the country trying to find allegations of mistreatment over a five-year period; no criminal conviction resulted. The Ministry of Defence spent more than £100 million on investigations and compensation relating to Iraq. Another £150 million was spent defending British soldiers from the allegations. A source told the *Daily Mail*, 'If it is anything like Iraq, in a few years there will be thousands of claims coming through. One of the cases includes a detainee who is complaining because he didn't like the food.'

Another example of the harm abstract theories about human rights cause was the penchant for human rights wars. It has been estimated that the cost of the most recent wars, primarily Iraq and Afghanistan, was between $3 trillion and $4 trillion. The cost to Britain of the war in Afghanistan was around £40 billion and 453 soldiers killed. Over 250,000 people died in such wars over a 15-year period. This is, as Robert Cooper, an adviser to Tony Blair urged for, 'a new kind of imperialism, one acceptable to a world of human rights and cosmopolitan values ... which like all imperialism aims to bring order and organisation but which rests today on the voluntary principle'.[164] Despite the penchant for human rights wars, the human rights theories and the legal profession's opportunism crippled the ability to fight such wars or defend the country. This was demonstrated by the lawyers, with judicial permission, bringing claims against Britain and its troops for alleged human rights breaches.

Wars have not necessarily been fought in defence of the national interest, but have been increasingly motivated by a determination to impose human rights theories on imperfect countries. Prime examples being countries affected by the so-called Arab Spring, and Syria in particular. While it might be welcome to see people who have been oppressed by a tyrant gain their liberty, that liberty cannot exist without law and order.

In January 2020, at an employment tribunal, Judge Robin Postle provided a major reinterpretation of rights. Of veganism, Postle said, 'It is clearly a view that meets all the requirements of a philosophical belief' as the principles were 'genuinely held' and were 'clearly cogent and worthy of respect'. Consequently, 'ethical vegans' should be protected under the Equality Act 2010. Of the ruling, the complainant's solicitor said, 'It will create room for dialogue and discussion about how ethical vegans are accommodated and respected.' The complainant, Jordi Casamitjana, moved to the UK in 1993 from Spain and acquired a UK passport in 2000. The ruling opened the floodgates for litigation for matters such as hotels failing to cater to vegan needs, hospital food and workplace complaints.

In June 2019, in yet another example of judicial power grabbing, the government announced it would halt the sale of arms to Saudi Arabia, following a Court of Appeal ruling that UK officials had not properly considered whether Saudi Arabia and its allies had broken international laws in their war in Yemen. Appeal Court judge and Master of the Rolls, Sir Terence Etherton, declared the government made 'no concluded assessments of whether the Saudi-led coalition had committed violations of international humanitarian law in the past, during the Yemen conflict'.

This judicial activism was lucrative for the legal profession. In January 2019, Martin Day, of the solicitors Leigh Day, admitted to the Commons defence committee that his firm had made £11 million from suing the Ministry of Defence on behalf of Iraqis who had alleged mistreatment.

However, judicial activism was positively harmful once it departed from the common sense of the public and wallowed in human rights theories. In May 2020, in response to a case where children were sent to live with a convicted paedophile, the former MP John Hemming wrote in the *Daily Mail*, 'Transparency is an instrument of justice and a weapon against abuse. When our civic institutions are forced to be open about their decisions, they are more likely to behave in humane, responsible and effective ways. Secrecy, on the other hand, allows cover-ups, bullying and dogma to flourish.' He further stated:

> 'As the late, great journalist and fellow open-justice campaigner Christopher Booker once wrote in this paper: "The rules, which in criminal courts require evidence to be put to a proper test, can be routinely ignored. Social workers and lawyers can trot out hearsay allegations which are accepted by the court as if they are proven fact." Our mature democracy, Britain, is supposed to have judicial fairness at its heart. But something has gone badly wrong in recent years...'

What has 'gone badly wrong' is the continued hegemony of political correctness.

Producer Capture

In *The Genesis of Political Correctness*, I highlighted an economic concept known as 'producer capture'. This applies where there is a monopoly. Instead of the monopoly organisation responding to customers and producing goods that customers want, the monopoly produces what it likes, and the consumers are trapped into buying whatever is produced. For example, in a car market, customers may want cars with sunroofs. In a competitive market with a choice of producers, those producers that make cars with sunroofs will sell more cars. However, with a monopoly, if the producer cannot be bothered to manufacture cars with sunroofs, since the customers can go nowhere else, then cars without sunroofs will continue to be bought. The monopoly does as it likes.

The same concept applies to the capture of public institutions by the politically correct. For example, would parents normally pay people to teach their children to say, 'Peace Be Upon Him', after saying, 'Mohammed'? Normally they would not – but they were. In December 2015, at a Christian state school in Worcester, in the UK, children were taught this in the Religious Education lessons. This, in a predominantly White school, was not because parents wanted to pay for teachers to teach this, but because the politically correct school decided to do so. The same ethos applies across a range of public institutions. Not only do they do as they like, but go so far as to sincerely believe they are morally superior in their political correctness. Ordinary people should be grateful for paying up. The politically correct are entitled to be well paid with public monies for showing ordinary plebs how racist those plebs are. The capture of public institutions enables the politically correct to get money via the tax system (including the BBC licence fee). Ordinary people have to pay up.

Another example in the UK was the banning of an advert for an electric cleaner. The Advertising Standards Authority accused the advert of perpetuating 'the stereotype that it was a woman's responsibility to take pride in the appearance and cleanliness of their home, and to clean up after other people'. Women take pride in the appearance and cleanliness of their homes. Would ordinary people pay for a quango to veto adverts on this basis voluntarily? No, they would not. The authority simply exceeded its remit and imposed political correctness upon the public. They just did as they liked.

Another good example is the overseas aid budget in the UK. This is a pet project of the UK's ruling Ponzi class and has been consistently unpopular with the public. The amount spent on overseas aid was fixed at 0.7 per cent of GDP and the main challenge was to find something to spend the money on. Those spending the money did as they liked.

The overseas aid budget increased to £14.5 billion in 2018, amounting to an average of £535 per household annually. By 2019, the budget reached £15.2 billion. The UK donated more than twice the G7 average of 0.29 per cent of gross national income. Pakistan was the largest recipient, receiving more than £400 million in 2017. Department for International Development (DfID) civil servants pocketed bonuses of up to £10,000, totalling £1.75 million in 2018. This constituted a six per cent increase on the previous year.

The UK's overseas aid to the world's most corrupt states rose more than one-third over five years, according to Transparency International. Aid to the worst 20 states reached almost £1.5 billion in 2018, and included Somalia, Syria, South Sudan, Yemen, North Korea, Sudan, Guinea-Bissau, Afghanistan, Libya, Burundi, Venezuela, Iraq, Congo, Chad, Angola, Turkmenistan, Haiti, Democratic Republic of Congo, Cambodia and Zimbabwe. Many of these states had substantial oil wealth and others had few historical ties with Britain. In many countries, extremist groups took the aid. For example, in Somalia, Al Shabab imposed 'taxes' on aid money, according to a CNN investigation.

MPs on the Commons public administration committee complained not enough was being done to ensure overseas aid was not being wasted, and no one knew if the money was well spent. It further criticised government moves to give more ministries the ability to spend money on aid via the Overseas Development Assistance scheme, and that those with less ability to assess the effectiveness of that expenditure would undertake such expenditure.

In June 2019, a report from the National Audit Office (NAO) revealed that over the previous four years, increased amounts of overseas aid was given to 'upper middle income' countries, despite commitments to target aid at the poorest. The amount had increased from six per cent of the total budget in 2014 to 14 per cent in 2017. The amount going to the least developed countries had fallen from 64 per cent to 58 per cent. In June 2020, the Commons international development committee found the amount of overseas aid spent on 'middle income' countries increased from 36 per cent to 45 per cent between 2014 and 2018. Although the DfID prioritised 33 poorer countries, other government departments spent around 75 per cent of their aid on middle income countries, including China, India and South Africa.

Also in June 2019, a report from the Independent Commission for Aid Impact (ICAI) condemned expenditure in the Newton Fund, which was managed by the Business, Energy & Industrial Strategy (BEIS). Much of the money was spent on student fellowships. None of the grants gave benefited institutions in poorer countries, the main beneficiaries being the university careers of individual students.

Grants awarded included £110,000 for a biography of the Boer War leader Paul Kruger, £98,810 for a Brazilian student to investigate divine images of Cicero (the Roman politician), and £72,816 for postgraduate studies of jazz music in South Africa. Almost 90 per cent of the expenditure in the Newton Fund occurred in the UK.

In April 2019, the OECD reported the UK was the only country that spent the target of 0.7 per cent of GDP on overseas aid. Out of the aid given by 29 major countries, £1 out of every £8 was given by the UK. The average figure for the G7 countries was 0.29 per cent. The USA, the world's largest donor, gave £25.7 billion, 0.14 per cent of GDP.

In July 2019, it emerged the DfID spent £21 million on a project, Connecting Classrooms through Global Learning, to British schools to link British and overseas children to discuss issues such as hunger and climate change. Another £17 million would come from the British Council. The scheme's aim was to: 'invest in a new generation of Global Britain ambassadors who are proud of the work the UK is doing to tackle global poverty'. The children were aged between seven to 14.

The UK's overseas aid to China included: £1.1 million to reduce salt intake, £984,000 on a study into air pollution, £70,315 to encourage shoppers to stop buying products made with pangolins (as they are an endangered species), £43,112 on improving the training of early years teachers, and £55,392 on a scheme to reform China's animal testing laws.

Overseas aid to India included £443,284 on improving weather forecasting, £81,091 on a text messaging scheme to give people health advice, £40,179 on an inquiry into using yoga to help prevent type-2 diabetes, £20,062 on how to use solar panels to power India's railways, and £25,878 promoting female employment in India's energy sector. The UK continues to give aid to India even though it will overtake the UK as the world's fifth largest economy, has a space programme and its own aid budget.

In April 2020, a report from the NAO urged the DfID to improve the management of spending on the promotion of gender equality. An amount of £4.2 billion was spent in 2018. NAO chief, Gareth Davies, said, 'Two years into the department's 12-year vision, interventions are already improving the lives of women and girls. However, if DfID is to achieve its ambitious aims, it needs to develop a clearer long-term plan for implementing its vision and continue to improve the accuracy and transparency of its performance information.'

In June 2020, Boris Johnson confirmed the UK's commitment to stick to giving away 0.7 per cent of national income in overseas aid. However, the DfID would be scrapped with the overseas aid budget being taken over by a revamped Foreign, Commonwealth and Development Office. Boris Johnson said:

> 'For too long, frankly, the UK's aid budget has been treated as some giant cashpoint in the sky, without any reference to UK interests, or to the values that the UK wishes to express ... It's no use a British diplomat going into see the leader of a country and urging him not to cut the head off his opponent, and to do something for democracy in his country if the next day another emanation of this government is going to arrive with a cheque for £250 million.'

Boris Johnson continued, 'We give as much aid to Zambia as we do to Ukraine, although the latter is vital for European security, and we give ten times as much aid to Tanzania as we do to the six countries of the western Balkans, which are acutely vulnerable to Russian meddling.' This money to Zambia, and the rest of the overseas aid, is not being spent in response to British public opinion. The commitment to spend o.7 per cent of national income in overseas aid is not the result of public opinion, but as a result of a Tory-led coalition government wanting to show off its globalist credentials. Giving away such huge sums of money is harmful not only to the UK but also to the recipient countries, not least due to the corruption and wastefulness it promotes. The whole exercise is an example of producer capture.

David Cameron described the decision to scrap the DfID as 'a mistake' and said, 'More could and should be done to co-ordinate aid and foreign policy, including through the National Security Council, but the end of DfID will mean less expertise, less voice for development at the top table and ultimately less respect for the UK overseas.' Tony Blair said he was 'utterly dismayed' and the decision was 'wrong and regressive'. Former aid minister Andrew Mitchell said the DfID's abolition was 'a quite extraordinary mistake [that would] destroy one of the most effective and respected engines of international development anywhere in the world'. Patrick Watt, policy director at Christian Aid, complained, 'Today's announcement is an act of political vandalism.'

The DfID had the highest average annual salaries in the civil service at £51,660 – £8,000 higher than the second best paid department. Unlike the Dutch, who ditched their aid target and found their aid was better spent, the UK would still spend money for the sake of it.

To test whether aid made any difference, the DfID spent £11 million on a scheme covering a group of villages in Ghana. The report into the scheme concluded that 'far from breaking the poverty trap, the project does not appear to have reduced poverty or hunger at all'. The report found that almost one-third of the money was spent on management and overheads, and there was 'large-scale' fraud involving a local partner.

In August 2020, the German Georg Eckert Institute launched an investigation into the use of £120 million British overseas aid for 'jihadi textbooks' used in Palestinian schools. In fact, it investigated Israeli textbooks that promoted peace and excluded mention of the inflammatory venom of the 'jihadi textbooks'. Marcus Sheff, of the Impact-se Israeli research institute, said, 'The review has been a comedy of errors from start to finish.'

After the scrapping of the DfID was announced in August 2020, a new overseas aid scheme was introduced to donate £6.85 million to improve working conditions in developing countries for those employed by Marks & Spencer, Primark, Sainsbury's, Tesco, Morrisons, Co-op, Waitrose and other large companies. The International Development Secretary, Anne-Marie Trevelyan, said, 'This new fund will strengthen vital supply chains for UK consumers, while supporting some of the most vulnerable workers in developing countries. It will make a real difference to people in the UK and abroad.' In other words, it was business as usual. Taxpayers' monies would continue to be spent on an expensive status symbol. The politicians would continue to do as they liked.

To give another example of producer capture, in June 2019, Theresa May pushed forward with her new law requiring the UK to reduce its greenhouse gas emissions to net zero, despite being warned by Philip Hammond, the then chancellor, that the cost of such a target would be £1 trillion. In addition, there would be the human costs in the change to our quality of lives, standards of living and the destruction of heavy industries, such as steel. Gas boilers for home heating would need to be banned, as would petrol and diesel cars. Air travel would need to be rationed. Red meat consumption would need to be restricted. May declared, 'now is the time to go further and faster to safeguard the environment for our children'. She also said, 'As the first country to legislate for long-term climate targets, we can be truly proud of our record in tackling climate change. This country led the world in innovation during the Industrial Revolution, and now we must lead the world to a cleaner, greener, form of growth. Standing by is not an option.'

The target was to reduce greenhouse gas emissions by 80 per cent of 1990 levels by 2050 – a target that was a struggle. The UK's greenhouse gas emissions had already fallen by 44 per cent since 1990. In fact, the UK was only responsible for less than one per cent of the world's greenhouse gas emissions and this amount was already falling. However, China and India were responsible for 27 per cent and 6.5 per cent respectively. Both China and India have been rapidly building new coal-fired power stations to fuel their industrialisation. Africa's greenhouse gas emissions are also increasing due to an increase in economic activity and a rapidly expanding population.

May's proposal would have no material effect on the world's greenhouse gas emissions. Nor is there any sense in destroying British industry simply to reduce the UK's gas emissions from one per cent to 0.9 per cent, say, if that simply means production and jobs are transferred to China and India, both of which use coal-fired power stations. Such an act would only increase the world's greenhouse gas emissions. May declared there was a 'moral duty to leave this world in a better condition than what we inherited'. The demise of British steel-making is a good example of the foolish consequences of so-called green policies (see Appendix Three).

Dame Carolyn Fairbairn, the director general of the Confederation of British Industry (CBI), approved of May's move and said it was 'the right response to the global climate crisis' and 'Climate leadership can drive UK competitiveness and secure long-term prosperity.'

At a G7 summit in August 2019, the UK announced it would spend £1.44 billion from its overseas aid budget on trying to get Third World countries to cut their carbon emissions. This is in addition to £720 million already committed in the UK's Green Climate Fund.

Despite Brexit and the UK's delay in implementing the referendum decision, in April 2019, Penny Mordaunt, the then International Development Secretary, wrote to the EU to object to the way in which British organisations were being frozen out of EU overseas aid contracts. One eighth of the EU aid budget was funded by the UK, and yet UK aid charities were being blackballed.

A major consequence of producer capture is not only that the various entities do as they like but also that the remuneration packages surge upwards. Whatever the effect of UK's policy of austerity on the wages of ordinary people, the British ruling Ponzi class continued to enjoy the high life – not least to enjoy lavish salaries. For example, in December 2018, figures from the *Daily Mail* showed that two-thirds of the chief constables in 39 English police forces had an annual salary greater than the prime minister's (£150,402). In addition, there were lavish pension contributions. Further, many chief constables enjoyed private healthcare, housing and car allowances. Twelve chief constables had a remuneration package in excess of £200,000.

In December 2018, the Taxpayers' Alliance revealed that the number of staff promoting health messages on £100,000 or more annual salary had increased from 223 to 266 in three years. The highest such salary was of £369,579 payable to the director of public health for Stoke-on-Trent council.

Government figures revealed that almost 500 officials in Whitehall were paid more than the prime minister.

In February 2019, figures from the Office for Students showed the average university vice chancellor's salary had reached £250,000 per year. The University of Bath topped the pay league with the vice chancellor being paid a basic salary of £470,000. In addition, there were some perks that seriously increased the total remuneration package, such as an accommodation allowance. Figures from the Taxpayers' Alliance in October 2019 showed that 3,600 university staff earn more than £100,000 per year, including 762 who earned more than £150,000.

In June 2019, High Court judges enjoyed a 25 per cent salary increase, taking their pay, including allowances, to £236,126, while circuit judges enjoyed a 15 per cent increase to £161,332 per year. The Ministry of Justice claimed there was a shortage of High Court judges. Supreme Court judges' salaries were increased from £221,575 to £282,741, while the Lord Chief Justice enjoyed an increase from £257,121 to £327,830.

Senior figures, including many who already earned more than the prime minister, at some charities (including RSPCA, Royal National Lifeboat Institution, British Heart Foundation, the National Trust, Macmillan Cancer Support, Guide Dogs, and the Royal National Institute of Blind People) were awarded five-figure salary increases in 2018. Simon Cooke, chief executive of Marie Stopes, enjoyed a jump in salary and bonuses totalling £434,000 compared to £300,352 in 2017. The London-based Save the Children International has at least 80 staff on six-figure salaries.

David Miliband had the title of President of the International Rescue Committee, a charity based in New York that was founded in 1933, and which has received £107 millions of British taxpayers' money over two years. In October 2019, Miliband's annual salary soared to $911,796 (around £741,883), an increase of no less than £195,314 over two years. His predecessor got $380,000 (around £309,400) per year. The 12 most senior employees at the charity enjoyed a £1.1 million increase to take their salaries to £4 million between them.

Simon Cooke, the chief executive of Marie Stopes International, enjoyed a salary of £434,000, including a bonus which doubled his pay. The charity received £48.2 million from the DfID and has six others on six-figure salaries.

In June 2019, despite sitting on a cash mountain of £850 million, just after the D-Day celebrations, the BBC announced it would remove free TV licences for 3.7 million pensioners over the age of 75. In the future, the BBC would charge all pensioners over 75 who did not receive pension credit. Hitherto, the over-75s had enjoyed free TV licences for around 20 years. The average age of the BBC viewer was 61.

This change came against a backdrop of controversy over the BBC profligacy such as lavish pay-offs, millions spent on taxi fares, more than £1 billion spent on new headquarters, high salaries for 'star' presenters and senior management (e.g. Gary Lineker was on £1.75 million per annum), local radio that competes directly with local commercial stations, large sums spent on international activities such as news channels. The BBC's generous pension scheme was forecast to need around an extra £2 billion by 2028.

In 2018, 139,719 people were prosecuted for not paying their licence fee, of whom 100,725 were women. Around 9,300 were found not guilty. Those found guilty got a criminal record and a possible fine of up to £1,000. In 2018, 65 were jailed for an average of 19 days.

In July 2019, the BBC's wage bill rose to £1.5 billion. Leading BBC presenters topped up their already lucrative earnings by moonlighting, particularly on the speaking circuit. Even an evening's effort could attract a five-figure sum and a full day in excess of £20,000. For example, Huw Edwards, on £495,000 BBC pay, was paid handsomely for hosting the Concrete Society Awards at London's Grosvenor House Hotel in 2015, and also the Fleet News Awards in 2017. Emily Matilis charges between £10,000 and £25,000 for herself. Fiona Bruce has been a key speaker for the Henley & Partners global citizenship conference. The firm helps the wealthy purchase citizenship in other countries. Huw Edwards received an estimated £400,000 for moonlighting over the previous five years. Jon Sopel, receives around £245,000 as BBC's North America Editor, and was paid for speaking at JP Morgan events. Sopel was paid £35,000 for speaking at one such event. The BBC's pay bill jumped by £1 million in 2019/20, with 76 presenters paid more than the prime minister.

Another gravy-train and a good example of producer capture is the HS2 high-speed rail project. The project was unpopular with the public, especially those whose homes would be blighted by the new railway track, but very popular with politicians. In 2012, HS2's cost was stated to be £34 billion. In May 2019, the House of Lords' economic affairs committee found the biggest beneficiaries of HS2 would be London commuters travelling to Milton Keynes. The committee warned the DfT forecasts of passenger demand were exaggerated and out of date. It further warned that costs were out of control. By June 2019, HS2's budget had surged to £56 billion. One estimate put the cost of the project at £106 billion. Almost a quarter of HS2's employees were getting six-figure salaries, with 112 getting more than £150,000, with 15 pocketing more than £250,000 per year. In August 2020, it was disclosed that the *average* pay of those working on the HS2 project was £94,824, according to the HS2's own 2019/20 annual report. The total pay bill was £134.2 million for 1,415 people. This was up from an average of £92,501 the previous year. The chief executive, Mark Thurston, received a basic salary of £617,296, with other bonuses and benefits taking his total remuneration to £659,416. To reach its intended speed of 225mph (Inter-City trains travel at 150mph), the trains would not stop frequently, would by-pass towns, and arrive in a to-be-built station in Birmingham that would not connect with other rail services. The aim was to get to the new station 25 minutes faster.

Not to be left behind, in March 2019, MPs received a 2.7 per cent increase in salaries – a £2,000 increase taking MPs pay to almost £80,000. MPs pay had increased by 20 per cent over the previous seven years. In June 2019, the cross-party Lords commission received demands from peers of more money in allowances. In particular, they wanted an increase in accommodation allowances to match the £175 per night that MPs get. This is equivalent to a 60 per cent rise in total, amounting to a tax-free payment of £70,000 for an average of 150 sitting days per year. Former Labour MP, Oona King, and now a member of the House of Lords, like many others, took an open-ended 'leave of absence' from the chamber, although she still styled herself as a member. King had moved to California. After the introduction of a £162 per day allowance for virtual voting in the House of Lords, the total number participating increased to 497 peers, being 137 higher than the average over the previous five years. There were roughly 800 peers. One peer said the increase of 40 per cent in those voting looked 'dreadful'.

The cronyism also applied with the promotion of communists. For example, in September 2019, in a programme about the rise of the Nazis, the BBC promoted communists as presenters for the programme. In particular, Ash Sarkar, who is neither a historian nor Holocaust expert but a journalist for Novara Media – a communist website linked to Momentum. Sarkar is a self-declared communist who responded to criticism by tweeting, 'I don't see why my support for boycotts, divestment and sanctions against the Israeli occupation of the West Bank should disqualify me from talking about the Communist Party of Germany, but hey, I guess we live in strange times.' She further stated that she 'reject[ed] wholeheartedly claims of anti-Semitism'.

In August 2017, the leading art critic, Sir Roy Strong, criticised the political correctness of the National Trust, which is supposed to preserve historic buildings. He said:

> 'A lot of it goes back to the direction it's being taken in. They've had two director-generals, both competent in their own way ... but too Left-leaning. They came out of the Civil Service and both were bent on what I call embracing the new inclusiveness – ticking the boxes and all the new management speak, which has poured out in all directions. So if you go to a National Trust house or property, you'll be almost told what to think or how to react. So much of what they're doing is like the Blair government in exile. It's ticking the boxes of the disabled, the aged, LGBT and the ethnic communities and the rest of it and something gets lost along the way.'

The situation at the National Trust worsened. In 2019, the National Trust announced it would downplay the role of families in the history of stately homes as this 'privileges heterosexual lives'. One senior curator complained that 'inherited and partial narratives' meant 'same-sex desire and gender diversity have generally been given little space'. In 2018, the Trust stopped using the terms BC and AD and instead used BCE and CE (Before Common Era and Common Era, respectively). The Trust's then chief executive, Dame Helen Ghosh, had to make it voluntary to wear rainbow coloured lanyards and badges, to mark the 50th anniversary of the legalisation of homosexuality, to avoid a mutiny by volunteer guides.

The Trust faced a member's revolt after it highlighted its supposed links to slavery to mark the UN's day to remember the slave trade. The Trust tweeted, 'Many of the places we care for have direct or indirect links to slavery, including objects made from materials obtained by forced labour.' The tweet was accompanied with pictures of 18th century mahogany furniture that was 'felled by enslaved Africans in dangerous virgin rainforest' and 'came at human cost'. Ivory and other items were included. The Trust has 5.6 million members.

The Trust took down the Ham House webpage as it was full of errors, such as a claim a family 'who supported and endorsed Britain's role in slave-trading' once owned the 17th-century house in London. However, experts disputed this. Tony Adler, a retired history lecturer and a volunteer helper at the house, said, 'It's just surmising and guilt by association. The Trust is becoming too political and is losing its way. It's a witch hunt of properties. What it really needs is a neutral historian to make sure details are historically correct.' Likewise, after posting an article on its website smearing Lord Curzon, the famous viceroy of India who had left many properties to the National Trust, the National Trust removed the article due to its many inaccuracies.

Professor Towler described his ongoing project at the National Trust, Colonial Countryside: National Trust Houses Reinterpreted, as 'a child-led history and writing project which seeks to make historic houses' connections to the East India Company and transatlantic slavery widely known'. A team of historians were working with 100 primary schoolchildren to examine 11 Trust properties for such links. The scheme received lottery grant funding to the tune of £160,000. In rejecting criticism, the Trust said, 'We always look for excellence, fairness and balance in the assessment of all aspects of the history at National Trust places, often working with external partners and specialists to help us.'

Previously, regarding the countryside, Professor Towler wrote, 'The countryside is a terrain of inequalities, so it should not surprise us that it should be seen as a place of particular hostility to those who are seen as not to belong, principally Black and Asian Britons.' Furthermore: 'Knowledge about gardens and plants, in particular botany, has had deep colonial resonances,' and 'This bird [the pheasant] is habitually represented as native to England's fields, hedgerows and woodlands [but it] is a global not a local bird.' Morris dancing also attracted her condemnation.

Other academics involved in the Colonial Countryside project were little better. One styled himself as Raj Pal 'damn black' on Twitter, and another, Marian Gwyn, opposed the new Museum of Military Medicine in Cardiff alleging it was 'effectively a monument to the British Empire and its armed forces' and 'to confront our imperial past and past conflicts is one thing, to try to use it as an attraction in such a location is an affront.' In fact, the museum was more focused on the work of Florence Nightingale, John Hall-Edwards and Geoffrey Keynes who, respectively, pioneered the use of X-rays and how to store blood.

Another academic involved in Colonial Countryside, Katie Donington, tweeted, 'The toppling of the statue of the slave trader Edward Colston is not re-writing history. It is not destroying history. It is making history.'

The Trust published a 115-page document setting out those properties alleged to have 'connections with colonialism ... including links with historic slavery'. The document alleged that 93 houses were linked to 'colonialism and slavery'. Even William Wordsworth's house, Allan Bank in the Lake District, is included for no other reason than Wordsworth's brother captained an East India Company ship to China.

Oliver Dowden, the Culture Secretary, told the *Daily Telegraph*, 'Churchill is one of Britain's greatest heroes. He rallied the free world to defeat fascism. It will surprise and disappoint people that the National Trust appears to be making him a subject of criticism and controversy.' The Trust had listed Churchill's home, Chartwell, along with the homes of others like Rudyard Kipling and Thomas Carlyle. A Trust spokesman said,

'The report does not make judgements about people or the places in our care but makes clear the deep and wide-ranging connections of colonialism and historic slavery across the centuries at our homes.'

Eventually, after a rebellion and moves to depose him, the National Trust chairman, Tim Parker, resigned. In a rare exercise in the UK of an organised people's revolt, a members group called Restore Trust tabled a motion of no confidence in the trust's AGM. A spokesman for Restore Trust said:

> 'What the National Trust needs now is a chair with a deep understanding and appreciation of our nation's heritage. We also call on the Board of Trustees to make this an open and accountable process so that their shortlist of potential candidates is published and they present themselves and their proposals for the Trust to members in open events in the coming months.'

In another example of producer capture, the Manchester Art Gallery removed the painting 'Hylas And The Nymphs' by the Victorian artist J. W. Waterhouse from display, stating it wanted to 'prompt conversations about how we display and interpret artworks'. The painting has young naked girls in a pool. The gallery's curator, Clare Gannaway, said the painting perpetuated 'outdated and damaging stories' that 'women are either femmes fatale or passive bodies for male consumption'. After an outcry, the painting was put back.

In September 2020, the Royal Academy of Dramatic Art capitulated to student pressure to remove George Bernard Shaw's name due to his beliefs about eugenics. The organisation continued to enjoy an income from royalties of Shaw's works.

Was any of this rampant political correctness by the National Trust and others in response to demands made by its ordinary members, volunteers and visitors? No. This was instigated by its management and imposed upon everyone else. As with producer capture, the National Trust does not face competition and so did as it liked, and will continue to do so until its members revolt and seize control, or until the management are sacked. Some members have started down that path.

The Capture of State Sector Organisations

The fact the first communist revolution occurred in a backward country, Russia, and the revolution failed to spread led to a questioning of Marxist ideology following WWI. In the forefront of this reappraisal was the Frankfurt School and the Italian communist Antonio Gramsci. The Frankfurt School focused not on the material (i.e. economic) issues prominent in Marxist ideology, but on the culture and superstructure of society to which Marxists had paid less attention.[165] George Lukacs, a Hungarian who the Nazis expelled from Germany, saw the Frankfurt School as an answer to the question 'Who shall save us from Western civilisation?'[166] The views of those creating the Frankfurt School were that the culture of Western societies was acting as a block on the communist revolution. The Frankfurt School focused more on Western culture rather than on examining classical Marxism, but nevertheless worked within a Marxist framework from the outset.[167] They sought to rework Marxism by combining it with Freud (1856–1939).[168] The Frankfurt School believed a new culture needed to be created to *increase* the alienation of the population. The philosopher Walter Benjamin said, 'Do not build on the good old days, but on the bad new ones.'[169] The Frankfurt School developed Critical Theory, which in its early manifestations was derived from Marxism. The objective of Critical Theory was to criticise in such a way as to debunk the objective of the criticism.

Both Lukacs and Gramsci focused more on the superstructure rather than the substructure, as Marx had done.[170] Gramsci was not a member of the Frankfurt School, but was a prominent communist in the 1930s. He became leader of the Italian communist party and argued that there needed to be

190

a long march through the institutions – including the government, the judiciary, the military, the educational system, and the media – before there could be a successful revolution. Gramsci also argued that alliances with other Leftist groups were necessary.[171] Lukacs believed that, for a new Marxist culture to be successful, the existing culture had to be destroyed: 'Such a worldwide overturning of values cannot take place without the annihilation of the old values and the creation of new ones by the revolutionaries.'[172] Despite their long-term approach, it should not be taken that the theorists of the Frankfurt School were more patient for a revolution than classical Marxists. With typical extremist logic, Max Horkheimer (1895-1973, and director of the Frankfurt School from 1930 to 1953) wrote:

> 'Present talk of inadequate conditions is a cover for tolerance of repression. For the revolutionary, conditions have always appeared right. What appears in retrospect a preliminary state or premature situation was once, for the revolutionary, a last chance to change. A revolutionary is with the desperate people for whom everything is on the line, not with those that have time ... Critical theory ... rejects the kind of knowledge that one can bank on. It confronts history with that possibility which is always concretely visible within it ... [Humanity] is not betrayed by the untimely attempts of the revolutionaries but by the timely attempts of the realists.'[173]

Habermas subsequently concentrated on communication and how it perpetuated capitalism. From the 1960s onwards, under the leadership of Habermas, the Frankfurt School revised critical theory to focus on what was believed to be advanced capitalism.[174] For Habermas, the task was 'to identify and reconstruct universal conditions of possible understanding'[175] and to establish that the basis of knowledge is language itself as it is the means by which reality is transmitted. As language is subjective, then so is knowledge.[176] Raymond Marrow and David Brown wrote, 'critical theory ... is ... nothing more and nothing less than a theory of the necessity of overcoming distorted communication as a part of an endless process of collective learning.' Habermas advocated that social theory must be critical and not only describe social reality but also criticise and try to change it. The theory therefore has a 'practical intent'.[177] Habermas regarded the critical theorist as being the 'psychoanalyst of the working class',[178] and believed 'the problem of language has today replaced the problem of consciousness'.[179] For Habermas, it is the transmission of culture and beliefs from one generation to the next and across society that needs to be prevented. False consciousness is deemed to be sustained by communication, and this communication should be targeted and controlled.

Habermas argued Marx's theories could no longer be relied upon to achieve revolutionary change for several reasons: with advanced capitalism the state and the economy are interlocked; the increase in living standards with advanced capitalism meant that economic grounds were no longer sufficient for revolution; and 'the proletariat as proletariat, has been dissolved' and cannot be relied upon as a revolutionary agent; and in Russia, Marxism had become a 'legitimation science'.[180] The response was for immanent critique to become 'total critique' – an attack on Western society.[181] Habermas saw those who experienced the most deprivation and were likely to be the least integrated into society as being the most likely supporters of revolutionary change.[182] Such unintegrated people needed to be radicalised and promoted into positions of power – i.e. they needed to take control of society's institutions, in particular state institutions. Critical theory is a means of justifying and promoting this.

The Frankfurt School's Marcuse argued:

'In the last analysis, the question of what are true and false needs must be answered by the individuals themselves, but only in the last analysis; that is, if and when they are free to give their own answer. As long as they are kept incapable of being autonomous, as long as they are indoctrinated and manipulated (down to their very instincts), their answer to this question cannot be taken as their own.'[183]

With this logic, the views of the people can be totally ignored as being invalid. Only the views of communists are valid due to the supposed communist superior intellect and understanding of society. Marcuse wrote:

'The basic idea is: how can slaves who do not even know they are slaves free themselves? How can they liberate themselves by their own power, by their own faculties? How can they spontaneously accomplish liberation? They must be taught and must be led to be free, and this the more so the more the society in which they live uses all available means in order to shape and preform their consciousness and to make it immune against possible alternatives. This idea of an educational, preparatory dictatorship has today become an integral element of revolution and of the justification of the revolutionary oppression.'[184]

Marcuse believed what was needed was 'the development of an effectively organised radical Left, assuming the vast task of *political education*, dispelling the false and mutilated consciousness of the people so that they themselves experience their condition, and its abolition, as vital need, and apprehend the ways and means of their liberation.'[185] Marcuse supported the 'long march through the institutions' (like Gramsci) and the strategy of 'working against the established institutions while working in them'.[186] One advantage of this, of course, is that the wealth of Western society is used to fund those whose aim it is to destroy Western society. Critical theory justified the capture of the institutions, and the capture of those institutions then further allowed a greater promotion of critical theory.

193

A good example of the capture of state institutions in practice is the experiences of Kathleen Stock in the UK. Stock was a lecturer at Sussex University and fell afoul of the trans mob after she wrote a book in questioning the importance of sex and gender identity. For Stock, biological identity mattered most, and those who were born men were not the same as those born women. Stock had also criticised the trans orthodoxy on a blog. On the trans issue, Stock was politically incorrect. She further was critical of self-ID, where people could declare themselves to be the opposite sex and then use the facilities of the opposite sex regardless of their physical sex. She said:

> 'Self-ID policies trade on a fantasy that suddenly putting on a dress or saying "I'm a woman" will change your basic nature. But, in fact, what was there before will be there after. Humans are humans, and if you make it the case that you can self-identify into a better situation than you were in – i.e. a woman's prison as opposed to a male prison, which are usually less intense, aggressive places – then some people will do it whether they're trans or not.'

For Stock, too little attention was focused on the consequences of self-ID for women.

The Inquisition came down hard and included protests and abuse. Stock resigned her job. She said, 'I was just hanging on. I was teaching from home. I saw the posters. I was advised to stay at home for my own protection. The police were coming round. I'm getting security stuff delivered to my house.' She was determined to keep teaching on Zoom. But she believed a statement her union branch issued made her position untenable: 'It was a pompous peroration about "standing with our trans and non-binary students against institutional transphobia".' She pointed out that the campus was 'literally saturated with positive messaging'.

Regarding the trans campaign and its intolerance of free speech and even free thought, Stock held the taxpayer-funded group Stonewall largely responsible. For several years, Stonewall visited both public and government sector organisations to vet their LGBT+ policies. This allowed Stonewall to foist their own views on those organisations. Stock pointed out Stonewall's interpretation of trans rights 'were embedded in national institutions, Government departments, the Crown Prosecution Service, the European Court of Human Rights, almost all our universities, schools and local authorities. Our national institutions have almost unwittingly been instruments to be used by extremists.'

Stonewall boasted that over 200 government departments and public bodies were a part of their 'diversity champions programme' scheme, which earned them millions of pounds per annum. The Ministry of Defence was the biggest spender, spending £80,312.

Another example of the power and extent to which the politically correct have taken over state institutions is the fight against the inclusion of Critical Race Theory (CRT) in school curriculums in the USA. One outcome of the Covid-19 pandemic was the parents had noticed their children were being indoctrinated with CRT ideology at school. It had been fed into the curriculum under the guise of 'Diversity, Equity and Inclusion'. A Fox News poll revealed that almost three-quarters of voters were 'extremely' or 'very' concerned about what was being taught.

There were confrontations at school board meetings when the unyielding school boards had to deal with angry parents. The response of those on the boards was to complain about being victims of domestic terrorism. In consequence, the National School Boards Association (NSBA) complained to law enforcement agencies, 'These heinous actions could be the equivalent to a form of domestic terrorism and hate crimes.' Within days, the Attorney General, Merrick Garland, sent a memorandum to the FBI, alleging 'there has been a disturbing spike in harassment, intimidation, and threats of violence' against school board members.

One parent, Maud Maron, a criminal defence attorney, and who described herself as a 'lifelong liberal', was outraged and circulated a letter attacking a letter sent by the NSBA to President Biden. That NSBA letter claimed 'America's public schools and its education leaders are under an immediate threat'. The NSBA letter wanted legal action under the 'Patriot Act in regards to domestic terrorism'. In her letter, Maud Maron complained:

> 'Perhaps the most outlandish aspect of all is the NSBA's risible complaint that parents are spreading lies about Critical Race Theory being taught in school. The letter states: "This propaganda continues despite the fact that critical race theory is not taught in public schools and remains a complex law school and graduate school subject well beyond the scope of a K-12 class."
>
> Are you kidding me?
>
> I read the classic Critical Race Theory textbook in law school. I would much prefer to have my children read that impenetrable tome than be subjected to the ideological grooming that takes place in their classrooms — a phenomenon that I and parents across the country witnessed over Zoom this past year-and-a-half. Why should our children — in class, in front of their peers — be required to discuss their sexual orientation? Give their pronouns? Renounce their "privilege"? Plumbing children for this kind of personal information is grotesque and inappropriate, and it has everything to do with the worldview of Critical Race Theory. Anyone who denies as much is lying.'

Not only were the school boards lying about teaching CRT, they were defiant, and wanted those parents who disagreed with them to face criminal prosecution for terrorism.

In both the UK and USA, the tactics were similar. Quietly, the politically correct infiltrated the institutions and imposed their cultural Marxist ideology upon those institutions and its users. When challenged, the Inquisition descended upon critics with force. In the UK, it was a campaign of vilification and persecution. In the USA, it was a determination to convict critics of being terrorists under the Patriot Act.

The Need for a Solidarity Tax

A key reason for the advance of political correctness is that its advocates do not face the financial consequences of their actions. They can carry out their activities on the public payroll. As Wayne Mapp has identified, the politically correct have infiltrated public institutions and thus acquired a legislative base with coercive powers – and all the funding that goes with that. The taxpayer funds them, and they have almost unrestricted access to public monies. The West's success thereby becomes its weakness. It is other people, ordinary families, who end up bearing the cost. This issue overlaps with the damage the Ponzi class caused (see *The Ponzi Class*, which details the costs of Ponzi economics and globalisation being dumped onto ordinary people and advocates a Solidarity Tax to help pay those costs). In the UK, ordinary families have already had to pay their share for Ponzi economics, of which the funding of political correctness is a part, be it in the form of lower pensions, university tuition fees, the seizure of old people's homes, lower wages, the inability to get social housing, etc. Meanwhile, the Ponzi class, including the politically correct, leads the high life with their incomes and assets untouched by the financial calamity they happily cause.

Former UK prime minister Margaret Thatcher remarked in 1976, 'Socialist governments traditionally do make a financial mess. They always run out of other people's money. It's quite a characteristic of theirs.' This is a telling point, even if it is not quite the whole truth. Socialists rarely run out of money altogether, because when they get a bit low, they start printing it. Nonetheless, Thatcher made an important point that remains relevant, especially with respect to the 'We' argument. Time and again on television, and during a general election campaign in the UK, ordinary people were presented with the 'we' argument: 'we' should be more generous in foreign aid; 'we' should accommodate more immigrants; 'we' should be more compassionate; and 'we' should build more houses; etc. But who is 'we'?

In everyday life, when someone is walking down a street and is greeted with an appeal to put money into a bucket for charity, they take a fiver, say, out of their pocket and put it in the bucket. That someone is £5 poorer, and the charity gains £5 for its cause. But when it comes to public monies, a different rule applies. Again and again, television studios are full of those (human rights activists, lawyers, politicians, journalists, members of pressure groups, and quangos) who happily demand 'we' should be doing all sorts of things and donating all kinds of monies without the slightest intention of forking out themselves. (Indeed, many are in receipt of public monies and have a vested interest in more being spent). No one is stopping these assorted worthies from donating money to whatever cause they are pontificating about if they want to do so. However, they have a far better idea. They have their eyes set on a big pile of cash known as taxpayers' monies. It is that which they wish to dip into. Even the public can be suckered into this notion and involve themselves in discussion programmes as to how 'we' should be spending more money on all sorts of things. But where does the money come from? It comes from ordinary members of the public. In particular, in the UK, it comes from the English.

In fairness, many of those advocating political correctness could well be keen to pay more tax. A Solidarity Tax allows them to do so. Such a tax could be levied at either 10 per cent or 20 per cent on targeted incomes such as television advertising, the BBC licence fee (preferably, the licence fee should be abolished), union subscriptions, subscriptions to business organisations, charity donations received for those charities promoting and engaged in political correctness, MPs' salaries, the salaries of senior civil servants, the salaries of senior executives of public bodies, the pensions of MPs and senior civil

198

servants, the block grant to Scotland and Wales, the salaries and pensions of others who have advocated political correctness (and called for mass immigration), the salaries of union officials, and all those high-minded judges with their lavish salaries and pensions, etc. Finally, there would be a need to impose a cost on those businesses employing immigrants to fully compensate for the additional costs to the country of those immigrants. A solidarity audit could be performed, with those firms employing immigrants being required to pay a sum equal to the cost of a house for each immigrant they have employed. The same could apply to universities and colleges for their foreign students.

Currently, there are those businesses which happily employ immigrants, sometimes in preference to available local people, paying lower wages and benefiting from the extra output with the increased profits that such employment entails. Yet the cost of housing the immigrants is dumped onto the public and the taxpayer. Many businessmen think this is a good thing, as well they might.

Periodically, the Tories announced there would be some new 'affordable' house-building programme, which would, over several years, result in a few hundred thousand new houses being built. For example, in August 2021, the Tory Government announced a plan to spend £8.6 billion in an Affordable Homes Programme to build 119,000 new houses – half of which would be sold and half rented. The aim was to build 180,000 new houses by 2026, with a total spend of £11.5 billion. The housing minister, Robert Jenrick, said, 'This huge funding package will make the ambition of owning a home a reality for families by making it realistic and affordable.' Compared to an *annual* immigration rate of 715,000 prior to the Covid-19 pandemic, with the new offer to allow millions of Hong Kongers into the UK, the new immigration partnership with India, and the Office for National Statistics (ONS) predicting that the UK population would surge to beyond 70 million by 2031, then 180,000 new houses over a five-year period is peanuts. It does not address the scale of the problem at all. Jenrick originally announced it in September 2020, and reported as a launch of plans. At that time, Jenrick said, 'This Government is helping hard-working families and prospective first-time buyers get their feet on the housing ladder in an affordable way.' The scheme was re-announced again as part of the October 2021 budget.

The Tories blithely assumed the taxpayer should fund this house building. It did not occur to them that the employers bringing the immigrants into Britain should pay. This is not outlandish. For example, mine owners built the pit villages in the 19th century for house miners, Unilever built the Port Sunlight housing village for its soap factory workers in the 1880s, and farmers to the present day have tied cottages to accommodate farm workers. For the Tories, a key role of the Welfare State is to supply free and low-cost housing to accommodate immigrant workers to save even foreign-owned multinationals the bother and costs of doing so.

A Migration Advisory Committee report in January 2016 disclosed that many hospitals and schools were hiring immigrants to 'undercut' British staff by paying the immigrants 'significantly less', with salaries being up to £6,000 a year less than an equivalent British worker. This 'saving' was not a saving to the taxpayer who had to provide housing for these immigrants, nor to the British people who find their salaries were forced down at the same time they have to cope with the increased housing shortage.

Likewise, universities and colleges enrol overseas students and pocket the fees while expecting the public and the taxpayer to foot the bill for housing those overseas students, many of whom do not return to their own countries once their courses are completed. University and college staff think this is a good thing and enjoy the extra income, as one can imagine. Those businesses, many of which are involved in a variety of tax dodging escapades (especially the multinationals), and those universities and colleges, benefit from the extra income by exploiting immigration. They should pay the bills for that immigration, including the housing costs, rather than, as is currently the case, expecting a whopping great subsidy. The extent of that subsidy should not be underestimated given the number of immigrants and because, according to Nationwide in December 2015, the average house price had reached £456,229 in Central London, or £146,086 in the North West. Substantial funds could be raised by insisting organisations that promote mass immigration pay for the costs of that immigration.

If sufficient revenues are raised, then it may be possible to compensate those British nationals who have been denied social housing, either in the form of a cash payment or a newly built house.

To put it into language that might appeal to the Left, what is needed is an irreversible transfer of wealth from those who advocate political correctness to the victims of political correctness. A Solidarity Tax is a way such a transfer might be achieved.

Political AIDs

Political correctness acts like a political version of AIDS. It weakens a society's culture, identity, and its ability to defend itself, thereby allowing any opportunistic, hostile entity to attack. Problems are not solved. The undermining of national culture and patriotism is as unremitting as are the intended consequences. An examination of Political AIDs will be broken down into culture, immigration, immigration and terrorism, UK grooming gangs, knife crime, and globalisation categories.

Cultural

For the politically correct, the attack upon national culture is a necessity. Patriotism is debunked and denigrated. On occasion, the anti-British sentiment of the ruling class can seem mild, such as when Suzy Klein accused those who complained at the inclusion of an Ibiza-style club music in the

Proms – a classical music festival – of being snobs, saying, 'These self-elected snobs and scaremongers are not there to fight for the universal power that great music unleashes – what they want is to "protect" classical music ... from the onslaught of mass entertainment.' Miss Klein was a presenter on BBC Radio 3, which survives courtesy of licence fee payers' money (this is yet another demonstration of producer capture) and which has been eclipsed by the independent Classic FM.

The Last Night of the Proms, traditionally a rousing patriotic event, has been a target for the politically correct for some time. *The Parekh Report* included the following 'presentation to the commission':

> 'The Rule Britannia mindset, given the full-blown expression at the Last Night of the Proms and until recently at the start of programming each day on BBC Radio 4, is a major part of the problem of Britain. In the same way that it continues to fight the Second World War ... Britain seems incapable of shaking off its imperialist identity. The Brits do appear to believe that "Britons never, never, never shall be slaves" ... [But] it is impossible to colonise three-fifths of the world ... without enslaving oneself. Our problem has been that Britain has never understood itself and has steadfastly refused to see and understand itself through the prism of our experience of it, here and in its coloniser mode.'

At the 2015 Last Night of the Proms, the American conductor Marin Alsop, called on the audience to tackle 'gender, racial, economic and ethnic inequality'. Such comments were totally inappropriate and irrelevant to the event. Patriotism was upstaged by political correctness.

In 2020, the BBC took a decision to refuse to sing the lyrics to *Rule Britannia*, and *Land of Hope and Glory* at the Last Night of the Proms. Other songs would be sung instead. A Finn conductor, Dalia Stasevska, and a South African singer were in agreement with this policy. A BBC source said, 'Dalia is a big supporter of Black Lives Matter and thinks a ceremony without an audience is the perfect moment to bring change.' Golda Schultz, a South African soprano for the Proms night, supported her: 'Dalia and I want to pay tribute to the culture that has invited us into its space, and also make sure we do something that speaks to the times we are living through.' In the event, the decision was reversed and a choir sang the words to both songs. However, the event attracted only 2.1 million viewers compared to a usual figure of 3.5 million.

Another example of the undermining the national culture and patriotism happened in February 2015, when Justin Welby, the Archbishop of Canterbury, told a German audience of his 'profound feeling of regret and deep sorrow' over the bombing of Dresden in WWII, which he said 'diminished all our humanity'. Angela Merkel never apologised for the Blitz.

Another example was when Travelodge removed bibles from its rooms in August 2014, citing a desire not to offend non-Christians. This was despite never receiving any complaints from guests. (This is a good example of critical theory in practice. Expert – i.e. communist – analysis had found that including bibles in rooms was racist, therefore it was racist. The accusation of racism was proof of guilt. The views of ordinary people were irrelevant).

Amazon decreed that *Tom and Jerry* should carry a warning that 'they contain some ethnic and racial prejudices that were once commonplace in American society'. The book *Tintin in The Congo*, written in 1930, was withdrawn from libraries and bookshops because it portrays Africans as primitive and ignorant. In November 2014, the singer Ellie Goulding was accused of racism for wearing a Red Indian costume to a Halloween party. In November 2014, a re-release of the Band Aid single was accused of being 'patronising' and of perpetuating negative images of Africa. This was entirely in keeping with the rejection of charity contained within above-mentioned *The Authoritarian Personality*. To his credit, band founder Bob Geldof was unmoved.

More controversially, in November 2014 during a by-election, the Labour Shadow Attorney General, Emily Thornberry, was forced to apologise and was then sacked following a tweet with a picture in which she mocked a man because he had hung some English flags outside his home. The MP later said she made the tweet because she had 'never seen anything like it'. In the internet furore that followed, one writer described Labour as being 'vacuum-packed lefty snobs'. The person Thornberry was sneering at said, 'She's a snob. What's she got, a three-storey townhouse in Islington? These flags can be found anywhere you look.' Thornberry was the wife of a high court judge and lives in a house worth more than £2 million. She claimed to be a victim of a 'prejudiced attitude towards Islington'.

Schools have been a particular target, even over innocent matters, such as nursery rhymes and singing. For example, in 2006, nursery school children at two centres in Abingdon and Oxford were banned from singing *Baa Baa Black Sheep*. Instead, they are being compelled to sing *Baa Baa Rainbow Sheep*. Stuart Chamberlain of the Oxford Sure Start Centre in Sutton Courtenay said, 'Basically we have taken the equal opportunities approach to everything we do. This is fairly standard across nurseries. We are following stringent equal opportunities rules. No one should feel pointed out because of their race, gender or anything else.'

This was not the first time that race zealots tried to ban or tamper with the nursery rhyme. Previously, attempts have been made to change it to 'green' or 'happy' sheep. In 1999, the Birmingham City Council banned the rhyme on the basis it was racially negative and likely to cause offence. In fact, the rhyme has nothing to do with race and is believed to have originated from the Middle Ages and relates to a tax the king imposed on wool.

The tolerance of anti-Whiteism could be unlimited. A memorial to the victims of the 7/7 London terrorist bombings of 2005 was defaced with slogans describing the terrorists as '4 innocent Muslims' and that '7/7 was an inside job'. The vandalism was done overnight, just before relatives were due to attend the memorial to commemorate the ninth anniversary of the bombings.

Immigration

The policies of mass immigration and multiculturalisation are front and centre of political correctness and are deeply damaging to a country as small and overpopulated as the UK. Despite the hostility shown by many in immigrant communities, public hostility to the policy, and the mounting unpaid bills arising from the policy, mass immigration remained received wisdom for a political establishment too feeble-minded and politically correct to defend the national interests. There is no better example than immigration and related issues to demonstrate the affliction of Political AIDs and the growth of the woke-Right.

The ONS predicted the population of Britain would reach 70 million by 2031, with 5.4 million immigrants settling. The population of England was 55,268,000 in 2016. An assessment in January 2020 from the ONS estimated that the Muslim population in England had reached 3,092,000 in 2016 – around 5.6 per cent of the population and up from 4.7 per cent in the 2011 census.

Brexit did not change the level of immigration, and figures to the year to the end of June 2018 showed 625,000 immigrants entered the UK. Andrew Green of Migration Watch UK wrote, 'For the last 15 years immigration has been adding one million to our population every three years – roughly the equivalent of Birmingham.'

In October 2018, the Home Secretary Sajid Javid announced there would be a new citizenship test, after condemning the current one as being a 'pub quiz'. Javid said he wanted immigrants to be questioned about tolerance, fairness and women's rights: 'It's about integration, not segregation. It's about signing up to those values that we share and live by together.' This was made for good reason. On 24 May 2019, the NAO revealed around 7,500 foreign students who had cheated in English language tests had been allowed to stay in the UK. The NAO described two test centres as being involved in 'organized cheating'. Stand-ins were believed to have sat the tests for the students.

In 2019, the number of Chinese students increased to 119,972 (with another 9,200 from Hong Kong), and the number of students from India increased to 37,540. Whereas UK or EU students paid £9,250 in student fees, those from elsewhere paid fees of up to £36,065.

By 2020, with Priti Patel as the Home Secretary, things had moved on. Patel's big ambition was to rush through a new points-based immigration system. In May 2020, documents published alongside the government's Immigration and Social Coordination Bill showed the government's points-based immigration system would increase Third World immigration into the UK by 30,000 annually, to work in jobs such as teaching and nursing, along with 20,000 family members, and another 25,000 students. Immigration from the EU was expected to fall by 80,000 annually at some time in the future.

Alp Mehmet, chairman of Migration Watch UK, said, 'The Government seem to be sticking to immigration proposals that have been overtaken by the Covid-19 crisis. The proposed system may well drive an increase in immigration.' Also in May 2020, ONS figures showed that Third World immigration into the UK reached a record in 2019. Jay Lindop of the ONS said, 'Overall migration levels have remained broadly stable in recent years, but new patterns have emerged for EU and non-EU migrants since 2016. For the year ending December 2019, non-EU migration was at the highest level we have seen, driven by a rise in students from China and India, while the number of people arriving from EU countries for work has steadily fallen.' Dr Ben Greening of Migration Watch UK said:

'Non-EU arrivals have reached new record levels and risk going up by leaps and bounds, once the pandemic has passed, should the points-based system be enacted. Coronavirus has already knocked out more than twice as many jobs as the financial crisis, according to one estimate. It is totally wrong in these tough times to scrap crucial safeguards for UK workers and to uncap work permits so that employers can hire an unlimited number of cheaper workers from overseas.'

By August 2020, ONS figures revealed that in the year to March, 715,000 immigrated to the UK, an increase of 100,000 over the previous year to March. Immigration from non-EU countries increased by 31 per cent to 437,000 – the highest since records began in 1975, when the figure was 93,000. The immigration minister, Kevin Foster, said:

'These figures demonstrate we are continuing to attract the brightest and best from across the globe, who come to the UK to work and study. We are introducing our new points-based system, which will attract the people we need to drive our economy forward and lay the foundation for a high-wage, high-skill, high-productivity economy. Through the Immigration Bill, the UK will have full control of our immigration system for the first time in decades.'

Worse, in May 2020, following a proposed new Chinese law to clamp down in Hong Kong, deputy prime minister Dominic Raab announced that 300,000 British National (overseas) passport holders would be allowed to enter the UK without a visa for up to 12 months, and they would then have a pathway to UK citizenship. Ultimately, there were up to 3.5 million Hong Kongers who either had British overseas passports or who might be granted one! Raab made his announcement in a television interview. There were no cost estimates for this move, nor any parliamentary debate of it. Subsequently, the offer was extended to include the qualifying Hong Kongers *and their families*. By January 2021, the estimate as to those eligible to come to the UK from Hong Kong reached 5.4 million, although government estimates remained that only 300,000 would do so.

The Ugandan Asians, admitted in 1972, numbered only 27,000. While Norman Tebbit, a Cabinet minister under Margaret Thatcher, was concerned in 1989 'Britain would be swamped by people of different culture, history and religion', he was now in favour of a potential 5.4 million Hong Kongers being transplanted to the UK. The *Daily Mail* editorial stated, 'Yes, this is potentially a massive commitment. Has the Government thought it through properly? Many eligible for sanctuary would stay put. But Mr Johnson must ensure any influx doesn't swamp housing, schools and hospitals.' The influx is certain to swamp housing, schools, hospitals, roads, railways, and everything else.

In an interview with the *Daily Mail*, Patel said, 'If you think what the British government did for Ugandan Asians, it's phenomenal, which is why, in particular sitting here, I feel so strongly about our moral commitment and responsibility to the people of Hong Kong. The Prime Minister, the Foreign Secretary and I are committed to creating a bespoke way for them to come here.' When asked if that would apply to more than two million of them, Patel nodded.

Patel further said, 'My family are international. We don't see colour, gender, race or stereotype. That is part of my motivation for becoming a Member of Parliament: I am not a stereotype. The Labour Party does not speak for me. I will not be defined by the Left because I am from an ethnic community.'

Patel's last comment may have been a response to Labour MPs' letter to her to complain about the way she said she had been called a Paki at school. The letter said, inter alia:

'We write to you as Black Asian and Ethnic Minority Labour MPs to highlight our dismay at the way you used your heritage and experiences of racism to gaslight the very real racism faced by black people and communities in the UK.

Our shared experiences allow us to feel the pain that communities feel, when they face racism, they allow us to show solidarity towards a common cause; they do not allow us to define, silence or impeded on the feelings that other minority groups may face.

Being a person of colour does not automatically make you an authority on all forms of racism. Some forms have become acceptable in our communities, others exist under the breaths and many are built on unconscious bias and systemic structures of power.

Rest assured, Asian and ethnic minority colleagues on this side of the house will not use their experiences to silence our black colleagues, but will use our shared experiences to stand behind them and support their voices to lead us on standing up against the distinct form of racism black communities in the UK and across the globe face.'

In addition to this attack, the letter betrayed a globalist, anti-White stance. This signified race war politics on a global level. On the internet, Patel was branded a 'coconut'.

The Tory commitment to increasing the level of mass immigration knew no bounds. In May 2020, the government agreed to a U-turn and scrapped fees charged to immigrant workers to use the NHS. Tory party figures had complained such fees would look 'mean-spirited'. The supposed reliance on immigrants to staff the NHS should be put into perspective. In March 2020, after a call to those NHS staff who had quit or retired since 2017 to rejoin to help combat the Covid-19 pandemic, 11,856 doctors and 7,510 nurses and midwives answered the call. Furthermore, there were another 715,000 who came forward as volunteers to help the NHS. Andrea Sutcliffe, of the Nursing and Midwifery Council, said she 'couldn't be prouder' of the returnees. To put this into perspective, in November 2019, a report from the Health Foundation forecast there was already a 44,000 shortfall in the number of nurses due to cuts in training and an increase in demand. Consequently, nursing assistants and nursing associates were filling the gaps. The report forecasted that if current trends continued, there would be a shortfall of 100,000 in the number of nurses. The report wanted a drive to bring in immigrant nurses. In 2016, a University of Southampton study revealed that for every 25 patients, substituting one qualified nurse with a lower-qualified person increased the likelihood of dying by 21 per cent. This is the consequence of not training sufficient nurses.

The pressure on public services mounted. In March 2020, Department for Education figures predicted there would be an extra 500,000 children in secondary schools by 2026. Currently, 17 per cent of schools were already at capacity, even after an extra 50,000 places created in 2019. Primary schools were under similar pressure. Professor Alan Smithers, director of the Centre for Education and Employment Research at Buckingham University, said, 'The baby boom fuelled by a rise in immigration and rising birth rates has now reached secondary schools.' A Department for Education spokesman said, 'We have created one million new school places this decade, the largest increase in school capacity in at least two generations, and the percentage of secondary schools at or over capacity has been cut from 28 per cent in 2010 to 17 per cent in 2019.'

Also in March 2020, the NAO reported that parts of southern England could run out of water within 20 years. One reason cited was a predicted seven per cent fall in the water supply due to climate change. The south east was already 'water stressed' as water consumption already outstripped supply in dry years.

The so-called 2018 Windrush scandal clouded the immigration issue. In this political scandal, a few immigrants from the Caribbean were badly treated. The pro-immigration lobby weighed in to promote the mantra the UK is racist. Announcing a compensation scheme of at least £200 million in April 2019, Sajid Javid said:

'The whole country was shocked by the unacceptable treatment experienced by some members of the Windrush generation. People who have built their lives in this country, people who have done so much for this

210

country, people who have every right to be in this country, they were told that they were not welcome. It was a terrible mistake and it should never have happened. And that it did is a matter of profound regret to myself, to my department [and] to the Government. That's why just under a year ago one of my first acts as Home Secretary was to stand at this despatch box and to say sorry on behalf of successive governments.

I didn't just say sorry to members of the Windrush generation, I also vowed to right the wrongs that had been done to them, and I sincerely hope that this compensation scheme being unveiled today goes some way into doing that.'

Satbir Singh, chief executive of the Joint Council for the Welfare of Immigrants, said, 'The Home Secretary's proposed baseline of £200 million will just not be enough to make up for all the hardship caused.' In June 2020, Priti Patel said the Windrush victims had been offered £1 million and the government would implement all 30 recommendations from a review, and, 'Over 12,000 people have been granted documentation by the task force, including over 5,900 grants of citizenship and the compensation scheme continues to make payments.' The recommendations included a programme of training for Home Office staff to understand Britain's colonial history, and the appointment of a Migrants' Commission. In October, Priti Patel announced all Home Office staff would receive compulsory training on Britain's 'history of migration and race'. (This explains why Priyamvada Gopal was invited to lecture Home Office staff – see above). Priti Patel said, 'The Windrush Generation have waited too long for justice and my resolve to deliver for them and their descendants is absolute.'

Even so, in June 2020, the EHRC launched a formal inquiry as to whether the 'hostile environment' policy towards illegal immigration complied with the Equality Act. EHRC chairman David Isaac said:

'The Windrush scandal and hostile environment policies have cast a shadow across the UK and its values. We are working with the Home Office to determine what must change so that this shameful period of our history is not repeated. The impact of Covid-19 and the killing of George Floyd by US police officers has resulted in urgent calls for action to end the systemic and entrenched race inequalities that exist in our country. The law requires that all public bodies must promote inclusivity and opportunity by considering the impact their policies have on ethnic minorities.'

Also in September, incredibly, the Migration Advisory Committee (MAC) called for the government to make it easier for employers to recruit immigrants for over 50 occupations including care workers, butchers, bricklayers, artists, archaeologists, welders and ballet dancers. The MAC chairman, Professor Bell, said, 'We remain particularly concerned about the social care sector – which is so central to the frontline response to this health pandemic – as it will struggle to recruit the necessary staff if wages do not increase as a matter of urgency.'

The problems of the scale of mass immigration were compounded by the tolerance of illegal immigration in both the UK and the USA. This is all the more disgraceful given the various organised crime rackets involved in people smuggling include ISIS, al-Qaeda and the Taliban.

In the UK, Tony Smith, the former head of the Border Force, said, 'The Government has not got a grip. For the migrants and people-smugglers, success breeds success. They see people getting into the UK … and it fuels the supply chain. We have got to say we will no longer tolerate this.' Of the Channel crossings, in May 2020, Smith gave evidence to the Commons home affairs committee, and said: 'This is becoming a major threat, I'm afraid, to the UK border.' He continued, 'We haven't really geared ourselves up to a major maritime threat like this in terms of our infrastructure, our powers, our response capability or our international response capability with France.'

In August 2020, Smith, said, 'If [asylum seekers] want to come to the UK they need to make their case on the French side and if they are found in the waterways or even make it as far as Dover we say "I'm sorry but you go back there and that's where you will be interviewed, on the French side".' This ignored that EU treaties are supposed to oblige asylum claims made in the first safe country reached by the immigrant – in which case, the UK should not have to receive those in France at all.

In August 2020, Dan O'Mahoney, a former Royal Marine of the Home Office appointed to lead the UK's response to the Channel crossings, said, 'We are determined to return those who do not have a legitimate asylum claim.' He added the crossings were 'facilitated by criminals who are making money exploiting migrants desperate to come to our country', and, 'France is a manifestly safe country with a fully functioning asylum system and refugees there can and should claim asylum.' In other words, the illegal immigrants would be allowed to make asylum claims and hence stay in the UK.

Revealingly, in August 2020, Admiral Lord West, a former First Sea Lord and Chief of Naval Staff, wrote (italics my emphasis):

> 'In recent years the Royal Navy has been depleted by savage funding cuts to the point where it can no longer monitor and guard these [UK] waters properly. In fact, despite the current influx of migrants, there is not one navy vessel currently patrolling the Channel.
> But it could be done, quickly and at a comparatively low cost. There is no need to send a grand Task Force. Britain already has ships known as Batch One offshore patrol vessels (OPV), such as HMS Tyne, Severn, and Medway. They were scheduled to be decommissioned but have been kept nominally in active service, though they would require full crews.

We also have HMS Clyde, another OPV, which was *taken out of service last December* and is now in dock. This gallant little ship, which helped guard the Falkland Islands for years, could be brought back to do the job she was built for.'

In other words, the government continued to take out of service naval vessels needed to patrol British waters, even when they knew the immigrant invasion was taking off, and in stark contrast to their own bluster.

The money involved in various schemes of illegal immigration was lucrative. In February 2019, BBC London News reported that immigrants were paying up to £2,000 to criminal fixers who would help them cheat the citizenship tests to allow them to stay in the UK and apply for British citizenship. Some used tiny earpieces so they could be told the answers to questions during the tests. In January 2020, a people-smuggling gang of 23 was charged £6,000 each to smuggle illegal immigrants (mainly Kurdish) into the UK. French and Dutch police arrested the gangsters.

The response from the authorities was half-hearted. In November 2018, a report from David Bolt, the Independent Chief Inspector of Borders and Immigration, found ports were 'not secured by any stretch of the imagination'. Border guards were not routinely checking vehicles for illegal immigrants. In September 2019, the government announced foreign students would be allowed to work in Britain for two years after graduation. The ultimate aim was to increase the number of foreign students by a third to 600,000 per year. Previously, students could only stay on for four months while they looked for a job, whereupon they could apply for a working visa. In December 2019, in giving judgement in a case, Mr Justice Jay in the High Court, ruled that fees of around £1,000 to register the children of foreign nationals for British citizenship were unlawful. The judge declared the Home Office 'failed to have regard to the best interests' of applicants and the fees were 'simply unaffordable' for many. The judge further declared the fees made children 'alienated, excluded, isolated'. Amnesty International UK assisted in the court application.

In January 2019, Home Office figures in a Civitas report revealed that between 2010 and 2016 80,813 people failed in their applications for asylum, yet only 29,659 (36 per cent) were deported. The report writer, David Wood, was in charge of immigration enforcement at the Home Office until 2015. He said:

> 'Once migrants reach the UK they are usually here to stay whether they have a valid claim to be here or not. This means that these numbers add to an ever-growing number of migrants in the country who have no lawful entitlement to be here. Furthermore, the failure to deal with this situation provides an incentive to further attempts to come to the UK by people who have no right to be here.'

In 2018, only 5,316 failed asylum seekers were deported, compared to 18,220 in 2016 when Labour was in office, and 10,394 when the Coalition government came to power in 2010.

In October 2018, James Hanratty, an immigration judge, said at the Henley Literary Festival:

> 'I had a case where a lady from Somalia came before me and her story was that she had found her husband on the doorstep of their house with his throat cut by the local warlord – so she had to flee to England. The Home Office barrister asked her to explain how this happened. He then said there seems to be a problem here as your husband came over to England 18 months ago and claimed asylum and you're saying he's dead on the doorstep in Mogadishu.
>
> There was a stunned silence but she had no answer and shouted at me. Then I found out that the solicitors acted for both the husband and for her, and so they knew

that the statement they had prepared for her was rubbish.

I reported it and the regulator unbelievably took no action saying that there was no damage to the public and "we're very busy". This was five years ago.'

Hanratty complained that smaller law firms involved in immigration cases tended to close down and then recommence under a different name when threatened with investigation. The judge complained the system was overwhelmed with crooked lawyers and the Solicitors Regulation Authority was doing nothing.

That the whole immigration system was riven with criminality makes the failure to control the borders more catastrophic. In April 2019, The *Daily Mail* (Sue Reid) reported:

'[Tolga] Binbuga, who came to Britain at the age of nine, but has never applied for British citizenship, has been convicted of robbery, burglary, assault, criminal damage and shoplifting. He has been fighting the Government against his deportation to Turkey for nearly five years – but thanks to a string of successful appeals to immigration tribunals, costing thousands of pounds apiece, he has succeeded in staying ... Day after day in our immigration courts, foreigners who have made their home in the UK, then abused our welcome by committing criminal acts, even serial rape and murder, game the overwhelmed system with the help of well-paid lawyers to wriggle out of being deported – sometimes for years, sometimes for ever because the system seems to forget them.'

One judge declared that as 'in various parts of London, gang culture is an accepted and widespread part of life for many young people', then Binbuga's [the so-called asylum seeker] association with one such gang was 'a good example of his

216

integration into one of the less savoury aspects of UK life'. One prisoner in nine was a foreigner.

The *Daily Mail* reported:

> 'In another case, a 40-year-old Albanian who arrived here illegally 20 years ago and has since been deported six times, appealed to stay. His request was turned down last September when he was found to have used nine false identities and four bogus nationalities during a crime spree in Britain that resulted in seven convictions for 19 offences, including burglary and motor vehicle theft. Yet the chances are he's still here.'

Even serious criminality was tolerated in the name of human rights. Citing Article 3 of the Human Rights Act (which prohibits 'torture or inhuman or degrading treatment'), a Sri Lankan who stabbed a man 21 times, killing him, was awarded the right to stay in the UK by the Upper Tribunal Immigration and Asylum Chamber. The killer had been refused asylum and yet had not been deported prior to committing murder, and had further convictions for assault. The killer, who claimed mistreatment for being a Tamil during the Sri Lankan civil war, had been diagnosed as a paranoid schizophrenic.

An Albanian killer, Astrit Mija, won the right to stay in the UK when the judge ruled he might 'harm others' in Albania if he were sent back. Mija killed his flatmate and spent 17 years in prison. He entered the UK falsely, claiming to be a Kosovan refugee. He claimed he needed medication for schizophrenia and the judge ruled he might be 'homeless and destitute' in Albania without family support.

Seven Nigerian stowaways who caused the tanker Nave Andromeda to be bordered by Special Boat Service (SBS) commandos off the Isle of Wight, lodged asylum claims to stay in the UK. The Crown Prosecution Service (CPS) dropped other chargers against them, claiming there was 'insufficient evidence'.

217

A 29-year-old immigrant from El Salvador won refugee status in the UK on the grounds that as a trans activist, police assaulted him in El Salvador and he suffered public abuse. The judge ruled, 'To be surrounded by men in authority, taunted, physically attacked and spat upon was surely an exercise in humiliation designed to punish the appellant for nothing more than being who they are. The power imbalance between perpetrators and victim, and the nature of the assault, made it of sufficient severity to constitute inhuman and degrading treatment.'

A flight to deport criminals to Jamaica was faced with 23 criminals being taken off the plane due to last-minute appeals on human rights grounds. Those removed, all immigrants, included a convicted murderer, two convicted of attempted murder, two rapists and a variety of drug dealers. David Olusoga supported the move to prevent deportation as did the Black actresses Naomie Harris and Thandie Newton, and a host of Labour luvvies, members and supporters.

One lawyer, working pro bono, tweeted, 'What a result, fresh reps [representations] submitted for our Jamaican client.' Another lawyer, who successfully stopped the deportation of a killer, got £93,500 in legal aid. Another £237,000 in legal aid was paid in respect to three killers who had been deported on the flight. In January, a judge freed one of those not deported, a drug dealer, pending the arrangements for a further attempt at deportation.

In August 2020, the Common Sense Group of 40 Tory MPs wrote to Boris Johnson to call for a 'root and branch' reform of the asylum system. They wanted an end to asylum claims from those who have crossed other safe countries, such as France. Sir John Hayes, a former security minister and the group's founder, said:

> 'The Human Rights Act in its current form in not fit for purpose. Of course, certain lawful entitlements, such as the right to a fair trial, are important ... but the Human Rights Act as it stands is being abused by a whole army

of lawyers. The majority of migrants crossing the Channel do not have the right to asylum when their cases are looked at, but even then it is very difficult to remove them without their cases becoming clogged up in the courts. Part of our manifesto was to create a Tory alternative to the bourgeois liberal hegemony. Now is the time to act because the public are sick of this.'

Also in August, Home Office figures showed the figures for deporting illegal immigrants and foreign criminals fell by one third in the 12 months to June 2020. Only 5,304 were deported, compared to 8,059 the previous year. In September, figures showed only 20 per cent of asylum claims from those crossing the Channel were granted. Even so, once in the UK, the prospects of being deported were slight. Meanwhile, although Facebook banned sites offering people smuggling, posts requesting help on how to get trafficked were still allowed. The National Crime Agency had many requests that posts be taken down rejected. Meanwhile, Dan O'Mahoney claimed the French had stopped over 200 boats crossing the Channel on one day alone. O'Mahoney told a House of Commons committee, 'We hear a lot of stories about migrants literally forced on to boats, who have no idea where they are when they get to the UK.'

By November 2021, the number crossing the English Channel to England had surpassed 20,000 that year so far, and looked set to exceed 30,000 by the New Year. Daily crossings could exceed 1,000.

While the UK's handling of the illegal immigration invasion across the English channel merely facilitated its continuance and escalation, President Biden's handling of immigration across the USA's southern border was widely regarded as a disaster. In January 2021, The White House website stated:

'President Biden is sending a bill to Congress on day one to restore humanity and American values to our immigration system. The bill provides hardworking people who enrich our communities every day and who have lived here for years, in some cases for decades, an opportunity to earn citizenship.'

On his first day in office, President Biden issued executive orders that revoked some of the Trump administrations immigration measures, including the ending of the travel bans and the cessation of 'extreme vetting'. Construction on the border wall was terminated (during the election campaign, Biden had promised not to build 'another foot' of the wall). A presidential memorandum instructed the secretary of Homeland Security to 'take all actions he deems appropriate, consistent with applicable law, to preserve and fortify DACA [Deferred Action for Childhood Arrivals]'.

The consequences of this were immediate and profound. In February 2021 alone, more than 100,000 tried to enter the USA – the highest level for five years. There were a record 3,500 unaccompanied minors in the Border Patrol detention cells. By May, the number trying to cross the southern border reached 180,034. By July, the figure was 210,000 and more than 19,000 unaccompanied children. The Department of Homeland Security said it expected apprehensions this fiscal year to likely be 'the highest ever recorded'.

Of President Biden's new immigration policies, Guatemalan President Alejandro Giammattei remarked, 'The message changed, to: "We're going to reunite families, we're going to reunite children." The very next day, the coyotes were here organizing groups of children to take them to the United States.'

Immigration and Terrorism

The ongoing determination of the authorities to equate opposition to fundamentalist Islam, the policies of multiculturalism and mass immigration with jihadist terrorism hampered the prosecution of the so-called war on terror in the UK. Also, the human rights of terrorists took precedence over the need to combat the growth of Muslim terrorism. Consequently, the terrorism steadily increased.

In December 2019, Home Office figures showed the total number of referrals to the Prevent programme of those deemed far-Right reached 1,389 – double the figure in 2015/16. Meanwhile, the number of referrals who were Islamic extremists fell from 3,197 to 1,404. There had been 254 far-Right new referrals compared to 210 Islamist ones. Scotland Yard Assistant Commissioner Neil Basu had claimed the far-Right was the UK's fastest growing threat. To put Basu's inflammatory claims into perspective, according to Europol, the number of those deemed right-wing and arrested for terrorism in 2017 in the EU numbered 20; those deemed left-wing numbered 36; whereas those described as 'Islamic/jihadist numbered 705. Those killed by right-wing terrorists numbered one, and no one was killed by a left-wing terrorist. Those killed by Islamic/jihadist terrorists numbered 62. Of the terrorist attacks either foiled or completed, right-wing terrorism accounted for five, left-wing terrorism accounted for 24, and Islamic/jihadist terrorism accounted for 265.

Scepticism about Prevent had existed for some time. The consultancy, the Behavioural Insights Team (BIT), conducted an investigation into the effectiveness of the Prevent scheme in 2018, and concluded Prevent was mostly ineffective, with almost all its various projects being a waste of money, time and effort. BIT found that a major problem was 'facilitators who were uncomfortable dealing with sensitive topics and would often refuse to engage if they were brought up' and teachers who were 'afraid to bring up race or religion with their students', believing it would be discriminatory. Furthermore, Prevent's own claimed a success rate of 90 per cent was 'not believable' nor was it supported by a 'sufficiently robust standard of evidence'. BIT found that Prevent's attempt to treat different extremism as the same was ineffective. The Home Office rejected the BIT report and did not publish it.

Despite three-quarters of those in prison for terrorist offences being Muslim terrorists, Muslim extremists accounted for only 22 per cent of those referred to Prevent, alleged far-right extremists accounted for 24 per cent. Muslim extremists receiving ideological mentoring on Prevent accounted for 24 per cent as opposed to the alleged far-right accounting for 43 per cent. The Henry Jackson Society's own report pointed out Prevent had been corrupted by false allegations of Islamophobia.

Basu's claims were not untypical. For example, on Newsnight, Kirsty Walk tried to drag the 'far-Right' into a report about a Muslim terrorist attack on London Bridge. Two people were killed in stabbing attacks before the police shot dead the attacker. Walk claimed that until *The Times* reported on the background of the attacker, we would not have known whether 'the ideology of the Right, the far-Right, or the ideology of radical Islam' motivated the attack. An interview with Sir Mark Rowley brought in the Christchurch killings in New Zealand and to discuss a need to stop the spread of information on the internet. Apparently, there was a need for a 'whole society approach' and not just a security response regarding radicalisation. This was total rubbish. We knew this terrorist had already been convicted and imprisoned – but the authorities let him back out again.

Of the early release of terrorist prisoners, Christopher Dean, the psychologist behind the Healthy Identity Intervention (HII) de-radicalisation programme, pointed out:

> 'People can get more reassured and confident about change and progress that people are making, but I think we have to be very careful about saying someone has totally changed or has been cured … Sometimes people move up two rungs, sometimes individuals may say "I've had my doubts" about this or that, and they may be willing to speak to people, but equally they may go down rungs as well.'

Former senior Home Office official Ian Acheson said that the HII scheme was 'easy to game or manipulate' and that it 'ignores or cannot really accommodate the theological foundations for violent extremism.' Acheson continued:

'There was a degree of false compliance with the HII course, which meant it would appear that people had improved or made progress, when in fact they might simply have been disguising their intentions in order for attention to pass on to someone else. I think we must accept that there may be a small number of people who are potentially ideologically bulletproof and do not wish to recant their hateful views.'

In December 2019, Nazeem Hussain, 34, who had been released from jail following a conviction for terrorism, was arrested for plotting a new atrocity. The arrest followed a government ordered crackdown after released jihadist Usman Khan murdered two people in an attack in London. Another 74 released jihadists were also under review. Figures from the Home Office revealed more than 350 convicted or suspected terrorists had been released from prison over the past seven years. The figures also showed the number of terrorist arrests had fallen by one fifth in the past year.

In December 2019, figures from the Henry Jackson Society showed one in seven jihadis jailed for terrorism had had their sentences reduced on appeal. Of those convicted of Islamic terrorism between 1998 and 2015, 40 out of 264 had their sentences reduced on appeal. At least seven were subsequently jailed again for breaking their licence conditions.

Dr Rakib Ehsan of the Henry Jackson Society said, 'For too long, woolly liberal judges have failed to take robust enough action over Islamic extremism.'

In August 2019, it was reported that if all other avenues have failed for illegal immigrants, many then claim gangs trafficked them and subjected them to modern slave conditions. Such a claim immediately cancels moves to deport them as victims. A Home Office source stated, 'Once a failed asylum seeker has used up every legal and administrative option to keep them in the country, an increasing number are then saying they are the victims of modern slavery. The wheels stop and we have to carry out an investigation.'

No matter the horror stories alleged, immigrants were prepared to return to their home countries when it suited them. On 29 May 2019, representatives of the Somali community said hundreds of Somali children had been sent back to Somalia to escape the UK's knife crime epidemic. The mayor of Islington estimated that two out of five Somali families in London had done this. Rakhia Ismail, a Somali refugee with four children, told the Victoria Derbyshire programme, 'Does the parent wait for her child to be killed? Or does the parent take a decision – quite drastic decision – to take him all the way back to wherever that child is from originally?'

In September 2019, there were reports of a Cabinet rift as Boris Johnson wanted to repatriate children from Syria, with Ben Wallace, the Defence Secretary, and Priti Patel, Home Secretary, being opposed. Around 30 children were in issue. In October 2019, in an article in the *Daily Mail*, arguing ISIS jihadi children should be brought back to the UK, Alibhai-Brown wrote, 'Yes, hard cases are the most testing a country can face. But how we deal with them demonstrates what sets a civilised nation such as Britain apart from savages like those of Islamic State.' The pressure to bring jihadists back to the UK remained.

Following the collapse of the ISIS caliphate in Iraq and Syria, some jihadists who had left the UK to join the ISIS genocide decided it now suited their purposes to travel back to the UK. For example, in February 2019, Mohammed Anwar Miah, who renamed himself Abu Obayda al-Britannia in the ISIS caliphate to which he had scuttled from Birmingham, and then been captured by the Kurdish-led SDF, announced:

'I want to go home. I'm proud to be British. Britain has got good human rights and that is a good thing. In an ideal situation I would like to take my wife and children back to Britain with me and just live a normal life. If she can live there and she's not allowed health care, OK so be

224

it. I've never claimed any benefits in my life. I've always worked for a living and paid taxes.'

Miah's wife is Syrian. Miah was born in Britain to a Bangladeshi mother. Miah stated, 'I have been to Bangladesh two or three times in my life. I don't have a Bangladesh passport, I only have one nationality – British.' (It should be noted he was vague as to the number of times he had been in Bangladesh. To be accurate, he did not have British nationality, he had British citizenship).

Another example is Adel Abdel Bary, an Egyptian released early from a 25-year prison sentence in the USA for his involvement in the al-Qaeda truck bombing of US embassies in East Africa, in which 224 were killed and thousands injured. He was immediately welcomed back into the UK.

Also in February 2019, was the cause célèbre of Shamima Begum, whose plight attracted great sympathy from the usual suspects. Begum was accused of being an ISIS operative who carried a Kalashnikov rifle, served in the morality police, and sewed suicide bombers into their vests. The UK government refused to re-admit her into the UK and stripped her of British citizenship. Begum complained, 'I feel like I've been discriminated against because everyone was saying I was a poster girl for ISIS. I'm being made an example of. I'm being punished right now because I'm famous.' On meeting her husband, she said, 'He told me that he was strict and he wanted a good housewife that stays inside. He didn't want someone who is Westernised and wants to always go out and stuff.' Of joining ISIS, Begum said, 'I don't regret it because it's changed me as a person. It's made me stronger, tougher. I married my husband – I wouldn't have found someone like him back in the UK. I had my kids. I did have a good time there. It's just at the end things got harder and I couldn't take it any more. I had to leave.' She even went so far as:

'But to kill people like women and children just like the women and children in Baghuz [ISIS's last stronghold] who

225

are being killed right now unjustly by the bombings – it's a two-way thing really, because women and children are being killed back in Islamic State right now. It's kind of retaliation. Their [ISIS's] justification [for Manchester] was that it was retaliation, so I thought "OK, that is a fair justification".'

Begum said, 'Mostly it was a normal life in Raqqa, with every now and then bombing and stuff. But when I saw my first severed head in a bin it didn't faze me at all. It was from a captured opposition fighter on the battlefield, an enemy of Islam. I thought of what he would have done to a Muslim woman if he had had a chance.'

Before fleeing to ISIS, Begum and the other girls had been watching ISIS videos of beheadings and ISIS propaganda videos. Tasnime Akunjee, the solicitor for the Bethnal Green jihadi brides, said, 'It is almost inconceivable that no agency has been investigated let alone held to account for the litany of failures that resulted in the Bethnal Green schoolgirls managing to travel to ISIS.'

Alex Younger, head of MI6, no less, said, 'British nationals have a right to come to the UK', including 'potentially very dangerous' fanatics. Of Begum, Corbyn said: 'She was born in Britain, she has that right to remain in Britain. On that return she must face a lot of questions about everything she's done. And at that point any action may or may not be taken. The idea of stripping anyone of their citizenship when they're born in Britain is a very extreme manoeuvre. I question the right of the Home Secretary to have these powers.' Regarding Begum's award of legal aid, former Labour leader Jeremy Corbyn said, 'She is a British national and, therefore, she has that right, like any of us do, to apply for legal aid if she has a problem. She has legal rights, just like anybody else does.'

In July 2020, following the judgement that Shamima Begum be allowed to return to the UK so she could appeal the decision to revoke her citizenship, Dr Alan Mendoza, executive director of the Henry Jackson Society, said, 'The deeply troubling implication of this judgement is that up to 150 terrorists are now legally entitled to enter the UK in order to appeal the decision in their case. This decision could have dramatic repercussions for our entire counter-terror strategy.' In the event, the UK's Supreme Court ruled the government had the right to block Begum's entry into the UK. Her sporadic television appearances and legal action continued. As of December 2021, Begum was still in Syria. However, another three who had had their British citizenship withdrawn successfully overturned the decision, despite the Home Office arguing they had dual citizenship. The Special Immigration Appeals Tribunal declared the move 'would make them stateless'. In November 2021, Yago Riekijk, Begum's husband, described the 'beautiful life' he and Begum had enjoyed in the ISIS caliphate. In a prison in northern Syria, he said he hoped to be reunited with Begum. He said he had 'got used to' the dead bodies that ISIS left in the streets. ISIS would 'leave the corpses to scare people'.

In June 2020, 25-year-old Libyan, Khairi Saadallah, killed three people in a knife attack in Reading. Police stopped him in the street the day before and returned him to his council flat. Police did not rule out the possibility the killings were homophobic. Saadallah yelled 'Allahu Akbar' as he attacked people. Saadallah was under psychiatric monitoring. According to relatives, he entered the UK as a tourist before claiming asylum. He had been granted five year's leave to remain in 2018. A cousin in Libya said, '[Saadallah] had been to the UK a number of times but at the end of 2012 he travelled there as a tourist and decided to stay and claim asylum. He was at risk of extremists in Libya because he liked to drink and socialise and didn't really lead a strict religious life. He did get in trouble in England but I can't ever imagine him getting drawn into something as serious as this.'

The Tory MP Lee Anderson pointed out, 'There is something wrong if an individual has come into this country illegally and been granted asylum and then goes on to be a security risk.' Maria Eagle, a former Labour minister, revealed in the House of Commons that Saadallah had been released from prison just 16 days before the killings: '[Saadallah] has been reported as being of interest to the security services as a potential terrorist sympathiser and was released well before the end of his sentence from prison.' To be precise, he had been reported, and was of interest to MI5, as someone who wanted to join ISIS. The case was closed due to lack of corroborating evidence.

Saadallah moved to the UK after the toppling of President Gaddafi. He had fought against the Gaddafi regime. Saadallah's older brother, Mohamed Saadallah, said:

> 'Khairi fought against Gaddafi in 2011 in Benghazi – when he was just 15-years-old – and after the war was over he went to the UK, aged 16. He is not a violent person. The reason he went to the UK was that he was upset with the way the Libyan revolution turned out, because it turned into a civil war. He did have some psychological problems, mainly as a result of his experiences in 2011 ... I don't believe what they're saying about him in the news – anything he would have done would have been in self-defence.'

His sister said, 'In Tripoli there were a lot of Gaddafi supporters who remained in positions of power after the war which was something that stuck with Khairi – he felt all his mates had died for nothing. He became obsessed with that to the extent he didn't want to stay in the country.'

However, a family source pointed out the Saadallahs had a close relationship with the Gaddafi family before the revolution in 2011. They were a wealthy family who lived in a gated three-storey home in Tripoli. They were close to Gaddafi's son Saif, with whom they socialised. They would be waved through the airport when returning from abroad. The father (who would regularly fly to Switzerland) had business dealings with the regime.

A friend from Bury recalled police often had to break up Saadallah's parties. Also, 'He did smoke cannabis a lot, though, when he was just hanging out. He said he'd been involved in the fighting in Libya and he'd had to leave because there was a risk of him being killed. He seemed proud of his time fighting – he would show off pictures of himself posing with guns.' Residents of the Bury house were asylum seekers under Serco supervision, on behalf of the Home Office, which supported asylum seekers in the community.

Following the Reading killings, Kevin Hurley, a former Surrey Police and Crime Commissioner and Detective Chief Superintendent in the Metropolitan Police, wrote an article in the *Daily Mail*, which began:

> 'As any man or woman in police uniform will tell you, neutralising the terrorist threat of individual Islamist extremists is almost impossible. Far-Right racist terrorists present their own problems, but they are generally easier to monitor because they tend to gather in places such as pubs and football grounds which can be more easily observed.'

So, within two sentences of his article, Hurley dragged an allegation of 'far-Right racist terrorists' into the matter of three people being killed by a Libyan immigrant.

Hurley described Saadallah as 'every surveillance team's nightmare' – even though he was well known and had been released early from prison. Saadallah was not a surveillance nightmare – he was in prison. The reasons for his release were not disclosed.

Hurley pointed out that whereas MI5 had only 4,000 employees, including cleaners and support staff, there were around 20,000 people of Middle Eastern and North African origin in the UK, regarded by MI5 as being a potential terrorist threat (other figures place the number in excess of 40,000). Many were also drug users and some 'typically ... have an unremarkable criminal record for theft or assault' and:

> 'Others are more directly menacing, and may be classed as having the potential to mount and attack like the one

we saw in Reading at the weekend ... I was hardly surprised to discover yesterday that he had already been convicted of a string of violent crimes. Naturally, now that MP Angela Eagle said in Parliament that Saadallah was released from prison only 17 days ago, questions will need to be asked about why an Appeals Court judge thought it wise to cut his prison sentence. But as someone who has served on the police frontline, I know fully well how tricky it is to snuff out terrorism before it takes place.'

Hurley pointed out that around the clock surveillance of one suspect requires four teams of 15 officers each. Covering 20,000 is therefore impossible.

In the House of Commons, Priti Patel said, 'If you abuse our hospitality and commit crimes in the UK we will do everything in our power to remove you. Tougher action is needed to speed up removals to deter foreign criminals from entering the UK. This is not always easy, there are barriers to overcome and that of course is something that we will be looking at through other legislative means.' This was all wind. Patel had a long track record of talking big and doing nothing. She is in favour of mass immigration from the Third World, and so is unlikely to object to the problems stemming from that policy.

Saadallah freely travelled between the UK and Libya several times. Libya has several terrorist training camps for jihadists, in particular Sabratha which has produced several terrorists who have committed acts of terror in Europe – e.g. Salman Abedi who killed 22 people at a concert in Manchester with a suicide bomb.

Also in June, the police shot dead an immigrant in Glasgow after he went on a rampage with a knife in a hotel housing asylum seekers. The attacker knifed a receptionist in the stomach before knifing two other hotel staff; one collapsed after staggering out of the hotel, the other was left with a 'big puncture wound'. The attacker charged through the hotel, knifing residents on the stairs and in the lift before being he confronted and stabbed a police officer in a struggle. Minutes later, an armed police unit arrived and opened fire.

The police denied that the attack was terror related, and said the assailant had been in a row about conditions at the hotel. There had been complaints about conditions for several days. Tensions had been rising about food and money. One said, 'Their financial support has been stopped so they are not getting any cash. People have been complaining about their mental health, that they are not getting enough food. This is not a terrorist issue. It is a depression issue. People have been saying for months that they are not well, they are not happy in the hotel.'

The impact of Political AIDs was effectively admitted in February 2020 when Ofsted's chief inspector, Amanda Speilman, warned on Sky News: 'In a school in Birmingham, we found some very, very rigid segregation that meant that boys were always put ahead of girls for everything. Children literally didn't see each other. We found books in the library saying men can beat their wives – provided they don't leave a mark – and that women aren't entitled to refuse sex to their husbands.' The school was theoretically a state school for all, but was in practice Islamic. Even the details of the reign of Queen Elizabeth I had been withheld from children in schools, Speilman said: 'Problems exist at a small minority of schools but the point is because of our sensitivities about religion, culture, ethnicity, we're very reluctant to say we've got some really tough issues.' In fact, ordinary people are prepared to complain about these issues, but the Tory Government condemns them for doing so. It is the Tories who have the problem and are the problem.

In reference to the gang rapes, Speilman said, 'There's no question that we're afraid. All the dreadful grooming gang stories – that shows vividly what happens when we censor ourselves. We desperately need everybody to be a little bit braver, calling things by their name, talking about what's there.'

UK Grooming Gangs

The UK stands out in its ongoing tolerance for the grooming, rape and gang rape of its young girls. No other Western country comes anywhere near being as depraved. For the authorities, who are steeped in political correctness and the promotion of mass immigration and multiculturalism, the mass paedophilia by Muslim gang rapists was an inconvenient truth to be covered up. The authorities, from the highest level downwards, cared little for the victims. Those who spoke out about the horror were dismissed as racists.

The result is that the grooming gang rape epidemic continued, as did the reluctance to deport the rapists. In May 2020, one victim of a Rochdale grooming gang, who had expected those who had raped her to be deported, came face to face with an abuser in the supermarket. The girl had been only 13 when she became pregnant by Adil Khan, 50. Khan and two other rapists, Abdul Aziz, 49, and Abdul Rauf, 51, were jailed for between six and eight years in 2012. They had been convicted of rape, abuse and torture of girls in Rochdale. All three had dual British and Pakistani citizenship, but their British citizenship was revoked. They finally lost their claims against deportation on human rights grounds in 2012 at the Court of Appeal in 2018. Even so, the Home Office had not deported them. Nine gang members were convicted, and police believed there were up to 47 victims. A Home Office spokesman said, 'We are committed to removing foreign national offenders wherever possible.' In May 2020, new figures showed 8,497 foreign-born criminals were still free in the UK and not deported.

Regarding Rotherham, the National Crime Agency (NCA) was invited after the Jay Report in 2014, which outlined the scale of the offending against children in the town. The agency now had more than 200 people working on Operation Stovewood, which had a budget in 2018 of just under £12 million, and was looking to increase this as it worked towards recruiting a staff of 250. The agency was engaged with 313 alleged victims and survivors and had identified 190 suspects. Asked how many years the operation would take, NCA regional head of investigations, Rob Burgess, said, 'Putting a time on it is not right, it's not fair in those circumstances. This is about pursuing the investigation to a point where, effectively, we've no longer got any victims that we can deal with. And, in reality that will take as long as it does.'

The Independent Office for Police Conduct upheld six complaints against South Yorkshire Police made by a victim of a Pakistani Muslim child rape gang. The chief inspector described the industrial child rape of English children in the area of Rotherham as 'Paki shagging that had been going on for 30 years.' Relating to grooming gangs, in January 2020, the Independent Office for Police Corruption said it could not identify the Rotherham police officer who had said, 'With it being Asians, we can't afford for this to be coming out [as the town] would erupt.'

A girl of 15 who had been gang raped repeatedly did not receive any help from the police. The victim told the police of 'one rape and incidents of sex with adult men as a minor' to police officers in 2011. The South Yorkshire Police did not record the crime. The girl made a second complaint months later, but the investigation was 'short-lived'. It was not until 2016 and 2017 her plight was taken seriously as part of another investigation. Nine men were put on trial, accused of a variety of charges against the victim between 2010 and 2011.

In the UK, the grooming, rape and gang rape of White, mainly English children, has been a problem for very many years – as has been the determination of the authorities to cover up the crime, despite the scale of it. No other country experienced anything approaching the scale of it. Ann Cryer, the former Labour MP for Keighley, wrote in the *Daily Mail:*

> 'It is almost 15 years since I first sounded a warning about the plight of young white girls being exploited by men from Asian communities in Britain. Yet on Wednesday evening, as I watched the TV news, it was clear to me there are broadcasters still reluctant to state the basic

facts about who the abusers are, for fear of appearing racist or Islamophobic.

Let us be clear, the men in the dock were mainly British-born from Pakistani, Bangladeshi, Iranian, Iraqi, Turkish and Indian communities, where I have seen a deep-rooted misogyny that perpetuates this form of abuse.

Some on the Left still refuse to accept that these are culturally rooted crimes, while religious and secular leaders in British-Asian communities are slow to come forward to condemn the men involved. No doubt I will be called racist for even pointing this out. It is nothing new.'

Ann Cryer recalled how, when an MP, seven women first appeared at her office one morning and explained that their daughters, mostly 12- and 13-year-olds, were being befriended by much older Pakistani men, lured to 'parties', and plied with drugs and alcohol before being sexually abused and raped. The women had the names and addresses of 65 men involved. After initial scepticism, it became clear to Ann Cryer that 'large-scale paedophile abuse was the norm for a section of the community' and it dated as far back as the eighties 'when it was first reported to the police' and that 'it was an open secret'.

When Ann Cryer took the matter to the police and social services, she expected disbelief but not to be 'flatly ignored by everyone' and that 'It was as if this crime was so toxic, no one could acknowledge its existence.'

In March 2018, it was revealed up to 1,000 children had been sexually abused and raped in the Shropshire town of Telford over a 40-year period. Telford has a population of about 170,000. In 2000, a 16-year-old girl and her sister and mother were killed in a fire started by a 26-year-old man who had got her pregnant. Another 13-year-old girl was killed in a car crash. Another girl died of a drug overdose after becoming a crack cocaine addict at the age of 12 while being abused by a grooming gang. One 14-year-old said she was groomed and abused and forced to have sex with several men 'night after night' in 'disgusting takeaways

234

and filthy houses'. The girl said nothing as she had been threatened the paedophiles would target her sisters and tell her mother she was a prostitute. There were numerous victims with similar experiences.

As with Sammy Woodhouse, a victim of the Rotherham child grooming gang, the police in Telford blamed the victims. An internal police memo stated that 'in most cases the sex is consensual'. Even in 2018, 46 girls in Telford were believed to be at risk.

A report by a barrister, David Spicer, into the grooming and sexual abuse of 700 girls in the North East of England, found the authorities were still allowing paedophile gangs to operate across the country. Various authorities had failed to even understand why White girls were being targeted and preferred to lock up the victims rather than confront the rapists and abusers. A gang of 18 paedophiles was believed to have assaulted 100 victims. The gang was eventually prosecuted for rape, sexual assault, trafficking, and inciting prostitution. The gangs operating in the Newcastle area were comprised of Bangladeshi, Indian, Iranian, Iraqi, Kurdish, Turkish, Albanian, and East European men. One 13-year-old had been gang-raped under a Kurdish flag.

In February 2018, the police claimed the numbers abused in Rotherham had increased to 1,510 and they needed 100 more officers besides the 144 presently engaged in the matter.

Sammy Woodhouse was refused compensation for the sexual abuse she suffered because she had allegedly given consent. She was only 14 when the 24-year-old Arshid Hussain groomed her for sex beneath the age of consent. Despite pregnancies, an abortion and then becoming a mother at 15, even when she was in social care, the Criminal Injuries Compensation Authority claimed she was a willing participant. A letter stated, 'I am not satisfied you were a victim of a sexual assault to which you did not in fact consent.' Sammy Woodhouse's claim for five years of 'intimidation, threats, and harassment' was rejected due to 'insufficient evidence'. After taking legal action, Sammy Woodhouse, now 32, was awarded an undisclosed amount.

By comparison, Abduirahman Mohammed, an illegal immigrant from Somalia, who had 30 convictions (e.g. burglary, possession of a knife, assaults and robberies), was awarded £78,500 on the grounds he had spent too long in detention awaiting deportation. He had been detained for 445 days. Aliou Bah, from Guinea, was awarded £110,000 for the same reason despite convictions for sexual assault. About 200 criminal illegal immigrants are awarded large sums of money every year in Britain. Up to 6,200 immigrant criminals were still free and at large in Britain at the time of writing and have not been deported.

Of the Rochdale rape victims of the Muslim grooming gangs, Lily Allen tweeted, 'Actually, there's a strong possibility they would have been raped or abused by somebody else at some point.' This tweet followed an earlier one in which she wrote, sarcastically, 'We should stop immigration because some brown men raped some white girls in Rochdale.'

In January 2020, a report surfaced as to a particularly vile scandal in Scotland – vile even by the UK's standards when grooming gangs are involved. Police in Glasgow shut down and then covered up a paedophile grooming gang, despite the members, consisting of 55 'asylum seekers or naturalized asylum seekers', having victimized at least 44 minors. Yet, despite successfully stopping the rapists, police kept the matter secret, choosing instead to keep the existence of the gang, along with the operation to shut them down, hidden from the public. *The Sun* obtained a briefing document from Police Scotland that revealed the members of the gang were from Iraq, Afghanistan, Pakistan, Egypt, Kurdistan, Morocco, and Turkey. Detective Inspector Sarah Taylor, from the National Child Abuse Investigation Unit, conducted a report and found that of the suspects, only 14 had been deported, eight were believed to be somewhere in the United Kingdom, one was in prison, one was pending deportation, and 22 were still in Glasgow.

The Labour MP Sarah Champion had previously described the gang rape epidemic of English girls as a 'national disaster' and demanded a task force to combat the 'horror'. She believed there could be as many as one million victims over a 30-year period.

Knife Crime

Knife crime is linked to both gang culture and drug dealing, with which non-Whites are disproportionately involved. In 2018, 1,144 children were arrested for carrying knives, including those as young as four. The growth of knife crime was linked to the growth in country lines gangs for selling drugs. In January 2019, a report from the National Crime Agency (NCA) estimated that up to 10,000 children as young as 11 were involved in county lines gangs. Some were believed to be pocketing £5,000 per day, with the crime calculated to be worth £500 million per year. Police had discovered 118 gangs with links to guns. The response from the authorities was feeble. Gaille Boia, who had killed someone to get a county lines phone, was awarded £52,000 in legal aid despite making £1,000 per day in running a county lines gang. He was convicted of manslaughter. Jen Lock, of Lives Instead of Knives, said, 'This sends out the message that crime does pay.' In March 2019, 21,484 people were caught with knives and other dangerous weapons (e.g. sharpened screwdrivers) in 2018. More than 60 per cent were let off without a jail sentence.

In May 2020, referring to the increase in knife crime in England and Wales to 45,627 in 2019, Priti Patel said, 'The figures are appalling. There is something so corrosive around knife crime that we absolutely have to break. There are things that we are doing. More officers – 100 per cent that is going to make a difference.' She further said: 'If you are caught with a knife, quite frankly, you will be going down and that is the right thing.'

In May 2019, the NCA director, Lynne Owens, warned that organised crime was costing the UK £37 billion per year. An NCA report revealed there were more than twice as many criminals involved in organised crime than soldiers in the Army. In August 2019, one county lines gang recruited 40 pupils, as young as 14, in the Kingsdown secondary school in Swindon, which has 1,200 pupils. In January 2020, even primary schools (children aged 4 to 11) were searching pupils for knives. For example, Darlington Council said one of its primary schools had a 'stop and search' policy, and Derbyshire Council had primaries using a 'risk-management approach' involving 'a period of searching with a parent on entry'.

In the final two months of 2019, there were 664 crimes involving machetes. This was up from around 100 per month for the same months three years previously. David Spencer of the Centre For Crime Prevention said, 'This huge growth in the use of machetes by hardened criminals is deeply troubling. There is absolutely no reason for anyone in the UK to own a machete. These new figures should hasten the outlawing of these brutal blades.' County lines criminals are resorting to machetes to spread fear. In addition, in May 2020, there was an increase in drug seizures in schools of a quarter over four years. There were 2,600 drugs cases reported to the police in England and Wales between 2016 and 2019.

Analysis from Scotland Yard and the National County Lines Coordination Centre showed that in the year to March 2020, 1,300 people involved with drug gangs in London were charged with over 2,000 offences, including 24 murders. 270 robberies, 160 assaults, more than 200 offences involving a weapon, and around 200 drug trafficking offences.

London gangs were estimated to account for approximately one-third of the county lines networks (for dealing drugs) in the UK. This meant the total extent of the criminality stemming from county lines was far higher.

A separate report revealed the drug dealers were using houses and empty hotels to sell their drugs rather than doing so on the streets. Dame Cressida Dick said, 'When violence breaks out between drugs gangs from somewhere like London it is very extreme, it is very shocking for people in market towns, villages and small cities.' She believed the tide was turning and said she was determined to destroy the gangs' business model.

An effective way to combat street crime was the use of stop and search. However, since this netted more Black people than White people, as Black people were more likely to be involved in street crime, then the tactic was curtailed amidst allegations of racism.

Globalisation

The extent of the Political AIDs and the grip of globalisation have led to the subversion of democracy. Globalisation is inherently anti-democratic, as the policy is focused on international organisations, the transfer of power to them, and the dismissal of the views and interests of the electorate. The Tory reaction to the Brexit vote is a prime example. The inability of the British ruling class to uphold the Brexit vote was an international embarrassment. Instead of 'taking back control' (the EU Vote Leave slogan), the UK, in 2020, had given up its representation in the EU and was subject to EU dictatorship in a transition period that was due to expire on 31 December 2020. The Brexit finally implemented was not one that the voters voted for and involved major concessions in both sovereignty and money. In *Turbo Brexit*, I wrote:

'Independence will be taken as consisting of three aspects. First, sovereignty and the ability of government to take decisions; equally important is their willingness to do so. A government might be sovereign, but if it continually defers decisions it should take to outside entities then that sovereignty becomes diluted or even worthless. Power is not the same as sovereignty, and the ability to implement a decision should be taken into consideration in the exercise of sovereignty.

Second, is military power and security. Is a sovereign, independent nation able to defend itself and its borders? Does it have the military capability to project forces to

239

support foreign policy objectives? Naturally, a puny military power will have less influence than a strong one.

Third, is the economy. Can the sovereign, independent nation pay its way? Can the government pay its bills and honour its obligations to its people? Currently, the British government cannot and successive governments have been dishonouring commitments to the public for a considerable time (the erosion of the state pension and social care being obvious examples). Can a country trade successfully and export sufficient goods and services to pay for imports? Currently, Britain cannot. Change is therefore necessary and this is an important reason for Turbo Brexit. Britain cannot afford to blunder on indefinitely as it is, as a member of the EU.'

Instead of simply leaving the EU and seizing the opportunity to reinstate the UK's independence and tackle the UK's many problems, the incoming prime minister in 2016, Theresa May, attempted to substitute a policy of creating a 'deep and special partnership' with the EU, rather than simply leaving. This proved as big a disaster as it was an act of treachery.

May proved herself to be a politically correct globalist. Globalisation is a policy in keeping with political correctness, as it undermines the nation state and the sense of nationhood. It transfers monies, power and governance to international institutions. National governments strive to adhere to international treaties, rules and interests and ignore national interests. Democracy is undermined if not ignored. Opposition to globalisation is widespread.

Immediately following the EU referendum, Lord Ashcroft, a pollster, immediately released an analysis of the result: 'How the United Kingdom voted on Thursday ... and why'. The report was highly informative. Of those who regarded themselves as English and not British, 79 per cent voted to leave, as did 66 per cent of those who considered themselves more English than British and 51 per cent of those who believed they were equally

English and British. Only 37 per cent of those who saw themselves as being more British than English voted to leave, as did only 40 per cent of those who said they were British and not English. Multiculturalism was regarded as a force for good by 71 per cent of Remain voters and a force for ill by 81 per cent of Leave voters. Globalisation was seen as a force for good by 51 per cent of Remain voters and a force for ill by 71 per cent of Leave voters. Immigration was seen as a force for good by 79 per cent of Remain voters and a force for ill by 80 per cent of Leave voters. It is notable that Remain voters were split down the middle on the issue of globalisation (51 per cent to 49 per cent), of which the EU is a part.

May's determination to thwart a genuine Brexit was obvious from the start of her premiership. She had no intention of simply leaving the EU, but instead manoeuvred to keep the UK involved to a very great extent. For example, In March 2017, May said:

> 'A number of MPs have used the term "divorce". I prefer not to use that term with regard to the European Union, because often, when people get divorced, they do not have a good relationship afterwards. MPs need to stop looking at this as simply coming out of the European Union and see the opportunity for building a new relationship with the European Union, as that is what we will be doing.'

For May, Brexit was not the people's rejection of globalisation, but an opportunity to extend it and replace subservience to the EU with subservience to a host of other international institutions like the UN and the WTO. Importantly, May craftily substituted a pro-EU policy in place of the Leave EU vote. 'Brexit means Brexit' was a useful slogan, but to May, Brexit meant a 'deep and special partnership with the EU'. In other words, the Leave vote should be replaced with a restoration of only a token sovereignty. Membership of the Single Market would be replaced with a comprehensive free-trade arrangement that, we were told, would require give and take (Britain would give, and the EU would take) and interim deals that would span many years. In the short to medium term, if not indefinitely, payments to the EU, free movement and subservience to the EU courts would continue.

A good example of May's globalism and political correctness was her speech to the UN in September 2016, shortly after she became prime minister. May began her speech by emphasising the global threats posed like 'war, political instability, abuses of human rights and poverty' and new threats such as 'global terrorism, climate change, and unprecedented mass movements of people'. She said, 'such challenges do not respect the borders of our individual nations and that only by working together shall we overcome them'.

May referred to the 'universal values that we share together' and Britain would 'honour our commitment to spend 0.7 per cent of our Gross National Income on development' and 'drive forward the implementation of the Sustainable Development Goals'. While she said, 'We will continue to stand up for the rules based international system and for international law', for her, national sovereignty was a secondary consideration.

May justified the phrase, 'we need this – our United Nations – to forge a bold new multilateralism', by claiming 'no country is untouched by the threat of global terrorism ... when extremists anywhere in the world can transmit their poisonous ideologies directly into the bedrooms of people vulnerable to radicalisation'. She said there would be 'the mass displacement of people, at a scale unprecedented in recent history' and 'when criminal gangs do not respect our national borders, trafficking our fellow citizens into lives of slavery and servitude, we cannot let those borders act as a barrier to bringing such criminals to justice'. She believed the United Nations was best placed to respond: 'as an international community, we must work together to adopt and implement the most comprehensive national action plans to tackle both the causes and the symptoms of all extremism'. She wanted to 'focus' on both violent and non-violent extremism, 'Islamist and neo-Nazi – hate and fear in all their forms'.

Having delved towards the cultural and racial friction, May then focused on immigration:

> 'Just as we need the United Nations to modernise to meet the challenges of terrorism in the 21st Century, so we also need to adapt if we are to fashion a truly global response to the mass movements of people across the world and the implications this brings for security and human rights.'

May openly sought to transfer control of immigration away from the nation state to international bureaucracies such as the UN. She said the 1951 UN Convention on Refugees and its 1967 protocol was a 'bedrock' and there were 65 million displaced people across the world, a figure which she readily admitted 'has almost doubled in a decade' – a fact that proved the failure of the UN and of which May did not grasp the implication.

(The 1951 UN Convention on Refugees, which is implemented alongside the European Convention on Human Rights and the UN Contention on Torture, commits a signatory to offer refuge to someone who has a 'well-founded fear of being persecuted for reasons of race, religion, nationality, membership of a particular social group or political opinion'.[187] The UN convention was introduced as a consequence of WWII and Nazism, as the 1930s restrictions in Germany meant German Jews had been unable to escape to safety. At the end of WWII, Europe had many refugees and holocaust survivors still living in refugee camps. The second paragraph of Article 1 states that the convention only applies to those who were refugees 'as a result of events occurring before 1st January 1951'.[188] This meant that the convention would only have a temporary effect to deal with a specific problem. However, in the 1960s, wars in Africa caused large numbers of refugees. This led to the resurrection of the 1951 convention and the introduction of the 1967 protocol, which simply removed half the sentence with the date limitation. The

UN convention was never intended to be used indefinitely in the way it has been, nor was it intended to be used to facilitate mass and illegal immigration).

May believed 'a managed and controlled international migration response' combined with 'investing to tackle the underlying drivers of displacement and migration at source' would allow the rejection of 'isolationism and xenophobia' and 'achieving better outcomes for all of our citizens'. This was political correctness. May dismissed the idea that government should also tackle the pull factors, such as the lack of border controls and so-called human rights nonsense that prevents illegal immigrants from being deported as 'isolationism and xenophobia'. For May, either someone believed in a 'controlled *international* migration response' or they believed in 'isolationism and xenophobia'.

May said, 'We must use our international law enforcement networks to track these criminals down (organised crime groups), wherever they are in the world, and put them behind bars where they belong':

> 'We need our law enforcement agencies to work together, with joint investigation teams working across multiple countries. Victims will only find freedom if we cultivate a radically new, global and co-ordinated approach to defeat this vile crime. Together we must work tirelessly to preserve the freedoms and values that have defined our United Nations from its inception.'

Once again, this is a globalist approach. May saw immigration control as a matter for international bureaucracies and not countries. She did not state Britain would take back control of its borders, despite the referendum vote.

> 'The United Kingdom has always been an outward-facing, global partner at the heart of international efforts to secure peace and prosperity for all our people. And that is how we will remain. For when the British people voted to

leave the EU, they did not vote to turn inwards or walk away from any of our partners in the world.'

Importantly, she said (italics my emphasis):

'Faced with challenges like migration, a desire for greater control of their country, and a mounting sense that globalization is leaving working people behind, they demanded a politics that is more in touch with their concerns; and bold action to address them. *But that action must be more global, not less.* Because the biggest threats to our prosperity and security do not recognise or respect international borders. And if we only focus on what we do at home, the job is barely half done. So this is not the time to turn away from our United Nations. It is the time to turn towards it.'

May was not alone in her globalism, and she and her ministers reinforced this through subsequent speeches and policies. The Tories revelled in it. May called a general election and proceeded to lose her majority. This was a disastrous result despite a huge lead in the polls when the election was called. Unlike the Labour manifesto, which contained some populist pledges to abolish tuition fees for students, the Tory one offered more austerity, political correctness and hid behind the 'Strong and Stable' slogan. They also launched a three-pronged assault on pensioners: the end of the triple lock on pensions, a means-testing of winter fuel payments, and a death tax to fund social care that became known as a dementia tax.

Having lost its majority, the May Government then gave in to any and every demand the EU made in the Article 50 negotiations. This split the Tory Party, and finally alienated public opinion when the date to leave the EU was repeatedly postponed.

While allowing EU immigrants to remain in Britain might be less problematic than trying to expel them, this largesse should not be ignored. For example, these EU immigrants occupy housing. The government estimated there were around 2.8 million EU immigrants. Migration Watch UK put the figure as more than 3.5 million by the time Britain was supposed to leave in 2019.[189] With around 92 per cent of these being of working age and with an average household occupancy rate of 1.92, then around 1,708,708 new houses would be required to increase the housing stock to meet the increased demand.[190]

Average house prices in England in March 2017 were £232,530. This average figure hides wide variations. Average house prices in London and the South East, where a disproportionate number of immigrants settle, were £471,742 and £311,514 respectively.[191] There were believed to be one million EU immigrants in London, and immigrants tend to settle in cities where the costs of housing are more expensive. To use ballpark figures, the cost of housing the EU immigrants was then at least £500 billion and could well be far higher. There is also the discrepancy between the official figures for the number of EU immigrants and the number of national insurance numbers issued (indicating the true number of immigrants was considerably greater). Furthermore, the numbers of non-EU immigrants worsened the strain on the housing stock. The children of immigrants, in turn, eventually need houses.

Britain has a desperate housing shortage, with immigrants taking over £1 trillion of housing stock. Britain does not have the resources to make good that cost, which, ultimately, is born by ordinary people in the form of higher costs for mortgages and rents, and lower standards of living by being denied home ownership, etc. Furthermore, there are the other costs of immigration as well. Yet the EU poured scorn on Britain's offer to confer residency rights on EU immigrants post-Brexit and even had the gall to demand up to £90 billion in a divorce payment! In reality, Britain should have billed them.

Worse still, by June 2021, more than six million EU citizens had applied for settled status, with another 58,200 applications coming in after the July 2021 deadline. The numbers applying were more than double the total EU citizens in the UK, according to government figures. The cost of housing these immigrants was around £1 trillion. Furthermore, the scale of the misestimation means the UK government has no clue who is in the UK – legally or illegally.

The Tory response to the Brexit vote demonstrated their ineffectuality. Their globalism and political correctness rendered them unable to govern properly. It is a further subversion of democracy. There are many other examples.

The Covid-19 pandemic presented an opportunity to try and resurrect a globalist agenda. A striking feature of the pandemic was that it was national governments that strove to combat the crisis and global institutions were useless, in particular the EU. Although it had its moments, the World Health Organization came in for criticism, especially given it was complicit in China's cover-up of the looming crisis. President Trump was not alone in criticising China for its responsibility for the spread of the Covid-19 virus. In March 2020, the Australian senator, Pauline Hanson, issued a statement:

'By refusing to take the appropriate steps required to prevent the evolution and spread of COVID19 coronavirus, China has put all human life, worldwide at risk. China must be called out and any attempts to attack or criticise people for referring to COVID19 as a "Chinese virus" should be pushed back on.

In recent history, it has been common to refer to viruses with reference to the area it originated. For example, MERS stands for Middle East Respiratory Syndrome. To the best of my knowledge, no one was ever called a racist for saying MERS. And the Spanish Flu was responsible for a global pandemic in 1918, but no one ever suggested the Spanish Flu was an offensive name. Attempts to hide the fact that COVID19 originated in China, shield China from criticism they rightfully deserve.

The threat of virus transmission from animals to humans caused by Chinese wet markets has been well documented for decades.'

There was an explanation for the WHO's failing. A report in *The Epoch Times* revealed that China controlled around one-third of the UN's agencies, and had placemen on the remaining agencies, including UNESCO. Former Assistant US Secretary of State for International Organization Affairs, Kevin Moley, described this ongoing takeover as 'the greatest existential threat to our republic since our founding'. He said, 'This is the fight of our lives. It is a struggle between Western civilisation and the Communist Party of China.'

Undeterred, in March 2020, former UK prime minister Gordon Brown announced, 'We need some sort of working executive.' Referring to his role in the financial crash of 2008, Brown continued, 'If I were doing it again, I would make the G20 a broader organisation because in the current circumstances you need to listen to the countries that are most affected, the countries that are making a difference and countries where there is the potential for a massive number of people to be affected – such as those in Africa.' He said the World Bank and the IMF needed an increase in their financial resources to cope with the impact of the crisis on low- and middle-income countries.

Later, a group of leaders and former leaders, including the three former British prime ministers Gordon Brown, Tony Blair and Sir John Major, called for a G20 summit and a £2 trillion fund to give to poor nations in response to the Covid-19 pandemic. They wanted 76 countries to no longer have to meet debt repayments. Gordon Brown said, 'Without a G20 leaders' meeting online soon and certainly long before the end of November, a vacuum in global leadership will open up just at the time when we need global action most – to avoid a second wave of Covid coming out of the poorest countries and to move the world economy from rescue operations to planning a global recovery.' In a letter, the leaders said, 'Without action from the G20, the recession caused by the pandemic will only deepen, hurting all economies and the world's most marginalised and poorest peoples and nations the most. Representing, as it does, 85 per cent of the world's nominal GDP, the G20 has the capacity to lead the mobilisation of resources on the scale required. We urge leaders to do so immediately.'

While many were calling for an enquiry into how the Covid-19 infection developed and China's culpability, Theresa May took a typically globalist line in an article, arguing, 'A highly infectious novel virus, life-threatening for many, might seem to be just the sort of thing countries would want to work together on. Instead, it has been treated as a national issue for countries to deal with alone.' May proceeded to condemn a populist approach that 'views the world through a prism of winners and losers and sees compromise and co-operation as signs of weakness'.

Rather than confronting China, May wanted 'to engage with China to ensure that it adopts higher standards on intellectual property, carbon emissions, human rights, and regional security'. May further repudiated President Trump's decision to stop funding certain international institutions, and said, 'Any frustrations we have about the performance of institutions like the World Health Organization should be channelled into reforming them, not denigrating the concept of international co-operation.'

May stuck resolutely to her globalist agenda. In an article for the *Daily Mail* in January 2021, May argued that 'once again' the shared values of the USA and the UK of 'respect for human dignity and human rights, freedom of speech and thought, representative democracy, equality and the rule of law' were 'under threat'. May argued this new threat was not only external from countries such as China and Russia, but also internal as the protest at the Capitol building in the USA had proved. May then referred to the jihadist attack near the House of Commons, when PC Keith Palmer was killed. For May, the Capitol building protest was 'an assault by a partisan mob whipped up by an elected president'.

May wrote, 'I set "Global Britain" as our foreign policy goal because I wanted to ensure that the UK did not turn in on itself or become isolated after Brexit.' Pointing out that the economic consequences of Covid-19 had yet to impact, May wrote:

'Last year the UK led a collective effort to fund global work on vaccines. Now, as countries close their borders in response to Covid, we must work collectively to find a way of living with the virus. This challenge makes the concept of Global Britain even more salient ... For this potential to be realised, there needs to be a change in world politics.

For too long we have been sliding toward absolutism in international affairs: if you are not 100 per cent for me then you must be 100 per cent against me. In this world there is no room for mature compromise. Indeed, compromise is seen as a dirty word. In fact, the opposite is true.'

May heralded the need for more compromise, rather than 'a few strongmen fac[ing] off against each other', and Britain should play 'a decisive role'. May continued:

'Threatening to break international law by going back on a treaty we had just signed and abandoning our position of global moral leadership as the only major economy to meet both the 2 per cent defence spending target and the 0.7 per cent international aid target were not actions which, in my view, raised our credibility in the eyes of the world ... The world does not owe us a prominent place on its stage. Whatever the rhetoric we deploy, it is our actions which count. So, we should do nothing which signals a retreat from our global commitments.'

The article was interpreted as a not too subtle attack on Boris Johnson, who promptly rejected the thrust of the article by pointing out what the UK was doing. When asked in the House of Commons whether the UK still provided moral leadership, Boris Johnson replied, 'Yes ... we continue to spend substantial amounts of money on aid to support international development and we will continue to do so this year despite the temporary cuts to the aid budget. We continue to provide more aid spending than almost any country in the world.'

Of far more importance, referring to stock market chaos in March, the Bank of England governor, Andrew Bailey, told Sky News, 'We basically had a pretty near meltdown of some of the core financial markets. We were seeing things that were pretty unprecedented, certainly in recent times. We were facing serious disorder.' The Bank of England reacted with £200 billion of quantitative easing (QE), of which Bailey said, 'I think we would have a situation where in the worst element, the Government would have struggled to fund itself in the short run.' In other words, the government would have been gone bust and been unable to pay its bills. Yet still the overseas aid flowed out and still the Tory backbenchers objected to the minor cuts in the scale of it. Yet still senior politicians were eager to splash trillions around in the Third World in response to the Covid-19 pandemic.

The Bank announced yet another £100 billion of QE, totalling £745 billion since the 2008 financial crisis. By May 2020, government debt had reached £1.95 trillion, after the government borrowed £55.2 billion in that month. Tax receipts plunged by 28.4 per cent in the year to May.

Figures showed the UK had the deepest fall in GDP of 20.4 per cent in the second quarter (April to June) of any Western country. By comparison, the USA had a fall of 9.5 per cent, Germany, 10.1 per cent, France 13.8 per cent, South Korea 3.3 per cent – while China had enjoyed growth of 11.5 per cent. The UK's fall wiped out 17 years of growth and reduced the UK to an economy smaller than in 2003.

The UK Government borrowed £221.4 billion in the first five months of 2020. A sum of £35.9 billion was borrowed in August, taking the national debt to £2.023 trillion – equivalent to £72,000 per household.

In June 2020, the government announced it was keen to end the triple-lock guarantee to the state pension (that the pension would increase each year in line with whichever was the highest: average earnings, or inflation, or 2.5 per cent). As sure as night follows day, they also announced on the same day there would be yet more QE – i.e. money printing. Once again, cutting back on the state pension was the first resort to balancing income and expenditure as the money ran out. Paul Dales, chief UK economist at Capital Economics said:

> 'May's further fall in inflation is probably only the beginnings of a prolonged period of very soft price pressure that we think will prompt the Bank of England to announce a total of £350 billion more QE, starting with £100 billion – or maybe even £150 billion – at today's policy meeting. This would push up the total amount of QE since the last financial crisis to almost £1 trillion.
>
> By pumping more money into the system this will boost demand and businesses can put their prices up.'

The total QE programme had reached £895 billion. Of this, £875 billion was for the purchase of government bonds, and £20 billion for the purchase of UK corporate bonds. In other words, £875 billion was to pay for government spending.

Boris Johnson's press secretary said, 'On the triple lock, these are unique and challenging economic circumstances and we cannot hide from that. As you know, decisions on tax and pension policy are set out at budget. But there are no plans to abolish the triple lock, and we will always stand by pensioners.'

Officials were concerned that due to wages being depressed in 2020, there might be a bounce back in 2021, thus leading to a larger than otherwise increase in the state pension in 2022. Some feared the total annual cost could be as much as £20 billion annually. Sir Steve Webb, a former pensions minister in the Cameron-led coalition government, said, 'Crudely applying the triple lock at a time of historic volatility in earnings could lead to huge state pension increases when many of working age have lost their job.' Steve Baker, a Tory member of the Commons Treasury select committee, said:

'We can't afford it. Obviously we need to look after pensioners, but in the current environment a double lock on earning and inflation would be far more affordable. We are looking at it running into three or four parliaments. We are looking at the public finances being in a genuinely catastrophic state. We are all going to have to make very hard choices. In a deflationary environment, a fixed minimum on pensions increasing will produce anger in those not seeing those benefits.'

The triple-lock was ended. The overseas aid gravy train continued.

Antisense

Antisense can be defined as being 'Marxist, malevolent, pre-meditated gibberish'. It goes well beyond nonsense and has a subversive intent. The aim is to replace common sense, facts and wisdom with gibberish laced with Marxism. It is a part of critical theory to replace established facts – reality – with gibberish, and thereby undermine society.

A good example is the following one of Mary Seacole. Controversially, the BBC children's programme *Horrible Histories* had a sketch in which the Jamaican-born Seacole was prevented from becoming a nurse during the Crimean War by Florence Nightingale, who held in the sketch that the role was 'only for British girls'. In the sketch, Seacole said, 'Four times me tried to join Old Lamp-Face's nurses in the Crimean War, and four times she said no.' Although Seacole was depicted as Black, she was, in fact, three-quarters White. She was proud of her Scottish heritage and considered herself to be White and Scottish.

This sketch was a complete lie and an invention. Seacole never applied for a job with Florence Nightingale and was not even medically qualified. However, a spokesman for BBC's children's television claimed the aim had been 'to open up a discussion about some of the attitudes of the time'. If such were the 'attitudes of the time', one wonders why the BBC had to invent lies about it. Eventually, even the BBC Trust admitted the sketch was 'materially inaccurate'.

In fact, Seacole travelled to Crimea to set up what might be described as a restaurant and bar, selling food and wine to officers. On arrival, she sought out Florence Nightingale and, according to Seacole's own memoirs, Florence Nightingale greeted her saying, 'What do you want, Mrs Seacole? Anything we can do for you? If it lies in my power, I shall be very happy.' Seacole wanted and was given a bed for the night before she continued on her journey to Balaclava.

Schoolchildren are even required to repeat the lies about Seacole to pass exams. For example, one GCSE paper required pupils to 'briefly describe the career of Mary Seacole'. To answer the question correctly, the pupils needed to lie. For example, Seacole's establishment was required to be described as a 'British hospital'. Furthermore, there are some children's books which completely misrepresent Seacole's status and activities.

But the Seacole saga did not end there. A Mary Seacole Memorial Statue Appeal, headed by Lord Clive Soley (a former Labour MP), was determined to erect a large statue 'to facilitate a memorial statue to commemorate Mary Jane Seacole; nurse and heroine of the Crimean War', with further plans for a 'memorial garden'. As is often the case, the appeal was unable to raise sufficient funds and experienced 'soaring' construction costs. Even so, a site was cleared and even 'blessed'. The site chosen was none other than St Thomas' Hospital, where Florence Nightingale founded the first nurse training school in the world. The Seacole statue's dimensions were so large it would dwarf the existing Florence Nightingale statue already at the hospital. The Seacole enterprise described Seacole as a 'Pioneer Nurse', which is something Seacole never claimed to be and was completely untrue.

Shamefully, George Osborne, the Tory chancellor, stepped in with public monies to bail out the scheme and £240,000 was pledged. This is to peddle a lie. A letter from the Nightingale Society to Osborne pointed out:

> 'The massive grant to the Mary Seacole statue is misplaced in three important respects: (1) Seacole was not a nurse, let alone a "Pioneer Nurse", nor ever claimed to be one (in her book, "nurses" are Nightingale and her nurses); (2) the place is wrong, as St Thomas' Hospital was for more than a century the home of the Nightingale School of Nursing, the first professional training school in the world, from which pioneers went out to bring the standards of the new profession to other countries. (3) It was Nightingale, not Seacole, who prepared briefs for committees, wrote and met with MPs and Cabinet ministers to press for reforms in nursing and health care.'

That someone such as Florence Nightingale, who did so much to save lives and develop the profession of nursing and who might normally be regarded as a true female role model, should be denigrated and smeared in this way demonstrates the malevolence and falsity of political correctness and those who practise it – including the Tories (demonstrating they are woke-Right). Further, to force schoolchildren to lie in order to pass exams regarding someone who is presented as being Black when she was not, presented as being a nurse when she was not, and someone who pioneered nursing when she did not, is antisense – Marxist, malevolent, pre-meditated gibberish.

Another example of antisense is the response to Islamist terrorism. For example, in the run up to the US 2016 presidential campaign, a Muslim committed mass murder in a homosexual bar in Orlando. The media, politicians and pressure groups tried to blur the fact this was an act of terrorism or, if it was an act of terrorism, then it was also a 'hate crime'.

Much of the reporting in Britain was taken up with a snooty denunciation of Donald Trump, who allegedly had responded to the murders in a manner and tone not befitting a president. In reference to a Donald Trump comment, Ed Miliband, a failed ex-Labour leader, wrote, 'Can there be a more heinous, self-serving, disqualifying statement about the murder of 50 people?' A quick answer to the question is to cite the question itself.

In fact, Donald Trump had been proved correct in his determination to confront radical Islam and in his willingness to restrict immigration. This was a common-sense approach rather than a politically correct one. It was also one likely to attract voter support.

BBC2 program, Newsnight, interviewed Pedro Julio Serrano, a gay activist from Puerto Rico and a 'senior advisor' at New York City Council. He regarded the mass murder as a hate crime and was hostile towards Donald Trump, who he lumped in with those he regarded as perpetuating hate and hence in some way responsible for the hate crime. He pointedly rejected the idea Donald Trump was right to advocate the restriction of Muslim immigration.

In Britain, one gay activist terminated a review of the day's newspapers on Sky News and walked out in anger at the murders not being described as homophobic attacks. Another prominent gay activist posted pictures of himself online holding a placard proclaiming solidarity with Muslims against the English Defence League (which was formed after Muslim extremists demonstrated against a parade for the return of troops from active service). Did these gay activists actually consider what they were doing?

The Orlando killer, who was from a wealthy family, was reportedly on an FBI watch list due to suspected extremism. The killer's father fancied himself as being the president of Afghanistan (from where he originated) and had released extremist videos on YouTube ('Our warrior brothers in [the] Taliban movement and national Afghan Taliban are rising up' and, just after the murders, 'God will punish those involved in homosexuality'). The killer rang the police three times just before and during the murder spree, claiming allegiance with Islamic State and al-Nusra extremists, and was 'laughing frantically' as he murdered. The killer was further alleged to have been using gay dating websites, and to have frequented the homosexual club involved where he had been trying to pick up gay men. In which case, the killer was not only a Muslim extremist but also an aspiring, if not active, homosexual – despite being married.

The evidence pointed towards the murders being another act of radical Muslim terrorism, or an extreme gay-on-gay act of violence, with the perpetrator being of dubious mental stability. It was not a homophobic attack by society in general on an oppressed gay community.

The attempts to impose a politically correct interpretation of what happened were wrong. It was the same reflex to impose dogma that led to the authorities, including the police, tolerating mass paedophilia in Rotherham; that led to judges corrupting human rights legislation to facilitate people smuggling, despite the people smugglers including organised criminals and terrorists (like ISIS); and that led to mass immigration despite the deaths of immigrants trying to invade the West and despite the known hostility of many of those immigrants to certain groups in particular, such as Jews and homosexuals, and the West in general.

Those gay activists who support other minorities in a hoped-for common cause against the host society, and hence support mass immigration of those who openly mean them harm, should take the trouble to rethink their political correctness. Those they claim to represent are being very poorly served. It is time that state funding for gay pressure groups was ended.

The allegation that any politician who warns of the danger of Islamist terrorism is the cause of that terrorism, and that the terrorists are motivated due to an atmosphere of hate created by those who warn of the dangers of Islam rather than being motivated by Islam, is antisense. It is an attempt to upstage the facts and impose a Marxist, malevolent, pre-meditated gibberish as the truth.

In the UK, a recent similar example was the murder of the Tory MP Sir David Amess in October 2021. The police eventually stated the murderer was a Somali with British citizenship, who had previously been on the anti-terrorist Prevent programme, and who had killed the MP in a frenzied attack with a knife and made no effort to escape the scene. The response from the media and politicians was to blame social media, which had allegedly created an atmosphere of hate. The television media were keen to describe the murderer as a British citizen, often not mentioning his Somali nationality, and continually dragged the far-Right into the reporting. Politicians were keen to increase social media censorship. Once again, the strategy was to upstage the facts with antisense.

In reference to military vehicles, including tanks, another example of antisense was the remark by General Sir Mark Carleton-Smith, at an arms fair in London, that, 'The challenge is to lead the world in the development of equipment which is not only battle winning but also environmentally sustainable.' He believed there was a need to put 'the army on the right side of the environmental argument'. Further, new recruits 'increasingly make career decisions based on a prospective employer's environmental credentials'. War is by its nature not environmentally climate friendly, and quite where the general thought he was going to find the charging points on a battlefield for the military vehicles was not explained.

A new phenomenon in political correctness is the rise of the trans campaign, and the sustained demands of gay pressure groups despite achieving almost everything they originally wanted. A primary target has been children. This is not only an example of producer capture.

A sinister aspect of the trans agenda is the aggressive promotion of antisense. A good example was the 'victory for transgender rights campaigners' relating to the introduction of 'new sex education lessons' to teach schoolchildren 'all genders' can have periods. This was approved by Brighton & Hove City

Council, UK, claiming to be trying to tackle stigma around menstruation. A council report stated, 'Trans boys and men and non-binary people may have periods. Menstruation must be inclusive of all genders.' The report recommended 'language and learning about periods is inclusive of all genders, cultures, faiths and sexual orientations'. For example, 'girls and women and others who have periods'. Bins for menstruation products would be available in all toilets for children. The council had recently introduced a 'Trans Inclusion Schools Toolkit' for teachers, which told them that not referring to children by their preferred pronoun or name might constitute harassment.

Another example of antisense was the proposed TV advertising campaign in the USA portraying menstruating men and boys. 'MENstruation for Period-Proof Underwear' was due to run on 18 channels. However, ABC, CBS and BBC America all rejected the ads.

The American Civil Liberties Union called for the provision of tampons in men's toilets. Their alleged aim was to prevent discrimination against 'every person who menstruates'. They complained, 'While free menstrual products are not uniformly provided in women's restrooms, they are almost never available in men's restrooms, even for pay.'

When someone put up some stickers in Oxford, England, stating, 'Woman: noun. Adult human female' and 'Women don't have penises', PC Plod treated the matter as a serious crime. Thames Valley Police appealed for witnesses, announcing that those responsible could be charged with a public-order offence.

Cheshire Police quizzed a man for half-an-hour after merely 'liking' a tweet deemed to be offensive to transgender people. The deputy chief constable of Cheshire police, Julie Cooke, took to Twitter to warn about the dangers of misgendering on 'Pronouns Day'. This is another example of producer capture. Would people pay the police and teachers to peddle such tripe? The problem is that they do via the tax system. State agencies get monies from taxes and just do as they like.

The Planned Parenthood, in the USA, recommended on its website that if a child asks why girls and boys are physically

259

different, the parents should raise the issue of transgender identity:

> 'While the most simple answer is that girls have vulvas and boys have penises/testicles, that answer isn't true for every boy and girl. Boy, girl, man and woman are words that describe gender identity, and some people with the gender identities "boy" or "man" have vulvas, and some with the gender identity "girl" or "woman" have penises/testicles. Your genitals don't make you a boy or a girl.'

This is antisense. Tim Wildmon, president of the American Family Association, responded, 'Gender is not fluid, either you have a penis or you don't. What Planned Parenthood is promoting here is just stupidity masked as sensitivity. If you're an adult and trying to talk to a child about whether they're really a boy or girl, you're at risk of harming them psychologically.' He believed that there was no reason to bring up the issue at such a young age 'unless a boy or girl is exhibiting behaviour or says that they're messed up about what they are'.

In August 2019, in Wichita, Kansas, a library got into a pickle over the issue of whether to automatically bar sex offenders from making presentations. It followed a rumpus over the revelation some of those involved in the Drag Queen Story Hour were convicted paedophiles and prostitutes. Thomas Witt, Equality Kansas director, objected, 'It's clear why they're checking for sex offences only: they're trying to label the LGBT population in this city as sex offenders, which is offensive in and of itself. These are public presentations in one of the most open and public places in the city of Wichita. I doubt very seriously it's a venue for predators.'

Cynthia Berner, library director, said she opposed letting sex offenders present to children but wanted to leave open the possibility of letting them participate in adults-only discussions. Pastor Craig Coffey, who protested the previous year's drag event and led the push for the new rule, said, 'Numerous incidents are being reported (nationwide) involving inappropriate contact between drag queen story hour participants and innocent children. Those of us opposing these types of ill-advised programming policies are not surprised, as we see this as a natural consequence of the LGBTQ agenda as it is directed toward progressive liberal indoctrination of our children.'

Incidents of 'inappropriate conduct' included drag queens teaching children to twerk, soliciting their email addresses, having children lay on them, and promoting homosexuality and gender fluidity. The San Francisco-based Drag Queen Story Hour openly stated that its aim was to capture the 'imagination and play of the gender fluidity of childhood' and presenting the children with 'unabashedly queer role models'. Dylan Pontiff, a Louisiana drag queen, bragged his aim was 'the grooming of the next generation'.

Pontiff, whose drag name is Santana Pilar Andrews, revealed his agenda at a meeting in September 2018 at the Lafayette City-Parish Council in Louisiana, when he said, 'This is going to be the grooming of the next generation. We are trying to groom the next generation ... I can go in and entertain adults in a club and also entertain a group of students and young children. I'm able to do that because I'm an adult and able to filter myself.' Many shook their heads in bewilderment at these remarks.

John Ritchie, director of TFP Student Action, said:

> 'Unfortunately, the Drag Queen Story Hour program is turning public libraries into platforms to advance the transgender revolution, places where pro-homosexual activists are given access to children as young as three. Instead of protecting the precious innocence of our children with wholesome stories, libraries are misusing our tax-dollars to harm their innocence. To attempt to dismantle and destroy the distinction between male and female is not only biologically ridiculous, but also a direct attack against God's plan for us and for the family.

Everyone who loves the family should wake up, pray and push back.'

Leslie Alexander, a local resident, told the *Lafayette Daily Advertiser* that the library should not have approved the drag queen story hour event without consulting the public:

'This is not about tolerance or anti-bullying. It is a direct and intentional effort to create gender confusion and doubt among very young children at the very time they need solid guidance and understanding. The intent is to plant a seed to make children more likely to question their sexuality or gender at a later age.'

Pontiff was not the first gay or trans activist to boast of his real intentions. For example, as far back as 1987, the homosexual activist, Michael Swift, wrote in the *Gay Community News*, 'We shall seduce them in your schools … They will be recast in our image. They will come to crave and adore us.' In 2011, US gay activist, Daniel Villarreal wrote for Queerty.com:

'Why would we push anti-bullying programs or social studies classes that teach kids about the historical contributions of famous queers unless we wanted to deliberately educate children to accept queer sexuality as normal? We want educators to teach future generations of children to accept queer sexuality. In fact, our very future depends on it. Recruiting children? You bet we are.'

In 2015, Canadian gay activist Sason Bear Bergman, a woman who identifies as a transgender man, wrote an article titled 'I Have Come to Indoctrinate Your Children Into My LGBTQ Agenda (And I'm Not a Bit Sorry)'. Bergman said, 'I am here to tell you: All that time I said I wasn't indoctrinating anyone with my beliefs about gay and lesbian and bi and trans and queer

262

people? That was a lie,' and that the aim was to make children 'like us' even if it 'goes against the way you have interpreted the teachings of your religion.'

A high-profile child activist, Nemis, known as 'Lactatia', is a young boy who dresses as a girl. His Instagram account, written by his mother, says, 'Choose Love. Be Proud. Smash the Patriarchy and be kind to one another, always! #pride #lovenothate #loveislove #nonbinary #thefutureisfluid'. He controversially posed for a picture dressed as a girl next to a naked male drag queen.

In June 2019, in the UK, a library in Southend-on-Sea introduced LGBT story readings for primary school pupils, some as young as five, to be given by drag artists. The local council supported the Drag Story Time idea. A spokesman said the event was to 'celebrate difference in a fun, safe, educational and age-appropriate environment'.

In November 2019, it was revealed David Lee Richardson, aka 'Miss Kitty Litter' – a drag queen who had been reading stories to children – had a conviction for prostitution in 1996. On social media, he was inclined to make 'perverse jokes and allusions to prostitution'.

An LGBTQ channel calling itself 'Queer Kid Stuff' sought to instruct toddlers, as young as 3-years-old, regarding gender 'transitioning'. The charity Educate and Celebrate, founded by Elly Barnes, 'transforms schools' into LGBTQ-friendly places by 'predominantly training teachers' to be 'confident in the language of gender identity and sexual orientation'. Barnes was open that the 'bottom line' was to train teachers to 'completely smash heteronormativity'.

Sarah Hopson, a primary school teacher from Warrington, told the BBC she conditions school children as young as six to accept LGBTQ ideology while they're young and impressionable, so they'll be less likely to accept a Christian view of sexuality later on in life: 'The more they can be accepting of "diversity" at this age – you're not going to face it further on, because the children will be accepting now and will be accepting this diversity around them.' The school introduced 'non-gender-specific' uniforms and its website declared 'any form of homophobia, transphobia and biphobia is unacceptable', and posts a code of conduct declaring 'respect' for anyone's 'gender identity', 'marriage', or 'sexual orientation'. Young children were required to write gay love letters. BBC Radio Manchester shared a video on its Facebook page showing six-year-olds being made to write love letters from one male story character to another male.

In November 2019, the board of the largest school in Ottowa asked kindergarten-age children about religion, gender identity and sexuality. One aim was to uncover how many might be gay.

Also in November 2019, in defence of a decision to invite an adult male entertainer, who performs at strip clubs, to spend the day with young school children, Anthony Lane, a school teacher at Willis High School in Texas, was openly contemptuous towards the parents of the schoolchildren, saying on Facebook:

> 'I believe that raising a child is the responsibility of the community, and that parents should not have the final say. Let's be honest, some of you don't know what is best for your kids. I have learned a ton about what is best for Ethan from his teachers, not the other way around. Parents believe they should be able to storm the school in the name of political and religious beliefs if something happens in the school that they are morally opposed to. They forget that we make a promise to prepare their children to live in a diverse world. We are not required to protect the misguided, bigoted views of their parents.'

Lane proceeded to tell parents to remove their children from the education system if they wanted them taught with their values, as the public system was 'not here to serve your archaic beliefs'. Not surprisingly, Lane deleted his post after it went viral and attracted adverse comment.

Teachers at the Austin Independent School District in Texas showed similar contempt. Trustees voted to introduce a radical sex education policy despite fierce opposition from parents. The policy included teaching children how to have anal and oral sex, gender issues and the LGBT movement. Children were encouraged not to use the terms 'mother' and 'father' as 'this can limit their understanding of gender into binaries and can exclude children who may not identify within these identities'. One parent complained, 'The curriculum is an attack on Christianity and family and on parental rights.' This complaint is, of course, true, and is the real agenda.

Activist Mommy highlighted the determination to indoctrinate children, the younger the better, and negate the influence of the parents in 2017. She drew attention to the UK's Drag Queen Story Time, that was held by seven nurseries by the London Early Years Foundation. The *Daily Mail* reported:

> 'Drag queens are being brought into taxpayer-funded nursery schools so that children as young as two can learn about transgender issues. The cross-dressers are reading nursery rhymes and singing specially adapted songs "to teach children about LGBT tolerance". Nursery bosses say the sessions are needed so that children can "see people who defy rigid gender restrictions" and grow up to combat hate crime.'

Activist Mommy wrote, 'So, let me get this straight: somehow confusing and most likely frightening toddlers will reduce hate crimes? Seriously? There could not possibly be any data to back this up because only in 2017 would anyone actually think it was OK for cross-dressers to read stories to nursery school children.' In the *Daily Mail*, a 'leading child psychotherapist' Dilys Daws said, 'There's this idea that's sweeping the country that being transgender is an "ordinary situation". It's getting so much publicity that it's getting children thinking that they might be transgender, when it otherwise wouldn't have occurred to them.' Norman Wells, director of the Family Education Trust, agreed: 'One of the most disturbing things about the transgender agenda is the way that it tries to distort our perception of reality and deny something as fundamental as the distinction between male and female.' In other words, it is antisense.

In addition to the story hour, there was also 'Halloween drag disco', face painting and 'high tea'. Thomas Canham, a Bristol University law graduate and part-time cross-dresser, instigated the scheme. He told the *Daily Mail* he 'dismisses traditional notions of masculinity as "meaningless"'. Canham claimed he wanted a 'safe space' where children would not be 'criticized for wearing a dress'. Included might be songs such as with Wheels On The Bus, 'the skirt on the drag queen goes swish, swish, swish'. Further, and tellingly, Canham said, 'The parents love it, and the children love it too – especially when you've got a six-year-old boy there in a princess dress which he isn't allowed to wear at home because his dad doesn't like it.' Is Dad wrong, and who is to judge?

Supplementing Drag Queens has been the emergence of Drag Kids, who perform provocatively and often in a sexualised setting. Men throwing money at boys is not unknown. In Toronto, Lactatia sashayed on a catwalk, as the audience showed its approval. Another performer, Miss Fluffy Souffle, decked out in a lilac wig and pink tutu, said afterwards, 'I kind of feel like no one was prepared for that!'

In the UK, the Scottish National Party MP, Mhairi Black, was criticised for visiting Glencoats Primary School in her constituency with a drag act called 'Flowjob'. Flowjob read to pupils aged four and five. Black branded her critics as homophobes and congratulated the school for hosting a 'great day'. However, the Renfrewshire council accepted the visit was 'not appropriate' and issued an apology.

One trick used in New Jersey was to introduce a new LGBT curriculum that was integrated into ordinary lessons such as history, maths, science, etc. The aim of this approach was to force the LGBT agenda onto children without their parents being able to opt out. In December 2019, the Stonewall campaign group pulled the same trick. Stonewall wanted children as young as five to be taught about lesbian, gay and transgender issues in every school subject with the rainbow flag used to help youngsters learn colours. In guidance issued to coincide with the launch of new sex and relationships lessons, Stonewall said teaching about LGBT people should be 'embedded' in timetables. In the USA, CNN reported:

> 'Illinois Gov. J.B. Pritzker signed into law a bill that ensures the contributions of LGBTQ people are taught in public schools. ... [The bill states] 'In public schools only, the teaching of history shall include a study of the roles and contributions of lesbian, gay, bisexual, and transgender people in the history of this country and this State. Equality Illinois, the state's largest LGBTQ civil rights advocacy organization, supported the bill and said the curriculum can have a positive effect on students' self-image and make their peers more accepting.'

The politically correct have long recognised the importance of history and its usefulness for propaganda purposes. A joke in the Soviet Union was, 'In the Soviet Union, the future is known; it's the past that is always changing.'

Another problem was sport, where men who claim to be women can compete with women and, due to their male physique, will mostly win. Even so, according to David Zirin, sports editor of *The Nation*: 'There is another argument against allowing trans athletes to compete with cis-gender athletes that suggests that their presence hurts cis-women and cis-girls. But this line of thought doesn't acknowledge that trans women are in fact women.' Rep. Ilhan Omar, in a letter to USA Powerlifting, claimed, 'The myth that trans women have a "direct competitive advantage" is not supported by medical science.' Sunu Chandy of the National Women's Law Center claimed, 'There's no research to support the claim that allowing trans athletes to play on teams that fit their gender identity will create a competitive imbalance.' Research does not trump common sense, and the idea that people cannot rely upon common sense and have an opinion is antisense. Men are stronger than women.

In the real world, meanwhile, Laurel Hubbard, a weightlifter from New Zealand, won several gold and silver medals at the 2019 Pacific Games in Samoa in three female categories. Hubbard was physically male.

In September 2019, Selina Soule failed to qualify for a track event in New England regionals after being beaten by two biological males, who claimed to be female. Selina Soule said:

> 'I've lost opportunities to compete at world-class tracks, [and] I've lost opportunities to compete in front of college coaches and gain attention, and I've lost opportunities to win titles. I know that I'm not the only girl who has missed out on opportunities. There are countless other girls who have lost meets, and titles, and their drive to compete as hard as they can because they know that they'll never be good enough to compete against these athletes.'

A leading noise on social media of the trans movement is the Canadian Jonathan 'Jessica' Yaniv, who is physically a male but describes himself as female. As Activist Mommy put it, he had not 'finally been arrested for the vast evidence of sexual harassment toward young girls, predatory desires to throw a topless pool party with children as young as twelve, or his gross abuse of Canada's human rights laws in forcing aestheticians to preform Brazilian waxes on his male genitalia'. At the time, in August 2019, Yaniv posted he 'had to miss out on a dip at the pool in his hometown of Langley, British Columbia because he forgot his tampons'. This, again, is a perfect example of antisense.

With a picture of himself, Yaniv tweeted: 'My period started so ya, couldn't go into the pool. But it was so much fun! Forgot my tampons in my other bag fml.' He soon took down the tweet when it attracted derision. Activist Mommy said:

> 'What else could possibly explain a grown man complaining on social media that he couldn't get in the

268

pool because he "forgot his tampons"? He is either hilariously delusional, or, equally as likely, he's going to ridiculous lengths to build up his "Jessica" persona while he continues to exploit society's love affair with the transgender movement for his own benefit.'

Yaniv's attention-seeking antics started to grate. In December 2019, after complaining that a gynaecologist had refused to treat him or other transgender patients, he tweeted: 'Are they allowed to do that legally?' Jay Cameron, a litigation manager at the Justice Centre for Constitutional Freedoms, had already told him that self-identification:

'...does not erase physiological reality. Our clients do not offer the service requested. No woman should be compelled to touch male genitals against her will, irrespective of how the owner of the genitals identifies. You could, of course, more or less say the same thing for gynaecologists. They are supposed to treat women's anatomy. That's what they specialize in – and it's why women visit them. A man may identify as a woman but – I'll try to explain this very slowly so Yaniv understands it – that does not magically turn his male body parts into those of a woman. Sorry. It just doesn't.'

Yaniv, who had already made more than a dozen other similar claims, lost a case before the British Columbia Human Rights Tribunal in Canada over a request for a bikini wax. The salon staff refused, which led Yaniv to make a claim for discrimination. The tribunal said Yaniv had 'manufactured the conditions for a human rights complaint, and then leveraged that complaint to pursue a financial settlement from parties who were unsophisticated and unlikely to mount a proper defence', and ruled, 'Human rights legislation does not require a service provider to wax a type of genitals they are not trained for and have not consented to wax.'

One 45-year-old sex offender, bald and bespectacled, claimed he identified as an eight-year-old girl, and that child pornography was a matter of free speech. In December 2019, it was announced Britain's first transgender couple were to allow their five-year-old child to start transitioning. They claimed they did not encourage this.

In the USA, by November 2019, there was some pushback. Republican State Representative Ginny Ehrhart, from Georgia, proposed a change in the law to make gender transition surgery on children illegal. This would include procedures such as mastectomy, vasectomy, castration, and a ban on the prescription of puberty-blocking drugs. In Texas, the Republican Representative Matt Krause likewise advocated legislative change to prohibit puberty-blocking drugs for children under the age of 18. In Kentucky, the Republican State Representative Savannah Maddox drafted a similar bill, saying: 'I am sure that many of you have read about the shocking case of this 7 yr old boy in Texas whose parents are in the midst of an ugly courtroom battle as a result of his mother's desire to transition his gender from male to female, but truth be told this has been in my mind and on my heart for quite a while.' On Facebook she wrote, 'I am a strong advocate for parents' rights – but it is not the right of a parent to permanently alter a child's gender or identity, even when based upon certain behaviours or the perceptions of a child's mind which has not yet had time to fully develop.'

This was in stark contrast to the stance Elizabeth Warren adopted. In an aborted bid to become a presidential candidate for the Democrats, Elizabeth Warren attracted the endorsement from a group of Black women who claimed President Trump's victory had 'laid bare what many Black women, gender non-conforming, and non-binary, and queer folk know deeply; that this nation embraces White supremacy and its evils, even at the expense of itself'. By comparison, the group described Elizabeth Warren as having 'a deep understanding of how racism and gender discrimination don't just compound income inequality but are actually central to maintaining the status quo' and urged

Elizabeth Warren to concentrate on 'rooting out the culture of White supremacy'. Elizabeth Warren was more than happy to receive such an endorsement, tweeting, 'Black trans and cis women, gender-nonconforming, and nonbinary people are the backbone of our democracy and I don't take this endorsement lightly. I'm committed to fighting alongside you for the big, structural change our country needs.'

Earlier, in February 2019, Elizabeth Warren had urged Arizona lawmakers to reject a bill aimed at protecting schoolgirls from having to compete with boys who claim to be girls. On Twitter, Warren described Arizona House Bill 2706 as 'cruel', saying, 'Trans athletes are not a threat. We need to protect trans kids – and all LGBTQ+ kids – and ensure they feel safe and welcomed at school. I urge the Arizona legislature to reject this cruel bill.'

In another example of some determined push back, in Texas, Leander City Council voted 5-2 to cease renting out space at the local library to prevent 'Drag Queen Story Time' for children. Troy Hill, the council's mayor, pointed out, 'We brought in $1,800 in rental fees and we spent $20,000 in security. That's not good math to me.'

Mary Elizabeth Castle, a policy adviser for Texas Values, a non-profit organisation promoting faith, family, and freedom, said of the drag queens: 'These are people who are actually employed at adult nightclubs.' Castle revealed, 'These drag queens are told to read stories, you know, about gender transitioning and about sexual orientation to young kids as young as infant age.' Castle believed the majority of people were opposed due to the costs and the desire 'to protect their children'.

This conflict between the views of the public, and the views of the minority pressure groups and their state allies, once again highlights the problem of producer capture. The libraries are doing what they like and are not providing a service the public want. Generally, young children are safer with women than with men. To be allowing male drag queens who perform in 'adult nightclubs' to 'read stories ... about gender transitioning and about sexual orientation' to 'infants' is reckless and antisense. It might suit the cultural Marxists to pursue such an agenda, but that agenda should have been firmly rejected by normal, right-thinking people.

Emilie Kao, director of the Richard and Helen DeVos Center for Religion and Civil Society at The Heritage Foundation, told *The Daily Signal* in an email: '"Drag Queen Story Hours" are contributing to the inappropriate and early sexualization of children. Parents, communities, and local libraries have the right to protect their children by refusing to host adult entertainment in spaces designed for kids.'

In the UK, the Labour leadership contender, Rebecca Long-Bailey, demanded a change under the 2010 Equality Act to remove exclusions from women-only spaces that exclude trans women from women's refuges. She said, 'I want a right to self id [identification] for trans people, it's not an easy journey to go on.' It was put to Ms Long-Bailey that female victims of domestic violence had spoken of their 'debilitating terror' and of the vital importance of a woman-only refuge. But she replied, 'We can't use that as an argument to discriminate against transpeople.'

A major issue with the trans movement was men using women's toilets. This even affected schoolgirls. The *Daily Mail* reported schoolgirls were skipping school and not drinking fluids (to prevent urination) to avoid using the girl's toilets that males also used:

> 'Parents and teaching staff told The Mail on Sunday that female pupils feel deeply uncomfortable or even unsafe sharing toilets with male students. The trend for single-sex toilets is driven by the wish to be more inclusive of children who identify as transgender and wish to use the same facilities as the opposite sex. But last night, doctors and politicians called on schools to halt the move towards unisex toilets to prevent any further harm to female pupils.'

Parents complained they had not been consulted about introducing unisex toilets. The *Daily Mail* reported:

> 'The latest row involves Deanesfield Primary School in South Ruislip, West London, where parents launched a petition last month against the introduction of unisex toilets. One angry mother, who has daughters aged four and eight at the school, said: "The cubicles were open at the bottom and top so older pupils can easily climb up the toilets and peer over." Stephanie Davies-Arai, from the parent campaign group Transgender Trend, said schools were being misinformed by "trans activist" organisations that they were breaking equality laws if they did not make toilets unisex. She said there were clear exemptions under the current equality laws that meant it was perfectly legal to have single-sex toilets.'

In May 2020, a 13-year-old schoolgirl forced Oxfordshire county council to scrap plans for transgender pupils to use any toilet or changing room they liked. The plan was part of a 'trans inclusion toolkit'. The schoolgirl said the plans threatened her safety, dignity and privacy and the council backed down when faced with court action supported by the Safe Schools Alliance. The unnamed schoolgirl said, 'I am very surprised the council never asked the opinion of girls in Oxfordshire about what we thought before they published the toolkit. Although they have withdrawn it now, they haven't apologised to me or said they were wrong. I would like to know what Oxfordshire country council is going to do to make schools a safe place for girls going forward.' Tanya Carter of the Safe Schools Alliance said, 'We welcome the decision from Oxfordshire country council to withdraw its Trans Inclusion Toolkit. However, we remain deeply concerned at the widespread undermining of child safeguarding and misrepresentation of the Equality Act that this case has revealed.' Once again, this is an example of both producer capture and antisense. A YouGov poll revealed less than four per cent of women supported gender-neutral toilets.

California took its own path. In February, Californian lawmakers were seeking to exempt some homosexual and child rapists from the state's sex-offender registry. Registration would be a matter for the judge. If the victim was within 10 years of age of the perpetrator, then the judge would have discretion. The proposals would allow a 24-year-old man to claim sodomy with a 14-year-old boy was consensual. One purpose of the proposals was to bring homosexual offences into line with vaginal intercourse in the name of equality.

Not to be left out, in August 2020, the BBC received some complaints about a programme on its CBBC channel aimed at children aged six to 12. The complaints concerned a scene of two girls kissing. The BBC said the decision to include the scene was 'taken very carefully and with much consideration' and was because 'the series could and should do more to reflect the lives of LGBTQ+ young people.' The idea that this reflects the lives of six- to 12-year-old children is antisense.

In the USA, New York City, California, Oregon, Washington state and New Jersey allowed parents to describe new-born babies as being gender 'X'. California issued sex education guidance to encourage teachers to discuss gender identity with children in kindergarten. This political paedophilia is antisense.

Intergenerational Equality

In *The Ponzi Class*, I pointed out that one of the most important aspects of Ponzi economics is the ability of the Ponzi Class to offload debts onto the public, with a redirecting of monies to pet projects. That has continued uninterrupted. A new term arose to justify this economic mismanagement called 'intergenerational fairness', which means that the standards of living of younger people should be increased by reducing the living standards of the elderly. Pensions were a key target.

By comparison, the UK was little interested in the plight of the elderly. For example, in December 2016, it was reported that 45 per cent of councils had stopped providing meals on wheels for vulnerable pensioners and another 20 per cent had significantly increased their charges. In February 2017, in a survey by ITV news, councils disclosed that those pensioners who needed home care were waiting for up to one year before that care could be provided. Social care was cut by six per cent in the previous year. In April 2017, more than 2,000 elderly people living in their own homes died over the previous three years before care visits could be arranged. Some had waited up to nine months.

In March 2017, the Commons Communities and Local Government Committee found that those pensioners in care homes who were 'self-funders' paid 43 per cent more on average than those the local councils funded for an identical service. The same committee recommended a new annual tax of £280 to fund social care.

In December 2016, an Institute for Public Policy Research (IPPR) report warned that by 2030, there would be a £13 billion shortfall in social care spending (estimated to reach £21 billion), as the number of those aged over sixty-five increased from 11.6 million to 15.4 million. In comparison, George Osborne, when Chancellor of the Exchequer in 2015, had said the foreign aid budget would need to be increased to £15.6 billion by 2020 and to a projected increase of £19 billion by 2030. In January 2017, David Mowat told MPs that families needed to take more responsibility for looking after their elderly relatives and could no longer rely on the state to do so. According to the Local Government Association, another £2.6 billion would be needed for social care by 2020.

What care the elderly got from the NHS was far from perfect, and the NHS was not quite the envy of the world it claimed to be. The number killed in the Liverpool Care Pathway (LCP) programme reached 130,000 per year. The programme involved withdrawal of treatment for very ill patients, curtailing, if not stopping, the provision of food and water, and heavy

275

sedation. Half of those on the programme had not given their consent. Hospitals had been offered extra monies for all of those put on the programme. It was phased out in the 12 months following July 2013 after widespread complaints of abuse. In Wigan, before the abolition of the LCP, nearly one in two hospital deaths were of those on the programme.

The scrimping regarding the elderly continued in new ways. In June 2017, the Oxfordshire Clinical Commissioning Group health trust instructed family doctors to reassess all patients over the age of 70 who were especially frail or with long-term conditions, to include 10 per cent of all care home residents. The purpose of the reassessment was to reduce 'inappropriate' prescriptions, with half the cost saved given to the doctors. The aim was to save £1.45 million per year. Professor Helen Stokes-Lampard, chairman of the Royal College of GPs, said the scheme 'will risk jeopardising the trust between doctors and their patients'.

The schemes to justify yet higher levels of taxation came against a background of the government's failure to honour its obligations to the people.

By comparison, in November 2016, The Social Mobility Commission produced a report that warned, 'The 20th century expectation that each generation would be better off than the one preceding is no longer being met' and that only one in eight children born in poorer households would achieve a well-paid job. The report said that middle-class families were on a 'treadmill', with falling earnings and higher house prices, and that those born in the 1980s were the first generation since World War Two (WWII) not to start their careers on higher salaries than their parents had.

Work and Pensions Secretary Damien Green said in September 2016:

> 'I absolutely accept that we need to look over time at the area of intergenerational fairness. But I do think we should step back from this view that we're being too generous to pensioners, because all these things are very

276

long term and if you look over the long term pensioner poverty in the 1980s was 40 per cent of pensioners. It's now down to 14 per cent. That's an enormous, beneficial social revolution.'

In February 2017, in response to a report from the Resolution Foundation, May's policy adviser, George Freeman MP, said, 'Intergenerational earnings and income fairness are a major issue for a 21st century sustainable political economy.' The executive chairman of the Resolution Foundation, Lord Willets, a former Tory Cabinet minister, said, 'The triple lock [which increases the state pension annually by the higher of inflation, wage growth or 2.5 per cent] is a very powerful ratchet pushing up pensions at a time when incomes of the less affluent half of working households are barely rising at all.' Intergenerational fairness was an issue about which Lord Willets was very keen.

The self-appointed Intergenerational Commission (IC) was 'run' by the Resolution Foundation, 'an independent think tank that works to improve the living standards of those in Britain on low-to-middle incomes'. The Policy Exchange was another organisation with a similar view.

The IC had a number of commissioners: David Willetts, Executive Chair of the Resolution Foundation (Commission Chair); Vidhya Alakeson, Chief Executive of Power to Change; Kate Barker, Chairman of Trustees, British Coal Staff Superannuation Scheme; Torsten Bell, Director of the Resolution Foundation; Carolyn Fairbairn, Director General of the CBI; Geoffrey Filkin, Chairman of the Centre for Ageing Better; John Hills, Professor of Social Policy at the London School of Economics; Paul Johnson, Director of the Institute for Fiscal Studies; Sarah O'Connor, Investigations Correspondent and columnist at the *Financial Times*; Frances O'Grady, General Secretary of the Trades Union Congress (TUC); Ben Page, Chief Executive of the pollsters Ipsos MORI; and Nigel Wilson, Group Chief Executive of Legal and General. The commission was widely drawn and included some surprising names of those who claimed to be conservatives and those who claimed to believe in a free society.

In Lord Willets' foreword, the report asserted that 'society is held together by mutual dependence between the generations' and welcomed the increased debate about 'fairness between the generations'. Willets asserted the 'generational contract' was in danger of policy drift. 'Generational progress' had 'stalled'. As the evidence of this was 'so powerful' there was 'an obligation to act'. The commission had 'risen' to meet this 'challenge' and had reached a 'consensus' that:

> 'We can deliver the health and care older generations deserve without simply asking younger workers to bear all the costs. We can do more to promote education and skills, especially for those who are not on the university route. We can and should provide more security for young people, from the jobs they do to the homes they increasingly rent. And we can promote asset ownership for younger generations so that owning a home and access to a decent pension are realities not a distant prospect in 21st century Britain.'

The foreword concluded that although the ideas put forward were 'not easy or comfortable', the problems alleged would not 'fix themselves' and so the commission hoped that 'as the important issues we identify are increasingly recognised, our proposals can be a useful guide to action'.

The executive summary defined the 'intergenerational contract' as being 'the principle that different generations provide support to each other across the different stages of their lives' and this affected not only families, but 'society as a whole', including government, and defined 'what the welfare state does'. For the commission, this contract was 'under threat, with widespread concern that young adults may not achieve the progress their predecessors enjoyed', although, 'While there is still much to do, opportunities for women, ethnic minorities and lesbian, gay and transgender people are much

278

better than for their predecessors.' Thus, of note from the outset, was a 'pessimism that dominates overall' not that younger people were worse off, but they were not as much better off as some ordained assumption would expect.

Pessimism was 'most marked' regarding 'housing, work and pensions'; these were, therefore, 'at the core' of the commission's work. For the commission, the financial crisis was the beginning of 'intergenerational anxiety' when 'young adults' had 'experienced incredibly poor pay outcomes' although employment had 'been strong'. Millennials, 'the generation born 1981–2000', had experienced unemployment levels 25 per cent lower than the baby boomers, 'born 1946–65', had at the same age.

The report alleged that where previous generations had higher real earnings than the previous one at the same age, now they had only 'similar earnings', although the report did acknowledge millennials were better off: 'But cohort-on-cohort pay progress has stalled, with the oldest cohort of millennials recording earnings at age 30 only slightly higher than the cohort born 15 years before them.'[192] This was due to the 'poor pay growth' since the financial crisis, although there was evidence the 'generational pay stagnation' had 'deeper roots' from before the crisis impacted.

Housing was identified as a major problem, with 'millennial families' being 'only half as likely to own their home by age 30 as baby boomers were by the same age'. This was due to higher house prices, tighter credit and low earnings growth (exacerbated by a longer period in education for many who therefore had not started earning sooner), and that 'In the 1980s it would have taken a typical household in their late 20s around three years to save for an average-sized deposit. It would now take 19 years.'[193] Home ownership for young families was stated as being the lowest in London.

Furthermore, 'an even bigger reduction in access to social housing means that four-in-ten millennial families at age 30 live in the private rented sector, four times the rate for baby boomers when they were the same age'. Whereas 'the silent

279

generation', 'born 1926–45', spent only eight per cent of their income on housing, now the millennials spent 'almost a quarter of the income on housing' at the same age.

The report alleged that even an improvement in the economy would still leave millennials unable to match Generation X, 'born 1966–80', until the age of 45. They would still be worse off than the baby boomers (the report contradicted itself when also saying, 'Far from showing significant generational progress, millennials' incomes have broadly tracked those of generation X to date'[194]. It also stated, 'Between 2001–03 and 2014–16, typical incomes grew in real terms by 38 per cent for Bangladeshi households and 28 per cent for Pakistani households, compared with 13 per cent for the White British group'[195]. Some would be helped by inheritances, but many would not, as almost half of the non-home owners aged 20–35 had parents who were also non-home owners.

The report alleged that although the incomes of younger people had 'faltered' following the financial crash, 'total household wealth' had grown rapidly in the 21st century. However, 'This is because unexpected house price and pension windfalls largely benefit older cohorts with existing wealth. These windfalls are unlikely to be repeated in future.' The report alleged the millennials were suffering higher 'income inequalities' and with the growing size of inheritances, then 'already-wealthy millennials were set to inherit more than four times as much as those with no property wealth'.

The report alleged an ageing population would mean 'public spending on health, care and social security is set to rise by £24 billion by 2030 and by £63 billion by 2040'. For the commission, this increase 'would put disproportionate costs onto younger generations who have borne the brunt of recent living standards pressures'. The report dismissed this as 'unsustainable in the long run' and 'unfair between the generations'. Therefore 'new answers' were needed 'to avoid breaching the intergenerational contract by either cutting essential support for older generations or putting unsustainable costs onto younger ones most affected by the financial crisis'. The report even went so far as to state, 'From housing to pensions and the labour market, we can reduce the challenges [the young generations] face and the risks that they bear'.[196]

The report said parents were helping their children buy their own homes ('bank of mum and dad'), more young adults were still living with their parents and 'the number of adults caring for elderly, ill or disabled relatives increased by 11 per cent in the decade to 2011'. However, 'so far the state has failed to adapt'. At this point, the report got to the crunch: 'Britain's booming stock of wealth is increasingly concentrated in older generations and that it is also increasingly lightly taxed'.

The report advocated some new taxes, tax changes, and bits and bobs of new spending schemes, such as £1 billion for a 'Better Jobs Deal' to be funded by 'cancelling 1p of the forthcoming corporation tax cut'. The report announced: 'in the long term we need to build more homes, year in, year out, in areas of strong housing demand, while increasing the number of affordable homes, to reduce housing costs'. Other than to recommend a '£1.7 billion building precept allowing local authorities to raise funds for house building', 'community land auctions' and 'compulsory purchase powers', the report did not explain how this recommended new house building was to be funded.

The crux of the report was the attention to 'the coming rise in intergenerational wealth transfers' which were 'an opportunity to show that Britain has something to offer young people, no matter who their parents are'. Therefore:

'We recommend abolishing inheritance tax and replacing it with a lifetime receipts tax that is levied on recipients with fewer exemptions, a lower tax-free allowance and lower tax rates. The extra revenues should support a £10,000 "citizen's inheritance" – a restricted-use asset endowment to all young adults to support skills, entrepreneurship, housing and pension saving. In the medium term, citizen's inheritances of £10,000 should be available from the age of 25 at a cost of £7 billion per

281

year. During an initial transition phase, gradually rising inheritances should be offered at older ages, starting with those turning 35 in 2020.'

The report boldly asserted this citizen's inheritance 'should be available from the age of 25 to all British nationals or people born in Britain'.[197] Given the free distribution of British passports to all and sundry, the refusal to control borders, and the proposed continuation of mass immigration, the potential consequences of this are eye-popping.

The report was bold in its proposed receipts tax:

'Each recipient should have a lifetime receipts tax allowance of £125,000 (rising with inflation). Beyond this threshold, any new gifts or inheritances received would be taxed – at significantly lower rates than the current system. Lifetime receipts above the allowance and up to £500,000 should be taxed at a basic rate of 20 per cent; with receipts above £500,000 being taxed at 30 per cent. Despite lower rates, this structure would raise an additional £5 billion initially, with revenues rising over time as inheritances grow and the lifetime allowances bed in.'

Gifts between spouses and small gifts (below £3,000) would remain exempt, although there would be caps applied for businessmen and agricultural property.

For the commission, the result of this 'would be profound' as 'a £10,000 boost today would at least double the wealth of more than six-in-ten adults in their late 20s', and 'would be enough' for a house deposit for a first-time buyer in 'half the regions and nations of the UK' or enough to fund a master's degree or 'significant retraining', or 'would add an estimated £45,000 to retirement savings pots if immediately invested in a pension'. Alternatively, it could bridge rental deposits when people move for work, or be used for business start-up funding 'for those in recognised entrepreneurship schemes'. The committee pronounced, 'Such an approach would represent a bold demonstration that the state's role in delivering the intergenerational contract can evolve for the 21st century.'

The cost of the citizen's inheritance was estimated to reach around £13.5 billion per annum by 2029. Given the total refusal to control mass immigration and the Tory Government's determination to increase it with their new points-based system and the commitment to allow up to around 5.4 million Hong Kongers and their families into the UK, this approximation is almost certain to be a gross underestimate. A whole new business model for people smugglers would have been created, with immigrants paying the various organised crime rackets (including jihadists) in the expectation of getting to Britain and qualifying for the citizen's inheritance once they have been given a British passport – if not before.

As the former Tory chancellor, Norman Lamont, succinctly wrote in the *Daily Mail*: 'In truth, the very idea of intergenerational inequality is bunk.' It is also antisense. Lamont made the point that after a lifetime's work, the elderly were bound to be more wealthy than those who had just finished their education, or were still in education. He said those who were older today had their own problems in their younger years with the inflation and unemployment of the 1970s and 1980s. In fact, pensioners had borne the brunt of the recession and private pensions have been decimated. More people are now working beyond retirement age due to low pensions. In February 2018, the number of women working in their 50s and 60s reached a high of 4.2 million.

In February 2018, figures from the OECD showed that at £122.30 per week – 29 per cent of the average wage – the UK state pension was the lowest in the developed world. By comparison, the Dutch paid a pension 100 per cent of the average wage, Portugal 94.9 per cent, Spain 81.8 per cent, France 74.5 per cent, Czech Republic 60 per cent, USA 49.1 per cent, Germany 50.5 per cent, Ireland 42.3 per cent, Poland 38.6 per cent and Mexico 29.6 per cent.

283

Importantly, as can be seen from the report, the argument is not that the younger generation today are worse off than their predecessors, but they are not as better off as were their predecessors compared to earlier generations. That is, the younger generation is not getting better off fast enough. This is not a credible reason to allow the state to help itself to ordinary people's money and is a pretty feeble excuse for doing so. People are born into a family. The family brings them up and provides for them. Ultimately, the next generation inherits the family wealth. People are also born into a nation and a country. They benefit from the level of civilisation that nation and country can provide and develop. That the state has ruined a country's economic development and civilisation is no excuse at all for those responsible, the ruling class, to then involve themselves in and help themselves to the family wealth of ordinary people. A ruling class that is too decadent and negligent to discharge proper stewardship of a country should be overthrown. It is the duty of the ruling class to preserve, develop and bequeath to the next generation the benefits of the country which are inherited. Due to patriotism being usurped by political correctness, presently, the ruling class does not see this.

The plan for this tax grab as a means of a redistribution of wealth with the 'citizen's inheritance' presumes that the state should interpose itself into family finances and the freedom of people to distribute their own money. This is not just cultural Marxism (aka political correctness), but classical Marxism.

The Plunder of the Welfare System

To state the obvious, for ordinary peoples across the West, the welfare system exists to act as a safety net for those in need. In many countries, it is a means of providing pensions for retirement. Then there is the provision of healthcare. The welfare system is central to increasing living standards, improving the quality of life, and reinforcing nation cohesion. To these ends, people are willing to pay taxes to fund the welfare systems. However, politicians are increasingly brazen in spending the taxes paid on pet projects while reducing welfare provision – often citing the need to cut costs. The result is that the welfare systems are being looted and standards of living are falling in consequence.

In February 2019, in the UK, the number of over 50s working increased to a record 10.4 million. Almost 500,000 women aged 65 or over were in work. A record 15.55 million women were working, according to the ONS, in August 2019. Three out of every four new workers were female. Only 1.78 million women were housewives.

ONS figures showed that those in work increased to 32.8 million at the end of 2019. This was an increase of 3.7 million since David Cameron took office in 2010. There was a record 20.7 million in full-time work. The self-employed reached a record total of 4.96 million. Those unemployed fell to 1.28 million (a rate of 3.8 per cent). The unemployment rate was roughly half that of France and a quarter that of Spain. The youth unemployment rate was 11.2 per cent (16-24-year-olds), whereas in Spain and Greece the rate was around one-third, one-fifth in France and 28 per cent in Italy.

These high employment rates were not enough for some. In August 2019, the Centre for Social Justice (CSJ) advocated the pension age be raised to 70 by 2028 and 75 by 2035. The CSJ believed that such a swindle, which is what it is, would increase economic output by £182 billion per annum.

Official estimates stated that increasing the average retirement age by one year would add one per cent to GDP. One million over-50s could find a job. A sum of £182 billion would constitute around nine per cent of GDP. Andy Cook from the CSJ said, 'Working longer has the potential to ... increase retirement savings and ensure the full functioning of public services for all.'

In November 2019, in a study by the ONS, 'Living Longer: Is Age 70 The New Age 65?', the case was advanced that the retirement age should be raised to 70:

'In the UK, 65 years of age has traditionally been taken as the marker for the start of older age, most likely because it was the official retirement age for men and the age at which they could draw their state pension. In terms of working patterns, age 65 years as the start of older age is out of date. There is no longer an official retirement age, state pension age is rising and increasing numbers of people work past the age of 65.'

Consequently:

'Longer lives mean people can continue to contribute for longer – through longer working lives, volunteering and possible providing care for family members, for example, grandchildren for individuals it might mean the opportunity to spend more time with family and friends and to pursue personal interests with more time for leisure activities. [But] more older people means increased demand for health and adult social services, and increased public spending on state pensions. The key to shifting the balance from challenge towards opportunity ... is for older people to be able to live healthy lives for as long as possible.'

The report anticipated that life expectancy would continue to rise.

It had long been recognised that social care for the elderly was underfunded. In July 2019, a House of Lords committee on economic affairs, chaired by Lord Forsyth, called upon the government to spend up to £8 billion per year on social care. Lord Forsyth said:

'Social care is severely underfunded. More than a million adults who need social care aren't receiving it, family and friends are being put under greater pressure to provide unpaid care, and the care workforce continues to be

286

underpaid and undervalued. The whole system is riddled with unfairness. Someone with dementia can pay hundreds of thousands of pounds for their care, while someone with cancer receives it for free.'

In August 2019, ONS figures revealed that dementia accounted for 12.8 per cent of the 541,589 registered deaths in England and Wales. In the previous two years, the government had spent £9.3 billion on dementia care, while families had paid £14.7 billion. More than 850,000 have dementia. A report from the charity, Independent Age, disclosed that 21,120 pensioners had sold their homes to pay for social care in 2018, compared to 11,880 in 2000. Elsewhere, it was reported that one third (31 per cent) of dementia patients had sold their homes. Furthermore, in October 2020, 17,000 pensioners were forced to sell their homes to pay for social care in the last year.

Almost two million people were looking after someone with dementia. The number was expected to increase to 2.8 million by 2035. A report from the NHS revealed that most carers of a relative were women and their mental health suffered and they were at a higher risk of depression, loneliness and other illnesses.

Pensioner poverty not only affected the pensioners themselves but also the whole family as what would have been inherited wealth was either seized by the state, or consumed to make ends meet. A report from HMRC revealed the amount paid in inheritance tax had more than doubled in a decade to reach £5.4 billion in 2018. In January 2019, figures from the Equity Release Council showed that almost £4 billion was released by older home owners the previous year – an increase of almost one third since 2017. In April 2019, Chris Knight of Legal & General Retirement said:

'Unlocking housing wealth in retirement is becoming a new normal and retirees are increasingly doing it for a range of reasons. From paying for home improvements to helping kids on to the property ladder and even covering the cost of care, lifetime mortgages are enabling retirees to really use their home as their pension.'

In July 2019, a report from the St James's Place wealth management group said, 'For those with a sufficient amount of wealth, the amount they expect to pass on is likely to be significantly impacted, with future retirees expecting to pass on £50,000 less of their retirement pot on average compared with current retirees.' The cause of the impact being the need to support both their parents and their children.

The cost of housing and its shortage continued to have a major effect on the quality of life. In 2018, around 10,600 40-year mortgages were taken out. The average property price was £226,798, which was more than eight times the annual income of the average worker. In May 2019, Hargreaves Lansdown produced figures showing that younger people were now more likely to downsize than those who were older, including those who lived in rented property. Spiralling costs of housing were to blame. Sarah Coles said, 'Generation Rent is being squeezed out of the property market and crammed into smaller and smaller homes. Tenants may be forced to keep downsizing in order to keep a lid on costs. When they eventually buy, they may have to downsize again in some areas to get onto the property ladder.'

In November 2019, an ONS report said, 'Over the last two decades, there has been a 46.3 per cent increase in the number of people aged 20 to 34 living with their parents, increasing from 2.4 million in 1999 to 3.5 million in 2019. This is equivalent to more than a quarter of young adults of the same age group living with parents in 2019. This number has not changed significantly since 2018.' A shortage of social housing is a major reason for this.

The burden of debt and its consequences was revealed in December 2019 when the Bank of England revealed one effect of the cut in mortgage rates was an increase in the birth rate. It was estimated that for every one per cent fall in the base rate, the birth rate increased by two per cent. Interest rates were cut from 5.75 per cent in July 2007 to 0.5 per cent in March 2009, leading to an increase in birth rates and an increase in the birth rate of 7.5 per cent over the following three years. This indicates that women would have more children if their quality of life and living standards were more secure.

The amount of personal debt (car finance, credit cards and personal loans) reached £9.9 billion in September 2019. Car loans accounted for 40 per cent of the total. Figures from the Department for Education revealed that 47 per cent of student debt would be written off by the taxpayer. An estimated 70 per cent of students would never earn enough to repay their student loans. The amount to be written off had increased to an estimated £7.4 billion.

Meanwhile, in August 2019, figures from the Government Expenditure and Revenue Scotland report showed the Scots received public spending £1,661 per capita higher than the rest of the UK, and paid £307 less in tax per capita. In August 2020, the latest figures showed Scotland had a deficit of £15.1 billion, 8.6 per cent of GDP, in 2019/20. The UK deficit as a whole was 2.5 per cent. Once again, to their own detriment, the English were subsidising others.

A pernicious aspect so far as the UK is concerned is that the anti-White agenda goes even further into an anti-English agenda. England is by far the largest country in the UK. Yet the English do not have equal voting rights, nor their own parliament, are expected to fund the various schemes and subsidies across the UK and the world, and are especially targeted as supposed oppressors. English subsidies to Scotland, Wales and Northern Ireland are in excess of £25 billion, for which there is little gratitude.

The greatest corrupting effect of the welfare systems in the West is not upon the behaviour of ordinary people, but upon the attitudes and behaviour of the politicians and the broader ruling classes. The welfare systems have become a justification for higher levels of taxation, of which ever increasing amounts are spent not on the provision of welfare to the nation, but on pet projects, including political correctness. Meanwhile, there are cuts in the provision of welfare to the ordinary people who pay the taxes.

Non-Crime

The UK's police determination to crack down on 'non-crime' stems from the Stephen Lawrence inquiry. An article on the BBC website explained, 'The police guidance on non-crime hate incidents was developed after the murder of the Black teenager Stephen Lawrence in a racist attack in 1993.' The purported aim is to deal with alleged hate incidents before they escalate into serious hate crimes. Each year more than 25,000 such non-crime hate incidents are logged by UK police. The bulk relate to race and disability.

The Metropolitan Police in London notoriously set out their own understanding on this issue, in a public notice titled 'What is a Hate Crime?' which answered (the word 'perceived' is key):

> 'In most crimes it is something the victim has in their possession or control that motivates the offender to commit the crime. With hate crime it is "who" the victim is, or "what" the victim appears to be that motivates the offender to commit the crime.
>
> A hate crime is defined as "Any criminal offence which is perceived by the victim or any other person, to be motivated by hostility or prejudice based on a person's race or perceived race; religion or perceived religion; sexual orientation or perceived sexual orientation; disability or perceived disability and any crime motivated by hostility or prejudice against a person who is transgender or perceived to be transgender."
>
> A hate incident is any incident which the victim, or anyone else, thinks is based on someone's prejudice

towards them because of their race, religion, sexual orientation, disability or because they are transgender.

Not all hate incidents will amount to criminal offences, but it is equally important that these are reported and recorded by the police.

Evidence of the hate element is not a requirement. You do not need to personally perceive the incident to be hate related. It would be enough if another person, a witness or even a police officer thought that the incident was hate related.'

A hate crime therefore is created by the perception of 'the victim or any other person'. As can be seen above, the willingness of the politically correct to manufacture allegations of hate is unlimited and, hence, so is the scope of hate crime.

The Met broke down hate crime into three types: 'physical assault, verbal abuse and incitement to hatred'. Physical assault was fairly straightforward and 'any kind is an offence' and 'a perpetrator may be charged with common assault, actual bodily harm or grievous bodily harm'.

Regarding verbal abuse, the Met advised:

'Verbal abuse, threats or name-calling can be a common and extremely unpleasant experience for minority groups. Victims of verbal abuse are often unclear whether an offence has been committed or believe there is little they can do. However, there are laws in place to protect you from verbal abuse. If you've been the victim of verbal abuse, talk to the police or one of our partner organisations about what has happened.'

People were urged to still report the incident even if they did not know who had abused them. The police deem a matter as incitement to hatred where matters are more open to mischief, not least because it is highly subjective:

291

'The offence of incitement to hatred occurs when someone acts in a way that is threatening and intended to stir up hatred. That could be in words, pictures, videos, music, and includes information posted on websites. Hate content may include:

- messages calling for violence against a specific person or group
- web pages that show pictures, videos or descriptions of violence against anyone due to their perceived differences
- chat forums where people ask other people to commit hate crimes against a specific person or group.'

Just who and how is someone condemned as guilty for being 'threatening and intended to stir up hatred'? For the politically correct, being politically incorrect is tantamount to hatred. As for chat forums, given the cancel culture rampant across social media, things have gone far beyond what even the Met has set out. This stems from the Met urging people to report 'hate incidents' even if there is no crime involved, so 'these are reported and recorded by the police'. Furthermore, by-standers can report such incidents, and 'evidence of the hate element is not a requirement'. Once again, this is antisense.

Therefore, all hate incidents have to be recorded. In London, one incident involved a bus driver who 'gave a racist look' and another incident concerned a woman who accused a man of standing 'intimidatingly' close to her because she was a 'non-conforming-gender-specific lesbian in a wheelchair'.

A police spokesman said, 'By recording and reviewing reports of hate incidents, police forces play a vital role in helping prevent hate crime.' Meanwhile, in April 2018, Scotland Yard admitted it had too few detectives to investigate murders. London's murder toll for 2018 had reached 55. A machete-related crime occurred every 90 minutes across Britain on average, with London experiencing by far the most. London's murder rate had overtaken New York and, excluding terrorism, had risen 38 per cent since 2014.

Until the end of the 20th century, the police were expected to protect the public from crime. In return, the public sacrificed their rights to defend themselves and to take matters into their own hands. Instead, a professional and impartial police force could be relied upon to uphold the rule of law. But now, as is evidenced by the Met's public notice regarding so-called hate crime, the police see it as their role to monitor public free speech and to compile lists of those deemed politically incorrect, regardless of whether any crime has been committed. This is happening under successive Tory governments.

Harry Miller, who set up the group Fair Cop, wrote in the *Daily Mail*:

> 'As research this month reveals, there is one certain way to stir the police into action: report a fellow citizen for saying something, or making some comment on social media, that constitutes an "incident" – or Non Crime Hate Incident (NCHI). In the past five years, it's now been revealed, 120,000 NCHIs have been recorded – and not one of them has been the subject of a proper probe. After all, by its nature, it is not a crime.'

These recorded incidents would be held on a person's police file for six years. The file's contents would be used and disclosed if the person applied for a visa or a job needing extended disclosure and barring service check – e.g. become a teacher. The police, in particular the College of Policing, treat the purpose of these records as a means of intimidation by a 'chilling effect'. NCHI guidance stated that police may even enter schools to issue warnings to children.

Police political correctness has not gone without criticism and has provoked ridicule. In October 2017, of the police, Mick Neville, a retired senior Scotland Yard detective, commented, 'They have forgotten what their purpose is', after the latest crime figures showed a surge in almost every type of crime and a 25 per cent increase in knife crime. Meanwhile, male police officers were posing in bear masks, painting their fingernails blue (in response to Vietnamese organised crime gangs operating nail salons across the whole of Britain), stroking puppies for stress release, driving bumper cars and even prancing around in red high heels (to highlight domestic violence) – and then posting photos of all this online. The Avon and Somerset Police urged those who felt victimised by adverse comments of their nail varnish (to highlight modern slavery) to report the matter as a hate crime. Drug squad officers were asking cannabis growers if they were victims of slavery. Neville observed, 'Too many modern chief constables have got more degrees under their belts than arrests. The people in charge have simply not done the job. The reason they do not investigate crime is they have never done it themselves. They are looking for cheap wins.'

In May 2018, police officers were pictured sporting multicoloured bootlaces to show their support for sexual and gender diversity on the International Day Against Homophobia, Transphobia and Biphobia (IDAHOTB). A number of government agencies were involved and gay pride flags were flown from government buildings.

In April 2018, there was a row when Chief Constable Peter Goodman decided to discontinue support for his force's male voice choir. He said, 'I have to say the Derbyshire Constabulary Male Voice Choir is way down my list of priorities. I want them to look and feel like the force we want to be, and frankly, a lot of quite old white men singing ... is not the kind of impression I want to create.'

In June 2018, Northampton Police promoted an 18-hour Ramadan fast for non-Muslim volunteers to show 'unity' with Muslims during Ramadan. The Northamptonshire Association of Muslim Police organised the event to 'send a powerful message' to local people. One officer who participated said, 'Fasting for the day with no food and water was quite an experience and I realised that it requires a significant level of dedication and self-control to do it. As part of my role, I want to get deeper into the community roots to help increase participation and recruitment from all parts of the community.'

Political correctness has consumed the police; they no longer represent the opinions or interests of ordinary people and are no longer capable of doing their jobs properly. The fixation with non-crime is merely a police attempt to use their powers to impose cultural Marxism upon society.

In the USA, the FBI defines a hate crime thus:

> 'A hate crime is a traditional offence like murder, arson, or vandalism with an added element of bias. For the purposes of collecting statistics, the FBI has defined a hate crime as a "criminal offence against a person or property motivated in whole or in part by an offender's bias against a race, religion, disability, sexual orientation, ethnicity, gender, or gender identity." Hate itself is not a crime – and the FBI is mindful of protecting freedom of speech and other civil liberties.'

The International Association of Chiefs of Police (IACP) has a similar definition to the FBI:

> 'A hate crime is a criminal offence committed against persons, property or society that is motivated, in whole or in part, by an offender's bias against an individual's or a group's race, religion, ethnic/national origin, gender, age, disability or sexual orientation.'

The IACP further set out what a hate incident is:

> 'Hate incidents involve behaviours that, though motivated by bias against a victim's race, religion, ethnic/national origin, gender, age, disability or sexual orientation, are not criminal acts. Hostile or hateful speech, or other disrespectful/discriminatory behaviour may be motivated by bias but is not illegal. They become crimes only when they directly incite perpetrators to

commit violence against persons or property, or if they place a potential victim in reasonable fear of physical injury.'

The Office for Democratic Institutions and Human Rights (ODIHR) pointed out that the FBI, 'as of 1 October 2020', had 'elevated hate crimes to its highest-level national threat priority' and thus increased the resources for 'prevention and investigations'.

Although under the Biden administration there was a greater priority given to hate crimes in the USA, there was no open move to redefine what constituted hate crime, and the distinction between hate crime and a hate incident remained. The police in the USA have yet to go as far as they have in the UK.

THE HEGEMONY

Institutional Aspects

As set out above, Wayne Mapp, when New Zealand's Political Correctness Eradicator, identified three features of political correctness. First, political correctness is 'a set of attitudes and beliefs that are divorced from mainstream values'. Second, 'the politically correct person has a prescriptive view on how people should think and what they are permitted to discuss'. And third, which he regarded as most important, political correctness is 'embedded in public institutions, which have a legislative base' and 'have coercive powers', and that 'It is this third aspect that gives political correctness its authority'. Wayne Mapp is correct in his analysis.

These three features are a part of the long march through, and capture of, the institutions. Producer capture is also relevant to this. Civil society, across the West, is under the control of the politically correct, who are using that control to impose their own minority views on everyone else. Obviously, the state institutions are the most important as they have the coercive powers, backed up by law, that can be used to impose the politically correct ideology upon the rest of society. Heretics can be criminalised.

Other parts of civil society are also important, particularly the charity sector and mainstream media. The various charities operating, more often than not, are naturally favourable to cultural Marxism, and are in receipt of taxpayer's monies from the state (in addition to funds raised from the public directly).

Libraries, schools, universities, the police etc. all are peddling and imposing a minority cultural Marxist viewpoint upon the public, and are contemptuous towards those who do not share their viewpoint.

Mainstream media is vital as it imposes a narrative upon society, not only through the news media but also through the underlying political stance on drama, children's programmes and documentary programmes. They set the agenda. Collectively, this comprises the institutional aspect of the hegemony of political correctness.

As with the BLM movement and in the UK, the murder of George Floyd did not spur a protest movement. Those believers in political correctness *exploited* the murder for their own agenda. The BLMUK had been set up in 2016 and preceded the murder by many years. Likewise, the march through the institutions brought those institutions under politically correct control long before that murder. All political parties in the UK either jumped on the bandwagon, or adopted a 'we support their aims but not their methods' line regarding the BLM and the toppling of statues.

The UK's civil society was openly supportive of BLM. The Church of England, the media (both social and mainstream), schools (both state and private), universities, a whole raft of charities and organisations such as the National Trust, Kew Gardens, Museums, Historic England, and local councils and their organisations all weighed in to demonstrate their devotion to political correctness, cultural Marxism and a hatred of Western civilisation. During the UEFA Euro 2020 football tournament, the English football team was on their knees prior to the kick-off. Other teams from Western Europe were little better. Eastern European teams were less craven.

This institutional surge in support of BLM, and the attendant, ongoing race war politics, meant politicians could betray their country and likewise support the anti-White agenda more freely, particularly the supposedly conservative ones. They encountered no criticism. For them, it was much easier to go with the flow. For many, they agreed anyway.

In the absence of any adverse criticism, the public acquiesced to the wall of propaganda being rammed at them. There were some demonstrations in opposition from those allegedly 'far-Right', but these did not alter the prevailing mood and were undermined by the police.

That part of the ideology of political correctness that had swept through the institutions and was responsible for the BLM surge was critical race theory. This poison featured on the radar in the USA during the presidential election campaign when President Trump belatedly issued orders to try and tame it. This was too late.

Critical Race Theory (CRT) emerged in the 1970s out of the perceived failure of Critical Legal Studies (CLS) to eliminate racism in the US jurisprudence. Legal scholars Derrick Bell, Alan Freeman, and Richard Delgado developed it initially. Whereas CLS focused on 'meritocracy', CRT focused 'directly on the effects of race and racism, while simultaneously addressing the hegemonic system of White supremacy on the "meritocratic" system'. CRT also has an activist agenda to implement so-called racial justice. CRT expanded out from legal research and into other areas of society – in particular into education:

> 'Critical Race studies in education could be defined as a critique of racism as a system of oppression and exploitation that explores the historic and contemporary constructions and manifestations of race in our society with particular attention to how these issues are manifested in schools. Critical Race studies in education then – like critical pedagogy – is ultimately concerned with employing multiple methods and borrowing from diverse traditions in the law, sociology, ethnic studies and other fields to formulate a robust analysis of race and racism as a social, political and economic system of advantages and disadvantages accorded to social groups based on their skin colour and status in a clearly defined racial hierarchy.'[198]

There are five aspects to CRT:

1 Counter-storytelling

Counter-storytelling can be defined as a method of telling a story that 'aims to cast doubt on the validity of accepted premises or myths, especially ones held by the majority'.[200] The idea is to give voice to marginalised groups by challenging the privileged, majority discourses, and thereby 'help us understand what life is like for others, and invite the reader into a new and unfamiliar world'.[201] These counter-stories might be personal stories or narratives, or other people's or a mixture of both.

The permanence of racism has been described as being the acceptance of a 'realist view' that, consciously and unconsciously, racism is a part of societal structure, and that such structures govern all political, economic and social aspects of society. These structures are responsible for White privilege.

Whiteness as property is the notion that Whiteness is treated as a property right, conferring ownership, the right to use, and the right of exclusion upon White people only. This allegedly has negative effects on non-Whites who find themselves dealing with institutions modelled by White people for their own benefit. (This argument demonstrates it is against the interests of the indigenous White populations to accept mass immigration of non-Whites, and reinforces the case that immigrant malcontents be deported).

Interest convergence is the description of the alleged civil rights gains made by non-Whites as being only due to those gains also being in White self-interests, and enjoyed by White people for decades, if not centuries. Gains that are not in the self-interests of White people are unlikely to be properly granted, if granted at all. (This argument does not apply to the UK, which has a non-White population stemming solely from mass immigration).

The critique of liberalism is a rejection of the ideas of colour blindness, the neutrality of the law, and incremental change. It is alleged the history of racism coincided with both colour blindness and neutrality and so both cannot tackle the problem, and the continuation of racism is proof of that. Racism and oppression cannot be remedied by ignoring race. Incremental change means change will only proceed at a pace agreeable to the White majority and so perpetuate inequality, racism and oppression.

As can be seen, the definition of racism has expanded beyond hatred, and embraced the concept of race more broadly, with CRT producing explanations for supposed race inequality and policies to achieve supposed racial justice. The CRT view was that racism was 'endemic in US society, deeply ingrained legally, culturally, and even psychologically'.[202] The liberal approach of colour-blindness was deemed ineffectual, meaning 'the everyday practices, patterns of inequality, and results of real-life struggles for racial justice' should be the focus.[203] Importantly:

> 'CRT is not so much whether or how racial discrimination can be eradicated while maintaining the vitality of other interests linked to the status quo such as federalism, traditional values, standards, established property interests, and choice. Rather, the new question would ask how these traditional interests and cultural artifacts serve as vehicles to limit and bind the educational opportunities of students of colour.'[204]

This change coincided with the impact in the UK of the Stephen Lawrence Inquiry, resulting in the charge against the police of institutional racism that focused on an organisation's failure as measured in outcomes, rather than racial abuse:

> '"Institutional Racism" consists of the collective failure of an organisation to provide an appropriate and professional service to people because of their colour, culture, or ethnic origin. It can be seen or detected in processes, attitudes and behaviour which amount to

301

discrimination through unwitting prejudice, ignorance, thoughtlessness and racist stereotyping which disadvantage minority ethnic people.'[205]

While President Trump spoke out against CRT during the presidential election campaign, the creed spread substantially under his administration. His attempts to stem the spread were taken in the dying days of his presidency. Once President Biden took over, it was business as usual, although some Republican state governors set about bringing the spread to an end. Those in favour of CRT were defiant. For example, the National Education Association (NEA) pledged to 'share and publicize' information about CRT, and had staff who would provide information to 'fight back against anti-CRT rhetoric'. The NEA further pledged to 'oppose attempts to ban critical race theory and the '1619 Project'. (The 1619 Project asserts that American history is one of slavery and White supremacy by arguing that in 1619, the year slaves were first brought to Jamestown, is the year of America's true founding rather than the Declaration of Independence in 1776). Also it pledged, 'NEA will research the organizations attacking educators doing anti-racist work and/or use the research already done and put together a list of resources and recommendations for state affiliates, locals, and individual educators to utilize when they are attacked.'

The NEA's moves debunked the allegations peddled by many Democrats and in the media that CRT does not exist. For example, the former Virginia governor, Terry McAuliffe, dismissed CRT as 'another right-wing conspiracy theory' that had been 'totally made up by Donald Trump'.

Economic Aspects

The economic aspects are central to the hegemony of political correctness. Without funding, the extravaganza would come to an immediate halt.

The manner in which political correctness is funded can be split into three parts: tax revenues, the welfare system and Ponzi economics. Ponzi economics is important as the resources hijacked are almost unlimited and the public does not properly see what is going on.

The Staatsvolk of the various Western countries, over centuries, built up their countries successfully. Those countries naturally reflected the culture and interests of those who built them. As the countries developed, the Staatsvolk were able to better themselves; to develop industries, a welfare system, a better standard of living, and a place of safety. This is the process of civilisation. However, there is a drawback. The central government introduced the welfare systems and funded them out of tax revenues. Consequently, taxation has steadily increased to fund the ever-expanding welfare commitments. Vast sums now flow into the government coffers, and politicians therefore have very substantial tax revenues available. Furthermore, politicians can borrow and even print money to fund government spending. Funding political correctness is not a problem, and politicians are deft at dreaming of new excuses to increase taxes still further (e.g. the intergenerational equality scam in the UK).

In the UK, the state pension is a particularly good example of what has gone wrong. People pay taxes (including the national insurance payments) in return for a state pension to retire upon. However, the payments are made annually throughout people's lives and the pension is payable many years hence. Put simply, the extra payments in taxes are made in return for an IOU that some politicians in a government of unknown beliefs and convictions in the future will honour the pension obligations. History has shown those future politicians will do no such thing. Time and again, the commitment to the state pension has been reneged upon. The amount of pension payable has been slashed from the original amounts, and the age at which the pension can be claimed has risen, and there are demands the pension age be substantially raised still further (as can be seen above, there were demands the pension age increase to 70). The UK's pensioners have been swindled. Then there is the ongoing plight of those in care homes, who not only have to fund their residence but also were treated appallingly during the Covid-19 pandemic.

Meanwhile, government spending on a host of other schemes and wheezes soared. Climate change (the UK is only responsible for less than one per cent of the world's total greenhouse gas emissions); foreign aid; subsidies to Scotland, Wales and Northern Ireland; and payments to the EU (which have continued post-Brexit), are all examples of large scale avoidable government spending.

The greatest drawback of the welfare systems of the West is that vast sums flow into the government coffers from taxation, borrowing and printing money, so politicians have plenty of money available to fund political correctness. The money taxed is not invested to provide for the future (such as for pensions) but is spent – too often on matters against the interests of the nation.

The second part of the funding of political correctness is the infrastructure of the welfare system itself. This particularly applies to mass immigration. Illegal immigrants enter a country and claim to be asylum seekers. Immediately, there are state-funded lawyers and pro-immigration charities on hand to assist. The illegal immigrants need to be housed. In the UK, this is achieved either by allocating social housing (supposedly for the benefit of the native population too poor to afford normal rented properties or to buy), or by putting the illegal immigrants up in hotels.

Irrespective of the merits of the claims for asylum, the illegal immigrants are rarely deported. They stay, still need to be housed, and have children. This all draws upon the welfare infrastructure, e.g. schools, hospitals, roads, railways, and housing.

This leads to the third part of how political correctness is funded: Ponzi economics. The welfare system, particularly regarding mass immigration, is run as a Ponzi scheme. The government takes money from those immigrants in work, who tend to be younger than the host population. The welfare benefits paid out, in the short term, are less than the tax revenues the immigrants paid. Therefore, the government is happy immigration is a good thing. But what of the extra demands immigration places on schools, hospitals, roads, railways and housing? The government either does not pay those bills, or makes a fanfare of the odd token gesture towards doing so.

Meanwhile, the accumulated liability for pensions is ignored. This is an unpaid bill that is an escalating debt some future government must deal with many years away. A Ponzi scheme will collapse ultimately due to the consumption of capital to meet debts as they fall due, but due to the promise of a profitable return, those debts are greater than the incoming capital in the long term. In the short term, the Ponzi scheme can survive by attracting an ever larger number of investors, but ultimately the scheme will not be able to attract sufficient investment capital to meet the debts as they fall due for payment. The scheme collapses, overwhelmed by large unpaid debts and paltry assets as the capital invested has been consumed.

Governments are different and have more leeway with Ponzi economics. Put simply, they do not pay the debts as they fall due. They just offload them as unpaid bills onto the public. Pensions are cut, welfare payments are cut, new schools are not built, hospitals are not built, roads and railways are not constructed, and the housing stock remains broadly the same despite the expanding population. As a result, the public pays. Pensioners are financially squeezed, as are others dependent on welfare. School classes get bigger, and consequently, the quality of schooling diminishes. Hospitals are stretched, doctor and dentist appointments difficult to get, and waiting lists get longer. Traffic jams get worse and the railway carriages get more packed. Living standards fall for many as they are priced out of having a home of their own (and so would ultimately become property owners with an asset they can pass on to their children) and have to pay increased rents in the private sector, assuming they can even pay that and are not forced to live with their parents.

Not only is the quality of life reduced, but these unpaid bills reduce the income and wealth of the public. Even sitting in a traffic jam can be quantified as a cost. Housing is more easily quantified as many lose out on the opportunity to become homeowners, and hence their children lose out on their inheritance.

Wages are depressed. Having to compete with low paid immigrants drives down wages. Especially if immigrants are shacked up in dormitories to avoid the costs of housing and maximise the money left to send back home (where costs are cheaper and the money goes far further). Worse, in the long term, productivity growth is reduced as employers use cheap immigrant labour rather than invest in more productive machinery. For example, as the then UK Chancellor of the Exchequer, Philip Hammond, pointed out, Britons have to work five days to do what German workers do in four. To put it another way, the income of British workers is only 80 per cent of what it should be if British productivity matched Germany's, and British workers would be 20 per cent better off if they did so. This is the cumulative cost of the corrupting effect of the welfare system on governance.

A very good example of the grip of Ponzi economics in the UK is the Office for Budget Responsibility's (OBR) 'Economic and Fiscal Outlook' report of March 2016 (in the run up to the EU referendum). In this report, the OBR examined the effect on the government surplus or deficit, going forward, of different levels of net migration into the UK. They had three scenarios: high, low and 'natural change' (or zero net migration) scenarios. In doing this, they made some assumptions (italics are my emphasis):

> 'In these scenarios, higher/lower migration leads to a higher/lower population and employment rate (because net inward migration is concentrated among people of working age). *We do not assume any change in average*

productivity per worker. The effect on the public finances is driven by population size (e.g. higher numbers of taxpayers or benefit recipients) and age structure (e.g. those of working-age pay more tax and do not receive child benefit or state pensions). *Since the Government has set departmental spending plans in cash terms, we do not assume that changes in population size lead to changes in departmental spending.'*[206]

According to the 2011 census, 26 per cent of Muslims had no qualifications, with the percentages for Hindus and Sikhs being 13.2 per cent and 19.4 per cent respectively. Yet the OBR assumed that there would be no difference in productivity between comparatively well-educated British people and immigrants, many of whom are from the Third World ('net migrants to the UK on average have the same age- and gender-specific characteristics as the native population, with the same employment rates and productivity and the same net contributions to the public finances'). Furthermore, with a steady inflow of cheap immigrant labour, employers can exploit that labour rather than invest in more modern production methods and so raise the productivity of their existing, indigenous workforce. Furthermore, the laws of supply and demand dictate an increase in supply will depreciate the cost of that supply. The more workers there are, the lower the wage rates. Furthermore, workers require welfare (such as schools and hospitals) and future pension provision – more advanced machinery to raise productivity does not. Machines do not need pensions.

The OBR justified the assumption that departmental spending would not change on the grounds they were 'fixed in cash terms at the levels set out in the November Spending Review and this Budget' and those levels were set for the 'next four years', so there would be no increase regardless of net migration. No extra spending on schools, hospitals, roads, railways, or for housing – at all. Not one penny.

The OBR were fixated with the size of the population as being the route to higher growth:

> '...the reason for potential output growth being revised down less than trend productivity in the UK but more than trend productivity in the US is largely due to developments in the labour market ... In the US, the CBO [Congressional Budget Office] expects it to have fallen significantly. Population growth has boosted potential output by more than expected in both countries, with net migration being the main factor in the UK.'

The OBR were open in their praise for net migration:

> 'Net international migration to the UK is an important driver of the economy's underlying growth potential. It affects it directly (via population growth) and indirectly (by contributing to changes in the employment rate, average hours worked or underlying productivity growth). Net migration has accounted for over half of UK population growth over the past 15 years and the ONS projects that this will remain so over the five years of our forecast period. Net migration to the UK has typically been concentrated among people of working age, which the ONS assumes will continue over the coming years. That means net migration leads to a higher employment rate and lower dependency ratio than would otherwise be the case.'[207]

In assessing the impact of net migration on the three scenarios, the OBR 'assumed that net migration affects potential output growth (via population and employment rate effects)' and that 'while real and nominal GDP growth vary in each scenario, inflation, average earnings growth, interest rates and the unemployment rate are unchanged'. Although, 'We have, however, assumed that given the very low responsiveness of housing supply in the UK to changes in demand, changes in population growth will feed through to changes in house prices.'

The outcomes of the three scenarios were that the high level net migration scenario produced higher GDP, the low migration scenario produced a less high level of GDP, and the zero net migration led to lower GDP and lower house prices.

It should be noted that the OBR adopted a statist approach and gave a good example of civic nationalism in practice. They examined the issue of net migration from the state's viewpoint and did not take any account of the interests of the public. English interests were ignored.

The idea more people will cause more tax is bunkum. To be exact, people are not taxed. What is taxed is their *income and expenditure*. What is needed is higher income. One person earning £50,000 will pay more tax than two people earning £25,000 each, and that one person will require less welfare and only one state pension. The case for net migration is garbage.

The so-called Office for Budget Responsibility set out a Ponzi scheme. They set out an example of Ponzi economics. In the short term, the state could pocket more money in taxes than it paid out in benefits, due to the assumed demographics of the immigrants. The state could then spend this 'profit'. The future liabilities arising with the net migration, such as pensions or the future population growth arising as the immigrants have children, were completely ignored and not quantified. Further, the OBR assumed whatever the level of net migration there was, there would be no increase in government spending to deal with that net migration, such as spending on schools, hospitals, roads, railways, housing and the whole infrastructure of local government. They assumed there would be no adverse impact on wage rates, productivity, inflation, or unemployment. They did acknowledge house prices might increase, due to the inevitable housing shortage, but did not quantify the financial impact of that upon the indigenous population or the adverse effect on that population's quality of life in the short or long term. Nor did they take any account of the social consequences.

This is Ponzi economics; it is a fraud, and it is key to the funding of political correctness.

The False Morality

The moral and political aspects of the hegemony of political correctness, its false morality, also consist of three parts: first, it is the basis of a false morality that has been accepted as the definition of morality across the West; second, this false morality is the trigger for the Inquisition against those deemed heretics; and third, the growth of the woke-Right has weakened opposition to political correctness. They have accepted that false morality of political correctness and supplanted the genuine conservatives.

The piety of political correctness is one of its attractions for many. Talk of diversity, racial justice, equality and human rights are all holy words that are highly appealing to wet liberals and do-gooders. They can embrace all these alleged causes without bothering to look behind at the actual consequences of the false morality. They need not confront the cultural Marxism that is political correctness. Diversity, in practice, means division and hatred. It means an open borders policy for immigration with no thought as to the financial consequences or the growth in terrorism the clash of culture brings. The ultimate result of demographic changes is too far away to be of any interest to them.

How can one disagree with the cause of racial justice? It of course presumes the status quo is racial injustice. It presumes the wealth and success of the West is something which Westerners should be ashamed of and Third World immigrants should take such wealth. It presumes White nations have no right to live in safety in their own countries.

Equality has been a demand of communists since that creed's inception. Equal *outcomes* for all the state imposes on the people for their own good. That the politics of envy resulted in the deaths of more than 100 million people in the 20th century and failed economies across the communist world is not something that need trouble the ruling classes or the global elite.

'Human rights' are the holiest of holy words. As can be seen above, judges are the high priests officiating how these holy words are interpreted. The outcome is an immigration system mired in criminality, greed (of both lawyers and people smugglers) and an illegal immigrant invasion. The consequences on the host nation are dramatic, with the grooming, rape and gang rape of English children being the most horrifying result. Impoverishment and the culture wars are an escalating disaster with demographic suicide the final result – unless there is change.

To supplement the analysis of the Frankfurt School's role in the development and power of political correctness, and the false morality of it, there are the matters Yuri Bezmenov raised. This defector from the KGB to the USA gave an interview ('"Useful Idiots" and the True Face of Communism') with G. Edward-Griffin in 1984 in which he explained how the KGB was primarily in the business of subversion – not espionage – and how they would subvert the West. Prior to his defection, Bezmenov worked for the KGB in India.

Bezmenov had little patience with those trying to appease the Soviet Union (USSR). He said, 'As long as the Soviet junta [keeps] on receiving credits, money, technology, grain deals, and political recognition, from all these traitors of democracy or freedom' there was 'no hope' of change in the Soviet Union. The communist dictatorship would survive and continue its activities as the West and the USA 'nourished' it. The West was nourishing 'its own destroyer'. The USA therefore needed to stand up to and stop the USSR 'unless you want to end up in [a] gulag system, and enjoy all the advantages of socialist equality, working for free, catching fleas on your body, sleeping on planks of plywood, in Alaska this time, I guess'. He therefore urged Americans to 'wake up' and 'force their government to stop aiding' the USSR.

The interview delved into the methods the KGB used, and Bezmenov revealed the execution of opponents and even potential troublemakers was ruthlessly applied. He cited the South Vietnamese city of Hue where thousands of those deemed to be aiding the South Vietnamese government and the Americans were quickly executed when the communists briefly conquered it during the Vietnam war. He said, 'Long before [the] communists occupied the city, there was [an] extensive network of informers, local Vietnamese citizens who knew absolutely everything about people who were instrumental in public opinion, including barbers and taxi drivers. Everyone who was sympathetic to [the] United States was executed.' This was routine for a communist revolution. Regarding India, he discovered the KGB had files of 'people who were doomed to execution' in the event of a communist revolution. These files included the 'names of pro-Soviet journalists with whom I was personally friendly', and also who were 'idealistically-minded Leftists who made several visits to [the] USSR. And yet, the KGB decided that in the event of "con-revolution", or drastic changes in [the] political structure of India, they will have to go'.

Bezmenov said the reason for the KGB's murderous ruthlessness towards Leftists and useful idiots was:

'Because they know too much. Simply, because, you see, the useful idiots, the Leftists who are idealistically believing in the beauty of [the] Soviet socialist or communist or whatever system, when they get disillusioned, they become the worst enemies. That's why my KGB instructors specifically made the point: never bother with the Leftists. Forget about these political prostitutes. Aim higher ... Try to get into large-circulation, established conservative media; reach the filthy-rich movie makers; intellectuals, so-called "academic" circles; cynical, egocentric people who can look into your eyes with [an] angelic expression and tell you a lie. These are the most recruitable people: people who lack moral principles, who are either too greedy or ...

312

suffer from self-importance. They feel they matter a lot. These are the people who[m] [the] KGB wanted very much to recruit.'

When asked if the useful idiots and Leftists might still serve some purpose, Bezmenov replied:

'No. They serve [a] purpose only at the stage of destabilization of a nation. For example, your Leftists in [the] United States – all these professors and all these beautiful civil rights defenders – they are instrumental in the process of the subversion only to destabilize a nation. When their job is completed, they are not needed any more. They know too much. Some of them, when they get disillusioned, when they see that Marxist-Leninists come to power – obviously they get offended – they think that they will come to power. That will never happen, of course. They will be lined up against the wall and shot.'

Bezmenov cited Nicaragua, Grenada, Afghanistan and Bangladesh where this had happened. The useful idiots and Leftists were either executed or imprisoned. With the same objective, in India, the KGB drew up lists of those to be executed, including 'most of the Indians who were cooperating with the Soviets, especially with our Department of Information of the USSR embassy'.

When asked what ideological subversion meant, Bezmenov explained it as a 'process, which is legitimate, overt, and open; you can see it with your eyes'. All that the mass media had to do was to 'unplug their bananas from their ears, open up their eyes, and they can see it'. It was nothing mysterious nor anything to do with espionage. He said James Bond was not relevant and was for the movies.

According to Bezmenov, only about 15 per cent of the KGB's time, money and manpower was spent on espionage whereas 85 per cent was devoted to the slow process of 'ideological subversion', often referred to as 'active measures' or 'psychological warfare'. The purpose of this subversion was to 'change the perception of reality, of every American, to such an extent that despite the abundance of information, no one is able to come to sensible conclusions in the interests of defending themselves, their families, their community and their country'. Importantly, he continued:

> 'It's a great brainwashing process, which goes very slow[ly] and is divided into four basic stages. The first one being 'demoralization'. It takes from 15-20 years to demoralize a nation. Why that many years? Because this is the minimum number of years which [is required] to educate one generation of students in the country of your enemy, exposed to the ideology of the enemy. In other words, Marxist-Leninist ideology is being pumped into the soft heads of at least three generations of American students, without being challenged, or counter-balanced by the basic values of Americanism – American patriotism.
>
> The result? The result you can see. Most of the people who graduated in the sixties – drop-outs or half-baked intellectuals – are now occupying the positions of power in the government, civil service, business, mass media, [and the] educational system. You are stuck with them. You cannot get rid of them. They are contaminated. They are programmed to think and react to certain stimuli in a certain pattern. You cannot change their minds, even if you expose them to authentic information, even if you prove that white is white and black is black, you still cannot change the basic perception and the logic of behaviour. In other words, [with] these people the process of demoralization is complete and irreversible. To rid society of these people, you need another 20 or 15 years to educate a new generation of patriotically-minded and common-sense people, who

314

would be acting in favour and in the interests of United States society.'

When quizzed if these would be the very people 'who would be marked for extermination in this country?', Brezmenov replied:

'Most of them, yes. Simply because the psychological shock when they will see in [the] future what the beautiful society of "equality" and "social justice" means in practice. Obviously, they will revolt. They will be very unhappy, frustrated people, and the Marxist–Leninist regime does not tolerate these people. Obviously, they will join the leagues of dissenters and dissidents ... In [the] future, these people will be simply squashed like cockroaches. Nobody is going to pay them nothing for their beautiful, noble ideas of equality. This they don't understand and it will be [the] greatest shock for them, of course.

The demoralization process in [the] United States is basically completed already ... actually, it's over-fulfilled because demoralization now reaches such areas where previously not even Comrade Andropov and all his experts would even dream of such a tremendous success. Most of it is done by Americans to Americans, thanks to [a] lack of moral standards ... exposure to true information does not matter any more. A person who was demoralized is unable to assess true information. The facts tell nothing to him. Even if I shower him with information, with authentic proof, with documents, with pictures; even if I take him by force to the Soviet Union and show him [a] concentration camp, he will refuse to believe it, until he receives a kick in is fat bottom. When the military boot crushes his balls, then he will understand. But not before that. That's the tragedy of the situation of demoralization.'

The next stage of subversion is 'destabilization'. In this stage, which would take only about two to five years, the focus is on the essentials: the economy, foreign relations and defence. Bezmenov expressed surprise at the extent to which the USA had fallen under the influence of 'Marxist-Leninist ideas'. The next stage is crisis, which could be engineered in as little as six weeks. Bezmenov cited Central America as a good example of the crisis stage.

After the 'crisis' stage, 'with a violent change of power, structure, and economy', there is the final stage of 'normalization'. Bezmenov described this as 'cynical expression borrowed from Soviet propaganda. When Soviet tanks moved into Czechoslovakia in 1968, Comrade Brezhnev said: "Now the situation in brotherly Czechoslovakia is normalized".' Bezmenov warned the USA should not allow 'all these schmucks to bring the country to crisis' with promises of 'all kinds of goodies and the paradise on earth' nor allow them to 'destabilize your economy' or put a 'Big Brother government in Washington' who will 'promise lots of things, never mind whether they are fulfillable or not.'

Bezmenov warned that although there were 'false illusions that the situation is under control, [the] situation is not under control. [The] situation is disgustingly out of control.' He said people were being led to think by 'politicians, media and educational system' they were living in peacetime. This was false. He said the USA was in a 'state of war: undeclared, total war against the basic principles and foundations of this system. And the initiator of this war ... [is] the system, however ridiculous it may sound, [it is] the world communist system – or world communist conspiracy. Whether I scare some people or not, I don't give a hoot. If you are not scared by now, nothing can scare you'.

When asked what could be done, Bezmenov answered:

> 'The immediate thing that comes to my mind is, of course, there must be a very strong national effort to

educate people in the spirit of real patriotism – number one. Number two, to explain [to] them the real danger of socialist, communist, whatever, welfare state, Big Brother government. If people will fail to grasp the impending danger of that development, nothing ever can help [the] United States. You may kiss goodbye to your freedoms [for] homosexuals, [for] prison inmates; all this freedom will vanish, evaporate in five seconds ... including your precious lives.'

This last comment was clearly targeted at the do-gooders.

Bezmenov further urged the public 'to force their government, and I'm not talking about sending letters, signing petitions, and all this beautiful, noble activity'. Instead, the government should be forced to stop aiding communism. Regarding the 'capitalists and wealthy businessmen', he said, 'I think they are selling the rope from which they will hang very soon. If they don't stop, if they cannot curb their unsettled desire for profit, and if they keep on trading with the monster of the Soviet communism, they are going to hang very soon.' Bezmenov concluded, 'I know it sounds unpleasant. I know Americans don't like to listen to things which are unpleasant, but I have defected not to tell you the stories about such idiocy as microfilm, James Bond-type espionage. This is garbage. You don't need any espionage any more. I have come to talk about survival.'

Bezmenov, using the alias Thomas Schuman while lecturing in Canada, presented a lecture called the 'Stages of Subversion' covering the matters of the interview above, in which he gave a few further details. In the lecture notes, regarding subversion, he wrote:

'Subversion on this level requires infiltration into domestic institutions of a nation as well as into her foreign policymaking bodies. Domestically, the aim of the subverter is to weaken the home defences, such as security services, police, army, civil service, other public services (transport, post office, hydro – if nationalized, etc.). The methods – discreditation of the administration of the most vital national services. Investigations of "wrong doings"; corruption affairs, sex scandals – implication of the national leaders and politicians in fraudulent or dubious affairs, smear tactics in media etc. Ridicule everything "patriotic" as psychotic. Describe every effort to reveal the activity of subverter (KGB et al.) as "paranoid". Discredit everyone, who can testify to public, media and parliament the true nature of subversion (immigrants from Communist regimes are shown to a nation as "emotionally unbalanced". Solzhenytsin "arrogant prophet and a profiteer" etc.).'

Internationally, the demoralisation process would seek to create a division between Western countries and with their allies, and to ensnare the West, or some of the countries, into useless treaties. Further, the aim would be to undermine the West economically by one-sided trade deals, economic espionage and takeovers, and dumping strategies designed to bankrupt manufacturing sectors (communist China has benefited greatly from all this in the 21st century).

The destabilisation stage would consist of the encouragement of workplace unrest, the agitation of pressure groups, the undermining of democratic institutions, tolerance of criminality, and a centralisation of government power. The aim being to 'create an atmosphere of insecurity and panic'.

In stage three, the 'crisis' stage, the aim would be to bring about economic collapse, strikes, civil unrest, and a growth of terrorism and crime. Potentially, a rival government would be formed or imported. Ideally, a communist occupation army would be invited to intervene.

In stage four, 'normalization', there would be the expulsion and execution of the previous leaders, military and security personnel. Any resistance would be denounced as an 'imperialist plot'. Press censorship would be imposed. Political opponents would be arrested and sent to concentration camps for those deemed 'enemies of the people'.

To resist subversion, Bezmenov said, 'It takes a unified national effort. Any democratic nation should cultivate such attitudes as devotion to one's country, patriotism, moral strength, working ethics, resurrection of all national traditional values.'

In the event, under President Reagan, the USA faced up to the Soviet threat and won the Cold War, strongly supported by the UK under Margaret Thatcher. That was a victory against the enemy without, there was no conclusive victory against the enemy within. Far from it, the Western communists were unashamed of their long-standing support for the gulag, slave-labour and the infested decrepitude of communism in practice, and were also undeterred by the various genocides that killed more than 100 million people. Instead, the Western communists embraced political correctness, rummaged around for other supposedly oppressed victims who they could use to buttress their falling support among the wider population, fastened upon race war politics in particular, and redoubled their efforts to destroy the West from within.

To give one example about the extent the demoralisation process has reached, in the UK the American pollster Frank Luntz carried out research that revealed 37 per cent regarded the UK as 'institutionally racist and discriminatory' and 41 per cent accepted the concept of 'White privilege'. These figures demonstrate that race war dogma has been accepted not only by the immigrant communities but also by a significant proportion of the indigenous British people. To focus on Labour voters and Tory voters, 48 per cent of Labour voters regarded the UK as being 'institutionally racist and discriminatory', while 19 per cent of Tory voters believed the same.

In the polling research, only five per cent of voters identified as being woke, although a quarter supported the cancel culture as they believed that those voicing racist or sexist views should face the consequences. Luntz believed the culture wars that had divided the USA would soon divide the UK to a similar extent.

The KGB subversion strategy, as Bezmenov set out, is entirely consistent with the strategy the Frankfurt School adopted – in particular Habermas' aim that people should be taught to hate their countries. The KGB and Habermas are at one. Bezmenov is correct in stressing the need for the West to enact fundamental change, and the need for an assertion of patriotic values rather than the false morality of political correctness.

That change must first get past the Inquisition. Political correctness, as the term implies, only allows one point of view. It is a belief system. Heresy is not allowed. The politically correct do not believe in free speech. There is none more outraged than a believer who encounters someone deemed a heretic. Deviation from political correctness triggers the Inquisition's denunciation and persecution. Name calling is a routine result. Heretics can lose their reputations and their jobs. Ultimately, criminal prosecution awaits.

This has had a profound effect on the political Right, with the growth of the woke-Right. These people, who often style themselves as conservatives, have accepted political correctness at face value, regard it as the basis of morality, fully support the Inquisition and strive to demonstrate their adherence to cultural Marxist ideology. This gutless betrayal is partly because they fear being called nasty names and believe the triumph of political correctness is inevitable, and partly because they believe they can gain from joining in the condemnation of those deemed heretics – which extends to a large part of the electorate and their own supporters. These phonies are not genuine conservatives and have retreated into classical liberalism (free trade, free markets and low taxation). In many cases, even classical liberalism is too much and they prefer their own version of a socialist economic policy. In the USA, they are known as Rinos (Republican In Name Only).

The importance of the emergence of the woke-Right cannot be underestimated. They dominate the right of politics and even the dissident Right in the UK. This means that the case against political correctness is not properly put and is only half-hearted.

320

A good example of this is Steve Bannon, who was closely involved with both the Conservative platform Breitbart and Trump's 2016 presidential campaign.

Speaking at the Oxford Union in November 2018, Bannon made some useful points and also an alarming revelation. Speaking off-the-cuff, he pointed out that the elites and the banking system had wrecked Western economies. He believed it was the reaction against the 'corrupt incompetent elite' that had led to the populist revolt and Donald Trump's victory in 2016.

Bannon said he saw three extinction-level events that posed a threat to the USA. First, the rise of China and deindustrialisation. He described China as 'a totalitarian, mercantilist regime'. Second, the $7 trillion spent on wars in the Middle East, and, third, the financial crisis. He regarded the populist revolt, including Brexit, as a product of these threats. He pointed out that big business wanted immigration in order to depress wages, and President Trump was committed to bringing back high value manufacturing jobs. Importantly, he pointed out a growth rate of 1.8 per cent was not normal, and a normal growth rate would be around 3.5 per cent.

In the long run, the difference between a growth rate of only 1.8 per cent and 3.5 per cent is major. The higher growth rate would produce far higher living standards and tax revenues. The UK's growth rate since the financial crisis of 2008 has been far lower than even 1.8 per cent. There has barely been any growth at all.

(Since 2007, the year before the financial crash, until the end of 2017, Britain's GDP increased by only 11 per cent. This was achieved by expanding the workforce by 8.7 per cent, and pumping £435 billion of printed money into the economy through Quantitative Easing and hence transferring the wealth of private pensions to the bankers, falling living standards, and an increase in household debt. In July 2018, ONS figures showed households took out £80 billion in loans in the previous year, while only £37 billion was saved in bank accounts. Households were spending more than they earned for the first time in 30 years. The excess spending amounted to £25 billion. The poorest families spent around two-and-a-half times their disposable income. This is Ponzi growth, and it is a fraud. Without this increase in debt-funded consumer spending, the UK would have been in recession).

Bannon rejected fascism as the answer and described it as being a combination of crony capitalism and a big state. Instead, he advocated 'economic nationalism'. He said Trump ran on a ticket of 'stop mass immigration and limit legal immigration, to get our sovereignty back, and, more importantly, to protect our workers'. He said, 'We are still going to have immigration. But we are going to limit it, because economic nationalism doesn't care about your colour, your ethnicity, your religion, your gender, your sexual preference. What it cares about is that you are a citizen.'

Having advocated 'economic nationalism', Bannon defined it. Crucially, he still advocated immigration – albeit more limited – and revealed he would allow economic nationalism to determine the make-up of those immigrants, who could be of any race, ethnicity, religion, etc. He did not advocate an Anglo-conformity immigration policy, and, in effect, rejected it. Consequently, he ignored the social and political costs of immigration and the need for social cohesion:

> 'Ethno-nationalism is ridiculous. It's stupid on the face of it. It's ridiculous. I've said it from day one. Ethno-nationalism is a dead end. It's for losers. Economic nationalism and civic nationalism binds you together, as citizens, regardless of your race, regardless of your ethnicity, regardless of your religion. That's what we stand for.'

These remarks from someone at the heart of the Trump campaign and, for a time, the Trump presidency, are a revelation. First, there is a dichotomy between the so-called civic nationalists and ethnic nationalists. In reality, there is only nationalism. Nationality is not the same as citizenship. Civic nationalism (or constitutional patriotism) is a Frankfurt School construct. Nationalism is not.

Second, Bannon is actually rejecting an Anglo-conformity immigration policy. For him, immigrants could be of any ethnicity, religion etc. and economic criteria should be the sole determinant of who is allowed to immigrate and become a citizen.

Third, Bannon's assertion that 'economic nationalism and civic nationalism' is sufficient to bind together all citizens, irrespective of cultural, ethnic or political differences, is wrong. Is Bannon unaware of the failure of the Ottoman empire in a 500 year timespan to build an Ottoman nation despite creating an Ottoman citizenship? Is he unaware the different ethnicities and religions eventually broke the Ottoman empire apart? Is he unaware of the bloodshed that still affects the former parts of the Ottoman empire to this day? Is he unaware of the failure of 100 years of imposed secularism by the Kemalist elite in Turkey that failed to instil a secular culture on the Muslim population? We are to presume he is unaware that Yugoslavia, after many decades of communist rule, disintegrated after a viscous civil war and ethnic cleansing; that the countries across North Africa are either under military dictatorship or are failed states (in particular Libya – despite its oil wealth); that other countries such as Syria, Iraq and Lebanon could not, in many decades, build a unified nation after the various wars between ethnicities and religions comprising those countries, which had been put together by drawing lines on a map; that Africa is riven with ethnic conflict (e.g. the Rwandan genocide); or even that Northern Ireland remains split between Catholics and Protestants.

Bannon advocated a Frankfurt School theory (civic nationalism) combined with one of his own (economic nationalism) – an exercise in wishful thinking and a dodge from rejecting cultural Marxism (launched by the Frankfurt School and of which civic nationalism is a part) and from the burden of advocating those policies necessary to keep the USA American.

He revealed himself to be woke-Right. This is someone who was at the very centre of the Trump revolution.

Bannon was not alone. Another influential figure in the Trump movement was Charlie Kirk, the founder of Turning Point USA, who claimed foreign students 'should staple a green card behind your diploma' after their courses were completed in order to immigrate to the USA. He was another who favoured mass immigration and campaigned for that policy. He subsequently backtracked.

In the USA, a nasty example of the woke-Right is the Lincoln Project. This organisation was publicly launched in December 2019 with a *New York Times* article. Those involved included 'some of the most prominent Never Trump Republicans', who, naturally, were anti-Trump *and anti-Trumpism*. The organisation was critical of the perceived takeover of the Republican Party by President Trump and complained that 'two views cannot exist in one party'.

The Lincoln Project quickly denounced and campaigned against perceived Trump supporters and also endorsed the presidential campaign of the Democrat candidate Joe Biden. The organisation ran some ads which were personal attacks on President Trump and his supporters. Swing states were targeted. One ad criticised Trump supporters for using the Confederate flag at Trump rallies and accused President Trump of receiving support from White nationalists.

Fundraising was a breeze. The Lincoln Project raised $87,404,908 for the 2020 presidential election and continued to attract funds afterwards.

On their website, the Lincoln Project describes themselves as 'Dedicated Americans Protecting Democracy', and of their mission:

> 'The fight against Trumpism is just beginning. The Lincoln Project launched with two stated objectives. The first was to defeat Donald Trump at the ballot box. The second was to ensure Trumpism failed alongside him. As we have seen, our fight against Trumpism is only

324

beginning. We must combat these forces everywhere and at all times. Our democracy depends on it.'

The website alleges: 'Tribalism in the country and hyper-partisanship in government has led to ever uglier examples of how our political system is failing. President Donald Trump and those who ascribe to Trumpism are a clear and present danger to the Constitution and our Republic.' In 2021, the Texas governor, Greg Abbott, was a particular target, as was 'the bloody tide of authoritarian populism'.

In the UK, the Tories support politically correct organisations such as the Conservatives Against Racism For Equality (see Appendix Four) and One Britain One Nation (see Appendix Five).

Another example of the woke-Right, in the UK, is the speed with which the then Tory prime minister, Theresa May, embraced the transgender madness. In October 2017, she told the Pink News awards: 'We are determined to eradicate homophobic and transphobic bullying. We have laid out plans to reform the gender recognition act, streamlining and de-medicalising the process for changing gender because being trans is not an illness and it should not be treated as such.' She further said:

'I am proud to be a member of one of the most diverse parliaments in the world and of the long way we have come as a country on LGBT+ issues – from the Sexual Offences Act 50 years ago to the Same Sex Marriage Act, which I was proud to sponsor as home secretary. But there is still much more to do and I am committed to seeing that work through – for instance, eradicating homophobic and transphobic bullying in schools, and reforming the Gender Recognition Act – so that we can build a better future for everyone in our society.'

This is complete rubbish. It is antisense. For someone to think they are in the wrong body *is* a medical issue. That she targeted children and supported the chemical and then surgical castration of boys and the removal of breasts of girls is bad enough, but to try and railroad through such acts beyond medical control is appalling. May is comprehensively brainwashed.

Another example in the UK is the fixation of and policy for dealing with climate change. In a speech to the UN in September 2021, Boris Johnson said:

'And I think it's very important that we in the developed world recognize our obligation to help less developed countries down this path, in all these technologies. And we've got to be honest, we in the United Kingdom, we in Britain, started this industrial hydrocarbon-based revolution. We were the first to send great puffs of acrid smoke into heavens on a scale big enough to derange the natural order. And though we were in fact, of course, doing something rather wonderful in one sense, we were setting in train a new era of technology that was itself to lead to a massive global reduction in poverty, emancipating billions of people around the world. I mean, the industrial revolution was a good thing fundamentally, but we were also unwittingly beginning to quilt the great tea cosy of carbon dioxide around the world.

And so we understand that when the developing world looks to us to help, we must take our responsibilities. And that's why two years ago, when I last came here, Mr. President, to UNGA [United Nations General Assembly], I committed that the UK would provide 11.6 billion pounds to help the rest of the world to tackle climate change. And I want you to know that in spite of all the pressures on our finances in the UK caused by COVID, we have kept that promise to the letter. And so I'm very pleased and encouraged by some of the pledges we've heard here at UNGA, including from Denmark, and now, a very substantial commitment from the United States that brings us within touching distance of that $100 billion pledge that we need every year. But we must go further

326

and we've got to be clear that government alone, government cash alone, is not going to be enough.

We must work together so that the international financial institutions, the IMF, the World Bank, are working with governments around the world to leverage in the private sector, because it is the trillions of dollars of private sector cash that will enable developing nations and the whole world, all of us, to make the changes necessary.'

According to Boris Johnson, the UK is to blame for global warming and the Third World is consequently entitled to expect even more subsidies from the UK. Further, his intention was to get hold of yet more monies from the private sector and 'international financial institutions' for yet more subsidies for the Third World. Apparently, the various countries of the Third World were not responsible for their own affairs and were not expected to act responsibly.

The version of history Boris Johnson advanced is pure political correctness. He exhibited a typical White-guilt complex. Once again, Westerners, the British in particular, were told to hate their countries. The UK did not start global warming, and given it was only responsible for around 0.9 per cent of greenhouse gas emissions, the UK was not responsible now.

The industrial revolution started in Britain decades before any other country. It began in the late 18th century. In 1750, the population of Britain (England, Scotland and Wales) was around 7.87 million. By 1801, it had risen to around 10.8 million (the world's population was around one billion at that time). By comparison, the populations of India and China, both of which are industrialising rapidly, in the 21st century are a little under three billion. It may well be the UK has had two centuries of being an industrial society, but the miniscule population of the UK compared to India and China in the 21st century means even two centuries' worth of emissions are nothing compared to what India and China currently emit annually. Furthermore, living standards in Britain in the 18th and 19th centuries were far lower than those in the 21st century. There were no fridges, freezers, computers, televisions, power stations, electricity, computers, modern lifestyles, aircraft or motor vehicles. The UK is not responsible for global warming, and the West is not obligated to pay for the Third World.

Furthermore, gas emissions do not stay in the atmosphere indefinitely. Plant life and the oceans absorb CO_2 in one or two centuries. The CO_2 emissions from the industrial revolution in Britain are no longer in the atmosphere.

Furthermore, the rise in global temperatures occurred mostly since the mid-20th century. There was little increase in the 19th century. The major increases occurred after 1980. These global temperature increases coincided not only with the industrialisation of many Third World countries *but also with their population explosions*. According to the United Nations Population Fund, the human population increased from 1.6 billion to 6.1 billion in the 20th century (it was still only 2.5 billion in 1950). At the same time, greenhouse gas emissions grew 12-fold. It is forecast the world population will grow to in excess of nine billion in the next 50 years, and to more than 11 billion by the end of the century – including a 3.5-fold increase in the population of Africa according to the UN, with its population increasing from 1.3 billion to 4.3 billion. Africa's population is currently just over 17 per cent of the world's population and is forecast to increase to 40 per cent by 2100. More than 80 per cent of the world's population is predicted to live in Asia or Africa by 2100.

By comparison, world population growth was very low up until 1700, at around 0.04 per cent per annum. In the 21st century, apart from the USA, the West's populations are either static or falling – and this is despite mass immigration into Western countries. The USA is experiencing population growth mostly due to mass immigration, and its population is expected to double by 2100.

The serious matter of uncontrolled population growth in the Third World was not an item on the COP26 agenda, nor was it mentioned in the final communique. It was completely ignored and not mentioned at all.

Boris Johnson's attempt to blame the UK for climate change is hogwash. Key to dealing with climate change is to slow the population increases across the Third World – especially Africa. The population of the UK could revert to living in caves and it would make no noticeable difference to greenhouse gas emissions. The Tories' fixation on the issue, their policies for dealing with it, and their encouragement of holding the UK as being responsible is an example of the woke-Right. To quote Bezmenov, the Tories were 'unable to assess true information' and 'the facts tell nothing' to them; their 'perception of reality' has been changed to such an extent they are unable 'to come to sensible conclusions in the interests of defending themselves, their families, their community and their country'.

Another example is that in the UK, in April 2021, MPs passed a motion in the House of Commons, which declared that Uyghur Muslims in the Chinese province of Xinjiang, were 'suffering crimes against humanity and genocide'. There are up to 20 million Uyghur Muslims in China. The prime mover in presenting the motion was Nus Ghani, a Pakistani immigrant from Kashmir and a Tory MP. Ghani said genocide was not just one act of 'mass killing', but was an act of 'in whole or in part' the destruction of a national, ethnic, racial or religious group and 'All five criteria of genocide are evidenced as taking place in Xinjiang. While we must never misuse the term genocide, we must not fail to use it when it's warranted.'

Ghani complained that although the UK government believed only a competent court could determine genocide, 'every route to a court is blocked by China'. Ghani said 'credible reports' had been made that 'up to two million people are extrajudicially detained in prison factories and re-education centres'. Furthermore, the Chinese government had imposed forced birth controls on Uyghur women.

Ghani had received particular support from the former Tory leader, Sir Iain Duncan Smith, who complained, 'At the United Nations it is impossible to get through to the International Court of Justice, it is impossible to get through to the International Criminal Court as China is not a signatory to that and therefore will not obey that.'

Tory rebels voted through the motion with Labour and Liberal Democrat support. Following the approval of the motion, Duncan Smith said, 'This is a historic moment. Even though the Government maintains that only a court can determine genocide, Parliament has chosen to disregard that and vote itself. This puts the UK Parliament in line with Holland, Canada and the US.'

When Duncan Smith was persuaded to champion the cause of the Uyghur Muslims and eagerly advanced the Commons motion they are victims of genocide, one wonders how much consideration he gave to the interests of the English. Ghani, of course, is representing the interests of her fellow Muslims, as per the Muslim Umma. English interests do not motivate her. Duncan Smith, and those other Tories supporting this, were so politically correct they were incapable of defending the national interest. They had been comprehensively brainwashed.

England is swamped with immigrants, both legal and illegal. Many of those illegal immigrants claim to be asylum seekers. Regardless of the merits of their variety of claims, few are ever deported. The UK has further committed to allow millions of Hong Kong Chinese to move to the UK (in practice this will mean England). What would happen if Uyghur Muslims arrived on England's shores and claimed asylum due to genocide? Given that parliament has already decided they are victims of genocide, it is a near certainty the Leftie judges would eagerly accept that and grant them asylum. The courts would accept they have a 'right' to claim asylum in the UK – this will apply to all 20 million of them.

There is also the debacle in Afghanistan, where a supposedly 300,000-strong Afghan army collapsed and the NATO countries decided to cut and run, thus allowing the Taliban to retake control of the country in a few weeks. After the defeat, in November 2021, Khalid Payenda, a former Afghan finance minister, told Radio 4's Today programme:

'My assumption is we never had 300,000 forces. The way the accountability was done you would ask the chief in that province "how many people do you have?" and based on that, you would calculate salaries and rational expenses. These would always be inflated ... [officials] would then surrender or make a deal with the Taliban saying why don't we just split the money [for wages and ammunition] 50-50.'

Payenda said that what troops there were often went unpaid, while generals were 'double-dipping' by pocketing the wages and taking bribes from the Taliban to surrender. In 2016, a US Special Inspector General for Afghanistan Reconstruction report stated 'neither the US nor its Afghan allies know how many Afghan soldiers and police actually exist, how many are available for duty, or, by extension, the true nature of their operational capabilities'. Despite all this, the NATO allies, in particular the Americans, did nothing to stop the corruption. The UK continued to pour aid into Pakistan despite reports Pakistan was supporting the Taliban. The West lacked the resolve to defend its own interests.

Afghanistan flipped from being a Western ally into being a jihadist rogue state. This created a clamour from many Afghans for asylum. The UK declared it would allow 25,000 to move to the UK and even granted asylum to a female Afghan football team. In October 2021, Sky News reported: 'Thousands of Afghan refugees – including former interpreters who worked for British troops and children without their parents – are stuck in hotels and hostels in the UK with no date for when they will be moved to permanent homes following their evacuation from Afghanistan.' The report continued with an interview with Colonel Simon Diggins, who warned that unless the promised 'warm welcome' for the Afghans included suitable housing, there would be a danger of radicalisation in response!

If there is any danger of radicalisation from any refugee, then they should not be let into the country in the first place.

The defence of the realm comes first, as do the interests of the host nation.

In another report, Sky News reported the suspicions voiced by locals who lived near the Faslane naval base in Scotland (where the UK bases its nuclear submarines). They were concerned as to the peculiar activities of an Afghan immigrant, Waheed Totakhyl, who was closely associated with the Taliban and had once called for the death of US troops. His brother was a senior Taliban commander. Totakhyl leased a farm near the nuclear base, and claimed, 'I rent [the farm] because I like to be a farmer and enjoy the weather ... of Scotland. I never done wrong in the UK. Whatever I've done, this is for my people, for my country.'

The locals were concerned about Afghan visitors to his farm. Totakhyl denied the claims, but admitted fellow members of Afghanistan's Hezb e Islami party had attended. Hezb e Islami is led by Gulbuddin Helmatyar, an Afghan warlord dubbed the 'Butcher of Kabul' and a supporter of the Taliban.

Totakhyl came to the UK in 2001. A photo on his Facebook profile shows him holding a rifle. He claimed the photo was taken during a visit to Bagram jail to visit his brother. Recent refugees had called for Totakhyl's deportation, given his continued support for the Taliban. Why was Totakhyl allowed into the UK and why was he not deported years ago?

In another example regarding the fall of Afghanistan, the BBC Radio 4 gave airtime to a certain Khola Hasan, a scholar at the UK Islamic Sharia Council, who, when asked about the return of the Taliban, said, 'Every single person I know as a Muslim – whether on social media or as friends – are celebrating.' Another guest, Miss Saqeb Jamal, was angry: 'They have been killing us for 25 years for going to school, voting and going to work. How can you say they are people? They aren't – they are killers. I am so angry. They took my childhood.' Hasan also claimed France was the enemy of Muslims as it had banned the burka and hijab in certain places. A Westernised Muslim, Dr Taj Hargey, wrote in the *Daily Mail*:

'For Miss Hasan to proclaim that Muslims in the UK are united in welcoming this seizure of power by religious zealots, and the resulting chaos, is both obscene and an affront to the British Muslim community. It is insulting, a travesty and a sign of just how pitifully ignorant she is. But for the BBC to give her a platform to air her doctrinal falsehoods, without then demolishing them with the real facts is unforgivable...

The BBC appeared terrified of contradicting Miss Hassan, simply because she is a Muslim woman and should therefore be allowed to assert any nonsense she likes without fear of contradiction...

I listened to [Hasan's] inarticulate tripe, wishing that the BBC still employed rigorous journalists instead of 'wokelings' who are afraid to question anything for fear of seeing sexist or racist.'

Dr Taj Hargey acknowledged Jamal had dismissed Hasan's claims as 'insane', but complained Hasan was allowed to ignore her and had the last word. He wrote, 'As a Muslim scholar myself, I regard the Hadith, Sharia law and fatwa as a toxic triad. But these are the cornerstones not only of Taliban theology and thinking but also of self-serving Islamic organisations that Miss Hasan is part of.' This might be true, but unfortunately, the majority of Muslims support Sharia.

Meanwhile, in the USA, the Jihad Watch website reported the Biden administration was having problems with Afghan refugees at Fort McCoy in Wisconsin. *The Wall Street Journal* reported: 'Every toilet on base was Western style, with a seat and toilet paper. But some Afghans are accustomed to restrooms that allow them to squat so they don't have to physically touch the toilet. It led to some cases of Afghans relieving themselves outside.' A Czech reported that this was normal in Afghanistan, where Afghan 'people in rural areas were found to defecate almost everywhere according to convenience. It is important to observe that particularly the rural population does not know or does not use toilet paper.' Some interpretations of Islamic law hold the use of toilet paper is banned. Jihad Watch stated, 'Muslim tradition teaches that toilets are possessed by demons and as a result followers of the religion may be reluctant to make contact with them because they have been taught that "Satan plays with the backsides of the sons of Adam". Islamic teachings encourage squat toilets and forbid men to urinate standing up because Mohammed "only ever used to urinate sitting down."' Soldiers of the Afghan army were liable to wipe their hands on the walls before rinsing their hands in the sink. At Kandahar Air Base, the toilets were segregated. One officer said, 'When they use our port-a-potties, they stand on the seats and it causes quite a mess. I think it's just a cultural thing.'

At Fort McCoy, there were complaints about the food. They did not like the 'hard rice'. There were also complaints of 'multiple cases of minor females who presented as "married" to adult Afghan men, as well as polygamous families.' This is considered normal in Afghanistan. One refugee, Bahrullah Noori, 'was arrested for trying to undress a 14-year-old boy and behaving inappropriately with a 12-year-old boy'. Another refugee was arrested after his wife accused him of trying to choke her. He had also threatened to send her back to Afghanistan 'where the Taliban could deal with her'. Many Afghans reportedly left the bases where they were housed rather than wait to be resettled.

The admission of Afghans into the West has two further consequences. First, in the USA, the news presenter Tucker Carlson highlighted the issue of chain migration. He pointed out that for every original refugee allowed into the USA, another 3.45 would follow in chain migration. He said that between 2005 and 2016, no less than 9.3 million immigrants had entered the USA citing family membership.

Second, in the UK, there is the problem of grooming gangs. The estimates for the number of victims vary wildly. One estimate is that there are around 250,000 victims in total. Another figure from Sarah Champion is that there could be as many as one million victims over a 30-year period. Official figures estimate that around 19,000 children were sexually groomed in the previous year. The Muslim population of the UK is in excess of three million, of whom around a third are children. Also, there are many who are elderly. Assuming that around a half the population is male, then there is around one million working-age male Muslims in the UK. Those one million, between them, are primarily responsible for the grooming and rape epidemic. They are responsible for around 19,000 child rape victims per year. Then there will no doubt be those victims who are not children. Put simply, the victim rate is about two per cent of the male Muslim population.

Knowing this, the Tories continue to allow male Muslims into the UK, and boast about how many refugees, asylum seekers, and other legal and illegal Muslim immigrants are let in. The Tory policy towards Afghanistan was almost identical to the USA's Democrats. Yet the Tories are supposed to be conservatives. They are not. They are woke-Right.

The most effective way of helping genuine refugees is to do so in their own or neighbouring countries. Regarding the purported morality of asylum seeking, I will quote an extract from *The Genesis of Political Correctness* regarding the UK's response to mass migration to Europe at that time:

> 'Fourth, the media's response to the immigrant invasion was to portray all immigrants, no matter where they were from, as refugees fleeing war and poverty and seeking a new life and that they all deserved sympathy and the right to barge into Europe. Cameron [the then Tory prime minister] was attacked for using the term "swarm" in reference to the numbers of immigrants. The Tory reluctance to take quotas of immigrants was met with continuous attack. The media simply assumed that anyone who claimed to be a refugee should be allowed to settle in Europe, and there was barely any analysis as to the best way to help genuine refugees. Those responsible for the news output were not simply news reporters; as per Habermas, they were the "cultural elite" managing

335

the views of ordinary plebs, the majority of whom were against accepting any more immigrants. As per Marcuse, right-wing or patriotic viewpoints were not tolerated.

A variety of EU and UN officials popped up repeatedly on television to denounce Britain's refusal to agree to take more immigrants and refusal to become a part of an EU quota system. The "cultural elite" did not see fit to query the UN officials as to their responsibility and their failure to deal with the immigrants.

It is not the case that the left-wing media bias is purely subconscious. In fact, there is a deliberate policy to exclude right-wing views. There is a ruling class monopoly on the definition of morality. This is a phoney definition. It is all very well for the politically correct to pose for photo opportunities, knee deep in the sea, clutching immigrant children just getting off a boat, before jetting back to Britain to demand that Britain take more immigrants, but this does not help genuine refugees. A genuinely compassionate report would explore why the UN was apparently so short of funds that it was turning away refugees and explore the wisdom of why Britain was spending money on Wimmin's issues in Africa from its bloated foreign aid budget while the UN was allegedly so underfunded. One can compare the morality of these journalists and others, who pose as champions of compassion for those in the Third World from a variety of television studios where they demand that "we", i.e. the taxpayer, should do more, with 19th century missionaries. Those missionaries, many of them young women, including nuns, ventured into the barely explored Third World to help the native population. They put their own lives at risk and made considerable personal sacrifices. The politically correct sacrifice nothing themselves, are extravagant in their largesse with other people's money and interests, and seek to use the plight of the refugees and immigrants for their own political ends.

The public reaction to the crisis was divided. Some were enthusiastic about accepting more immigrants. However, public opinion was overwhelmingly out of step with the ruling class: 45 per cent considered the figure of 20,000 Syrian immigrants to be too high; 27 per cent supported the decision to allow in 20,000; only 15 per cent wanted more than 20,000. This anti-immigration view was not reflected in the news output of the media, "the cultural elite". In fact, Eurostat figures showed that, of the 213,000 immigrants logged as arriving in the EU, only 44,000 were from Syria.

The media were not alone in condemning the Tories, as 84 Church of England bishops signed an open letter to Cameron demanding that he let in at least 50,000 Syrian immigrants. This followed another letter by numerous judges and 300 lawyers a week earlier likewise demanding that the number of Syrian immigrants be increased.

One of the bishops, the Right Reverend David Walker, the Bishop of Manchester, remarked that it would be "a sad reflection" on society if ordinary people did not welcome more Syrians. Although the Archbishop of Canterbury offered a cottage and the Manchester diocese offered an empty vicarage, the bishop balked at welcoming refugees into his own house, which has six bedrooms and is owned by the church. The bishop explained: "Refugees need ... a place where they can be with their families, not try to share the breakfast table with a couple whose language they don't understand and whose culture is alien to them."

In October 2015, a leaked Home Office document put the cost of allowing in Syrian refugees at more than £24,000 per immigrant per year (£8,520 cost to the local councils, £12,700 in benefits and £2,200 for medical expenses). This figure is an underestimate as it does not take into account the impact on ordinary English families, such as on the cost of lower wages or the inability to get social housing. It also doesn't take into account other factors, such as was evidenced by a doctors' report which revealed that 1 in 20 so-called asylum seekers are HIV positive, the infection being particularly bad for those from Zimbabwe, the Democratic Republic of Congo, and Somalia, but also for the obvious inevitable costs of the spread of the infection into the UK population as a whole. Accepting the £24,000 figure, the total figure for 20,000 immigrants is therefore around £480 million per year. This should be compared to the poorest in the LDCs [less developed countries] who survive on around a dollar a day – around £240 per year. That £24,000 would provide for 100 of the poorest people in the LDCs for a year; the £480 million would provide for almost two million people in their own countries.

Also, by comparison, following a tsunami in December 2004, an appeal was made for funds, and it was set out that £5 will provide 100 litres of purified water to a refugee family, £12 will vaccinate a child for life against six killer diseases, £15 will buy a hot meal for 125 people in an emergency feeding centre, £25 buys plastic shelter and food parcels for two families for two weeks, £30 buys enough water purification tablets to give 320 children a litre each, £59 buys tarpaulin shelters for 10 families, £100 buys a tent for one refugee family, or food parcels to feed 60 families for one month, and £250 provides emergency food and shelter for 100 people.

If these bishops, lawyers, and others were sincere in their loudly proclaimed determination to help refugees, then they would be rushing through laws to prevent the people smuggling activities as fast as possible – not aiding and abetting those activities. Any objective analysis clearly shows that shipping people to overcrowded Western countries is the worst possible way to help the poor. What the bishops and lawyers are trying to do, along with a whole host of others, is to show off. They wish to parade their moral superiority (in other words, the motive is snobbery), and, for the communists, to foment a race war in Britain.'

The impact on the Third World should not be overlooked. Those paying organised crime rackets, including al-Qaeda, ISIS and the Taliban, to smuggle them across a multitude of countries, continents and oceans to the West have money. They are the wealthier and more middle class elements of their home countries, which are impoverished by the drain of resources and skills. The enrichment of organised crime rackets, especially the terrorist ones, leads to the growth of corruption and the expenditure of money on bombs, bullets, drug smuggling and dealing, and the slave trading of non-Muslim captured women. All of this is courtesy of the easy access to taxpayers' monies by the politically correct. This is moral degeneracy.

In the UK, the Tories have not taken back control of Britain's borders post-Brexit. Then there is the migration 'partnership' with India – with its population around 1.38 billion. The Tories have accepted the false morality of political correctness as the basis of morality, and their supposed opposition to it is flimsy. What they are not doing is defending British or English interests, or even understand that they should be. They are brainwashed. They are not morally superior. They are practising barbarists.

CONCLUSION

As the West now moves into the post-populist political environment, the resilience of political correctness to withstand the voter's revolt is incredible, at first glance, and understandable with some investigation. The various ways in which it affects our lives have expanded, become more shrill – and there is no effective pushback.

In 2016, both the UK and the USA experienced a voter's revolt and an unequivocal breakthrough against the establishment. The Republican Party in the USA had a new president, who was had a far more radical programme than that to which the party was used, and the party controlled both houses of Congress and a large number of state governorships. Yet President Trump failed to deliver on his pledge to build a wall along the southern border, and the ideology of political correctness ran rampant. The president became mired in fending off numerous ridiculous allegations culminating in impeachment proceedings. His administration lacked cohesion and many of his appointees left or were sacked. The Republicans lost control of the House of Representatives. The BLM protests following the killing of George Floyd were widespread and violent.

This is not to ignore that President Trump did have some solid achievements, particularly regarding foreign policy where he contained the dangerous North Korea and where he made serious progress regarding Israel and its relations with several neighbouring Arab countries. He implemented tax cuts, and the economy was booming. He further took steps and imposed tariffs to tackle the USA's trade deficit. There was a reduction in immigration. Then the Covid-19 pandemic struck, and the economy nosedived due to the lockdowns and the safety of Americans was at stake. In the following presidential election, the Democrats won after widespread election malpractice, controversy and fraud (about which the courts, including the

Supreme Court, refused to show interest). Historians might conclude that President Trump was on course to victory, but that he was unlucky.

By comparison, the UK had a decisive victory for Brexit in the EU referendum in 2016, but what followed was an international embarrassment. The Tories had a nervous breakdown as the majority of Tory MPs wanted to thwart the vote. Following David Cameron's immediate resignation, the new prime minister, Theresa May, had no intention of honouring the referendum result and sought to fudge the issue by agreeing a new 'deep and special partnership' with the EU that would minimise any recovery of sovereignty and keep the UK embroiled in EU affairs. To convince the EU to agree to this, despite being repeatedly told by the EU they were not, May offered large bribes of money and accepted the EU's demands for and terms of an unnecessary withdrawal agreement that was clearly not in the UK's best interests. As the saga was strung out, with the Brexit date being repeatedly postponed, with a shambolic House of Commons and the intervention of judges who were extending their powers, May finally lost the confidence of both the public and the Tory Party. She was replaced with Boris Johnson, who had headed the Vote Leave campaign. Boris Johnson bodged Brexit and pushed a poor deal through the parliament. The result is that an imperfect Brexit was implemented. But Brexit had been achieved and the referendum vote was finally implemented after many years.

In both the UK and the USA, and across the West, political correctness remained the dominant political creed. Far from being driven back from its dominant position, it continued to spread.

The underlying thought process of political correctness is communism – as interpreted by the Frankfurt School. In *The Genesis of Political Correctness*, I focused on three key works: *The Authoritarian Personality*; the 'Repressive Tolerance' essay; and the 'Citizenship and National Identity' essay. *The Authoritarian Personality* was an attack on mainstream conservatism and set out a rationale for mass brainwashing of

342

the population – naturally citing the need to oppose Nazism, Fascism and a new far-Right as a justification. The 'Repressive Tolerance' essay took matters further, and advocated the positive abolition of free speech for conservative views only, and the promotion of left-wing views and those deemed revolutionary. The 'Citizenship and National Identity' essay was an attack on the nation state and nationhood. Particularly, it made the case for using immigrants and ethnic minorities to undermine social cohesion and the culture of the nation states of the West. In examining the 'Citizenship and National Identity' essay, I delved into the divide between civic nationalism (aka constitutional patriotism) and ethnic nationalism, and examined the differences between citizenship and nationality.

Passport citizenship is insufficient to hold countries or empires together. It is nationality that binds together a country. It is therefore key that people are not seduced by the candyfloss language the Frankfurt School and their followers used. Both Marcuse and Habermas openly admitted they wanted to supplement class war politics with race war politics, and that is what the West is now experiencing. The Staatsvolk of the various countries of the West need to assert their rights and not be intimidated.

To take the 16 basic concepts of political correctness in turn, the three features of political correctness, as Wayne Mapp identified, explain why political correctness is different to other ideologies and ideas. First, the creed is a minority viewpoint not only divorced from mainstream society but positively hostile to it. Second, and easy to miss, is that the creed is prescriptive. The politically correct feel entitled to instruct others how to behave and what they are allowed to believe. This is fundamental. The politically correct are ideologues who are firmly convinced they should instruct the public and institutions of society what they are permitted to do and think. Deviation is not to be tolerated. The politically correct are not advocating what they want to do, but are advocating what everybody else should be allowed to do. Third, which Wayne Mapp believed was key, the politically correct captured a legislative base which enabled them to follow through on their prescriptive ideology. They not only believed they should instruct others what they might do and think, but were actively engaged in imposing those instructions on society as a whole. Wayne Mapp believed 'a clear programme' was required to reverse political correctness and 'to remove the viewpoints and language of the politically correct from the institutions of government' otherwise nothing will 'materially change' other than 'the most obvious examples of government silliness', and that: 'Removing the power of the politically correct means removing their institutional and legislative base.' Despite the Brexit vote in the UK, or the election of President Trump in the USA, there was no determined effort made to achieve this in either country.

The second basic concept, the two wings of political correctness and the opposing patriotic stance, highlight the two wings of political correctness: the liberal wing, who advocate the candyfloss language at face value, and the communist wing who believe in the communism that political correctness is and welcome the damage it does. The importance of this is that protests from patriots that political correctness causes harm will have no effect on the communists who intend to cause harm. It might affect the liberal wing differently save for that they have embraced the creed notwithstanding the harm it causes. All the talk of human rights, justice and the search for equality persuades the liberal wing, who are in deep denial of the communism they advocate. They are useful idiots who fancy themselves as being morally superior to the rest of us. They are snobs. They are bigots in the truest sense in that their minds are closed. They have been brainwashed and impervious to reality – just as Bezmenov warned.

The third basic concept is that of the barbarist. This is important. Collingwood, as did other philosophers, examined the relationship between civilised societies and barbarian ones. He described the different aspects of civilisation: an entity, a process, and the contrast with more backward societies. Rightly, he pointed out the relationship between civilisation and barbarian societies was relative. However, Collingwood went

344

further and contrasted a barbarian with a barbarist. A barbarian was someone who was uncivilised, possibly through no fault of his own and possibly stemming from being born into a less civilised society. A barbarian might wish to become civilised and acquire the benefits of civilisation.

By contrast, a barbarist, who may be in a relatively barbarian society or a civilised one, positively rejects civilisation and seeks to destroy it. A barbarist seeks to barbarise civilisation. Collingwood believed this was impossible. With respect, Collingwood was wrong. Barbarists can destroy civilisation as an entity, and there are many historical examples of this. With the destruction of civilisation as an entity, the destruction of the process of civilisation follows.

Political correctness is a barbarist creed with an objective of destroying and barbarising the West. The West needs to recognise this and square up to the barbarists and destroy the poison they advocate.

The fourth basic concept is the Inquisition. The aptly named cancel culture is but one manifestation of this. Even the outcome of the electoral process can be affected if the vote is not one the politically correct approve. Both the Brexit vote and President Trump's election were debunked. Ordinary political activists faced the prospect of losing their access to the main social media platforms, if not worse. The censorship across social media is ever increasing. Children were targeted. Language and words were more restricted. Certain films were subjected to adverse comment. A particular cause célèbre was the trans issue – both to impose the righteousness of the campaign to encourage more people, including children, to undergo sex change surgery, and to demonise anyone who did not agree with this. Even feminists and lesbians fell afoul of the Inquisition when they objected to the erosion of safe spaces for women.

The Inquisition was prosecuted by government, the police and judges, the media (both mainstream and social), charities and even business corporations. Writers and books could be banned (as even J. K. Rowling discovered, although she battled her way out).

The fifth basic concept is the weighty issue of race war politics and the anti-Whites, which has created hatred and division beyond the Frankfurt School's wildest imagination. It is steadily getting worse. Even those immigrants elected to high office are open in their hatred of the West. CRT has been adopted across state sectors. The slave trade of centuries ago has become an excuse for the destruction of statues and demands for reparations. History is rewritten. In the UK, the British Empire is demonised and England is now in the process of being treated as no different to Rhodesia – even by the Tories. Muslim terrorism has become an ongoing fact of life, along with the attempt to excuse it. In the UK, the grooming gangs that are raping and gang-raping English children continue, regardless. The supposed victim status of immigrant communities is matched by the demands for more special treatment, more allegations of racism (of which there are many types), and more anti-White ethnic cleansing. The BLM organisations of both the UK and USA successfully exploited the death of George Floyd. An anti-White agenda was relentlessly pursued.

The sixth basic concept is closely related to the fifth: the power of culture. Culture is deeply ingrained and not easily changed. Where there is a clash of cultures, then there can be trouble. The promotion of mass immigration and multiculturalism should be viewed as deliberate trouble-making and a barbarist activity. When religion is involved, then the likelihood of conflict is even greater. The history of the Ottoman empire and Turkey are prime examples of the power of culture.

The seventh basic concept is closely related to both the fifth and sixth: assimilation vs. integration. Parekh and Kymlicka's theorising 20 years ago, malevolent though it was, has been superseded by far worse. The open hatred towards the West and its peoples is revolutionary in its agenda. Steeped in critical theory, it is open communism. In both the UK and the USA,

Western culture is relentlessly condemned. There is no effort to assimilate immigrants who are encouraged to see themselves as victims. The scale of immigration means the West is being colonised.

The eighth concept is the corruption of human rights. 'Human rights' are the holiest of holy words for the politically correct, and the definition of those words is decided by judges – the high priests of political correctness. The judges have openly treated human rights as their vehicle to impose their own political views on society, and are openly contemptuous of majority opinions. The result is that the understanding and implementation of human rights has been corrupted into a lawyer's enrichment scheme to promote the anti-West, anti-White, anti-patriotic dogma of wilful stupidity.

The ninth basic concept is producer capture. Originally, this was an economic problem where monopoly firms produced what they liked rather than what customers wanted. Today, it also applies to a range of state and other institutions that treat the receipt of tax income as a means of allowing them to disregard the opinions and interests of those who would otherwise be their customers. They can just do as they like. The concept can be further extended to monopolistic organisations divorced from having to rely upon sales income.

The capture of state sector organisations is the tenth basic concept, naturally closely related to the ninth concept, and is in keeping with the problem Wayne Mapp identified of the politically correct acquiring a legislative base. Both the Frankfurt School and Antonio Gramsci, an Italian communist, advocated this strategy. It has been carried through very successfully, for them, and has met with almost no real opposition.

The eleventh basic concept is the need for a Solidarity Tax. That Leftists in general are very extravagant with taxpayer's money, combined with a large flow of it into government due to the need to fund the welfare system, means large sums are wasted and the first instinct of the Left is to help themselves to other people's money rather than foot their own bills. One ruse is the 'we' argument to advocate expenditure. 'We' need to do this and spend that. By 'we', the Left means the taxpayer. They have no intention of being out of pocket themselves.

Whereas in previous centuries people, sometimes of humble means and origins, might have done good both in their own countries or abroad, at their own expense, today, television studios are filled with those (human rights activists, lawyers, politicians, journalists, members of pressure groups and quangos) who prefer to demand they should help themselves to yet more taxpayer's money to fund their big ideas. It should be noted that those philanthropists whose statues have been pulled down were philanthropic with their own money and not taxpayer's money.

Then there is the habit of 'funding' political correctness, in particular mass immigration, by means of Ponzi economics. The politically correct do not pay the bills their big ideas incur and simply dump the unpaid bills onto the public, and issue IOUs that might be paid many years hence while they squander the taxes paid now. This needs to change, and a Solidarity Tax is one means to achieve it.

To put it into language that might appeal to the Left, what is needed is an irreversible transfer of wealth from those who advocate political correctness to the victims of political correctness. A Solidarity Tax is a means by which such transfer might be achieved.

The twelfth basic concept is that of Political AIDs. It weakens society's ability to fend off hostile entities. Social cohesion and political stability are remorselessly undermined. Instead of patriotism, people are taught to hate their countries and are less willing to defend them as a result. The opposition to political correctness is reduced and becomes half-hearted.

Political AIDs affect law and order. Terrorism has grown, as has street violence and organised crime. The police response to this is feeble, if not apologetic. Excuses are made, such as people being radicalised. Victims of grooming gangs are blamed and the problem of Muslim grooming gangs denied or glossed over.

The cultural effects of Political AIDs can seem mild, if irritating. But the continued onslaught on national culture weakens society and undermines patriotism. The continued policy of mass immigration is highly damaging. Despite the popular opposition to that policy, the policy remains and is expanded. For a country as small as the UK to be promoting the immigration of millions of Hong Kong Chinese is grossly irresponsible. The Tories are too mired in human rights theories, and too desperate to show off their self-appointed moral superiority, and willingness to sacrifice British interests, to respond to the immigration crisis intelligently. The Tories could not even secure the borders and illegal immigrants invaded England across the English Channel. Organised crime rackets controlled Britain's borders. President Biden fared no better in his policy regarding the USA's border with Mexico when grandstanding became the policy.

One of the consequences of mass immigration was the problems with terrorism. Political AIDs rendered the response to even ISIS jihadists wishy-washy. The war on terror was not properly prosecuted. Things were so bad, prior to ISIS, the French dubbed the English capital Londonistan.

The UK distinguished itself in its depravity with its tolerance of the grooming, rape and even gang rape of English children by immigrant, mainly Muslim, grooming gangs. These gangs had been operating for decades, and authorities covered up their activities. That instinct to cover up this ongoing abomination remained. Even when convicted, the rapists were not deported afterwards.

Likewise, the UK's response to its knife-crime epidemic was half-hearted. Once again, the desire to be anti-racist was a factor. The stop and search tactic was reduced, as was its effectiveness.

Political AIDs also revealed itself with the inability to implement the Brexit vote and with the obsession with globalisation. The Tories were reluctant to re-establish the UK's independence. Prime Minister Theresa May corrupted the Brexit vote with her globalist obsessions. Simply leaving the EU was

349

too complicated for her. Immigration was a global problem requiring a globalist response. For May, the response to the disquiet of the UK public was 'more global, not less'. Such an attitude is totally incompatible with the vote for Brexit.

The Covid-19 pandemic revealed the limitations of globalisation, as it was the national governments that had to deal with the crisis, and the global institutions were found wanting. Despite this, the UK's leading globalists were keen to globalise the pandemic's management, preferably with a few trillion pounds to give away to the Third World.

The thirteenth basic concept is antisense. Antisense is Marxist, malevolent, pre-meditated gibberish. It goes well beyond nonsense. This has found its element in the trans issue, where 'stupidity' is not a strong enough term to describe the various wheezes. 'All genders' do not have periods. Men do not need tampons. Neither men nor boys need period-proof underwear. So what if not putting 'free menstrual products' in men's restrooms is discriminatory? There is no demand from the public for 'Pronouns Day' and the public are not exorcised about misgendering. The whole trans issue is stuffed with antisense.

Trying to indoctrinate children with a blurring of the difference between the two genders is not celebrating diversity, nor is encouraging boys to be chemically castrated then surgically so, and girls to have the breasts suppressed and then cut off and all the rest of the surgery. It is evil, promoted by evil people. It is not the children themselves nor the doctors who are pushing the trans issue. It is the various political agitation groups. Drag Queen Story Hour is irresponsible. Generally, children are safer with women.

The fourteenth basic concept is the ruse of intergenerational equality. Put simply, this is a scam to encourage young people to be envious of old people and to redistribute older people's wealth to young people – with the state officiating and pocketing monies into the bargain. Furthermore, is the determination in the UK to welch on the commitment about the availability of and amount of the state pension. The pension triple lock was abolished for one year in 2021. There has been nothing more than a duplicitous promise to better fund social care in the UK. Pensioners will still continue to lose their homes. The Tories are circling the assets of pensioners like vultures.

Intergenerational equality is simply bog-standard, classical Marxism. It is surprising so many so-called conservatives and free marketeers support it.

The fifteenth basic concept is the plunder of the welfare system, and is closely related to the fourteenth concept. The UK has an appalling record of taking money via from the tax system to fund welfare benefits, and then reneging on those commitments. Put simply, the public are swindled. Pensioners have been the greatest losers. The English are treated worse of all, and are funding even greater subsidies to Scotland, Wales and Northern Ireland – thus awarding more welfare benefits to those countries than the English get.

The biggest adverse effect of the welfare systems in both the UK and the USA is the corrupting effect on the political establishment and not the effect on ordinary people. Governments have been corrupted by the easy access to more taxes, to be spent as they like, by making promises of welfare they have no intention of honouring.

The sixteenth basic concept is non-crime. PC Plod does not tolerate so-called hate incidents and politically incorrect speech. Police monitor what people say on social media. Those who have broken no laws can still be penalised if the police take exception to those views, and may even try to prosecute, anyway. This even applies to children. Thus the police impose the Inquisition and free speech is disallowed.

In the chapter 'The Hegemony', I examined the three broad categories of the reasons for the triumph and spread of political correctness that help explain why the basic concepts persist: the institutional aspects, the economic aspects, and the false morality.

The three features of political correctness Wayne Mapp identified are the core of the damage done by the institutional aspects: the creed is divorced from 'mainstream values' and positively hostile to those values. Political correctness is prescriptive, in that believers concentrate on dictating how the public should live and be allowed to think. It is a bullying creed. Worse, as Wayne Mapp pointed out, the creed is 'embedded in public institutions, which have a legislative base'. The politically correct not only set out how everyone else should live, but are in a position to impose their views on everyone else whether they like it or not. This is also a result of the communist strategy of the long march through the institutions, and the result of producer capture. Civil society is politically correct. This would not have happened had those on the Right been more alert to the danger and its importance.

The consequences of this institutional capture are not confined to the legislative base and the ability to prosecute the Inquisition, but also, as demonstrated both regarding the George Floyd protests and the speed of the adoption of the trans issue, as examples, is that as the institutions are controlled with those who have a politically correct outlook, then those institutions act in unison to likewise reproduce that outlook. Many organisations adopting CRT training reinforced this. Hence, the BLM street protests, despite their violence in the USA, and the toppling of statues, are instantly presented as acceptable. This is how the police treat the matter, as did other local authorities and many politicians, and it was how the mainstream news media reported it – almost without dissent. The cultural Marxist propaganda was fed directly into people's homes.

With the trans issue, there had been little attention paid to it apart from the odd snigger at the idea of there being a multitude of sexual identities. Yet, suddenly, the cause swept across Western civil society in a matter of weeks. The public was swamped with antisense propaganda and demands surrounding trans. These demands did not come primarily from those with gender dysphoria themselves (although some did), nor from the medical staff treating such people, it came from political activists and swept through the institutions that, in turn, promoted it.

The matter of child sex in the UK in the 1970s and early 1980s was promoted by the Paedophile Information Exchange (PIE), which had successfully infiltrated into parts of the Labour Party and human rights groups. Prominent Labour Party figures were briefly associated with the PIE campaign. PIE wanted to legalise sex with children. This demand did not come from the children themselves. We did not witness schoolchildren waving placards demanding to have sex with middle-aged men. We witnessed middle-aged men demanding the right to have sex with children. The arguments were not about the right of children to have sex with middle-aged men, but about middle-aged men wanting it to be legal for them to have sex with children.

The same applies to the trans issue. We do not see schoolboys waving placards and demonstrating for the right to be castrated, or of schoolgirls demanding their genitals be surgically altered or removed. Nor do we see doctors waving placards and demanding more children are chemically castrated or have their breasts suppressed. What we do see is a variety of political zealots encouraging children to be uncertain as to their gender and to encourage those uncertain to opt for chemical and then surgical procedures. Even the Tory prime minister, Theresa May, wanted the matter de-medicalised! It was the capture of the institutions that enabled the politically correct to prevail on the trans issue.

The economic aspects enabling the funding of political correctness can be split into three parts: access to taxpayer's money, the facilities of the welfare system, and Ponzi economics. It is often commented upon, especially by free market liberals, that the welfare system corrupts the work ethic and breeds a dependency culture. But this corrupting effect, true at least in part, is dwarfed by the corrupting effect on politicians and the government as a whole. The need to fund the welfare system now means that taxes are far more widely applied than before, thus raising vast sums in tax revenues. This steady inflow of taxes has proved too tempting for politicians and political zealots, and they have been as greedy as they have

353

been ruthless in seizing large sums of those tax revenues to spend on themselves and their pet projects. Political correctness in all its forms is one such pet project.

To take immigration as an example, when an immigrant enters a Western country (legally or illegally) and makes a claim for asylum, immediately monies are made available. The asylum seeker gets money for his upkeep and that of his family (if they have come as well). Immigration pressure groups get funding to campaign for such people. Lawyers get paid for making the case as to why the asylum claimant should be allowed to stay. Judges and case workers get paid for dealing with the claims. Taxpayer's money is available and the money flows.

Then there are the facilities of the welfare system to draw upon. The asylum seeker needs to be housed. Children need to be sent to school. Illnesses needs to be treated. So it goes on. All of these things can be made available because the facilities of the welfare system are already there to be drawn upon.

Then there is Ponzi economics. The extra demands on the welfare system from asylum claims do not necessarily attract extra funding – at least in the short term, if not indefinitely. The extra schools are not built, nor the extra hospitals and social housing. The existing facilities become more over-stretched. The school class sizes get larger, the hospitals get more crowded and less willing to admit patients, the traffic jams get longer and more frequent, and the railways more crowded. Importantly, the existing housing stock fails to meet the extra demand. Consequently, the housing shortage means the indigenous population, the Staatsvolk who founded the country and are funding it, get pushed out of property ownership. The government simply offloads unpaid bills onto the public who have to endure a reduced quality of life and face the extra bills for housing rent, higher house prices, higher rail fares, poorer education for themselves and their children, poorer healthcare, lower wages, etc.

Meanwhile, governments find they struggle to afford to meet their obligations due to financial pressures and so commitments are not met. Welfare payments to the indigenous population are cut, including pensions. Roads do not get built, nor rail networks, hospitals or schools. Defence spending is cut. The quality of life for the core nation is needlessly and recklessly traduced. Living standards fall either from where they should have been, or absolutely as pay rates falter if not fall.

The false morality of political correctness is the third aspect of its hegemony. This aspect also consists of three parts: it has become accepted as the basis of morality; deviation from that false morality is the trigger for the Inquisition; and far from opposing political correctness for its intolerance and cultural Marxism, the woke-Right have displaced genuine conservatives and are intent on either abiding by the creed or, at best, implementing their own version of it. The result is little effective opposition and is a part of the Political AIDs concept identified above.

It has been said that 'those who stand for nothing fall for anything'. The woke-Right are proof this saying is true and have fallen for the candyfloss words of the false morality that is communism in practice.

The constant chatter using controlled language is accepted. It is churned out from state institutions, charities, business corporations, backed up by law and the police, and is common across all mainstream media outlets. It is everywhere.

Those who adhere to the candyfloss language and embrace political correctness are treated as being compassionate and high minded. The piety is a part of the strength or political correctness, and it allows believers to feel good about themselves. The support for racial justice, social justice, economic justice, climate justice, human rights, celebrating diversity, tolerance, equality, and compassion is difficult to resist for the liberal do-gooders and woke-Right. They do not bother to look at what is actually being advocated or the financial consequences of it on the public. They live for the moment.

A desire to do good and to be seen to do good is not the same as actually doing good. To turn a blind eye to the consequences of what is being advocated is not good but morally degenerate. A desire to be seen as morally superior is not moral superiority – it is snobbery. The liberal wing of political correctness is comprised of a such a collection of snobs. Instead of adulation, they deserve condemnation. A fawning media ensure that deserved condemnation is never put. The attempt to control social media and impose a politically correct orthodoxy on that too makes things even worse. Nowhere is the snobbery challenged. Even books can be suppressed.

An obvious flaw in the piety, which the liberals and woke-Right choose not to see, or the media choose not to mention, is that despite all the high-minded searches for justice, equality, etc., in order to supposedly do good, it is necessary to do harm. The supposed benefits of political correctness are measured in how much harm is caused to so-called oppressors – be they capitalists, Westerners, Whites, pensioners and a host of others. These oppressors are demonised and persecuted. The capitalist system is the cause of racism. The West is only wealthy due to the slave trade, and White people thus benefit from White privilege. Pensioners are too wealthy and there is a need for generational justice. So it goes on. The solution to which is reparations or the bog-standard communist call for the redistribution of wealth.

A particular example presently is the alleged need to fight climate change, and the need for climate justice. Back in the 1980s, there was a recognition there was a hole in the ozone layer above the poles. The cause of this was identified (the use of CFCs) and measures taken to tackle the problem. These measures worked effectively and the hole in the ozone layer is gradually disappearing. This was done without the zealotry or malice that surrounds alleged climate change.

In the 21st century, the preponderance of scientific opinion is that certain gases, including carbon dioxide, are responsible for trapping heat and thus warming the planet, which will ultimately lead to damaging climate change. Some allege the evidence of that climate change is already upon us. There are dissenting opinions from some scientists and these people have been branded climate change deniers. Most might agree it would be

356

prudent to take reasonable measures to reduce greenhouse gas emissions. But the politically correct have monopolised the issue of climate change (in the UK, Green activists attracted many defectors from the communist party with the collapse of communism at the end of the Cold War) who have adopted a more zealous and confrontational approach. Disagreeing with the proposed measures to fight climate change is not allowed. There are protests that have closed down London and motorways, causing severe disruption. There are demands for all sorts of new taxes and laws to force ordinary people to do as the climate activists demand. In the UK, energy prices have been forced up, thus jeopardising the jobs of those in heavy industries such as steel. Coal, gas and oil production is restricted and new methods, such as fracking, opposed. Power stations are not built and coal-fired power stations are closed (by the autumn of 2021, the UK experienced major increases in energy prices). There are demands for central heating boilers to be banned and replaced with inefficient heat pumps. There is a wild demand to force people to use only electric cars, despite there being insufficient charging points or power generation to cope. The thrust of the agenda is to disrupt the lives of ordinary people as much as possible. The more they are harmed, the more good the zealots consider they have done.

Likewise, with the issues of immigration and race, the aim of the politically correct is not to act in the interests of the host nation or to foster good race relations, but to foster a hatred of the host nation, a sense of victimhood amongst ethnic minorities and immigrant communities, and to use anyone with a victim status to overthrow society. Mass immigration, CRT, BLM, the taking down of statues, re-writing of history, and general demonisation of White people are all examples of this. The more malevolence there is, the more pious the politically correct consider themselves to be. The more allegations of racism that are made and invented, the more morally superior the accusers supposedly are. As Collingwood pointed out, the barbarist considers himself to be superior to the civilised person.

Deviation from the false morality triggers the Inquisition. In the UK, police officers are paid to watch social media to censor alleged hate speech. Those deemed heretics can be prosecuted, or lose their jobs. The purpose of the Inquisition is to enforce the false morality and its narrative, and to terrorise those who have opinions of their own.

The KGB approach Bezmenov explained, was consistent with that of the Frankfurt School, although the KGB was more structured and practical. They had a plan to destabilise a country and bring about a communist revolution. The KGB was utterly ruthless and willing to execute those deemed opponents and even their supporters if they were deemed potential opponents.

Bezmenov rightly pointed out that ideological subversion was a 'process, which is legitimate, overt, and open; you can see it with your eyes' and that all the media had to do was to 'unplug their bananas from their ears, open up their eyes, and they can see it'. It does not take too much effort to notice the pulling down of statues and the demonisation of the West. The media report these things, but they do not treat them as being subversive. They prefer to talk about the right to protest. The media definitely ignores the effect of the steady infiltration the politically correct make into state institutions. Cultural Marxism values corrupt the values of patriotism. This is reflected by the state's redefinition of British culture, as if it is nothing more than abstract theories about human rights, democracy and political correctness! In the UK, all immigrants have to do is pass a 'pub quiz', or cheat their way through that quiz, and they are deemed to share British values and are awarded British citizenship. This is subversion.

British culture is not about abstract theories of human rights, or supposed shared values of democracy, gay rights or positive images for women. British culture is, as it is for national cultures generally, about national history – British history, and the achievements of our ancestors and kin.

It is about the British monarchs, such as Alfred the Great, Edward Longshanks, Richard the Lionheart, Edward III, Henry V,

Henry VIII, Queen Elizabeth I (who, wearing a silver breastplate, addressing her troops preparing to fight the Spanish Armada, said: 'I know I have the body but of a weak and feeble woman, but I have the heart and stomach of a king, and of a King of England too, and think foul scorn that Parma or Spain, or any Prince of Europe should dare to invade the borders of my realm'), Queen Victoria and Richard III, who 'alone, was killed fighting manfully in the thickest press of his enemies' at the Battle of Bosworth Field. It is about Oliver Cromwell. It is about Britain's prime ministers such as Walpole (Britain's first prime minister), Pitt the Younger, and Winston Churchill, who led Britain during her darkest hour in WWII.

It is about the Royal Navy and all her commanders, such as Sir Francis Drake, Sir Walter Raleigh, and Admiral Lord Nelson (who died in action at the Battle of Trafalgar). It is about Britain's generals such as the Duke of Marlborough, the Duke of Wellington (and Picton, Ponsonby and de-Lancey who all died at the Battle of Waterloo, and Uxbridge who lost a leg), Auckinleck and Montgomery (who respectively won the first and second battles of El Alamein in WWII) and not forgetting The Black Prince – nor those generals and commanders who died leading their men into battle during WWI (more than 200 generals were killed, captured or wounded during WWI). It is about Fighting Mac and Lord Kitchener who finished the Mahdists at the Battle of Omdurman – not forgetting Lieutenants Bromhead and Chard and all those brave men who stood fast at Rorke's Drift and redeemed British honour.

It is about the explorers such as Captain Cook, Dr Livingstone, Ernest Shackleton, and Scott of the Antarctic. About the British Empire and all the empire builders such as Wolfe of Quebec (whose dying words were: 'Then, tell Colonel River, to cut off their [the French] retreat from the bridge. Now, God be praised, I die contented'), Clive of India, Cecil Rhodes, Sir Alfred Milner, Lord Curzon, and General Gordon of Khartoum – and all the humble people and missionaries whose names we do not readily know.

It is about the Victorian era, Pax Britannica, and all Queen Victoria's ministers, social reformers and Victorian heroes, such as the great statesmen of Lord Palmerston and Joseph Chamberlain.

It is about Britain's great inventors, innovators, architects and engineers across the centuries, such as Alan Turing and the very many during the Victorian era – not least of which was Isambard Kingdom Brunel. And Britain's musicians be they Handel, Elgar, Ralph Vaughan Williams, George Butterworth (who was awarded the Military Cross and died in action in the Battle of the Somme), Vera Lynn, Ken Dodd, The Beatles, Cliff Richard, The Rolling Stones, The ELO, The Kinks, Led Zeppelin, Mott the Hoople, Oasis, David Bowie and Elton John – to mention but a few. And the Last Night of the Proms. And Britain's artists such as Turner and Constable. And Britain's writers such as the Bronte sisters, Charles Dickens, William Shakespeare, Rudyard Kipling, J. K. Rowling, and Rupert Brooke ('If I should die, think only this of me: That there's some corner of a foreign field, That is for ever England') – and actors and actresses such as Cary Grant, Richard Burton, Michael Caine, Roger Moore, Laurence Olivier, David Niven, Gary Oldman, Sean Bean, Hugh Grant, Bob Hope, Peter Cushing, Christopher Lee, Jeremy Irons, Peter Sellers, Dirk Bogarde, Helen Mirren, Joanna Lumley, Diana Rigg, Elizabeth Taylor, and Vivien Leigh.

It is about the stiff upper lip, stoicism, the Dunkirk spirit, an element of bloody-mindedness (when necessary), the V-sign (originating from the Battle of Agincourt), the British sense of humour and self-depreciation, the *Carry On* films, the *St. Trinian's* films, the Hammer Horrors, Benny Hill, *Monty Python*, *Dr Who* (excluding recent versions), *Blakes 7*, *Dad's Army*, *The Sweeney*, *Only Fools and Horses*, *Fawlty Towers*, *The Avengers*, a cup of tea, roast beef and Yorkshire pudding, and fish and chips. It is about films such as *Zulu*, *Excalibur*, *I'm All Right Jack*, *Two-Way Stretch*, *Carlton-Browne of the F.O.*, *The Battle of Waterloo*, *The Wild Geese*, *The Long Good Friday*, *The Rocky Horror Picture Show*, *Where Eagles Dare*, the *Lord of the Rings* films, the *Harry Potter* films and a whole host of James Bond features.

It is about 1066, our island culture, a history of success, and of leading the world rather than being repeatedly invaded and conquered – and about all those who died in battle defending our country and way of life. It is about our desire for freedom and Magna Carta. It is about the English language, our pubs, our sporting events, national holidays, and about Christmas. It is about the daughter nations of Canada, Australia, New Zealand and our American cousins of the USA.

Other countries have their own distinct national culture in the same way. Habermas' openly stated aim of brainwashing people to hate their countries should be rejected, along with the KGB programme. As Bezmenov recommended, 'there must be a very strong national effort to educate people in the spirit of real patriotism'. One might normally expect the conservative Right to initiate such a national effort, but that will not happen. The mainstream conservative Right has been replaced with the woke-Right. At best, the woke-Right do little more than complain at the excesses of political correctness and prefer to implement their own version of it. Being globalists, there is an overlap between the anti-nation state stance of the cultural Marxists and the anti-nation state aspect of the policy of global free trade, which ignores national boundaries and treats the world as one single market despite the different stages of development and various national cultures. The woke-Right will never stand up to the politically correct, whose approval they seek, and prefer to advocate nice things such as low taxes, higher government spending, and more immigration – especially if they believe they are rescuing asylum seekers. The impact on and interests of the host nation are ignored.

The interaction between the various different concepts of political correctness, and with the different aspects, together form the strength of the creed and explains its continued hegemony. The trans issue is a perfect example of how comprehensive this hegemony is.

Gender dysphoria has been a minor matter for years. Doctors have been treating, without controversy, those, previously, mainly men, who reject their gender and believe they should be female. Not all such cases resulted in surgery, as there are many cases of the mental problem being successfully treated differently. However, in the 21st century, all of a sudden, gender dysphoria is dismissed as a term to be replaced with trans as a gender (along with a host of other supposed genders), accompanied by a multiplication of girls afflicted with this problem, and there is a ballyhoo, with much name calling directed at those who do not accept the trans agenda. If a 16-stone male identifies as a girl, anyone who does not agree with him is prejudiced and risks the wrath of the Inquisition. The condition is supposedly no longer a matter of gender dysphoria of an individual, but of the prejudice of the general population. The trans process is to be de-medicalised – as the then Tory prime minister, Theresa May, advocated.

That such a crackpot orthodoxy swept the West is bewildering. The obsession fits the matters Wayne Mapp set out and who identified the three features of political correctness. The stance is a minority view and divorced from mainstream public opinion. It is prescriptive in that it dictates how the public should react to those who are trans, particularly the various stages of it. Due to the capture of the legislative base, the law and how it is interpreted promotes the politically correct view. Human rights are routinely cited as a reason to adhere to trans demands. The steady takeover of state institutions and civil society meant that all these institutions acted in unison to impose a politically correct view that was pro-trans. Public opinion and hence democracy was ignored. The issue is barbarist, in that it is harmful to society, not only in the harm done to those who need medical help for gender dysphoria, but also wider society, which is demonised as being prejudiced. The Inquisition descends upon heretics, including those feminists who might normally be regarded as supporters of political correctness (an example of Bezmenov's analysis and how the KGB would ruthlessly deal with troublemakers). For the

362

police, this was an opportunity to treat critics of the politically correct view of the trans issue as being guilty of non-crime, which would not be tolerated. Non-criminals could expect phone calls if not a visit from the police, who would check their thinking. Social media was monitored. The Inquisition even descended upon those who disputed the antisense of the trans campaign (men do not need tampons).

The control of language became a trigger for the Inquisition, both regarding the trans issue and generally. Institutions almost vie with one another as to how restrictive, if not daft, they can get with banning words and even inventing new ones. The more unpalatable the language control is, the prouder the politically correct are as to what they have done.

The mammoth issue of immigration also triggers a variety of concepts and aspects of political correctness. Once again, the pro-immigration fanatics are divorced from mainstream public opinion. Across the West, public opinion is opposed to mass immigration to varying degrees. The politically correct view is prescriptive, and control of the institutions enables the pro-immigration agenda to be rammed down the public's throat. The two wings of political correctness act in unison, but the communists delight in the damage the policy does. That policy is barbarist in that Third World cultures are introduced into civilised society. The Inquisition aggressively stamps down on dissent. Dissenters are branded racists. Race war politics and an anti-Whiteism are to the fore. The Anglo-conformity model of immigration has been ditched as has assimilation. Multiculturalism is promoted along with steady ethnic cleansing of Whites from state organisations and civil society.

Crucially, the plundering of tax revenues funds the policy of mass immigration, the plundering of the facilities of the welfare system, and, essentially, Ponzi economics, where unpaid bills are simply offloaded onto the public. Consequently, for example, public services are overstretched and there is a major housing shortage.

Opposition to the policy of mass immigration is ineffectual and phoney. The woke-Right have decided to go with the flow,

363

and those in the dissident Right focus on illegal immigration, and, possibly, fundamentalist Islam about which the big talk is not matched by the advocacy of big solutions.

The interpretation of human rights, freely cited, has been corrupted beyond antisense as an excuse to admit an unending flow of those who claim to be asylum seekers no matter how feeble their claim or as to how many continents, oceans and countries they have crossed to reach their desired destination.

The closely related policy of multiculturalism draws in the same interactions. The policy is divorced from mainstream opinion and is highly prescriptive, requiring the public to likewise accept the policy – or else. The capture of the state institutions and civil society, along with a strong legislative control via the courts and a variety of laws, enables the policy to be imposed across society, with the Inquisition reaching its most active. The policy is barbarist in that it denigrates civilised values and venerates uncivilised ones. The grooming gang rape culture of the UK is one example of the clash between different cultures. The idea of assimilation is treated as almost criminal and racist.

The various schemes and wheezes to promote the multiculturalisation process cost money, and once again is funded by a mix of taxpayer's cash, drawing upon the facilities of the welfare state, and Ponzi economics. The passing of laws to force the private sector to comply not only costs money but also stirs up resentment.

Front and centre of cultural Marxism is race war politics and anti-Whiteism. This concept interacts with other concepts too. It is divorced and positively hostile to mainstream public opinion. It is highly prescriptive, and benefits hugely from the legislative base and the long march through the institutions. It is barbarist. It relies upon the Inquisition to impose its dogma upon societies, and to persecute opponents and even those who are merely not adherents – resorting to non-crime allegations when possible. As per Marcuse, it positively lauds cultures hostile to the West and Whites. Western and national culture is denigrated. Obviously, assimilation is rejected, instead 'integration' – in practice this means ethnic cleansing as Whites are replaced with

364

non-Whites – is advocated. The holy words of 'human rights' are frequently bandied about to justify policies and demands, and cited in law. The various organisations implementing this concept benefit from either or both of the capture of state sector institutions and producer capture, meaning they could not care twopence what ordinary people want or think. Given the damage done by the spendthrift nature of the concept, a Solidarity Tax is highly appropriate so those who advocate race war politics and anti-Whiteism pay their bills rather than plundering the welfare state and offloading unpaid bills onto the public. The concept of antisense is heavily involved, as is the portrayal of the younger immigrant generations as victims of intergenerational inequality.

Not only is the opposition to race war politics and anti-Whiteism so feeble as to be barely visible, but that feebleness is endemic in the woke-Right. Even the dissident Right are half-hearted.

An important related issue affected by the various concepts and aspects of political correctness is the war on terror. President George Bush used this term following 9/11 to describe the USA's response and its determination to confront those responsible. Race war politics was influential in the hours after the attack, as some Muslims living in the West were supportive of the atrocities. Some remain so to this day, and deny that al-Qaeda was responsible.

In the UK, leading commentators from the Muslim community sought to excuse the terrorism, and likewise the subsequent bombings in London (e.g. Yasmin Alibhai Brown). The media continued to promote those commentators. Both the terrorists and their apologists are barbarists. ISIS, al-Qaeda and other fundamentalist Muslim terrorists are as barbarist as one can get – *and their apologists are little better.* No civilised society would tolerate such savagery or the immigration of it. Once again, the concept of Political AIDs and the rise of the woke-Right explains the steady weakening of the opposition to Muslim terrorism and the failure to defeat it.

Repeatedly, in the UK, immigrants commit terrorist acts. The refusal to secure the borders is the reason for this. Attention has been given to not using offensive language to describe the terrorism. For example, the terrorists are more likely to be described as 'militants' than 'terrorists'. This has the intended effect of glossing over how evil these people are. Also, they are not described as Muslim, and the terrorism is presented as being not of Islam, the religion of peace, when in fact it is entirely of Islam.

Race war politics both creates the environment for the terrorists and the excuse for their terrorism. The terrorists at times are described as having mental health issues, possibly as a result of the failure of the West to treat them properly (i.e. it is the victims of terrorism who are to blame), when in fact the savagery is an integral part of Islam and has been for centuries. It is the clash of cultures, mass immigration and multiculturalisation that creates the friction that would otherwise not be there.

The terrorists are adept at exploiting human rights laws, as are their lawyers who are in receipt of funding from the welfare system. In the UK, far from deporting the terrorists, like other immigrant criminals, Muslim or not, the judges find excuses to keep them in the country and even bring them into the UK if they are overseas or deemed to have been deported wrongly. The cause célèbre of Shamir Begum is a good example. Begum left the UK of her own volition, travelled to Syria to join ISIS, married an ISIS fighter and had children (all of whom died). Reportedly, she played an active part in ISIS terrorism, including sowing suicide bombers into their explosive vests. After the ISIS caliphate was overrun, she nonchalantly explained in an interview that she was unfazed when she first saw a bin containing severed heads of ISIS victims, and justified the Manchester bombing as being in response to what the West had done to ISIS. She did this at a time when she was demanding to return to the UK. Fortunately, she was stripped of her citizenship. In the UK, her supporters present her as being a victim of grooming (which the UK allowed), a victim of being stateless, and a victim of being denied her day in a British court.

It is a false morality to exploit human rights laws and eagerly pocket welfare monies to promote the immigration of barbarists into the UK, no matter how heinous their activities. Begum's supporters might consider themselves to be morally superior, but they are not. There are even Tory MPs who support her demands to be let into the UK.

Given the synergy and power of political correctness, and its various basic concepts and aspects, it is not surprising that support for BLM and critical race theory swept across society so quickly and easily. The capture of the institutions and the availability of funding was a powerful boost to cultural Marxism. As Kathleen Stock highlighted regarding Stonewall and the trans issue, Stonewall had funding from the taxpayer and was quietly presented as an expert opinion as it visited and indoctrinated organisations. Adherence to whatever Stonewall said was deemed sophisticated and enlightened – if not a legal necessity. The false morality was uncontested and 'embedded' in national institutions. The same applies to CRT.

The basic concepts of political correctness show how its different facets impact society. The three aspects of the creed's hegemony – institutional aspects, economic aspects, and the false morality – show how the various concepts managed to withstand the populist revolts of both the UK and USA in 2016. The interaction of the concepts and aspects renders the creed robust to opposition.

Of the three different aspects, only the government can tackle the institutional ones. Campaigners might be able to play a part, particularly if they fight back in a particular organisation, such as the UK's National Trust. But it is only government that can make a big difference. Therefore, voters need to eye the manifestos of those who they might be tempted to vote for to see whether those politicians have any de-Marxification programme to purge political correctness from government and wider society. The politically correct need to be stripped of their legislative base.

The economic aspects also are primarily a matter for the government. It is the government that doles out the taxes people pay to fund the welfare system. The government needs to stop throwing money around at those who are hostile to the West. The politically correct need to be defunded. They further need to be denied access to the facilities of the welfare system. Part of this would be to prevent situations arising that would lead to that access being sought. For example, legal aid can only be granted if the law, often human rights law, gives rise to a court application, and, currently, on behalf of someone who may not even be a citizen.

Ponzi economics is crucifying living standards across the West. Unpaid bills are being dumped onto the public without hindrance. The voters are aware of the strain on public services, but are less aware of the extent of it and how it is happening. In the UK, the demand for more 'affordable housing' is the response to the housing shortage, and thus higher house prices, but this does not address the nature of the problem or the scale of it. Building a couple of hundred thousand affordable (i.e. cheap and subsidised) houses over a five-year period is not a credible response to an annual immigration rate of 715,000, with illegal immigration in addition. That employers in the past built houses to accommodate their workers needs to be pointed out to the public and contrasted with the welfare dependent multinationals of today, which expect to exploit cheap immigrant labour, expect the welfare system to house and subsidise the wages of that labour, and then expect to use all manner of tax dodging wheezes to avoid paying tax. There needs to be a Solidarity Tax to introduce some to the real world and get them to pay their bills. We need a 'Bill the Bums' campaign. The way in which Ponzi economics is impoverishing the public needs to be highlighted and explained.

Some time ago, someone described today's liberal-Left as being the spoilt brat of the welfare state. Stuffed with their own importance, sense of entitlement and of theories about rights, they glibly assume that, courtesy of the welfare state, there is an unending amount of taxpayers' monies to which they

368

can help themselves in furtherance of their own agenda. In *The Genesis of Political Correctness*, I wrote, 'Like vampires, communists lurk in dark places away from the sunlight of public awareness. For them to succeed, it is important that their activities are not recognised until it is too late. So they crawl about various government, charity, and other public organizations, feeding off ordinary peoples' monies.'

It is already long overdue that the liberal–Left, the liberal wing of political correctness, be introduced to something called reality. It takes more than their snobbery to pay bills. Both the UK and the USA are running substantial government and trade deficits. The policy of globalisation, in all its forms, has devastated the UK and US economies, and living standards are either static or falling. There will no doubt be much bawling and shouting, but the liberal–Left has to be faced down. We need to get real. As for the communists and the communist wing of political correctness, both they and their agenda need to be exposed. No longer should they pass themselves off as experts on their chosen topic, as they infiltrate society. They need to be subject to the sunlight of public awareness and their access to public monies terminated.

The false morality of political correctness is not solely a matter for government, and the aspect falls firmly into the domain of the dissident Right. It is a campaign issue. Those on the Right who cannot make the moral case against political correctness, not least stemming from its heritage, and all its many forms, need to vacate politics. The Right has lost the moral argument and has given up even trying to make that argument. That needs to change. The Right needs to engage the moral argument and win that argument by convincing the public, the victims of political correctness, that the creed is evil and should be disposed of.

The 1970s are an example. Then, there were three ideological battles to be fought in the UK and the USA. First, there was the Cold War – the conflict between the West and the USSR. This was not won until President Reagan won it – as Bezmenov demonstrated in his interview. Second, there was the battle between capitalism and socialism (this affected the UK more than the USA). That battle was being steadily lost until Margaret Thatcher became prime minister in 1979. Eventually, the Tories stood up to the unions and denationalised state industries. Third, there was the fight between the failing orthodoxy of Keynesianism and monetarism. Milton Friedman and other free market economists engaged in that fight outside government. That fight was ideologically won and then influenced government policy.

An important similarity between Keynesianism and political correctness is that both rely upon repression. Despite the convoluted (and unconvincing) theory, what Keynes advocated was a burst of inflation. After his death, the Keynesians developed the original theory into Keynesian demand management. The problem with this is that it presumed a trade-off between inflation and unemployment and that trade-off broke down. The inflation wilfully inserted into the economy steadily increased, as did the adverse economic consequences. The response was to introduce repressive measures such as price and wage controls to prevent the effects of inflation. Those repressive measures failed and eventually Keynesian orthodoxy was overthrown.

Likewise, political correctness is openly hostile to public interests and thus provokes an angry public response. This is understandable given the communism of the creed, and that the aim is not to adopt policies in the people's interests, but to adopt the people to fit in with the ideology of the policies. The reaction of the politically correct to the inevitable anger provoked is to introduce repressive measures to prevent both freedom of speech and even freedom of thought, and to control people's behaviour. Conflict is inevitable. As with Keynesianism, there has to be a determined attempt to overthrow the orthodoxy.

To simply react to the latest politically correct outrage by describing it as being 'political correctness gone too far', or 'political correctness gone stark raving bonkers/mad' does not constitute opposition to it at all. Another favourite reaction is to declare of the politically correct that he/she 'shares their aims, but not their methods'. These often-used cliches, at best, are merely expressions of exasperation and take the creed at face value. Taking it at face value confers a degree of morality upon a barbarist false morality. To say it has 'gone too far' or 'gone stark raving bonkers/mad' is to balk at the extent of its implementation and not its cultural Marxism. No genuine Conservative would ever agree with the aims of political correctness. It is the creed that is to be rejected and not merely the manner of its implementation.

The hegemony of political correctness is its false morality. That the Conservative Right has not been prepared to challenge that false morality, and have in many cases embraced it, is the primary reason for its success. To expose the creed for what it is would also destroy the case for its funding and for its institutional base. The fight between patriotism and political correctness is the fight between good and evil. It is as clear cut as that.

APPENDIX ONE
Home Office Report

The recently published Home Office report (frequently referred to as a paper – presumably due to its inadequacy) into the grooming–gang rape epidemic that has swept the UK, came with a foreword from the Home Secretary, Priti Patel (italics my own emphasis):

'*An External Reference Group*, consisting of independent experts on child sexual exploitation, reviewed and informed this work. While this is a Home Office paper, *it owes a great deal to the experts who provided honest, robust and constructive challenge.* I am grateful to them for their time and their valuable insight. *The paper sets out the limited available evidence* on the characteristics of offenders including how they operate, ethnicity, age, offender networks, as well as the context in which these crimes are often committed, along with implications for frontline responses and for policy development. Some studies have indicated an over-representation of Asian and Black offenders. However, *it is difficult to draw conclusions about the ethnicity of offenders as existing research is limited and data collection is poor.* This is disappointing because community and cultural factors are clearly relevant to understanding and tackling offending. Therefore, a commitment to improve the collection and analysis of data on group-based child sexual exploitation, including in relation to characteristics of offenders such as ethnicity and other factors, will be included in the forthcoming Tackling Child Sexual Abuse Strategy.'

In paragraph 3, the External Reference Group (ERG) was described as 'made up of experts on child sexual exploitation and abuse across a range of sectors, including representatives of victims and survivors, law enforcement, academia, the third sector, and parliamentarians'. The members of the ERG are listed:

- Chief Constable Simon Bailey QPM (National Police Chiefs Council lead on child protection)
- Dr Helen Beckett (Director, The International Centre: Researching child sexual exploitation, violence and trafficking, University of Bedfordshire)
- Sarah Champion MP (Member of Parliament for Rotherham)
- Rosina Cottage QC (Barrister QC and member of the Sentencing Council)
- Donald Findlater (Director of Stop It Now!, Lucy Faithfull Foundation)
- Imran Khan MP (Member of Parliament for Wakefield)
- Dr Sophie Laws (Deputy Director Research and Evaluation, Centre of expertise on child sexual abuse)
- Anne Longfield (Children's Commissioner for England)
- Fay Maxted (CEO, The Survivors Trust)
- Trevor Pearce CBE QPM (Chair of UK Anti-Doping, previously Director General of the National Crime Squad and the Serious Organised Crime Agency)
- Sheila Taylor MBE (CEO, NWG Network)
- Sammy Woodhouse (CSE [child sexual exploitation] Survivor and Campaigner)

Paragraph 4 says, 'The ERG had an advisory role in the development of this paper, and as such, all comments from the ERG were considered carefully, but not all were taken onboard. The final paper is ultimately a Home Office product and does not reflect the position of all ERG members.' Priti Patel's comment about how the report 'owes a great deal to the experts' immediately following her comment about how the ERG 'reviewed and informed this work' should be taken as being disingenuous.

Paragraph 5 states (italics my own emphasis):

'Throughout their discussions, ERG members were clear that group-based CSE is an important issue that warrants significant government attention. *However,* they recognised that this is a complex and nuanced area. The group recognised the difficulties in defining group-based CSE, particularly as a form of abuse that is distinct from other types of CSE and child sexual abuse more generally. *The group agreed that these definitional challenges contribute to a lack of robust research and data in the public domain* on group-based CSE. *It was also highlighted that much of the evidence available is now quite old and therefore is unlikely to represent current thinking and understanding* of group-based CSE. The ERG was *broadly supportive* of the aims of this paper in *trying to achieve a rounded picture* of the nature of offending with a mix of data, research and more illustrative detail from case studies and local reviews.'

In other words, the ERG were spoken down to and bullied into accepting the issue was far too complicated for the experts to actually do anything constructive, other than to talk about it and demand more research. The carefully crafted form of words in the paragraph should be noted.

Paragraph 8 states (italics my own emphasis):

'The group *expressed differing views* in relation to *the scope of the paper, including how tightly drawn the definition of group-based CSE should be* for the purposes of this paper. *Some members* felt that the paper needed to position group-based CSE more clearly in the context of wider CSA, and *highlighted the risk that a narrow focus on CSE by groups could contribute to failures to*

> *recognise and tackle other forms of CSA [child sexual abuse] and CSE that have received less attention.'*

In other words, the ERG itself was split sufficiently to warrant mention. That split included an objection from some (or someone) as to the determination to impose a definition of the scope of the report. The paragraph reveals there was a determination, including by some on the ERG, to prevent the report focusing on grooming gangs.

Paragraph 9 states (italics my own emphasis):

> 'The ERG also *did not reach consensus* around how the evidence should be presented, *particularly with regard to cultural and community contexts.* While this has been a central consideration both in the development of the paper and the research that informed it, *the available evidence is weak and robust data is scarce. Some, but not all, members of the group wanted to see more explicit detail on manifestations of group-based CSE when perpetrated by offenders from certain communities, particularly Pakistani communities, given the involvement of Pakistani-ethnic offenders in a number of high-profile cases and the recognised need for specific responses to specific threats.* In finalising the paper, we have sought to be as specific as we can be, *despite the lack of available evidence on cultural drivers in particular.'*

The disagreement as to the report's purpose is reflected throughout. Paragraph 25 states: 'This paper considers the evidence base for characteristics of group-based CSE offending in the community' and 'We have focused primarily on offending by adults against children, although some of the cases we examined involved offenders who were under the age of eighteen.'

Paragraph 28 states:

376

'The primary aim of this paper is therefore to present as comprehensive an assessment as possible of this form of abuse, using the best available evidence. We intend for this paper to be useful to leaders and practitioners wishing to better understand the characteristics of group-based offending in order to develop targeted responses. The paper outlines the main challenges local and national agencies face in responding to group-based CSE, sets out implications for national and local responses, and highlights necessary future work in this area, including new research.'

Paragraph 37 states: 'For the avoidance of doubt, our work has focused on child sexual exploitation perpetrated by groups, as per the above definition, which therefore includes what commentators sometimes describe as "grooming gangs".'

Paragraph 50 states:

'The work that has informed this paper was aimed at better understanding the characteristics of group-based child sexual exploitation offenders and offending, and this paper reflects that emphasis. Our ultimate aim is to prevent sexual exploitation, and to ensure better safeguarding and support for victims and survivors. We consider it important therefore to present these findings in the context of a broader understanding of who experiences child sexual exploitation and how it affects them.'

The report devotes four paragraphs to bemoaning the available data. Paragraph 65 states:

'Throughout our work on group-based CSE ... a consistent challenge has been the paucity of data. This lack of good quality data limits what can be known about the characteristics of offenders, victims and offending behaviour, as data is only available on the small proportion of known cases. It is therefore important that the data that is available is of high quality and shared effectively between different agencies. Several factors contribute to this.'

It should be noted that the 'known cases' are dismissed as a 'small proportion' of a total. That is a highly subjective statement that is the opposite of the facts as to the scale of the epidemic. Paragraph 66 says because of 'under-reporting', 'Many victims cannot or do not disclose their abuse to the authorities, and nor is it identified by safeguarding professionals, so the abuse remains uncovered.'

Paragraph 67 states, 'In our work to improve the recording and collation of data on group-based child sexual exploitation, we have found that a lack of clarity around definitions of groups, gangs, and sexual exploitation contribute to inconsistencies in recording. There remains confusion amongst practitioners around what constitutes group-based CSE.'

Paragraph 68 states: 'Even where CSE is identified, the data relating to CSE is still often inconsistently recorded. For example, research has found that information is often recorded inconsistently about victims and offenders, with different agencies focusing on different aspects when recording information. Police data in particular suffers from a lack of consistency in recording.'

None of this nit-picking goes to the substance of the issue.

Under the heading 'Ethnicity', the report presents 'key findings' (italics my own emphasis):

- *'Research on offender ethnicity is limited, and tends to rely on poor quality data. It is therefore difficult to draw conclusions about differences in ethnicity of offenders, but it is likely that no one community or culture is uniquely predisposed to offending.*
- A number of studies have indicated an over-representation of Asian and Black offenders in group-based CSE. *Most of the same studies show that the majority of offenders are White.'*

Paragraph 75 elaborates further on the issue:

> 'There is a limited amount of research looking at the ethnicity of perpetrators of group-based CSE, which makes it difficult to draw conclusions about whether or not certain ethnicities are over-represented in this type of offending ... Data in this space is reliant on "known" or identified offending behaviour, therefore limiting our understanding of group-based CSE in its entirety ... Law enforcement data can be particularly vulnerable to bias, in terms of those cases that come to the attention of the authorities, and this can impact on the generalisability of such data. This can also lead to greater attention being paid to certain types of offenders, making that data more readily identified and recorded ... Police-collected data on ethnicity uses broad categories and requires the police to assign an ethnicity rather than it being self-reported by offenders. Data is therefore not always accurate ... Data on ethnicity are not routinely or consistently collected by police forces and other agencies ... many research and evidence collections have a lot of missing or incomplete data.'

Paragraph 81 states (italics my own emphasis):

'While some of the research set out above suggests that there are high numbers of offenders of Asian or Black ethnicities committing group-based CSE offences, it is not possible to say whether these groups are over-represented in this type of offending. As set out in paragraph 75, research to date has relied on poor-quality data with a number of weaknesses. *It remains difficult to compare the make-up of the offender population with the local demography of certain areas*, in order to make fully informed assessments of whether some groups are over-represented. Based on the existing evidence, and our understanding of the flaws in the existing data, *it seems most likely* that the ethnicity of group-based CSE offenders is in line with CSA more generally and with the general population, *with the majority of offenders being White*.'

The report's assertions and hints about the 'local demography', or that an alleged 'lack of ... data in the public domain' due to 'definitional challenges', and that what evidence is available 'is unlikely to represent current thinking and understanding', are no more than dishonest sophistry. There is no evidence 'the majority of offenders [are] White'. The Home Office should not embark on an exercise of trying to find (i.e. fabricate) evidence to 'represent current thinking and understanding'.

There is no evidence of there being a multitude of White grooming gangs. The same cannot be said of those from particular immigrant communities. The report is a brazen cover up. Of note, is the fact the terms 'Muslim', 'Islam', the 'Koran', 'immigrant', 'immigration' or 'English' (the overwhelming majority of victims are English) are not mentioned even once in the report. The overwhelming majority of those committing these heinous crimes are Muslims, many of whom immigrated to the UK. That they are picking on White children would indicate a racial motive and/or a contempt for those regarded as infidels, and this should be investigated and not ignored.

380

Despite the report complaining about a 'lack of robust research and data in the public domain', there have been reports and belated police investigations into the abuse, and there is evidence 'in the public domain'. For example, there is the photograph showing the faces of many of the offenders, and there are many other photographs. A casual look on Wikipedia is also informative.

The list of grooming gang offenders convicted in Bristol names Liban "Leftback" Abdi, Mustapha "Greens" Farah, Arafat "Left Eye" Osman, Abdulahi "Trigger" Aden, Mustafa Deria, Said "Target" Zakaria, Mohamed "Deeq" Jumale, Jusuf "Starns" Abdirizak, Sakariah "Zac" Sheik, Abdirashid "Abs" Abdulahi, Omar Jumale, and Mohamed "Kamal" Dahir.

In Derby, those convicted were Abid Mohammed Saddique, Mohammed Romaan Liaqat, Akshay Kumar, Faisal Mehmood, Mohammed Imran Rehman, and Graham Blackham.

In Halifax, those convicted were Hedar Ali, Haider Ali, Khalid Zaman, Mohammed Ramzan, Haaris Ahmed, Tahir Mahmood, Taukeer Butt, Amaar Ali Ditta, Azeem Subhani, Talib Saddiq, Sikander Malik, Mohammed Ali Ahmed, Aftab Hussain, Mansoor Akhtar, Sikander Ishaq, Aesan Pervez, Furqaan Ghafar, Basharat Khaliq, Saeed Akhtar, Naveed Akhtar, Parvaze Ahmed, Izar Hussain, Zeeshan Ali, Kieran Harris, Faheem Iqbal, and Mohammed Usman.

In Newcastle, 'the 18 gang members ... convicted of nearly 100 offences' were Mohammed Azram, Jahangir Zaman, Nashir Uddin, Saiful Islam, Mohammed Hassan Ali, Yasser Hussain, Abdul Sabe, Habibur Rahim, Badrul Hussain, Mohibur Rahman, Abdulhamid Minoyee, Carolann Gallon, Monjour Choudhury, Prabhat Nelli, Eisa Mousavi, Taherul Alam, Nadeem Aslam, and Redwan Siddquee.

In Oxford, those convicted were Kamar Jamil, Akhtar Dogar, Anjum Dogar, Assad Hussain, Mohammed Karrar, Bassam Karrar, Zeeshan Ahmed, Bilal Ahmed, Mustafa Ahmed, Assad Hussain, Kameer Iqbal, Khalid Hussain, Kamran Khan, Moinul Islam, Raheem Ahmed, Alladitta Yousaf, Haji Khan, Naim Khan, Mohammed Nazir, Tilal Madhi, Salik Miah, and Azad Miah.

For Peterborough, those convicted were Hassan Abdulla, Renato Balog, Jan Kandrac, Yasir Ali, Daaim Ashraf, Mohammed Abbas, 'Unnamed Child', Muhammed Waqas, Zdeno Mirga, and Mohammed Khubaib.

For Rochdale, those named were Shabir Ahmed, Mohammed Sajid, Kabeer Hassan, Abdul Aziz, Abdul Rauf, Adil Khan, Mohammed Amin, Abdul Qayyum, and Hamid Safi. Another ten, unnamed, in a second grooming gang were subsequently convicted.

Grooming gangs and the determined attempts by authorities to cover up have badly affected Rotherham. Those named in various trials are Razwan Razaq, Umar Razaq, Zafran Ramzan, Mohsin Khan, Adil Hussain, Qurban Ali, Arshid Hussain, Basharat Hussain, Bannaras Hussain, Karen MacGregor, Shelley Davies, Sageer Hussain, Basharat Hussain, Ishtiaq Khaliq, Masoued Malik, Waleed Ali, Asif Ali, Naeem Rafiq, Mohammed Whied, Basharat Dad, Nasser Dad, Tayab Dad, Mohammed Sadiq, Matloob Hussain, Amjad Ali, Zalgai Ahmadi, Sajid Ali, Zaheer Iqbal, Riaz Makhmood, Asghar Bostan, Tony Chapman, Khurram Javed, Mohammed Imran Ali Akhtar, Nabeel Kurshid, Iqlak Yousaf, Tanweer Ali, Salah Ahmed El-Hakam, Asif Ali, Aftab Hussain, Abid Saddiq, Masaued Malik, Sharaz Hussain, Mohammed Ashen, and Waseem Khaliq.

Of the Jay report into the horror of what happened in Rotherham and the attempts, including violent attempts, to intimidate witnesses, victims and those raising the alarm, Wikipedia states:

'The police had shown a lack of respect for the victims in the early 2000s, according to the report, deeming them "undesirables" unworthy of police protection. The concerns of Jayne Senior, the former youth worker, were met with "indifference and scorn". Because most of the perpetrators were of Pakistani heritage, several council staff described themselves as being nervous about identifying the ethnic origins of perpetrators for fear of being thought racist; others, the report noted, 'remembered clear direction from their managers' not to make such identification. The report noted the experience of Adele Weir, the Home Office researcher, who attempted to raise concerns about the abuse with senior police officers in 2002; she was told not to do so again, and was subsequently sidelined.'

Little has changed in the Home Office.

It is blindingly obvious the overwhelming majority of those named are from immigrant communities and are Muslims. The allegation in the Home Office report of 'the majority of offenders being White' is a barefaced lie to distract attention from the real culprits. The report is a cover-up. The grooming, rape and gang rape of mostly English children continues. Priti Patel should resign.

APPENDIX TWO

THE SINGH INVESTIGATION
Independent Investigation Into Alleged Discrimination

The Singh Investigation into alleged Islamophobia in the Tory Party was launched following the last Tory leadership campaign, when one of the candidates, Rajid Savid, a Muslim, in a live television debate, demanded such an investigation and all the other candidates followed suit. Shame on them.

Professor Swaran Singh is conducting the investigation and has lived in the United Kingdom for over thirty years after arriving during the first Gulf War. He claimed to have 'experienced first-hand the pernicious manifestations of racism within certain parts of British society'. A colleague had even told him to 'go home' if he did not like it in the UK (one wonders why a colleague would say that?) As a psychiatrist, he claimed to have 'witnessed the damage done to people's health and lives by racism, discrimination, bullying and harassment'. Although he conceded, 'much has changed for the better ... perhaps not enough has changed, and not everywhere'. Professor Singh is a former equality and human rights commissioner.

The Tories set up the investigation 'following discussions with the Equality and Human Rights Commission' (EHRC). The EHRC approved the terms of reference.

The investigation revealed: 'Over the six years 2015 to 2020 (inclusive of both years), the Party's central database recorded 1,418 complaints concerning 727 incidents of alleged discrimination; i.e. an average of 237 complaints relating to 122 incidents per year in a party with 200,000 members (latest CCHQ figure).'

For most normal people, that would have been the end of the matter. Out of a 200,000 membership, there were '122 incidents per year'. Around two-thirds of these incidents related to allegations of Islamophobia, and around three-quarters related to activity on social media. This is an infinitely small number (the incidents being around 0.0006 per cent of the membership).

The report listed four items as 'specific cases'. One, a statement that 'There were examples of anti-Muslim discrimination by individuals and groups at local association level'. Two, the investigation had uncovered 'one serious allegation of direct discrimination at local association level whose investigation showed serious failings in the complaints process'. Three, there was 'a perception among some respondents' there had been incidents that 'suggest[ed]' the Tories were 'insensitive to Muslim communities'. A previous London mayoral campaign was cited and comments made by Boris Johnson. Four, the investigation had 'heard powerful testimonies about the adverse impact of perceived or actual discrimination on a victim's wellbeing and self-confidence, and concerns that making a complaint may lead to negative consequences such as being seen as a "troublemaker"'. None of those making these 'testimonies' 'were willing to be identified'.

This is the best the investigation could come up with. Regarding a public call for evidence, Professor Singh said:

> 'The Independent Investigation is reaching the end of its initial examination of the Conservative Party's handling of past complaints of discrimination. We are now calling for further evidence that we may not already have seen to ensure that we are aware, as far as realistically possible, of all evidence relating to alleged discrimination within the Party. We need to determine whether all important evidence of discrimination has been considered

in the framework of the Party's existing complaints process.'

The Muslim Council of Britain (MCB) was not very cooperative, although it did make a submission. This is after the MCB had written to the EHRC 'to formally request an EHRC Investigation into whether the Conservative Party had breached its obligations under the Equality Act 2010'.

In a letter to the investigation, the MCB made some demands, including: 'Deny membership to those with a history of far right and extreme views: There is evidence of Party membership from individuals from bodies that are known to be hostile towards ethnic minorities and especially Muslims. A real policy of change, coupled with improved due diligence, will reduce risk of those with racists views entering the Party.'

The Muslim Engagement and Development (MEND) organisation also made a submission, as did Hope Not Hate, which published and submitted a 'dossier':

> 'The submission included an analysis of the Party's disciplinary processes and recommendations for improving procedural and cultural issues related to anti-Muslim discrimination in the Party. Hope Not Hate also included the results of its own survey of Party members' views on Muslims, and included 40 case studies of Conservative councillors, MPs and activists accused of anti-Muslim acts.'

This exercise was merely an invitation for anti-conservatives and the politically correct to make allegations against the Tory Party, and the making of those allegations constitutes evidence the Tories are Islamophobic. The investigation drew attention to the definition of Islamophobia:

'On 27 November 2018, the All-Party Parliamentary Group on British Muslims published its working definition of Islamophobia, namely: "Islamophobia is rooted in racism and is a type of racism that targets expression of Muslimness or perceived Muslimness". This definition was adopted by the Labour Party, the Liberal Democrats, the Scottish National Party and many local councils but it was rejected by the Conservative Government.'

The investigation also stated: 'Theresa May, former Conservative Prime Minster, said in her 2002 Conference speech: "Our base is too narrow and so, occasionally, are our sympathies. You know what some people call us – the Nasty Party."'

The investigation focused on the supposed failings of the Tory Party's procedures for handling complaints. It recommended some measures the party should take and laid out timetables (of weeks and months) to be adhered to:

'We recommend that the Party publishes an Action Plan within six weeks of the publication of this report. This Action Plan should clearly set out the Party's actions, timescales for implementation and measures of success for each of the recommendations accepted by the Party. Should the Party choose not to accept any particular recommendations, it should give clear reasons for its non-acceptance. The Party should follow up the Action Plan by publishing a six-month Progress Report prepared by the Party, followed by a One-year Review prepared by the Investigation or some other appropriate body, to determine the extent to which the recommendations have been implemented.'

Furthermore:

388

'The Investigation recommends that all major political parties consider, in discussion with the EHRC, the creation of a cross-party, non-partisan, and independent mechanism for handling complaints of discrimination against their parties or party members on the basis of Protected Characteristics. This could be similar to the current Parliamentary Independent Complaints and Grievance Scheme for Sexual Misconduct.'

In fact, there is no comparison to the parliamentary scheme regarding sexual misconduct, as sexual misconduct is not a matter of ideological contention – how to react to the scale and consequences of Muslim immigration is.

As can be seen from the bullying 'recommendations', there is a move to subordinate the Tory Party to unelected, unaccountable and politically correct pressure groups. Once a country has adopted a regime, whereby only politically correct people are allowed to stand for office, then that country ceases to be a democracy.

The Muslim Baroness Warsi, who has been making allegations of Islamophobia against the Tories for years, despite being a member of the Tory Party, said the report's recommendations were 'good and should be implemented' but also said: 'I think we now need an independent Equality and Human Rights Commission investigation because there are flaws to this report.' The investigation concluded that although 'anti-Muslim sentiment' remained 'a problem within the party', there was 'no evidence' the party was institutionally racist.

MEND dismissed the report as a 'whitewash' and said the investigation did not acknowledge 'the root causes of this bigotry' and demanded an EHRC investigation to 'determine whether any breaches of law have taken place'.

Conservative co-chairman Amanda Milling said the party accepted all the recommendations:

> 'On behalf of the Conservative Party I would like to apologise to anyone who has been hurt by discriminatory behaviour of others or failed by our system. We held this investigation to address these allegations to make sure that any instances of discrimination are isolated and to look at how we can improve and strengthen our complaints process. The Conservative Party will continue to take a zero-tolerance approach to discrimination of any kind and take immediate action to improve our handling of complaints. It is clear that there have been failings in our complaints process and we will begin work on implementing the recommendations set out by the investigation.'

Sajid Javid also wanted the recommendations to be implemented in full.

Handing over the running of the Tory Party, including the vetting of party membership and candidates, to a collection of politically correct, Labour supporting race zealots is the last thing the Tory Party should do.

APPENDIX THREE

Britsh Steel is a good example of the damage climate change nuttiness can do. In *The Ponzi Class*, I wrote:

'The demise of British Steel is a sad testimony to the disaster of the takeover culture stemming from the City and successive British governments. British Steel was making good profits and was investing in new production methods. By contrast several European steel producers were dependent upon government subsidies and those governments were reluctant to reduce surplus capacity. The subsidies enabled those less efficient producers to undercut British Steel. Even so, by 1997 British Steel was the second largest producer in Europe with an output of 17 million tonnes – only 0.5 million tonnes less than Germany's Thyssen Krupp.

In 1999, British Steel merged with the Dutch company Hoogovens to form the largest producing steel company, now called Corus, in Europe and the third largest in the world (behind POSCO of South Korea and Nippon Steel). The merger was a disaster with falling output and increasing losses. Despite the merger, the Dutch part of Corus had maintained its own supervisory board which vetoed decisions, demanded extra investment for the Dutch side of the business, and was accused by the British unions of trying to preserve Dutch jobs at the expense of British ones.

Corus was taken over by Tata Steel in 2007. Half the cost of the takeover was a loan secured against the assets of Corus. The capacity of 18.2 million tonnes that Tata took over from Corus is a small part of the 120 million tonnes that Tata aims to have worldwide by 2015. That the plight of Britain's steel industry was of minor concern to Tata and of little concern to the Tory Government was shown by the demise of the Redcar steel plant, which had been sold by Tata to the Thai firm SSI in 2011. As a result of a number of factors, including electricity costs on average 82 per cent higher than EU competitors, not least due to climate change levies, other green costs, the inclusion of plant and machinery in business rates, and the fact that China had been dumping surplus steel production onto the European market, led to the permanent closure of the Redcar plant in October 2015.

The steel industry's energy costs were so high because in order to comply with the Climate Change Act, which Britain unilaterally adopted, Britain must reduce the use of carbon-based energy and, due to the 'carbon price floor', cannot cut the price of carbon-based energy even if its costs fall – as they have. Consequently, along with the dash for unreliable and expensive green energy, accompanied by the closure of cheap electricity from coal-fired power stations, the energy costs for Britain's heavy industries is roughly twice that of other European countries such as France and Germany (which is currently building a number of new coal-fired power stations). Consequently, British industry cannot compete. The new nuclear power station at Hinkley will only make matters worse. The cost of the agreed 'strike price' of Hinkley's output is roughly twice the current wholesale cost of electricity, and this price is further index-linked to inflation for the next 35 years. Furthermore, Hinkley's 3,200 Megawatts of capacity will cost as much to build as 50,000 Megawatts of gas power station capacity.

The Tories did not allow the fact that China was a communist state and therefore able to fix the costs of its steel production, nor the fact that other countries are supporting their steel industries, to interfere with their commitment to globalisation. Chinese steel producers are heavily subsidised and are dumping surplus production onto world markets at less than their own cost of production. Chinese surplus capacity was 340 million tonnes in 2014, which is more than double the demand for steel in the entire EU.

The numbers employed in the steel industry have collapsed from 200,000 in the 1970s to less than 20,000 in 2015. Other steel plants, especially the Tata owned one at Scunthorpe, were also under threat of closure. The steel firm, Caparo, went into administration. Of the Redcar plant, Alexander Temerko, deputy chairman of the oil rig maker OGN and a major customer, said: 'The closure of SSI's Redcar plant is a damning indictment of the government's ineptitude when it comes to supporting UK heavy industry. A business like ours can use more than 100,000 tons of steel per year, but the opportunities for synergy and collaboration have been wasted by successive energy ministers, who have turned their backs on UK oil and gas suppliers, pointing to EU regulations and claiming their hands are tied'. It was only after the closure of the Redcar pant that the Tory Government finally asked the EU for permission to assist the British steel industry meet the unnecessarily high energy costs. Other European countries have been willing and able to assist their own steel industries without EU obstruction. The Tories are simply using the EU as a cover for their true agenda, which is their policy of unilateral free trade and globalization. Gary Klesch, who had withdrawn from a deal to buy the Scunthorpe plant in the summer of 2015, said that Scunthorpe's 6,000 workers were 'being led to the slaughterhouse' by politicians.

The Tory Government was somewhat embarrassed when it was revealed, just after the Redcar plant had closed, that the Ministry of Defence had entered into a £3.8 billion deal to use Swedish steel for an order for 589 Ajax armoured vehicles and three naval offshore patrol ships. Once again the British government put unilateral free trade theories ahead of the national interest and the livelihoods of ordinary people. That the British war effort at the outbreak of WWII was crippled by the inability to produce or buy the required amount of steel needs to be remembered, and that it was only US Lend-Lease that bailed Britain out.'

– *The Ponzi Class: Ponzi Economics, Globalization and Class Oppression in the 21st Century*, page 274.

APPENDIX FOUR
CONSERVATIVES AGAINST RACISM FOR EQUALITY

The Tory MP, Steve Baker, is the chairman of a new faction of the wokerati: the Conservatives Against Racism For Equality (CARFE – as it styles itself). This group was co-founded by Albie Amankona – 'a member of Brentford & Isleworth Conservatives, TRG [Tory Reform Group] and LGBT+ Conservatives' and someone who is 'passionate about how the Conservative party can appeal to minority groups & young voters'. The other co-founder was Siobhan Aarons, who is a 'TRG Board Member' and also 'co-Chair of the Conservative Friends of the Caribbean, as well as a committee member of her local association'.

The CARFE website explains the organisation intends to reach out to the 'entire party' and 'across society'. Further, the organisation was founded 'in the wake of the disproportionate impact of Covid-19 on ethnically diverse communities, the fallout from George Floyd's killing and Britain's divisive BLM protests'. The home page states:

> 'Conservatives Against Racism For Equality (CARFE), is Britain's first centre-right organisation dedicated to race-relations. Racism can only be tackled if we reach out to all sides of politics. Racism is not a matter of left and right, it is a matter of right and wrong; that's why CARFE seeks to create a centre-right, common sense approach to race-relations. This narrative can't be controlled by the left, nor can Conservatives appear silent on issues of race as the demographics of our electorate changes.'

By 'the demographics of our electorate changes', they mean the continued mass immigration and colonisation of England by

Third World immigrants. This colonisation is the result of government policy.

CARFE seeks to merge the Tory stance on immigration and related issues with the left-wing one. That is, the Tories seek to join the politically correct to an even greater extent than is already the case. Tory policy will be forged as much by a variety of race war groups and the Labour Party as it is by the Tories. This is the woke-Right in action.

CARFE urges all Tories to 'take the following pledge':

> '**RACISM**
> If we see it,
> we'll call it out.
> If we're made aware of it,
> we'll call it out.
> If we discover it,
> we'll call it out.'

The mind boggles. The home page continues:

> 'It is who we are as people, not the colour of our skin that defines us. We are at a turbulent time as we face society's reaction to racial prejudices and biases that unfortunately exist to this day. George Floyd's killing has brought out the feelings of confusion and hurt that have lain just under the surface for so many people of colour. Right across the world, people are angry about racial injustice and societies around the world should take note of that energy, including here in the UK.'

The website rambles on about Covid-19 and how ethnic minorities were more badly affected, and that '40 per cent of the poorest UK households are Black households, ethnic minorities account for 50 per cent of children incarcerated in young offender's institutes and Black mothers are 5 times more likely to die in childbirth than White mothers. Statistics like this are unacceptable.'

Therefore, CARFE:

> '... are pushing to address racial disparities and we are committed to tackling the injustices faced by ethnic minorities. We will play our part to repair the hurt by raising awareness of social injustice and we pledge our commitment to level-up the inequality in health, education, justice, housing and career outcomes. Violence and vandalism are not the answer but we must break down the barriers that stop us as Conservatives engaging meaningfully in race relations. We have a role to play to rid ourselves of prejudice and injustice.'

To be blunt, this group is politically correct, and the ideology advocated is pure cultural Marxism. Even for those unimpressed with the Tories, it is a wonder to watch a couple of entryists lead the whole party down the race war route.

Accusing people, institutions and countries of being racist is neither constructive nor intelligent.

Equality is a communist obsession. Equality of opportunity has traditionally been a liberal and conservative belief. There will always be a degree of inequality. Some people are cleverer than others. Some are luckier, or have more supportive families and colleagues. Some make lifestyle choices that prioritise, for them, a better quality of life rather than a higher income. Others may well be less well off because they have spent a large part of their income on high living. It is not the role of any government to seek to impose supposedly equal outcomes for all.

CARFE exists solely on the assumption that the UK, and England in particular, is racist – as are the indigenous British, the English in particular (England is where the overwhelming majority of ethnic minorities immigrate to and live).

The CARFE cliché that 'It is who we are as people, not the colour of our skin that defines us', is of course true. The English, Germans, French, Italians etc. might all be White, but they are still distinct nations, with distinct histories, loyalties and culture.

CARFE portrays the ethnic minorities as victims and alleges 'racial injustice' and 'anger' across the world, and that the ethnic minorities are poorer and more likely to be imprisoned, but does not even acknowledge the justified anger of the English. The immigrant communities are more likely to be poorer as they have moved to the UK from poorer countries, often illegally, and if they object to more of their members being imprisoned, then perhaps those criminals should stop committing crime.

An estimated minimum of 250,000 mostly English children have been groomed, raped and/or gang raped by Muslim grooming gangs (the Tory Government disputes this – see Appendix One). The English are being denigrated, casually accused of being racist, experience their country being taken away from them, are denied democratic equality within the UK and experience lower standards of living due to mass immigration – not least the housing shortage created by mass immigration means they are increasingly less likely to be able to afford their own homes.

Of some surprise are the veiled threats. Comments such as 'people are angry about racial injustice and societies around the world should take note of that energy, including here in the UK', and 'Violence and vandalism are not the answer but we must break down the barriers that stop us as Conservatives engaging meaningfully in race relations' are veiled threats and a justification of violence and hatred. The murder of George Floyd has nothing to do with the UK, and nor has the USA's history of immigration.

What is needed is justice for the English, not more anti-English race war politics.

APPENDIX FIVE
ONE BRITAIN ONE NATION

A recent incarnation of so-called civic nationalism (a Frankfurt School construct) is One Britain One Nation (OBON). Punjabi immigrant, Kash Singh, founded this organisation. OBON's website states, 'Kash Singh is the Chief Executive and Founder of One Britain One Nation (OBON). As Chair and founder of the British Indian Association, he was responsible for bringing together thousands of people from diverse backgrounds.'

The Tories support OBON and gave it state funding. Identity is important to OBON. Its website states:

> 'One Britain One Nation brings us together, not to focus on our differences but to celebrate the values we share: tolerance, kindness, pride, respect, and a tremendous desire to help others. Today's Britain boasts a wonderful array of cultures. It is our multicultural identity that makes Britain so unique. Our diverse cultures are inextricably linked by the sole fact that we are British. It is this fact that has prompted OBON to reinforce and revive what collectively unites us. OBON aims to give a new impetus for the creation of a harmonised society, to make Britain an international model of moral rectitude.'

Were multiculturalism so wonderful, there would be no place for OBON. The website continues (italics my emphasis):

> 'Our ideal is based on a set of values, a spirit, a way of living and a state of mind that is ultimately about shared values of tolerance, respect, fair play, a belief in freedom and democracy. It is about *seeking to create a single culture* that embraces and accommodates differences

without over-emphasising and reinforcing them. It is one which is inclusive, meaningful and capable of *restoring civil pride* and creating unity of purpose with a strong shared sense of belonging for all our people. It is a national mission with a patriotic vision that unifies people with *a common bond of working for the future of our country*.'

OBON is not advocating assimilation of immigrants, but manufacturing a 'single culture' to replace British culture. Given most immigrants settle in England, it is English culture that is under attack. The aim of 'restoring civil pride' would not be necessary unless something had gone wrong. The English have no problem with their patriotism or civil pride. The comment about a 'common bond' to work for the future of the country is disingenuous. In part it is a territorial grab and in part flawed in that such a common bond is too weak to hold together a country.

OBON's mission is set out as being to 'promote the concept of responsible citizenship; to instil a sense of personal pride in all our citizens of being British and create a real sense of collective identity regardless of one's background'; to 'facilitate, inspire and strengthen the spirit of inclusion and involvement and social responsibility in all our communities in an effort to promote peaceful, respectful coexistence in citizens who will play a more active part in the wellbeing of our Nation'; to provide 'role models' for 'our youth'; and 'To recognise, acknowledge and value our diverse communities and their cultural heritage while aiming to facilitate and harness their integration into mainstream Britain.'

The candyfloss language should not obscure the agenda to replace English national culture in England with a theoretical construct that promotes immigrant cultures. There is no reason the English should support this and they should not.

Worse, in pursuit of its mission, OBON is targeting primary schoolchildren. The website states:

> We need the support of your school to celebrate the day in the spirit it is intended and as outlined in the OBON DAY 2021 brochure but to do the following as a MUST please: **At 10am on Friday 25th June 2021.** Encourage every child in your school to clap for a minute to recognise, embrace and pay tribute to all those people who helped during the Covid 19 pandemic crisis. Sing the OBON DAY 2021 anthem written by school children at St John's CE Primary School, Bradford titled **"We are Britain and we have one dream to unite all people in one Great Team"**.

Yes, they even have a silly song. The Scottish First Minister, Nicola Sturgeon, initially thought it was all a 'spoof'. It was also described as a 'barmy brainwashing event'.

It is appalling that primary schoolchildren are being dragged into politics and exploited in this way. It is equally appalling the Tories are actively involved.

Extremists do target children. The communists did, the Nazis did, and ISIS are doing so too.

1   Herbert Marcuse, *Repressive Tolerance*, essay, 1965, page 11

2   Herbert Marcuse, *Repressive Tolerance*, essay, 1965, page 11

3   Martin Schoolman, *The Imaginary Witness*, The Free Press, New York, 1980, page 319

4   Douglas Kellner, *Herbert Marcuse and the Crisis of Marxism*, Macmillan Education Ltd, Basingstoke, 1984, page 303

5   Martin Schoolman, *The Imaginary Witness*, The Free Press, New York, 1980, page 303

6   RG Collingwood, *The New Leviathan*, Oxford University Press, New York, 1992, page 346

7   RG Collingwood, *The New Leviathan*, Oxford University Press, New York, 1992, page 347

8   Tim Newark, The Barbarians; *Warriors and Wars of the Dark Ages*, Blandford Press, Poole, 1986, page 49

9   Arthur Ferrill, *The Fall of the Roman Empire: The Military Explanation*, Thames and Hudson, London, 1986, page 99; and Edward Gibbon, *The Decline and Fall of the Roman Empire*, volume 3, Dent & Sons Ltd, Great Britain, 1981, page 322

10   AHM Jones, The Later Roman Empire 284–602, Volume 1, Basil Blackwell, Padstow, 1986, page 183; and Edward Gibbon, *The Decline and Fall of the Roman Empire*, volume 3, Dent & Sons Ltd, Great Britain, 1981, pages 351, 358 and 373

[11] RG Collingwood, *The New Leviathan*, Oxford University Press, New York, 1992, page 353

[12] RG Collingwood, *The New Leviathan*, Oxford University Press, New York, 1992, pages 354 and 355

[13] RG Collingwood, *The New Leviathan*, Oxford University Press, New York, 1992, page 372

[14] RG Collingwood, *The New Leviathan*, Oxford University Press, New York, 1992, page 373

[15] RG Collingwood, *The New Leviathan*, Oxford University Press, New York, 1992, page 380

[16] RG Collingwood, *The New Leviathan*, Oxford University Press, New York, 1992, page 381

[17] RG Collingwood, *The New Leviathan*, Oxford University Press, New York, 1992, page 381

[18] RG Collingwood, *The New Leviathan*, Oxford University Press, New York, 1992, pages 381 and 382

[19] RG Collingwood, *The New Leviathan*, Oxford University Press, New York, 1992, page 385

[20] RG Collingwood, *The New Leviathan*, Oxford University Press, New York, 1992, page 385

[21] RG Collingwood, *The New Leviathan*, Oxford University Press, New York, 1992, page 386

[22] *Catholic Encyclopedia*, http://www.newadvent.org/cathen/01267e.htm

[23] Richard Murphy, *Collingwood and the Crisis of Western Civilization*, Imprint Academic, Exeter, 2008, page 2

[24] RG Collingwood, *The New Leviathan*, Oxford University Press, New York, 1992, page 351

[25] AHM Jones, *The Later Roman Empire 284-602, Volume II*, Basil Blackwell, Padstow, 1986, page 1026

[26] AHM Jones, *The Later Roman Empire 284-602, Volume II*, Basil Blackwell, Padstow, 1986, pages 1030 and 1031

[27] Correlli Barnett, *The Collapse of British Power*, Alan Sutton, Great Britain, 1984, page 107; and Sidney Pollard, *Britain's Prime and Britain's Decline: The British Economy 1870-1914*, Edward Arnold, Great Britain, 1989, page 235

[28] Beate Jahn, Barbarian Thoughts: Imperialism in the Philosophy of John Stuart Mill, *Review of International Studies*, 31:3 (2005), page 609

[29] AHM Jones, *The Later Roman Empire 284-602, Volume II*, Basil Blackwell, Padstow, 1986, page 1064

[30] Edward Gibbon, *The Decline and Fall of the Roman Empire*, volume 6, Dent & Sons Ltd, Great Britain, 1981, page 449

[31] Douglas Kellner, *Herbert Marcuse and the Crisis of Marxism*, Macmillan Education Ltd, Basingstoke, 1984, page 303

[32] Martin Schoolman, *The Imaginary Witness*, The Free Press, New York, 1980, page 303

[33] Jurgen Habermas, Citizenship and National Identity: Some Reflections on the Future of Europe, *Theorizing Citizenship*, edited by Ronald Beiner, State University of New York, Albany, 1995, page 255

[34] *Collins English Dictionary*, Second Edition, Collins, Glasgow, 1986

[35] Reza Aslan, No God But God: *The Origins, Evolution and Future of Islam*, Arrow Books, London, 2006, page 79

[36] Reza Aslan, No God But God: *The Origins, Evolution and Future of Islam*, Arrow Books, London, 2006, page 79

[37] Ayaan Hirsi Ali, *Heretic: Why Islam Needs A Reformation Now*, Harper, New York, 2015, page 99

[38] Peter Townsend, *Questioning Islam: Tough Questions & Honest Answers About the Muslim Religion*, Amazon, Great Britain, 2014, page 47

[39] Peter Townsend, *Questioning Islam: Tough Questions & Honest Answers About the Muslim Religion*, Amazon, Great Britain, 2014, page 47

[40] Peter Townsend, *Questioning Islam: Tough Questions & Honest Answers About the Muslim Religion*, Amazon, Great Britain, 2014, page 48

[41] Reza Aslan, No God But God: *The Origins, Evolution and Future of Islam*, Arrow Books, London, 2006, page 68

[42] Reza Aslan, No God But God: *The Origins, Evolution and Future of Islam*, Arrow Books, London, 2006, page 71

[43] Reza Aslan, No God But God: *The Origins, Evolution and Future of Islam*, Arrow Books, London, 2006, page 163

44 Reza Aslan, No God But God: *The Origins, Evolution and Future of Islam*, Arrow Books, London, 2006, page 24

45 Ayaan Hirsi Ali, *Heretic: Why Islam Needs A Reformation Now*, Harper, New York, 2015, page 77

46 Ayaan Hirsi Ali, *Heretic: Why Islam Needs A Reformation Now*, Harper, New York, 2015, page 92

47 Reza Aslan, No God But God: *The Origins, Evolution and Future of Islam*, Arrow Books, London, 2006, page 159

48 Ayaan Hirsi Ali, *Heretic: Why Islam Needs A Reformation Now*, Harper, New York, 2015, page 94

49 Ayaan Hirsi Ali, *Heretic: Why Islam Needs A Reformation Now*, Harper, New York, 2015, page 134

50 Reza Aslan, No God But God: *The Origins, Evolution and Future of Islam*, Arrow Books, London, 2006, page 162

51 William Montgomery Watt, *Islamic Fundamentalism and Modernity*, Routledge, London, 1989, page 24

52 William Montgomery Watt, *Islamic Fundamentalism and Modernity*, Routledge, London, 1989, page 31

53 Peter Townsend, *Questioning Islam: Tough Questions & Honest Answers About the Muslim Religion*, Amazon, Great Britain, 2014, page 268

54 Peter Townsend, *Nothing To /Do With Islam? Investigating the West's Most Dangerous Blind Spot*, Amazon, Great Britain, 2016, page 80

55 Ayaan Hirsi Ali, *Heretic: Why Islam Needs A Reformation Now*, Harper, New York, 2015, page 159

56 Reza Aslan, No God But God: *The Origins, Evolution and Future of Islam*, Arrow Books, London, 2006, page 168

57 Ayaan Hirsi Ali, *Heretic: Why Islam Needs A Reformation Now*, Harper, New York, 2015, page 139

58 Ayaan Hirsi Ali, *Heretic: Why Islam Needs A Reformation Now*, Harper, New York, 2015, page 140

59 Reza Aslan, No God But God: *The Origins, Evolution and Future of Islam*, Arrow Books, London, 2006, page 170

60 Ayaan Hirsi Ali, *Heretic: Why Islam Needs A Reformation Now*, Harper, New York, 2015, page 11

61 William Montgomery Watt, *Islamic Fundamentalism and Modernity*, Routledge, London, 1989, page 6

62 Ayaan Hirsi Ali, *Heretic: Why Islam Needs A Reformation Now*, Harper, New York, 2015, page 80

63 Peter Townsend, *Questioning Islam: Tough Questions & Honest Answers About the Muslim Religion*, Amazon, Great Britain, 2014, page 252

64 Ayaan Hirsi Ali, *Heretic: Why Islam Needs A Reformation Now*, Harper, New York, 2015, page 15

65 Ayaan Hirsi Ali, *Heretic: Why Islam Needs A Reformation Now*, Harper, New York, 2015, page 140

66 Reza Aslan, No God But God: *The Origins, Evolution and Future of Islam*, Arrow Books, London, 2006, page 243

67 Peter Townsend, *Nothing To /Do With Islam? Investigating the West's Most Dangerous Blind Spot*, Amazon, Great Britain, 2016, page 162

68   Reza Aslan, No God But God: *The Origins, Evolution and Future of Islam*, Arrow Books, London, 2006, page 81

69   Peter Townsend, *Questioning Islam: Tough Questions & Honest Answers About the Muslim Religion*, Amazon, Great Britain, 2014, page 228

70   Peter Townsend, *Questioning Islam: Tough Questions & Honest Answers About the Muslim Religion*, Amazon, Great Britain, 2014, page 229

71   Reza Aslan, No God But God: *The Origins, Evolution and Future of Islam*, Arrow Books, London, 2006, page 84

72   Peter Townsend, *Questioning Islam: Tough Questions & Honest Answers About the Muslim Religion*, Amazon, Great Britain, 2014, page 221

73   Peter Townsend, *Questioning Islam: Tough Questions & Honest Answers About the Muslim Religion*, Amazon, Great Britain, 2014, page 222

74   Ayaan Hirsi Ali, *Heretic: Why Islam Needs A Reformation Now*, Harper, New York, 2015, page 117

75   Ayaan Hirsi Ali, *Heretic: Why Islam Needs A Reformation Now*, Harper, New York, 2015, page 118

76   Peter Townsend, *Nothing To /Do With Islam? Investigating the West's Most Dangerous Blind Spot*, Amazon, Great Britain, 2016, page 128

77   Peter Townsend, *Nothing To /Do With Islam? Investigating the West's Most Dangerous Blind Spot*, Amazon, Great Britain, 2016, page 2

78   Peter Townsend, *Nothing To /Do With Islam? Investigating the West's Most Dangerous Blind Spot*,

Amazon, Great Britain, 2016, page 2

79 Peter Townsend, *Nothing To /Do With Islam?
    Investigating the West's Most Dangerous Blind Spot*,
    Amazon, Great Britain, 2016, page 2

80 Peter Townsend, *Nothing To /Do With Islam?
    Investigating the West's Most Dangerous Blind Spot*,
    Amazon, Great Britain, 2016, page 2

81 Peter Townsend, *Nothing To /Do With Islam?
    Investigating the West's Most Dangerous Blind Spot*,
    Amazon, Great Britain, 2016, page 113 and 114

82 Ayaan Hirsi Ali, *Heretic: Why Islam Needs A
    Reformation Now*, Harper, New York, 2015, page 183

83 Ayaan Hirsi Ali, *Heretic: Why Islam Needs A
    Reformation Now*, Harper, New York, 2015, page 19

84 Ayaan Hirsi Ali, *Heretic: Why Islam Needs A
    Reformation Now*, Harper, New York, 2015, page 192

85 Ayaan Hirsi Ali, *Heretic: Why Islam Needs A
    Reformation Now*, Harper, New York, 2015, page 190

86 Peter Townsend, *Nothing To /Do With Islam?
    Investigating the West's Most Dangerous Blind Spot*,
    Amazon, Great Britain, 2016, page 118

87 Ayaan Hirsi Ali, *Heretic: Why Islam Needs A
    Reformation Now*, Harper, New York, 2015, page 185

88 Ayaan Hirsi Ali, *Heretic: Why Islam Needs A
    Reformation Now*, Harper, New York, 2015, page 19

89 Ayaan Hirsi Ali, *Heretic: Why Islam Needs A
    Reformation Now*, Harper, New York, 2015, page 21

90   Cigdem Nas, Intercultural Dialogue Between Civilizations: Turkey as a Bridge?, *European Union and Turkey: Reflections on the Prospects for Membership*, edited by Nanette Neuwahl, Haluk Kabaalioglu, Marmara University, Istanbul, 2006, page 164

91   Paul Kubicek, Turkey's Inclusion in the Atlantic Community: Looking Back, Looking Forward, *Turkish Studies*, volume 9, No 1, page 23

92   Cigdem Nas, Turkey-EU Relations and the Question of Identity, *The European Union Enlargement Process and Turkey*, edited by Muzaffer Dartan, Cigdem Nas, Marmara University, Istanbul, 2002, page 224

93   Burak Bekdil, *Gatestone Institute*, 22nd October 2016

94   Robert Jones, *Gatestone Institute*, 16th November 2016

95   Joby Warrick, *Black Flags: The Rise of ISIS*, Corgi Books, London, 2016, page 346

96   Joby Warrick, *Black Flags: The Rise of ISIS*, Corgi Books, London, 2016, page 368

97   'Video purports to show Turkish intelligence shipping arms to Syria', Reuters. 29 May 2015

98   Joby Warrick, *Black Flags: The Rise of ISIS*, Corgi Books, London, 2016, page 372

99   Jessica Stern and JM Berger, *ISIS: The State of Terror*, William Collins, London, 2016, page 41

100   Patrick Cockburn, 'Turkey duped the US, and Isis is reaping the rewards', @indyworld, 30 August 2015

[101] Robert Jones, *Gatestone Institute*, 3rd September 2016

[102] 'Russia Warns World Over ISIS Heroin Trade', valuewalk. 2015-12-16

[103] Kasim Cindemir, *Gatestone Institute*, 26th December 2016

[104] *Onedio* (Ankara), 26th August 2014

[105] David Phillips, Research Paper: Turkey–ISIS Oil Trade, Columbia University's Institute for the Study of Human Rights, 15th December 2015

[106] Despite US–led campaign, ISIS Rakes in Oil Revenue, *Associated Press*, 23rd October 2015

[107] Joby Warrick, *Black Flags: The Rise of ISIS*, Corgi Books, London, 2016, page 413

[108] Patrick Cockburn, 'Whose Side is Turkey On?', 24 October 2015

[109] ISID petrolu uc guzergahtan Turkiye'ye gidiyor, *Cumhuriyet*, 2 December 2015

[110] ISIS Oil Trade Full Frontal: Raqqa Rockefellers, Bilal Erdogan, KRG Crude, And the Israeli Connection, *Zero Hedge*, 29th November 2015

[111] Aykut Erdogdu yolsuzluk baglantilarini belgeleriyle anlatti, *Cagdas Ses*, 21 October 2015

[112] Opposition MP says ISIS is selling oil in Turkey, *Al–Monitor*, 13th June 2014

[113] Syria conflict, Russia accuses Erdoğan of trading oil with IS, *BBC News*, 2nd December 2015

[114] Meet the Man Who Funds ISIS: Bilal Erdogan, The Son of Turkey's President, *Zero Hedge*, 26th November 2015

[115] Are These The Tankers Bilal Erdoğan Uses To Transport ISIS Oil?, *Zero Hedge*, 30th November 2015

[116] Italya savciligna Bilal Erdoğan sikayeti, *Rota Haber*, 4th December 2015

[117] Adam Justice, 'Isis: Israel accuses Turkey of funding Daesh for oil and failing to fighting terrorism', 27 January 2016

[118] Burak Bekdil, *Gatestone Institute*, 27th September 2016

[119] Burak Bekdil, *Gatestone Institute*, 22nd October 2016

[120] Burak Bekdil, *Gatestone Institute*, 1st January 2017; and Uzay Bulut, *Gatestone Institute*, 3rd November 2018

[121] Andrew Finkel, *Turkey: What Everyone Needs To Know*, Oxford University Press, New York, 2012, page 99

[122] Bhikhu Parekh, Cultural Diversity and Liberal Democracy, in David Beetham (editor), *Defining and Measuring Democracy*, Sage Publications, London, 1994, pages 200–201

[123] Bhikhu Parekh, Cultural Diversity and Liberal Democracy, in David Beetham (editor), *Defining and Measuring Democracy*, Sage Publications, London, 1994, page 201

[124] Bhikhu Parekh, Cultural Diversity and Liberal Democracy, in David Beetham (editor), *Defining and Measuring Democracy*, Sage Publications, London, 1994, page 201

[125] Bhikhu Parekh, Cultural Diversity and Liberal Democracy, in David Beetham (editor), *Defining and Measuring Democracy*, Sage Publications, London, 1994, page 201

[126] Bhikhu Parekh, Cultural Diversity and Liberal Democracy, in David Beetham (editor), *Defining and Measuring Democracy*, Sage Publications, London, 1994, page 202

[127] Bhikhu Parekh, Cultural Diversity and Liberal Democracy, in David Beetham (editor), *Defining and Measuring Democracy*, Sage Publications, London, 1994, page 202

[128] Bhikhu Parekh, Cultural Diversity and Liberal Democracy, in David Beetham (editor), *Defining and Measuring Democracy*, Sage Publications, London, 1994, page 203

[129] Bhikhu Parekh, Cultural Diversity and Liberal Democracy, in David Beetham (editor), *Defining and Measuring Democracy*, Sage Publications, London, 1994, page 204

[130] Bhikhu Parekh, Cultural Diversity and Liberal Democracy, in David Beetham (editor), *Defining and Measuring Democracy*, Sage Publications, London, 1994, page 205

[131] Bhikhu Parekh, Cultural Diversity and Liberal Democracy, in David Beetham (editor), *Defining and Measuring Democracy*, Sage Publications, London, 1994, page 206

[132] Bhikhu Parekh, Cultural Diversity and Liberal Democracy, in David Beetham (editor), *Defining and Measuring Democracy*, Sage Publications, London, 1994, page 206

[133] Bhikhu Parekh, Cultural Diversity and Liberal Democracy, in David Beetham (editor), *Defining and Measuring Democracy*, Sage Publications, London, 1994, page 206

[134] Bhikhu Parekh, Cultural Diversity and Liberal Democracy, in David Beetham (editor), *Defining and Measuring Democracy*, Sage Publications, London, 1994, page 207

[135] Bhikhu Parekh, Cultural Diversity and Liberal Democracy, in David Beetham (editor), *Defining and Measuring Democracy*, Sage Publications, London, 1994, page 207

[136] Bhikhu Parekh, Cultural Diversity and Liberal Democracy, in David Beetham (editor), *Defining and Measuring Democracy*, Sage Publications, London, 1994, page 207

[137] Bhikhu Parekh, Cultural Diversity and Liberal Democracy, in David Beetham (editor), *Defining and Measuring Democracy*, Sage Publications, London, 1994, page 208

[138] Bhikhu Parekh, Cultural Diversity and Liberal Democracy, in David Beetham (editor), *Defining and Measuring Democracy*, Sage Publications, London, 1994, page 208

[139] Bhikhu Parekh, Cultural Diversity and Liberal Democracy, in David Beetham (editor), *Defining and Measuring Democracy*, Sage Publications, London, 1994, page 210

[140] Bhikhu Parekh, Cultural Diversity and Liberal Democracy, in David Beetham (editor), *Defining and Measuring Democracy*, Sage Publications, London, 1994, page 211

[141] Bhikhu Parekh, Cultural Diversity and Liberal Democracy, in David Beetham (editor), *Defining and Measuring Democracy*, Sage Publications, London, 1994, page 212

[142] Bhikhu Parekh, Cultural Diversity and Liberal Democracy, in David Beetham (editor), *Defining and Measuring Democracy*, Sage Publications, London, 1994, page 213

[143] Bhikhu Parekh, Cultural Diversity and Liberal Democracy, in David Beetham (editor), *Defining and Measuring Democracy*, Sage Publications, London, 1994, page 216

[144] Bhikhu Parekh, Cultural Diversity and Liberal Democracy, in David Beetham (editor), *Defining and Measuring Democracy*, Sage Publications, London, 1994, page 217

[145] Bhikhu Parekh, Cultural Diversity and Liberal Democracy, in David Beetham (editor), *Defining and Measuring Democracy*, Sage Publications, London, 1994, page 205

[146] Parekh Report, London, Profile, 2000, paragraphs 3.28–3.30

[147] Brian Barry, *Culture and Equality*, Harvard University Press, USA, 2001, page 292

[148] Shola Mos-Shogbamimu, *This is Why I Resist: Don't Define My Black Identity*, Headline Publishing Group, London, 2021, page 16

[149] Shola Mos-Shogbamimu, *This is Why I Resist: Don't Define My Black Identity*, Headline Publishing Group, London, 2021, page 28

[150] Shola Mos-Shogbamimu, *This is Why I Resist: Don't Define My Black Identity*, Headline Publishing Group, London, 2021, page 32

[151] Shola Mos-Shogbamimu, *This is Why I Resist: Don't Define My Black Identity*, Headline Publishing Group, London, 2021, page 14

[152] Kehinde Andrews, *The New Age of Empire*, Allen Lane, 2021, page 26

[153] Kehinde Andrews, *The New Age of Empire*, Allen Lane, 2021, page 26

[154] Robin DiAngelo, *Nice Racism: How Progressive White People Perpetuate Racial Harm*, Penguin, 2021, page 27

[155] Robin DiAngelo, *Nice Racism: How Progressive White People Perpetuate Racial Harm*, Penguin, 2021, page 29

[156] Kehinde Andrews, *The New Age of Empire*, Allen Lane, 2021, page 83

[157] Shola Mos-Shogbamimu, *This is Why I Resist: Don't Define My Black Identity*, Headline Publishing Group, London, 2021, page 194

[158] Kehinde Andrews, *The New Age of Empire*, Allen Lane, 2021, page 84

[159] Kehinde Andrews, *The New Age of Empire*, Allen Lane, 2021, page 208

[160] Kehinde Andrews, *The New Age of Empire*, Allen Lane, 2021, page 206

[161] Kehinde Andrews, *The New Age of Empire*, Allen Lane, 2021, page 84

[162] Ann Coulter, *Adios America*, Regency Publishing, Washington, 2015, page 94

[163] Melanie Phillips, *Londonistan*, Gibson Square, London, 2006, page 70

[164] Simon Jenkins, *Daily Mail*, 12th September 2015

[165] Martin Jay, *The Dialectical Imagination: A History of the Frankfurt School and The Institute of Social Research, 1923-1950*, page 84

[166] William S Lind, *'Political Correctness': A Short History of an Ideology*, edited by William S Lind, Free Congress Foundation, 2004, page 5

[167] Raymond Marrow and David Brown, *Critical Theory and Methodology*, Sage Publication, London, 1994, page 15

[168] William Lind, *The Origins of Political Correctness*, speech, 2000, page 4

[169] Michael Minnicino, The New Dark Age, The Schiller Institute, Vol 1, No 1, 1992, page 8

[170] Raymond V Raehn, *'Political Correctness': A Short History of an Ideology*, edited by William S Lind, Free Congress Foundation, 2004, page 9

[171] Gerald L Atkinson, What Is The Frankfurt School (and its effect on America)?, *Western Voices World News*, 2009, page 4

[172] Raymond V Raehn, *'Political Correctness': A Short History of an Ideology*, edited by William S Lind, Free Congress Foundation, 2004, page 10

[173] Rick Roderick, *Habermas and the Foundations of Critical Theory*, MacMillan Publishers Ltd, London, 1986, page 137

[174] Raymond Marrow and David Brown, *Critical Theory and Methodology*, Sage Publication, London, 1994, page 16

[175] Raymond Marrow and David Brown, *Critical Theory and Methodology*, Sage Publication, London, 1994, page 151

[176] Raymond Marrow and David Brown, *Critical Theory and Methodology*, Sage Publication, London, 1994, page 154

[177] Rick Roderick, *Habermas and the Foundations of Critical Theory*, MacMillan Publishers Ltd, London, 1986, page 7

[178] Rick Roderick, *Habermas and the Foundations of Critical Theory*, MacMillan Publishers Ltd, London, 1986, page

59

[179] Rick Roderick, *Habermas and the Foundations of Critical Theory*, MacMillan Publishers Ltd, London, 1986, page 73

[180] Rick Roderick, *Habermas and the Foundations of Critical Theory*, MacMillan Publishers Ltd, London, 1986, page 44

[181] Rick Roderick, *Habermas and the Foundations of Critical Theory*, MacMillan Publishers Ltd, London, 1986, page 45

[182] David Held, *Introduction to Critical Theory*, Hutchinson & Co (Publishers) Ltd, London, 1980, page 277

[183] Herbert Marcuse, *One Dimensional Man*, Routledge & Kegn Paul Ltd, London, 1964, page 6

[184] Martin Schoolman, *The Imaginary Witness*, The Free Press, New York, 1980, page 302

[185] David Held, *Introduction to Critical Theory*, Hutchinson & Co (Publishers) Ltd, London, 1980, page 75

[186] Martin Schoolman, *The Imaginary Witness*, The Free Press, New York, 1980, page 319

[187] Harriet Sergeant, *Welcome to the Asylum*, Centre for Policy Studies, London, 2001, page 7

[188] Harriet Sergeant, *Welcome to the Asylum*, Centre for Policy Studies, London, 2001, page 7

[189] Migration Watch UK, 'The Rights of EU Nationals in the UK Post-Brexit', October 2014, updated 20th March 2017

[190] Migration Watch UK, 'Household Projections and Immigration', March 2006

[191] HM Land Registry, UK House Price Index (HPI) for March 2017, 16th May 2017

[192] A New Generational Contract, The final report of the Intergenerational Commission, page 37

[193] A New Generational Contract, The final report of the Intergenerational Commission, page 55

[194] A New Generational Contract, The final report of the Intergenerational Commission, page 105

[195] A New Generational Contract, The final report of the Intergenerational Commission, page 108

[196] A New Generational Contract, The final report of the Intergenerational Commission, page 119

[197] A New Generational Contract, The final report of the Intergenerational Commission, page 210

[198] Lynn, M., & Parker, L. (2006). Critical race studies in education: Examining a decade of research on US schools. The Urban Review, 38, 257–290

[199] Jessica T DeCuir and Adrienne D Dixon-Smith, *'So When It Comes Out, They Aren't That Surprised That It is There': Using Critical Race Theory as a Tool of Analysis of Race and Racism in Education*, Educational Researcher; Jun/Jul 2004; 33, 5; ProQuest Psychology

[200] R Delgado and J Stefancic, *Critical Race Theory: An Introduction*, New York University Press, New York, 2001, page 144

[201] R Delgado and J Stefancic, *Critical Race Theory: An Introduction*, New York University Press, New York, 2001, page 41

[202] WF Tate, *Critical race theory and education: History, theory, and implications, in* M.W. Apple (Ed.) Review of Research in Education, Vol. 22 (page 234). Washington DC: American Educational Research Association

[203] Celina Su, Cracking Silent Codes: Critical race theory and education organizing, City University of New York, Discourse: studies in the cultural politics of education, volume 28, No. 4, December 2007, page 532

[204] William F. Tate IV, *Critical Race Theory and Education: History, Theory, and Implications*, Review of Research in Education, Vol. 22 (1997), page 234

[205] W Macpherson, *The Stephen Lawrence Inquiry*, CM 4262-I. London: The Stationery Office, page 321

[206] Office for Budget Responsibility, *Economic and Fiscal Outlook March 2016*, Her Majesty's Stationary Office, London, paragraph 1.50

[207] Office for Budget Responsibility, *Economic and Fiscal Outlook March 2016*, Her Majesty's Stationary Office, London, paragraph 5.43

Printed in Great Britain
by Amazon

21462764R00241